'This is a well-considered and thoughtfully written text providing a much-needed perspective on the nexus between theory and practice in relation to customer experience in fashion retail, a field often lacking in the academic rigour which is addressed thoroughly in this book. It provides the academic criticality of use to students and academics alike in the fields of retail marketing, brand marketing and fashion.'

Professor Liz Barnes, *Head of Manchester Fashion Institute,*
Manchester Metropolitan University, UK

'Dr Alexander's book provides a much-needed reference touch-point for both students and those leaping into industry, at a time when the emergence of new technologies, communication paradigms and spaces for brand engagement mean that so many of the traditional rules and codes of customer service in retailing have been widely thrown into disarray.'

Katie Baron, *Trend and Foresight Director at Stylus Innovation, UK*

'The book *Customer Experience in Fashion Retailing: Merging Theory and Practice* brilliantly combines both theoretical and practical knowledge around customer experience in the fashion sector. It gives a holistic and global perspective on this surely specific segment in the retail sector. It is a must read for all involved in fashion.'

Dr Katelijn Quartier, *Professor, Retail Design Lab, Hasselt University, Belgium*

'Dr Alexander's new work *Customer Experience in Fashion Retailing: Merging Theory and Practice* is a comprehensive retail recipe book for the future. Leveraging her decades-long experience in the space, both practical and academic, Dr Alexander lays out all the ingredients necessary to understand and contemplate retail of the future, one that puts the consumer right at the heart of the experience.'

Michelle Poole, *Brand President, Crocs*

T0298535

Customer Experience in Fashion Retailing

This text provides a holistic, integrated and in-depth perspective on the growing field of customer experience (CX), in a fashion context.

Merging three core perspectives – academic, creative agency and retailer – the book takes a chronological approach to tracing the evolution of customer experience from the physical store, to omnichannel through channel convergence to consider the future of fashion retailing and customer experience. Beginning with the theoretical perspective, customer experience evolution in a fashion retail context is traced, considering the definition of customer experience, physical retail, the digitalisation of customer experience, omni-channel retail, in-store technologies and envisioning future retail CX. The retail creative agency perspective looks at how to locate and design customer experience journeys, designing harmonised CX across retail brand environments online and offline, responsible retailing and taking a human-centric approach to create visceral, well-being-based experiences. Finally, the retailer perspective explores real-life case studies of great customer experience from international brands, including Zara, Nike, Ecoalf, To Summer and Anya Hindmarch. Pedagogical features to aid understanding are built in throughout, including chapter objectives and reflective questions.

Comprehensive and unique in its approach, *Customer Experience in Fashion Retailing* is recommended reading for students studying Fashion Retail Management, Customer Experience, Retail Design and Visual Merchandising, Fashion Psychology and Fashion Marketing.

Bethan Alexander is Reader in Fashion Retailing and Marketing and Research Lead at the Fashion Business School, London College of Fashion, University of the Arts, London. Bethan's scholarly research interests span Multi-Sensory Fashion Retailing, Customer Experiences Online and Offline, Innovative Retail Formats, Retail Technologies and Future Retailing. Results of this research have been published in various academic journals and books in the fashion, retail, marketing and business disciplines. She champions research-informed teaching and leverages her extensive networks in collaborating with industry and academics internationally. Bethan is a published author, mentor and thought leader. She wrote Part 1 (Chapters 1 and 2) on theoretical perspectives of customer experience, as well as the Anya Hindmarch and Loanhood case studies.

Mastering Fashion Management

The fashion industry is dynamic, constantly evolving and worth billions worldwide: it's no wonder that Fashion Business Management has come to occupy a central position within the Business School globally. This series meets the need for rigorous yet practical and accessible textbooks that cover the full spectrum of the fashion industry and its management.

Collectively, *Mastering Fashion Management* is a valuable resource for advanced undergraduate and postgraduate students of Fashion Management, helping them gain an in-depth understanding of contemporary concepts and the realities of practice across the entire fashion chain - from design development and product sourcing, to buying and merchandising, sustainability, and sales and marketing. Individually, each text provides essential reading for a core topic. A range of consistent pedagogical features are used throughout the texts, including international case studies, highlighting the practical importance of theoretical concepts.

Postgraduate students studying for a Masters in Fashion Management in particular will find each text invaluable reading, providing the knowledge and tools to approach a future career in fashion with confidence.

Luxury Fashion Brand Management
Unifying Fashion With Sustainability
Olga Mitterfellner

Fashion Business and Digital Transformation
Technology and Innovation across the Fashion Industry
Charlene Gallery and Jo Conlon

Customer Experience in Fashion Retailing
Merging Theory and Practice
Edited by Bethan Alexander

Luxury Fashion Marketing and Branding
A Strategic Approach
Alice Dallabona

Creativity and Innovation in the Fashion Business
Contemporary Issues in Fashion Design and Product Development
Helen Goworek and Fiona Bailey

For more information about the series, please visit https://www.routledge.com/Mastering-Fashion-Management/book-series/FM

Customer Experience in Fashion Retailing

Merging Theory and Practice

Edited by Bethan Alexander

LONDON AND NEW YORK

Designed cover image: Designed by Harmony Closs, BA (Hons) Graphic Design, Camberwell, UAL

First published 2024
by Routledge
4 Park Square, Milton Park, Abingdon, Oxon OX14 4RN

and by Routledge
605 Third Avenue, New York, NY 10158

Routledge is an imprint of the Taylor & Francis Group, an informa business

British Library Cataloguing-in-Publication Data
A catalogue record for this book is available from the British Library

ISBN: 9781032456553 (hbk)
ISBN: 9781032453002 (pbk)
ISBN: 9781003378099 (ebk)

DOI: 10.4324/9781003378099

Typeset in Sabon
by codeMantra

Access the Support Material: www.routledge.com/9781032453002

Heartfelt thanks to everyone that generously contributed chapters and case studies to the book. Incorporating industry practitioners, academic colleagues and alumni, your collective global experiences and expertise of customer experience have greatly enriched the book. I would also like to thank my amazing family for their unwavering love, support and patience – Graham, Tallulah and Matilda. Finally, but most poignantly, to my parents, Jean and Bryan, who were always my greatest advocates, this book is dedicated to them.

Contents

Figures

Tables

Contributors

Bethan Alexander

Affiliation: Reader in Fashion Retailing and Marketing, Fashion Business School, London College of Fashion, University of the Arts, London, UK

Biography: Bethan is Reader in Fashion Retailing and Marketing and Research Lead at the Fashion Business School, London College of Fashion, University of the Arts, London. Her scholarly research interests span Multi-Sensory Fashion Retailing, Customer Experiences Online and Offline, Innovative Retail Formats, Retail Technologies and Future Retailing. Results of this research have been published in various academic journals and books in the fashion, retail, marketing and business disciplines. She champions research-informed teaching and leverages her extensive networks in collaborating with industry and academics internationally. Bethan is the main author and editor of this book. She wrote Part 1 (Chapters 1 and 2) on theoretical perspectives of customer experience, as well as the Anya Hindmarch and Loanhood case studies.

Nicola Arcenas

Affiliation: Design Strategist at Wozere Studio, Madrid, Spain

Biography: Nicola is a Service Designer graduate from the University of Navarra. Her work encompasses a wide range of categories in both the digital and physical spheres within the design realm. She currently works as a Design Strategist at Wozere Studio. Nicola co-wrote the Ecoalf case study.

Ben Butling

Affiliation: Trends Analyst at GWI, London, UK

Biography: Ben Butling is a Trends Analyst and an alumnus of the Fashion Business School at London College of Fashion, University of the Arts, London. His research focuses on the intersection between fashion retail experiences and consumer well-being, with his most recent work exploring restorative retail practices. Ben wrote the Aesop case study.

Laura Costin

Affiliation: Manchester Fashion Institute, Manchester Metropolitan University, UK

Biography: Laura is a Senior Lecturer who specialises in Fashion Communications and joined Manchester Fashion Institute, MMU, in 2016. Prior to this Laura worked in the fashion industry for ten years in a variety of roles in PR and marketing. Laura co-wrote the Glossier case study.

Rocío Elizago
Affiliation: ISEM Fashion Business School, University of Navarra, Spain
Biography: Rocío, after finishing her MA in Fashion Retail Management at London College of Fashion (UAL, United Kingdom), started her PhD in Applied Creativity at the University of Navarra, Spain. Her academic research interests are kidswear and fashion retailing. Rocío combines her work as a teacher and researcher with the development of her children's fashion brand Litel Family. Rocio co-wrote the Zara case study.

Ying Gao
Affiliation: Project Manager in the Merchandising Planning Department, YI Concept Fashion Company, China
Biography: Ying is an alumnus of the Fashion Business School, London College of Fashion, University of the Arts London. She is currently working in product lifecycle planning, which involves pre-planning, R&D, operations, marketing and retail. Ying wrote the To Summer case study.

Christina Herbach
Affiliation: Partner at Yonder Consulting, London, UK
Biography: Christina is a consumer insights, innovation strategy and experience design expert with over 12 years' experience in the retail industry. As a Partner at Yonder Consulting, she blends insight, strategy and imagination to deliver business impact. Christina wrote Chapter 3 on placing people at the heart of customer experience journeys.

Valeria Iannilli
Affiliation: Professor and Faculty member of Design Department. Head of the Fashion Design Program (BA and MSc), Politecnico di Milano, Milan, Italy
Biography: Valeria's research interests concern retail design processes as the expression of brand identity. Her current research investigates the impact of digital transformation on the retailing experience by focusing her attention on omnichannel customer experience and the new phygital concept and format. Valeria co-wrote the Sunnei case study.

Anna Mangas
Affiliation: Manchester Fashion Institute, Manchester Metropolitan University, UK
Biography: Anna is a lecturer specialising in Fashion Communications. Before joining Manchester Fashion Institute in 2015, Anna worked in a range of brand marketing roles for pureplay and multichannel fashion retailers. Anna co-wrote the Glossier case study.

Silvia Pérez-Bou
Affiliation: ISEM Fashion Business School, Madrid, Spain
Biography: Silvia is an architect. She has a Masters in Transport, Territory and Urbanism, and a PhD from the Polytechnic University of Valencia, Spain. She is Assistant Professor in ISEM Fashion Business School and the School of Architecture at the University of Navarra, where she teaches Sustainability and Circular Design. She is also Academic Director of Fashion Business Administration, FBA Master at ISEM, Spain. Silvia co-wrote the Ecoalf case study.

Andrew Quinn

Affiliation: Creative Director, Seen Studios

Biography: As Creative Director, Andrew oversees the creative output of all projects at Seen Studios. Studios' retail design offer ranges from strategically led design retail environments, experiential programming and store activations as well as creating content for brands for their physical, digital and social channels. Andrew wrote Chapter 4 on designing harmonised customer experience for brand environments.

Natascha Radclyffe-Thomas

Affiliation: Professor, EdD FRSA, British School of Fashion, GCU London

Biography: Natascha was named in *The SustainabilityX® Magazine*'s inaugural Global 50 Women In Sustainability Awards™ 2022. As Professor of Marketing and Sustainable Business Natascha's research focuses on sustainable and circular fashion. Natascha is a National Teaching Fellow and Vice Chair of the UN Principles for Responsible Management Education UK and Ireland. Natascha wrote the Raeburn Lab case study.

Javier Antón Sancho

Affiliation: Academic at University of Navarra, Spain

Biography: Javier graduated as an Architect (2006) and has a PhD (2016) from the University of Navarra, Spain. He has a Masters in Critical, Curatorial and Conceptual Practices in Architecture (2014) from Columbia University. He is Professor in the Degrees of Design and Architecture at the University of Navarra, Spain. Javier co-wrote the Ecoalf case study.

Patricia Sanmiguel

Affiliation: Associate professor, School of Communication and ISEM Fashion Business School, University of Navarra, Spain.

Biography: Patricia's academic research interests focus on Digital Marketing, Consumer Behaviour (especially Millennials, Z and Alpha generation), Consumer Experience and Influence Processes among consumers. The results of this research have been published in several academic journals and books in the disciplines of fashion, marketing and business. Patricia co-wrote the Zara case study.

Kate Shepherd

Affiliation: Co-founder and Strategic Director of The Future Collective, UK

Biography: Kate is an expert in design thinking, future forecasting and digital and design innovation who has strategically led award-winning design teams for companies. Her passion lies in the intersection between design and innovation trends and shifts in consumer culture. In 2019, she co-founded the strategically led creative consultancy The Future Collective. Renowned for their mission Design for Better, she has collaborated with many notable brands, including Audi, Coach, Vans, adidas, Michael Kors, Jimmy Choo and Versace. Kate wrote Chapter 5 on creating visceral and human-centric customer experiences.

Alessandra Spagnoli

Affiliation: PhD, Assistant Professor and faculty member, Design Department, Politecnico di Milano, Milan, Italy

Biography: Alessandra's research interests concern the management of design-driven processes in the field of Cultural Heritage and CCI, the exploration of new paradigms, narrative structures and languages in the retail design domain, the experimentation of innovation trajectories and new technologies for the enhancement of cultural capital. Alessandra co-wrote the Sunnei case study.

Rosemary Varley
Affiliation: Fashion Business School, London College of Fashion, UAL
Biography: Rosemary (MPhil) is an experienced academic and Associate Lecturer at the London College of Fashion, University of the Arts, London. Previous roles at LCF's Fashion Business School include Subject Director and Research Coordinator. Her teaching expertise includes fashion retail and marketing strategy, retail management and product management and she has published textbooks, case studies and academic papers in these areas. Rosemary wrote the Nike case study.

Foreword

I have long said that the industry that needed to embrace the Experience Economy more than any other is retail. There is a such a crying need out there for engaging, memorable and personal retail experiences – no more so that now, in a post-pandemic retail landscape that was catapulted into chaos when governments closed stores. The rapid pivoting to online sadly caught many retailers flat-footed with global retail casualties as a result. Those that survived learned hard and fast lessons about making retailing experiential or facing the threat of extinction. Bethan Alexander's book therefore couldn't be more timely, dedicated not only to the industry that arguably suffered the most during COVID-19, but to fashion, one of the most dynamic, creative and volatile sectors of the retail industry.

For the last 25 years we have been trailblazing about the Experience Economy, where goods and services are no longer enough, but what consumers crave are experiences that engage them in an inherently personal way. We conceived this as the Progression of Economic Value, which, in short, depicts the succession of value from the Agrarian Economy (based on commodities) to the Industry Economy (based on goods), to the Service Economy, to what now is most important and prominent, the Experience Economy. The currencies of today's Experience Economy are time, attention and money; retailers therefore need to stage memorable, distinctive experiences that engage customers on an emotional level. The best way for retailers to generate demand for their store offerings is with an experience so engaging that consumers cannot help but spend time within the store, give the place their attention and then purchase the merchandise as memorabilia for that experience. And ideally that experience should be so engaging that customers are willing to pay admission for the place, or places within the place, i.e. for experiencing the experience. While this might seem a bold leap for many retailers, this book offers some excellent examples of fashion retail brands working to create a plethora of such innovative, admission-worthy experiences for its customers.

Customer Experience in Fashion Retailing offers readers the chance to do a deep dive into fashion retail experiences from both the retailer and consumer perspectives. It provides a new, ground-breaking and integrated approach to this topic by intersecting academic, retailer and retail creative agency viewpoints for succeeding in today's Experience Economy. The compilation of chapters, cases and questions prompts readers to consider the similarities and differences in approach and imagine future retail experiences, an essential strategy in a fast-moving industry such as fashion.

The publication of this book is timely and welcome. I'm delighted to endorse it as a specialist resource that complements *The Experience Economy* and other experience-based books available in this exciting field. The more individuals, students, consumers, teachers, practitioners, retailers, brands and enterprises that read about and practise truly memorable, distinctive experiences the better (and more exciting) the retail industry will become.

Joseph Pine II
Co-author of The Experience Economy and Co-founder of Strategic Horizons.

Preface

Continuous change has always been a core characteristic of retailing, its recent acceleration unprecedented, due to the global pandemic, digitalisation, channel evolution, consumption patterns and consumer demands. Whilst customer experience has been recognised by retailers and scholars for many years as important in both creating and delivering customer value whilst enabling competitor differentiation, today it is widely acknowledged as a strategic imperative for retailers to survive and thrive in a highly competitive market, like fashion.

The fashion industry is one of the biggest and most important globally. It is a vital value-creating industry for the world economy. If it were ranked against individual countries' GDP (gross domestic product), it is suggested that the global fashion industry would be the seventh largest economy in the world. In addition, the fashion industry is recognised for being innovative, often one of the first to experiment with new business models and to create, craft, test and trial new retail formats and customer experiences in order to stand out in a highly fragmented and cluttered market.

I spent 17 years working in the fashion industry for a range of international brands with responsibility for leading and enhancing customer experiences through product, retail and brand marketing activations. I've spent the last 17 years in academia, teaching and researching on customer experience applied to fashion. I noticed a gap in the literature for harnessing the scholarly and practitioner perspective on this important subject, whilst leveraging my experience, expertise and personal passion on it. For these reasons, it made sense to focus on this dynamic, fun and highly creative industry. The main aim of the book is to provide students, academics and practitioners with diverse knowledge and understanding about the growing field of retail customer experience in a fashion context.

The book is dedicated to fashion customer experiences, explored through both theory and practice by melding academic, retail creative agencies and retailer viewpoints, to offer a holistic and global perspective on the topic. There are several other books on retail, brand or customer experience available that are valuable to studying the subject, but the content of this book is dedicated to providing an integrated, in-depth view on fashion retail customer experiences specifically, which makes it unique. Furthermore, given the ascendance and complexity of the subject, the book diverges from most existing competitor books by including three distinct but coherent parts.

Part one is the theoretical perspective, which chronologically and thematically traces the evolution of customer experience from the physical store to omnichannel retailing, through channel convergence enabled by digitalisation; the chapter closes by envisioning future retail customer experience.

Part two takes the retail creative agency perspective. It includes three points of view on customer experience through the lens of strategists and designers who practice day-to-day the conception and creation of compelling retail environments, both on- and offline, in generating and enhancing customer experiences. Each practitioner takes a different aspect of customer experience, yet logically builds on and complements each other. Christina, Partner at Yonder Consulting, focuses on placing people at the heart of customer experience journeys, Andrew from Seen Studios looks at designing a harmonised customer experience for retail brand environments and Kate, co-founder and strategic director of The Future Collective, explores creating visceral and human-centric customer experiences.

The **third and final part** is the retailer perspective, whereby fashion retail customer experiences are brought to life through a collection of ten global case studies that have been written by a range of international scholars and alumni of London College of Fashion, who now work in the fashion industry. The cases have been carefully selected to ensure variety across geography, market level, channel and product category. Covering retailers from Australia, China, Italy, Spain, the US and the UK, from fashion, sports and beauty and from mass market to luxury, they serve to showcase best practices in retail customer experience. The case studies contain learning objectives and end with questions intended to probe enquiry, provoke discussion and deepen student learning. Linkages between each part – theoretical, practitioner and case studies – are made to help scaffold and extend the learning.

This is the first known book that takes this novel, 360 degree approach to fashion retail customer experience. It has been designed for different potential audiences. It offers a novel and dedicated read for undergraduate and postgraduate students requiring critical theory as well as robust applications of fashion retail customer experience, for academics who teach a module or individual lectures on the subject, and for practitioners, who want to expand their understanding, access tools to scaffold their thinking or reflect upon current industry practice.

Through the coalescing of theory and practices and taking a collaborative approach, I am proud to have produced a salient and relevant book, featuring an excellent cross-section of examples. Through a collection of chapters and case studies by different authors, I have striven to achieve a coherent, consistent tone of voice, whilst allowing for individual expertise and experience to be expressed and communicated. I hope you enjoy reading it as much as I enjoyed designing and writing it.

Bethan Alexander

Part 1

Theoretical perspectives on retail customer experience

Introduction

Part 1 anticipates and responds to scholarly calls for new research perspectives towards customer experience and customer experience management (CEM), particularly in the context of retail places, channels and touchpoints (Grewal et al., 2009; Maklan and Klaus, 2011; Schmitt and Zarantonello, 2013; Bagdare, 2016; Lemon and Verhoef, 2016; Bustamante and Rubio, 2017; Grewal et al., 2017; Grewal et al., 2020; Hänninen et al., 2021). This theoretical perspective offers a reconceptualisation of the physical store within omnichannel fashion retailing, particularly in connection with the experiential dimensions of physical place and virtual space, and, through their convergence, enabled and enhanced by retail technologies. Furthermore, the concept of Experiential Retail Territories (ERTs), introduced in Chapter 2, extends the territorology construct into the area of retailing (Brighenti, 2010; Kärrholm, 2012). The section concludes by contextualising the ERTs concept through three significant drivers of retail experience futures: hyper-phygital, hyper-personalised and hyper-responsible.

Customer experience theoretical context

Schmitt and Zarantonello (2013) categorise 'experience' research into five distinct areas: *consumer experience* (e.g. Carbone and Haeckel, 1994; Schmitt, 1999, 2003; Arnold et al., 2002), *offline and online experience* (e.g. Kotler, 1973; Mehrabian and Russell, 1974; Bitner, 1992; Turley and Milliman, 2000; Bäckström and Johansson, 2006; Verhoef et al., 2009), *consumption experience* (e.g. Holbrook and Hirschman, 1982), *service experience* (e.g. Helkkula, 2011) and *brand experience* (e.g. Pine and Gilmore, 1998; Schmitt, 1999; Brakus et al., 2009; Schmitt and Zarantonello, 2013; Khan and Rahman, 2015a). Whilst acknowledging the growing field, Schmitt and Zarantonello criticise the lack of integration across contexts, leading to narrow and singular perspectives, and call for future research to take a multidisciplinary and holistic approach.

Whilst practices of experiential retailing are widespread (Pine and Gilmore, 1998, 1999, 2019; Gilmore and Pine, 2002; Schmitt, 2003; Kim et al., 2007; Mikunda, 2007; Lemon, 2016; Briedis et al., 2020), scholarly attention to the phenomenon arguably remains underdeveloped (Verhoef et al., 2009; Bagdare and Jain, 2013; Schmitt and Zarantonello, 2013; Khan and Rahman, 2015a; Bustamante and Rubio, 2017), especially in relation to the changing role and configuration of physical retail, and from a dynamic, omnichannel perspective (Bäckström and Johansson, 2017; Botschen and Wegerer, 2017; Hagberg et al., 2017; Bruce et al., 2023; Sharma and Dutta, 2023; Pusceddu et al., 2023), the customer experience journey (Berry et al., 2002; Bagdare, 2016; Lemon and Verhoef, 2016; Ieva and Ziliani, 2018; Grewal et al., 2020; Roggeveen and Sethuraman, 2020; Poorrezaei et al., 2023) and the facilitation of customer experience through in-store technologies over time (Grewal et al., 2020; Hoyer et al., 2020; Bonfanti et al., 2023; Quinones, et al., 2023). Moreover, retail experience research predominantly focuses on the antecedents of in-store experience (e.g. Grewal et al., 2009; Puccinelli et al., 2009; Verhoef et al., 2009; Bagdare, 2013; Meng et al., 2023), its consequences (e.g. Bitner, 1992; Baker et al., 2002; Babin et al., 2003; Arnold et al., 2005; Andreu et al., 2006; Jones et al., 2006; Ballantine et al., 2010; Brun et al., 2017; Prentice et al., 2019) and, more recently, the need for a holistic approach towards customers' experience (Verhoef et al., 2009; Maklan and Klaus, 2011; Petermans et al., 2013; Spence et al., 2014; Ballantine et al., 2015; Sachdeva and Goel, 2015). However, in this literature, studies dedicated to digitally enhanced customer-centric experiences in-store have been criticised as being lacking (Khan and Rahman, 2015b; Bäckström and Johansson, 2017; Alexander and Blázquez Cano, 2019; Biswas, 2019; Poorrezaei et al., 2023; Sharma and Dutta, 2023) and scarce within the fashion industry (Khan and Rahman, 2015a; Varshneya et al., 2017; Colombi et al., 2018; Mosquera et al., 2018; Lynch and Barnes, 2020). Therefore, this theoretical section seeks to fill this scholarly lacuna.

Customer experience industry context

This book on customer experience takes the fashion retail sector as its context. Globally, this sector is valued at USD 1,734 billion[1] (Euromonitor, 2023) and comprises footwear, men's, women's and children's clothing, sportswear, beauty, jewellery, accessories, luggage and bags and lingerie, across segments from 'value' to 'luxury' (Amed and Berg, 2020). It employs more than 300 million people worldwide across the value chain, ranks second in consumer goods globally (behind packaged food) in terms of industry value size and growth (Euromonitor, 2021) and would be the seventh-largest economy if ranked against individual country GDP (Amed and Berg, 2020; Gazzola et al., 2020). Furthermore, as the fashion retail sector is recognised as being digitally innovative and experimental (Mosquera et al., 2018; Pantano and Vannucci, 2019; Lynch and Barnes, 2020), it is a highly suitable context to explore the future of experiential retail places and spaces.

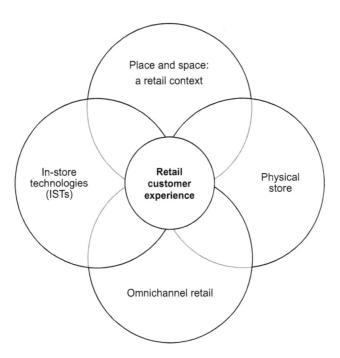

Figure 0.1 Multidisciplinary literature informing Part 1.

Source: Authors own.

Before the COVID-19 global pandemic, many physical stores were already struggling, and, consequently, a retail 'apocalypse' was predicted by some scholars (Helm et al., 2020; Paul and Rosenbaum, 2020). Indeed, the impact of COVID-19 further destabilised the sector, with global retail sales declining by 19% in 2020 (Amed and Berg, 2020; Euromonitor, 2021), and by exacerbating and accelerating already existing trends towards online consumption. It is generally accepted that the clothing and footwear sector was among the worst affected by the pandemic, with physical store sales contracting by 29% year on year, due to measures such as lockdowns and social distancing, combined with the unprecedented growth of online fashion sales (Euromonitor, 2021). In 2020, global online retailing grew by 14.4% to USD 1,819 billion as consumers shifted to purchasing online (GlobalData, 2020). Today, post the pandemic, 30% of global clothing sales is through online channels, meaning that 70% of sales still take place physically (Euromonitor, 2023), giving credence to the importance of harnessing both the online and offline channels in shaping customer experience. Market volatility and transformation, both pre- and – significantly – post-pandemic, call for new (re) conceptualisations of physical retail within channel and touchpoint proliferation (Mende and Noble, 2019; Hoyer et al., 2020; Jocevski, 2020), which this theoretical perspective section acknowledges, investigates and forecasts. Figure 0.1 depicts the multidisciplinary literature fields informing Part 1.

1

Customer experience evolution in a fashion retail context

From mono- to omnichannel

Bethan Alexander

> What people really desire are not products but satisfying experiences.
>
> (Abbott, 1955:40)

CEM has received extensive scholarly and practitioner attention over the past four decades and is increasingly seen as a strategic imperative for retailers (Verhoef et al., 2009; Klaus and Maklan, 2013; Khan et al., 2020). Given the rapidly changing retail landscape, the need to understand, manage and offer better customer experiences is a priority for retailers and academics alike (Bustamante and Rubio, 2017; Mahr et al., 2019; Gartner, 2021). Yet, despite rapid advances in experiential research, in terms of construct and methods, further exploration is called for (Bagdare, 2013; Petermans et al., 2013; Sachdeva and Goel, 2015; Stein and Ramaseshan, 2016; Bäckström and Johansson, 2017; Becker, 2018). This chapter discusses the scholarly evolution of the retail customer experience, from mono-channel (physical store) to omnichannel (seamless integration across channels and touchpoints) contexts. In doing so, it highlights emerging trends in the literature, to incorporate a more holistic approach towards customer experience(s) (Verhoef et al., 2009; Ballantine et al., 2015; Bäckström and Johansson, 2017; Becker, 2018), moving from a provider- to consumer-centric perspective that focuses on the customer journey (Lemon and Verhoef, 2016; Becker and Jaakkola, 2020; Poorrezaei et al., 2023), from simple retailer-customer dyads to ecosystems (including other actors; e.g. family, friends, influencers) involving multiple channels and touchpoints, with implications for the physical store (Addis and Holbrook, 2001; Heinonen et al., 2010; Akaka et al., 2015; Becker, 2018), and the increasing integration and use of technology in amplifying retail customer experience (Blázquez, 2014; Poncin and Mimoun, 2014; Alexander and Kent, 2022). Consequently, this chapter takes an evolutionary rather than static perspective on experience. First, customer experience is defined and its theoretical developments are expounded. Next, the evolutionary developments of customer experience within retail settings is explored and examined, from a focus on physical stores to their digital transformation from mono- to multi- then omnichannel retailing, with phygital retailing enabled through emergent retail technologies.

Definitions and conceptualisations of customer experience

Significant efforts have been made to define and conceptualise customer experience, yet the literature remains fragmented with a lack of consensus, both within academic silos and across multiple disciplines (Jain et al., 2017; Chevtchouk et al., 2021; Poorrezaei

DOI: 10.4324/9781003378099-2

et al., 2023). Experience literature can be found in the fields of philosophy (e.g. Dewey, 1938), marketing and consumer research (e.g. Holbrook and Hirschman, 1982; Schmitt, 1999), cognitive science (e.g. Pinker, 1997), design science (e.g. Wright et al., 2003; Norman, 2004) and management practice (e.g. Pine and Gilmore, 1999), each assigning different meanings to the construct, with different conceptions and little integration (Petermans et al., 2013; Schmitt and Zarantonello, 2013). Most scholars agree that Holbrook and Hirschman (1982) were influential in viewing consumption from an experiential perspective, arguably instigating the scholarly stream of research on experience, but this research, it has been suggested, has lacked definitional consensus (Carú and Cova, 2003; Schmitt and Zarantonello, 2013; Poorrezaei et al., 2023).

Since then, scholars and practitioners have described the experience construct using a variety of terms and dimensions, relating to different contexts, including service, product, consumption, customer, brand and retail experience, as indicated in Table 1.1. These descriptions tend to overlap or be subsumed within each other, making delineation between terms ambiguous (Jain et al., 2017; Chevtchouk et al., 2021). Whilst all terms outlined in Table 1.1 share experience dimensions of cognition, behaviour and affect, few share sensorial dimensions and only 'customer experience' includes the social dimension. As the retail environment is seen as a setting where social interactions take place, the social context and thus the social dimension of customer experience is deemed important (Gentile et al., 2007; Vargo and Lusch, 2008; Johnstone, 2012; De Kesyer et al., 2015).

Thus, for the sake of clarity, this chapter draws on the broadest definition and dimensions by using the term customer experience. Defined as the customer's cognitive, affective, emotional, social and physical responses to the retailer (Verhoef et al., 2009:32), it is holistic, interactional and multidimensional in nature and marked by a level of uniqueness, from the ordinary to extraordinary (Carú and Cova, 2003; Verhoef et al., 2009; De Keyser et al., 2015; Poorrezaei et al., 2023; Puscedddu et al., 2023).

Customer experience and its management have gained prominence as a subject for research enquiry. Many scholars have emphasised the importance of managing the total customer experience across the purchase journey to create value and competitive advantage and improve customer satisfaction and loyalty (e.g. Schmitt, 2003; Gentile et al., 2007; Grewal et al., 2009). CEM involves systematically designing, orchestrating and measuring the customer's entire experience (Carbone and Haeckel, 1994; Berry et al., 2002; Hwang and Seo, 2016; Poorrezaei et al., 2023), and has become a strategic priority for retailers as a key determinant of success (Frow and Payne, 2007; Verhoef et al., 2009; De Kesyer et al., 2015; Marketing Science Institute, 2022).

Physical retail: in-store customer experience

Many conceptions and discussions of customer experience until the 1990s were primarily focused on the physical retail store, specifically store design, in effecting purchasing behaviours (Hänninen et al., 2021). Hirschman and Holbrook's (1982) seminal study defined hedonic consumption as those facets of consumer behaviour that relate to the multisensory, fantasy and emotive aspects of consumption in-store (Bäckström and Johansson, 2006). In contrast with the long-focused view on utilitarian aspects of the shopping experience, based on task-related, rational product purchases (Babin et al., 1994), hedonic consumption is driven by fun, entertainment and enjoyment (Jones, 1999; Alba and Williams, 2012).

Table 1.1 Key terms, definitions, dimensions and authors in experience-based research

Term	Indicative definition	Dimensions	Other authors
Consumption experience	"Consumption experience is seen as involving a steady flow of fantasies, feelings and fun. A subjective state of consciousness with a variety of symbolic meanings, hedonic responses and esthetic criteria" (Holbrook and Hirschman, 1982:132)	Cognitive Affective Behavioural	Mehrabian and Russell (1974); Donovan and Rossiter (1982); Hirschman and Holbrook (1982); Arnold and Price (1993); Holt (1995); Richins (1997); Turley and Milliman (2000); Addis and Holbrook (2001); Carù and Cova (2003); Joy and Sherry (2003); Alba and Williams (2012); Jantzen et al. (2012); Antéblian et al. (2013); Woodward and Holbrook (2013); Chaney et al. (2018)
Service experience	"The cognitive, affective and behavioural reactions associated with a specific service event" (Padgett and Allen, 1997:52)	Cognitive Affective Behavioural	Bitner et al. (1997); Jones (1999); Froehle and Roth (2004); Grace and O'Cass (2004); Pullman and Gross (2004); Arnold et al. (2005); Patricio et al. (2008); Heinonen et al. (2010); Zomerdijk and Voss (2010); Brocato et al. (2012); Klaus and Maklan (2012); Juttner et al. (2013); Chandler and Lusch (2015); Jaakkola et al. (2015); Vargo and Lusch (2016); Voorhees et al. (2017); Bueno et al. (2019); Mahr et al. (2019); Roozen and Katidis (2019)
Product experience	"Experience can be characterised as all the thoughts, emotions, activities, and appraisals that occur during or as a result of an event" (Goode et al., 2010:276)	Cognitive Affective Behavioural	Hoch and Ha (1986); Hoch (2002); Aurier and Guintcheva (2014); Berger et al. (2018)
Brand experience	"Subjective, internal consumer responses that are evoked by brand-related experiential attributes when consumers search for, shop for, and consume brands" (Brakus et al., 2009:53) "Experiences are distinct economic offerings... an experience occurs where a company intentionally uses services as the stage, and goods as props, to engage individual customers in a way that creates a memorable event" (Pine and Gilmore, 1998:97–98)	Sensory Affective Intellectual Behavioural Memorable Personal Entertainment Educational Escapist Aesthetic	Iglesias et al. (2011); Khan and Rahman (2015a, 2015b, 2016); Schmitt et al. (2015); Atwal and Williams (2017); Khan and Fatma (2017); Hepola et al. (2017); Saari and Mäkinen (2017); Andreini et al. (2018); Chevtchouk et al. (2021); Mondal and Chakrabarti (2021)

(Continued)

Table 1.1 (Continued)

Term	Indicative definition	Dimensions	Other authors
Retail experience	"Retail customer experience is the sum total of cognitive, emotional, sensorial and behavioural responses produced during the entire process, involving an integrated series of interactions with people, objects, processes and environment in retailing" (Bagdare and Jain, 2013:792)	Cognitive Emotional Sensorial Behavioural Joy Mood Leisure Distinctive	Baker et al. (1992); Jones (1999); Babin and Attaway (2000); Andreu et al. (2006); Bäckström and Johansson (2006); Healy et al. (2007); Naylor et al. (2008); Jones et al. (2010); Bäckström (2011); Bagdare (2013); Bagdare and Jain (2013); Bagdare (2016); Bäckström and Johansson (2017); Triantafillidou et al. (2017); Grewal and Roggeveen (2020)
Customer/ consumer experience	"Experiences provide sensory, emotional, cognitive, behavioural and relational values that replace functional values" (Schmitt, 1999:57)	Sensory (sense) Affective (feel) Cognitive (think) Physical (act) Social (relate)	Carbone and Haeckel (1994); Novac et al. (2000); Berry et al. (2002); Gilmore and Pine (2002); Shaw and Ivens (2002); Schmitt (2003); Frow and Payne (2007); Gentile et al. (2007); Meyer and Schwager (2007); Grewal et al. (2009); Puccinelli et al. (2009); Palmer (2010); Rose et al. (2012); Maklan and Klaus (2011); Klaus and Maklan (2013); Petermans et al. (2013); Schmitt and Zarantonello (2013); Andajani (2015); Sachdeva and Goel (2015); Bilgihan et al. (2016); Stein and Ramaseshan (2016); Schmitt et al. (2015); Yakhlef (2015); Hwang and Seo (2016); Lemon (2016); Parise et al. (2016); Bustamante and Rubio (2017); Jain et al. (2017); Varshneya et al. (2017); Becker and Jaakkola (2020); Khan et al. (2020); Roggeveen et al. (2020)

Source: Author's own.

Customer experience dimensions

Marking a shift from generic experience construct development to the retailing context more specifically, a myriad of retail customer experience theorisations have followed, focusing on the dimensions that influence customer experience and behaviours in-store (e.g. Baker et al., 2002; Bäckström and Johansson, 2006; Grewal et al., 2009; Vehoef et al., 2009). According to Bäckström and Johansson (2017), these comprise

- *Personal dimensions*, including consumer shopping motivation, attitude, mood and involvement (e.g. Holbrook and Hirschman, 1982; Babin and Darden, 1995; Tauber, 1995; Spies et al., 1997; Mathwick et al., 2001; Soars, 2003) as well as gender and financial means (Jones, 1999);
- *Retail dimensions*, including store design, atmospherics, social aspects, service and price (e.g. Turley and Milliman, 2000; Baker et. al., 2002; Grewal et al., 2009; Puccinelli et al., 2009; Verhoef et al., 2009);
- *Situational dimensions*, including the type of store, season and culture (Verhoef et al., 2009; Bäckström and Johansson, 2017);
- *Macro-level dimensions*, including economic and political (Grewal et al., 2009).

Over the years extensive scholarly attention has been given to personal and retail-related dimensions in-store, especially in relation to hedonic and utilitarian consumption value, with particular emphasis given to the former (Holbrook and Hirschman, 1982; Babin et al., 1994; Jones, 1999), and to *atmospherics*, referring to tangible and intangible in-store cues that can be designed or altered in order to create emotional and behavioural consumer responses (Kotler, 1973; Puccinelli et al., 2009).

Kotler (1973) advanced the notion that the place where the product is purchased was a significant feature in consumption experience, arguably more important than the product itself in influencing how people react and act (Bitner, 1992). This paved the way for numerous studies on overall store atmospheric elements and their role (e.g. Baker, 1987; Bitner, 1992; Babin and Attaway, 2000; Turley and Milliman, 2000; Ballantine et al., 2010; Krishna, 2012; Bagdare, 2013; Spence et al., 2014; Sachdeva and Goel, 2015), as well as the effects of specific atmospheric (sensory) elements (Alexander and Nobbs, 2016; Biswas, 2019), such as *sight cues* (e.g. Bellizzi and Hite, 1992; Halsted, 1993; Babin et al., 2003; Van Rompay et al., 2012; Reynolds-McIlnay et al., 2017), *sound cues* (e.g. Milliman, 1982; Garlin and Owen, 2006; Morin et al., 2007; Jain and Bagdare, 2011; Knoferle et al., 2012, 2017; Biswas et al., 2014), *touch cues* (Krishna et al., 2010; Martin, 2011; Hultén, 2012), *smell cues* (e.g. Spangenberg et al., 1996; Madzharov et al., 2015; Lin et al., 2018; Roy and Singh, 2022) and *taste cues* (e.g. Lindstrom, 2005; Hultén, 2009; Rodrigues et al., 2011; Wiedmann et al., 2013).

Here, the retailers' service experience was recognised as being crucial in seeking to control and add materiality to the abstract nature of in-store atmosphere, thereby positively influencing consumers' product and service evaluation (Hoffman and Turley, 2002; Bäckström and Johansson, 2006). This approach to the physical environment was coined as the *servicescape* (Bitner, 1992), with more recent expanded conceptions as the *experiencescape* (O'Dell, 2005), describing places where human interactions, pleasure, entertainment and enjoyment occur (Tresidder and Deakin, 2019; Tasci and Pizam, 2020). Research into store atmosphere concludes that positive retail environmental features influence consumers' subjective experience, especially pleasure and arousal, and lead to approach behaviours, for example, increasing dwell time, money spent, impulse purchasing, merchandise value and patronage intention while improving consumer relationships and customer experience (e.g. Mehrabian and Russell, 1974; Donovan and Rossiter, 1982; Babin and Attaway, 2000; Baker et al., 2002; Puccinelli et al., 2009; Verhoef et al., 2009).

However, whilst contributing to our initial understanding of customer experience in retail, these early studies arguably fail to fully acknowledge the more holistic aspects of customer experience and how consumers experience and interact with retail environments (Bäckström and Johansson, 2017) in five key ways, discussed next.

Limitations of traditional customer experience conceptions

Traditional conceptions of CX first fail to fully consider the *social dimension* of the servicescape or more holistic approaches to in-store experience (Verhoef et al., 2009; Spence et al., 2014; Ballantine et al., 2015). Interactionally, customer experience derives from human (e.g. employees, other consumers) and non-human (e.g. self-service technologies) interfaces. However, without an interaction, there is nothing to experience (De Keyser et al., 2015; Biswas, 2019), yet the retail environment's social nature has received less attention (Rosenbaum, 2006; Johnstone and Conroy, 2006; Johnstone, 2012; Alexander, 2019). Indeed, many recent scholars support Verhoef et al.'s (2009) contention that customer experience is holistic in nature, involving multiple dimensions, whilst acknowledging its subjective nature, and call for further empirical studies that take an interconnected approach (e.g. Petermans et al., 2013; Sachdeva and Goel, 2015; Bäckström and Johansson, 2017). This sentiment relates to Part 2, with practitioners (Chapters 3–5) emphasising the importance of an audience-centric approach and social involvement in customer experience optimisation.

Second, customer experience is now no longer limited to the customer's interaction in-store but is impacted by a combination of experiences that evolves over time, across channels during the *purchase journey* (Lemon and Verhoef, 2016; Bäckström and Johansson, 2017). With growth in digital channels, novel ways of organising the physical store are necessary and require investigation (Bell et al., 2014; Grewal et al., 2017; Gauri et al., 2021); however, empirical consumer and retailer perspectives on this remain scarce (Bäckström and Johansson, 2017; Bruce et al., 2023; Poorrezaei et al., 2023).

Third, *customer experience is dynamic*, with past and current experience impacting future experience, yet the dynamics of customer experiences over time has also received little attention in retailing research (Verhoef et al., 2009; De Keyser et al., 2015).

Fourth, the use of *technology in-store* has been accepted as influencing customer experiences, with scholars referring to it as an important atmospheric tool (Blázquez, 2014; Poncin and Mimoun, 2014) and responsible for propelling omnichannel capabilities (Herhausen et al., 2015; Cai and Lo, 2020) in the past ten years or so, which is absent from early theorisations. The way people experience retail is being transformed through technologies and the lines between human and machine are becoming increasingly blurred (Lemon, 2016; Jocevski, 2020; Bonfanti et al., 2023; Chang et al., 2023).

Fifth, prior studies focus on retailer-customer dyads, thereby arguably failing to reflect the complex, multidimensional, multichannel and touchpoint nature of today's *customer experience retail ecosystem*. This is where traditional views on customer experience in retail environments that focus on atmospherics and more recent conceptions diverge (De Keyser et al., 2015; Bäckström and Johansson, 2017; Roggeveen et al., 2020). Current scholars recognise the shift from provider- (i.e. retailer control) to consumer-centric conceptions of customer experience that takes place as part of a longer journey across different channels, arguably impacting on the relevance of earlier studies in the context of today's omnichannel retail environment (Becker, 2018; Becker and Jaakkola, 2020; Roggeveen et al., 2020). This paradigm shift reflects Vargo and Lusch's (2004) notion of co-creating value collaboratively with customers over an extended time frame. This embodies an evolution of retailing beyond products, services and post services to the most important expression of the retailscape – customer experience (Pine and Gilmore, 1999; Maklan and Klaus, 2011). The move from a mono-physical store to omnichannel convergence and customer experience is discussed next.

The digitalisation of retail customer experience: convergence online and offline

Over the past three decades, retailing has radically transformed due to digitalisation. The role of the physical store has changed from a place of transaction to a showroom and a place to interact, as the emergence and development of online retailing has enabled different and more meaningful customer experiences (Brynjolfsson et al., 2013; Hänninen et al., 2021). Consequently, conceptual and empirical retail research on customer experience has grown (e.g. Bolton et al., 2018; Paul and Rosenbaum, 2020; Chevtchchouk et al., 2021). Huuhka et al. (2014) and Hänninen et al (2021) offer a cogent synthesis of the evolution of retailing over the past three decades (see Figure 1.1), from mono-physical channel to multi- and then omnichannel retailing precipitated by advances in information and communication technology, broadly falling into three phases.

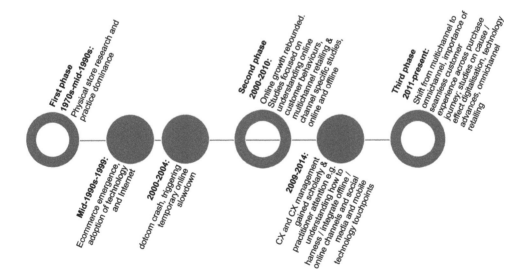

Figure 1.1 Chronology of retail evolution from physical to omnichannel: 1970–present.

Source: Authors own, based on Huuhka et al., 2014 and Hänninen et al., 2021.

Phase 1: 1990s – siloed channel proliferation

E-commerce burgeoned in the mid-1990s as retailers used information and communication technology and the internet, transforming buying behaviours and business processes (e.g. Reynolds, 2000; Grewal et al., 2009; Gerea et al., 2021; Hänninen et al., 2021). This channel shift destabilised traditional retailing, with the acceleration of e-commerce reducing the customer's need to visit a physical store. The term 'marketspace' was coined to depict the real-time interactivity and global connectivity realised by the internet (Dutta et al., 1998).

Phase 2: 2000–2010 – rise of multichannel – retailer-centric

Multichannel retailing dominated practitioner and academic attention during this period, yet inconsistencies in both definitions and characteristics led to confusion in its progressive conceptualisation – with emerging terms like multi-, cross-, and omnichannel retailing (Picot-Coupey et al., 2016). It is generally accepted that multichannel retailing refers to the design, deployment, coordination and evaluation of different channels (i.e. online, offline, etc.), yet with siloed structures and no integration or synergistic management of them (Neslin et al., 2006; Rigby, 2011; Gallino and Moreno, 2014). Multichannel became superfluous when the same customers were using more than one channel. Moreover, with the proliferation of channels, issues of definitional delineation, integration, coordination and synergies became paramount (Herhausen et al., 2015; Picot-Coupey et al., 2016; Cai and Lo, 2020). Channel integration is defined as the degree to which different channels interact with each other (Bendoly et al., 2005), which is conceived as a continuum, based on the level of integration intensity – from none (multichannel) to partial (crosschannel) to full (omnichannel) (Lewis et al., 2014; Picot-Coupey et al., 2016). Given the often overlapping channel conceptions and meanings, which has caused confusion (Picot-Coupey et al., 2016; Yrjölä et al., 2018a; Hu and Tracogna, 2020), Table 1.2 presents a synthesis of the main theoretical contributions in the field of retailing, arranged by thematic classification and temporal channel evolution from multi-, cross- to omnichannel. Whilst it can occur from offline to online or from online to store, the focus of this chapter is the offline; that is, the physical store providing access to and knowledge and experience of the online store and digital touchpoints (Herhausen et al., 2015).

Scholarly retail studies during this phase shifted to understanding online customer behaviour, the emergence of multichannel retailing conceptions (Mathwick et al., 2001; Arnold and Reynolds, 2003; Verhoef et al., 2009) as well as channel-specific studies, offline (e.g. Sweeney and Soutar, 2001) or online (e.g. Childers et al., 2001; Ahn et al., 2007). Simultaneously, customer experience and CEM gained increasing interest from scholars and practitioners alike, with growing realisation of the importance of channel and touchpoint convergence across the customer journey, in enhancing customer experience (e.g. Verhoef et al., 2009; Grewal et al., 2009; Puccinelli et al., 2009; Verhoef et al, 2015; Lemon and Verhoef, 2016; Becker, 2018; Hänninen et al., 2021), its significance giving rise to a special issue on retail customer experience in the *Journal of Retailing* in 2009.

The growing importance of the customer experience construct was indicated by the increasing number of scholarly publications between 2012 and 2014, as indicated in Table 1.2, yet most were limited to quantitative enquiry, covering aspects of antecedents, measurement and consequences of consumer experience (e.g. Bagdare, 2013; Bagdare

Table 1.2 Theoretical evolution: from multi- to omnichannel retailing

Theme	Multichannel 2000+	Crosschannel 2005+	Omnichannel 2011–present
Concept development	Berman and Thelen (2004); Neslin et al. (2006); Sousa and Voss (2006)	Chatterjee (2010)	Rigby (2011); Levy et al. (2013); Bell et al. (2014); Beck and Rygl (2015); Hansen and Sia (2015); Chopra (2016); Rey-Moreno and Medina-Molina (2016); Ailawadi and Farris (2017); Chen et al. (2018); Galipoglu et al. (2018); von Briel (2018); Ye et al. (2018); Cai and Lo (2020); Mahadevan and Joshi (2021); Mishra et al. (2021); Sharma and Dutta (2023)
Channel management/ integration	Otto and Chung (2000); Schoenbachler and Gordon (2002); Payne and Frow (2004); Balasubramanian et al. (2005); Bendoly et al. (2005); Tate et al. (2005); Verhoef et al. (2007); Kwon and Lennon (2009); Yan et al. (2010); Chiu et al. (2011); Herhausen et al. (2015); Pauwels and Neslin (2015); Hossain et al. (2019)	Chatterjee (2006); Falk et al. (2007); Brynjolfsson et al. (2009); Lee and Kim (2010); Schramm-Klein et al. (2011); Avery et al. (2012); Lewis et al. (2014); Cao and Li (2015); Huang et al. (2016)	Pawar and Sarmah (2015); Cummins et al. (2016); Picot-Coupey et al. (2016); Huré et al. (2017); Park and Lee (2017); Rodriguez-Torrico et al. (2017); Saghiri et al. (2017); Sopadjieva et al. (2017); Bell et al. (2018); Cao and Li (2018); Hosseini et al. (2018); Shen et al. (2018); Wiener et al. (2018); Yrjölä et al. (2018a/b); Zhang et al. (2018); Jocevski et al. (2019); Alexander and Blázquez Cano (2019, 2020); Tyrväinen and Karjaluoto, (2019); Xu and Jackson (2019); Quach et al. (2020); Gao et al. (2021); Gasparin et al. (2022); Hübner et al. (2022); Neslin (2022); Nguyen et al. (2022)
Consumer behaviour/ customer journey	McGoldrick and Collins (2007); Schröder and Zaharia (2008); Kwon and Jain (2009); Gensler et al. (2012); Wolny and Charoensuksai (2014); Melis et al (2015); Pantano and Viassone (2015); Rapp et al. (2015); Bèzes (2016); Hu and Tracogna (2020); Jo et al. (2020)	Piercy (2012); Heitz-Spahn (2013); Cao (2014)	Juaneda-Ayensa et al. (2016); Gao and Su (2017); Barwitz and Maas (2018); Kazancoglu and Aydin (2018); Larke et al. (2018); Mosquera et al. (2018); Kang (2019); De Borba et al. (2020); Lee (2020); Lynch and Barnes (2020); Mishra et al. (2021); Sahu et al. (2021); Tueanrat et al. (2021); ben Mimoun et al. (2022); Lazaris et al. (2022); Salvietti et al. (2022); Poorrezaei et al. (2023)

(Continued)

Table 1.2 (Continued)

Theme	Multichannel 2000+	Crosschannel 2005+	Omnichannel 2011–present
Retail strategy	Brnjolfsson and Smith (2000); Rangaswamy and van Bruggen (2005); Neslin and Shankar (2009); Zhang et al. (2010); Hübner et al. (2016)		Brnjolfsson et al. (2013); Piotrowicz and Cuthbertson (2014); Lazaris and Vrechopoulos (2014); Verhoef et al. (2015); Hagberg et al. (2017); Huré et al. (2017); Berman and Thelen (2018); Shen et al. (2018); Yrjölä et al. (2018b); Savastano et al. (2019); Gauri et al. (2021); Asmare and Zewdie (2022); Barbosa and Casais (2022)
Customer experience	Burke (2002); Jones and Runyan (2013); Blázquez (2014); Alexander and Alvarado (2017)		Bhalla (2014); Cook (2014); Hoepner et al. (2015); Blakeney (2016); Melero et al. (2016); Mirsch et al. (2016); Ieva and Ziliani (2018); Tyrväinen and Karjaluoto (2019); Hickman et al. (2020); Klaus (2020); Shi et al. (2020); Verhoef (2021); Chang and Li (2022); Rahman et al. (2022)

Source: Author's own.

and Jain, 2013; Khan and Rahman, 2015a, 2016; Bueno et al., 2019). Verhoef et al.'s (2009) earlier customer experience definition was extended to reflect the onus on the purchase journey, as a "multidimensional construct focusing on a customer's cognitive, emotional, behavioural, sensorial, and social response to a firm's offering during the customer's entire purchase journey" (Lemon and Verhoef, 2016:71).

Customer experience continued to be recognised as strategically important, with greater attention given to understanding how retailers could best harness and integrate their offline and online channels during this period (Cachon and Lariviere, 2005; Rigby, 2011; Brynjolfsson et al., 2013; Bustamante and Rubio, 2017; Huré et al., 2017). Retailers experienced the advantages of blending offline and online retailing in the pursuit of integrated retail – that is, the benefits of uniting services of accessibility and assortment with personal inspection and immediate gratification (Badrinarayanan et al., 2012; Herhausen et al., 2015).

Phase 3: 2011-today – rise of omnichannel – customer-centric

By the mid-2010s, traditional physical stores started to see declining footfall as consumer purchase behaviours shifted and conventional retailers were errant in not embracing newer digital ways of driving consumers to the store (e.g. via social media), whilst increased use of new interaction touchpoints, specifically social media and mobile technology, continued to challenge and change the retail customer experience (Ailawadi and Farris, 2017; Ieva and Zilani, 2018; Larke et al., 2018). By the late-2010s, the online channel was firmly entrenched in retailing, and academic and practitioner theorisations of multichannel had been widely displaced by omnichannel retailing, as retailers acknowledged the need to offer a seamless customer experience across the purchase journey, regardless of channel (Lemon and Verhoef, 2016; Sopadjieva et al., 2017; Tyrväinen and Karjaluoto, 2019; Mahadevan and Joshi, 2021). Rigby's (2011:4) first practitioner-oriented definition of omnichannel retailing as "an integrated sales experience that melds the advantages of physical stores with the information-rich experience of online shopping" was pioneered by scholars Brynjolfsson et al. (2013) and Bell et al. (2014) by taking retailer competitive advantage and customer-focused perspectives, paving the way for burgeoning areas of further research in the domain (Cai and Lo, 2020; Hickman et al., 2020; Mishra et al., 2021; Salvietti et al., 2022; Poorrezaei et al., 2023).

Growing capabilities and the significance of smartphones has accelerated the implementation of omnichannel strategies by retailers (Ailawadi and Farris, 2017). Consequently, as consumers have become accustomed to using different channels in their 'journey', so they are influenced by behavioural, cognitive and emotional factors and interactions (Verhoef et al., 2015; Grewal and Roggeveen, 2020; Mele et al., 2021). In this scenario, traditional retailers are shifting from a 'bricks and mortar' to a 'bricks and clicks' format by adopting multiple touchpoints to communicate and transact with customers (Hübner et al., 2016; Jocevski, 2020). Whilst advances have been made in our understanding of CEM, within the customer journey and decision stages (pre-purchase, purchase and post-purchase), ongoing consideration is required, specifically on the nonlinearity of the purchase journey, with consumers jumping between stages and channels, and each shaped by contextual, environmental, societal and individual factors (Lemon and Verhoef, 2016; Grewal and Roggeveen, 2020; Mele et al., 2021; Poorrezaei et al., 2023).

Conception and definition of omnichannel retailing

The concept of omnichannel therefore represents a shift in the retail paradigm (Verhoef et al., 2015; Jocevski et al., 2019), from a retailer- to a customer-centric approach, enabling consumers to access, compare, choose, purchase and return goods more readily and seamlessly (Hsieh et al., 2012; Wagner, 2013; Blázquez, 2014; Piotrowicz and Cuthbertson, 2014; Baxendale et al., 2015; Stein and Rameseshan, 2016; Ailawadi and Farris, 2017; Gauri, 2021; Ylilehto et al., 2021). Verhoef et al. (2015:3) define omnichannel management as the "synergetic management of the numerous available channels and customer touchpoints, in such a way that the customer experience across channels and the performance over channels are optimized". Yet, despite a surge of academic interest in the concept in the past five years, research remains fragmented (Mahadevan and Joshi, 2021), with a scarcity of studies examining how an omnichannel retailing approach affects the customer experience (Verhoef et al., 2015; Ye et al., 2018; Hickman et al., 2020; Poorrezaei et al., 2023) and few studies providing an understanding of the opportunities and challenges of omnichannel for the physical store (Picot-Coupey et al., 2016; Barann et al., 2020; Jocevski, 2020; Bruce et al., 2023).

Many studies at this time focused on the cause and effect of digitalisation, technology advances and omnichannel retailing (e.g. Beck and Rygl, 2015; Rapp et al., 2015; Verhoef et al., 2015; Hagberg et al., 2016), yet the physical store is conspicuous by its relative absence in this literature stream (Bäckström and Johansson, 2017; Hänninen et al., 2021). The adoption of online, multi- and omnichannel naturally resulted in a shift in research focus, yet the physical store remains the main channel choice for many consumers (Hagberg et al., 2017; Avsar, 2021; Mahadevan and Joshi, 2021; Euromonitor, 2023). What was initially signalled as a physical retail apocalypse (Helm et al., 2020; Paul and Rosenbaum, 2020) has shifted to a recognition that the role of the physical store is being redefined, with the need for more research to understand the future of the physical store space, its multidimensionality features, its further evolution and influence on customer experiences (Bäckström and Johansson, 2017; Bustamante and Rubio, 2017; Reinartz et al., 2019), especially since the COVID-19 pandemic (Gerea et al., 2021; Hänninen et al., 2021; Bruce et al., 2023). This is crucial as retailers continue to invest in in-store technologies to enhance customer experience and engagement (Shankar et al., 2020; Ylilehto et al., 2021; Bonfanti et al., 2023; Pusceddu et al., 2023).

Towards omnichannel retailing through in-store technology

Technology is reshaping the retail landscape (Grewal et al., 2017; Helm et al., 2020; Roggeveen and Sethuraman, 2020; Shankar et al., 2020; Quinones et al., 2023). A significant enabler of retail change over the past two decades has been digital transformation, as such technologies have become more pervasive (Reinartz et al., 2019; Ylilehto et al., 2021). In recent years, the blurring of channel boundaries has accelerated, with traditional offline stores investing in their online service offer to drive convenience and assortment, whilst online retailers have been investing in physical stores to drive customer experience (Reinartz et al., 2019; Ratchford et al., 2022; Pusceddu et al., 2023). The modern retail landscape is defined by constantly changing consumer expectations and increasing customer touchpoints, which demands channel unification (Foroudi et al., 2018; Raconteur, 2021a/b). The physical store has become increasingly integrated with digital channels to offer a connected, personal experience in the consumer's 'phygital' shopping journey (Blázquez, 2014; Fernández et al., 2018; Mosquera et al., 2018). Technology-based service delivery systems in-store have become an integral part of shopping and are shown to impact on customer experience (Verhoef et al., 2009; Grewal et al., 2017; Larke et al., 2018; Hossain et al., 2019). Today, when customers can check their phones to see product assortments and prices from home, physical stores have to differentiate themselves (Gauri et al., 2021) if they are to retain a role.

The ascendance of phygitality

While the term phygital is not new to retail practitioners or researchers, its meaning remains contested and underdeveloped (Klaus, 2021; Batat, 2022; Bonfanti et al., 2023; Lee et al., 2023). It is widely assumed that its conception dates back to 2007 when Australian advertising agency Momentum first coined the term to describe the connection between physical and digital ecosystems (Ilius, 2023). Since then, the usage of the term has proliferated amongst practitioners with tardy scholarly attention culminating in 2021 (Mele et al., 2023). Many argue that its conceptual vagueness has perpetuated scholarly confusion and restricted its development (Klaus, 2021; Batat, 2022; Lee et al., 2023; Mele et al., 2023). A recent 'phygital' word search on Google and Google Scholar outputted 4.5 million and 4,680 results, respectively. Moving from the dominance of the word being used as an adjective to a noun, Klaus (2021:1) conceptualises "phygitality" as a new form of "hybrid consumption experience", which integrates customer interactions online and offline (i.e. syneresis of physical and digital) (Batat, 2022; Lee et al., 2023). Phygital experiences are perceived as a merging, multidimensional ecosystem that creates a continuum in consumer value (Batat, 2022). Therefore, phygital CEM involves continuously aligning a retailer's resources with those of its customers, with the experience being co-created by both (Jacob et al., 2023).

Phygital discourse can be broadly categorised into six areas: context (e.g. retail, tourism, luxury, fashion) (e.g. Iannilli and Spagnoli, 2021; Klaus, 2021; Kim et al., 2022; Hyun et al., 2022; Pangarkar et al., 2022; Lawry, 2023), channel, places and spaces (e.g. Duhan and Singh, 2019; Akter et al., 2021), objects and applications (e.g. Tom Dieck and Han, 2022; Mele et al., 2023), customer journey (e.g. Mele et al., 2021; Mele and Russo Spenda, 2022; Jacob et al., 2023; Mele et al., 2023), shopping experience (e.g. Ballina et al., 2019; Batat, 2019, 2022; Samir and Soumia, 2020; Silva and Cachinho, 2021) and wider benefits afforded to customers – empowerment, satisfaction, patronage, happiness, marketplace immersion and increased accessibility (e.g. Banik, 2021; Mishra et al., 2023; Lee et al., 2023) and companies – enhanced brand image consistency, customer relationships, resource alignment and leveraged capabilities (e.g. Homburg et al., 2017; Siebert et al., 2020; Talukdar and Yu, 2021; Jacob et al., 2023; Lee et al., 2023). Much of the extant discourse has attracted recent criticism for limiting the phygital construct to channels, seen as 'a part' of CX, rather than taking a more holistic customer-centric approach that extends beyond economic (purchase) and functional (channel) boundaries (associated with omnichannel retailing) (e.g. Klaus, 2021; Batat, 2022; Pangarkar et al., 2022; Bonfanti et al., 2023; Lawry, 2023; Lee et al., 2023), regardless of what channel or technology contributes to the experience (Klaus, 2021). In expounding the concept, Batat (2022:10) defines phygital as a holistic and integrative ecosystem that adopts a consumer standpoint as a starting point and then integrates a combination of physical, human, digital and media content elements, platforms, technologies and extended realities, among others; the goal of phygital is to offer unique and compelling customer experiences that should guarantee a coherent continuum in the delivery process of consumer value provided from digital to physical and vice versa.

Two conceptual frameworks offer utility in the advancement of phygitality. The 'Phygital CX framework' (PH-CX) (Batat, 2022:11–12) depicts that CX is created by shifting from physical to digital (i.e. digitalisation) and from digital to physical (i.e. physicalisation). Along this continuum, digital technologies provide customers an immersive experience with higher levels of emotional, symbolic and social value (Bonfanti et al., 2023). Second, the 'ADO framework' (based on antecedents, decisions and outcomes) (Mele et al., 2023) offers a holistic interpretation for phygital transformation, whereby antecedents (A) comprise phygital resources (objects and applications) and phygital context (place/space), which, in turn, affect decisions (D) during the phygital customer journey, which then enable phygital experience outcomes (O). Both models envision phygital as extending beyond channel integration, as a nexus or hybrid that is still emerging and developing. These frameworks align with Alexander's notion of ERTs, explained further in Chapter 2. The shift towards hyper-phygital fashion experiences and practices is discussed further in Chapters 2, 4 and 6.

In-store technologies: definition, types, integration, impact

In-store technologies are defined as "different devices that facilitate the shopping process at various points in the store" (Mosquera et al., 2018:66) and "digitise and enhance the customer experience" (Lorente-Martinez et al., 2020:2) by enabling consumer interaction. Research on in-store technologies has gained increasing attention over the past 20 years, yet remains an emerging field, with most papers published over the past five years and with few accepted theoretical frameworks, adoption models or technology taxonomies (Dekimpe et al., 2020; Wolpert and Roth, 2020; Grewal et al., 2021; Ylilehto et al., 2021). Existing studies primarily focus on consumer intention to adopt or use technologies (e.g. Venkatesh and Davis, 2000; Curran et al., 2003; Montoya-Weiss et al., 2003; Meuter et al., 2005; Weijters et al., 2007), ownership and control (e.g. Beck and Rygl, 2015; Inman and Nikolova, 2017; Bèzes, 2019), the consequences of usage on satisfaction, loyalty and engagement (e.g. Holloway and Beatty, 2008; Kim et al., 2013), cost and service measurement (e.g. Zeithaml et al., 2002; Parasuraman, 2000; Parasuraman et al., 2005; Roggeveen and Sethuraman, 2020) and, to a lesser extent, retail management strategies towards integration (e.g. Hagberg et al., 2017; Pantano et al., 2018; Roy et al., 2018; Tom Dieck and Han, 2022) and their contribution towards store atmospherics (e.g. Poncin and Mimoun, 2014; Pantano, 2016; Roggeveen et al., 2020).

From a customer perspective, technologies are seen to positively influence the shopping experience, increase store attractiveness and buying behaviour (Lee and Leonas, 2018; Savastano et al., 2019; Ha, 2020; Ylilehto et al., 2021), whilst enabling retailers to improve the digital information on customer behaviours and thereby data-driven decision-making, optimise operations and facilitate channel integration (Inman and Nikolova, 2017; Grewal et al., 2020; Chang et al., 2023; Quinones et al., 2023). They are known to facilitate both utilitarian and hedonic consumption experience through self-checkout (Lee, 2015; Fernandes and Pedroso, 2017; Bonfanti et al., 2023) smartphones and retail apps (Shankar et al., 2010; Kim et al., 2013; Pantano and Priporas, 2016; Fuentes et al., 2017; Perry et al., 2019) and virtual reality (VR) and augmented reality (AR) technologies (Rese et al., 2017; Watson et al., 2018; Jin et al., 2021). However, most existing studies focus on a single technology type, rather than several, and their interrelated influence on the total customer experience (Blázquez, 2014; Wolpert and Roth, 2020). In terms of technology types, radio-frequency identification (RFID), digital signage and self-service technologies are considered the most prevalent and pervasive in service settings (e.g. Weijters et al., 2007; Dennis et al., 2010; Chen, 2012; Eastlick et al., 2012; Wang et al., 2013; Renko and Druzijanic, 2014; Bhattacharya, 2015; Roggeveen et al., 2016; Venkatesh et al., 2017; Willems et al., 2017; Hauser et al., 2019; Lee and Lyu, 2019; Pantano and Vannucci, 2019; Alexander and Kent, 2021; Ha, 2020). The relatively few studies that take a general approach to in-store technologies serve to offer an index and classification of technologies and retailer prioritisation towards them (Willems et al., 2017; Inman and Nikolova, 2017; Hagberg et al., 2017; Pantano and Vannucci, 2019; Baier and Rese, 2020; Wolpert and Roth, 2020), with most acknowledging the role of technologies in the future of physical retailing, but there remains a dearth of research in this area (Hwangbo et al., 2017; Grewal et al., 2017; Dekimpe et al., 2020; Quinones et al., 2023).

Despite the accelerated pace at which technology is permeating retailing (Grewal et al., 2017; Roggeveen and Sethuraman, 2020; Shankar et al., 2020), and its progress being a strategic issue for many retailers (Pantano and Vannucci, 2019; Wolpert and Roth, 2020; Quinones et al., 2023), scholarly research on the impact of technology on the total customer experience remains nascent and could be considered work in progress due to the incongruence between different channels in the physical store that may generate negative experiences (Verhoef et al., 2009; Bäckström and Johansson, 2017; Alexander and Kent, 2021). Indeed, recent trade journals, market reports (BoF, 2020; Bridges, 2021; The Future Laboratory, 2023; Euromonitor, 2023) and interactions with fashion retailers support the view that omnichannel frictions remain, with limited "buy online return to store" or "buy from store return to any store" service capabilities, despite recognised rapid retailer advances and investment in digitalisation since the pandemic (industry interviews with the author, 2021; see also Alexander and Kent (2022), for seven friction points of the shopping journey). Moreover, Bäckström and Johansson's (2017) study revealed that while many retailers emphasised innovation and advanced technologies in-store, in practice most prioritised traditional values such as personnel, layout and display over technological investment. These inconsistencies are particularly evident in the fashion sector, where scholars refer to fashion retailers' innovativeness towards in-store technologies (Colombi et al., 2018; Pantano and Vannucci, 2019), conflicting with some practitioner perspectives (Stephens, 2018; Thomson, 2019; Fish, 2020; McKinsey, 2020; Euromonitor, 2023; The Future Laboratory, 2023).

Research into in-store channel integration has demonstrated continuous evolution facilitated by technologies, yet prior studies have tended to take a cross-sectional approach thereby limiting their ability to assess changes in retailer technology adoption and customer experience (e.g. Iman and Nikolova, 2017; Willems et al., 2017; Pantano and Vannucci, 2019; Yadav and Pavlou, 2020), or the possible usage of new technologies (Pantano et al., 2018; Shankar et al., 2020), despite strong consumer appetite

(Grewal et al., 2020). Further studies are required to engage with retailing dynamics (Dekimpe and Gyskens, 2019) in order to gain a more nuanced understanding of the impact of technologies and their future evolution (Souiden and Ladhari, 2019; Paul and Rosenbaum, 2020). This is a necessity – especially for physical stores – in order to avoid becoming obsolescent (Mende and Noble, 2019), to meet the high service, personalisation and convenience expectations of consumers (Grewal et al., 2020; Grewal and Roggeveen, 2020; Euromonitor, 2023; The Future Laboratory, 2023) and anticipate future unified spatial experiences (Hoyer et al., 2020; Bruce et al., 2023). The leveraging of technologies in-store to generate phygital experiences is exemplified in the case studies in Chapter 6.

References

Abbott, L. (1955) *Quality and competition*. New York: Columbia University Press.

Addis, M. and Holbrook, M.B. (2001) 'On the conceptual link between mass customisation and experiential consumption: An explosion of subjectivity.' *Journal of Consumer Behavior*, 1(1), pp. 50–66.

Ahn, T., Rhu, S. and Han, I. (2007) 'The impact of web quality and playfulness on user acceptance of online retailing.' *Information Management*, 44(3), pp. 263–275.

Ailawadi, K.L and Farris, P.W. (2017) 'Managing multi- and omni-channel distribution: Metrics and research directions.' *Journal of Retailing*, 93(1), pp. 120–135.

Akaka, M.A., Vargo, S.L. and Schau, H.J. (2015) 'The context of experience.' *Journal of Service Management*, 26(2), pp. 206–223.

Akter, S., Hossain, T.M. and Strong, C.A. (2021) 'What omnichannel really means.' *Journal of Strategic Marketing*, 29(7), pp. 567–573.

Alba, J.W. and Williams, E.F. (2012) 'Pleasure principles: A review of research on hedonic consumption.' *Journal of Consumer Psychology*, 23(1), pp. 2–18.

Alexander, B. (2019) 'Commerce, culture and experience convergence: Fashion's third places.' *Journal of Services Marketing*, 33(3), pp. 257–272.

Alexander, B. and Nobbs, K. (2016) 'Multi-sensory fashion retail experiences: The impact of sound, smell, sight and touch on consumer-based brand equity,' in Vecchi, A. and Buckley, C. (eds.) *Handbook of research on global fashion management and merchandising*. IGI Global, pp. 420–443.

Alexander, B. and Olivares Alvarado, D. (2017) 'Chapter 8: Convergence of physical and virtual retail spaces: The influence of technology on consumer in-store experience,' in Vecchi, A. (ed.) *The book of advanced fashion technology and operations management*. Hershey, PA: IGI Global, pp. 191–219. https://doi.org/10.4018/978-1-5225-1865-5.ch008

Alexander, B. and Blazquez Cano, M. (2019) 'Futurising the physical store in the omnichannel retail environment,' in Piotrowicz, W. and Cuthbertson, R. (eds.) *Exploring Omnichannel retailing: Common expectations and diverse realities*. Springer Press. ISBN 978-3-319-98272-4.

Alexander, B. and Blazquez Cano, M. (2020), 'Store of the future: towards a (re)invention and (re) imagination of physical store space in an omnichannel context', *Journal of retailing and consumer services*, Vol. 55, pp.1–12. DOI: https://doi.org/10.1016/j.jretconser.2019.101913

Alexander, B. and Kent, A. (2018), Retail Environments. In Petermans, A., Kent, A. Eds. Retail Design. Routledge Publishing. ISBN: 9781472467836. Chapter 5, pp. 62–86.

Alexander, B. and Kent, A. (2021) 'Tracking technology diffusion in-store: a fashion retail perspective.' *International Journal of Retail & Distribution Management*, 49(10), pp. 1369–1390. https://doi.org/10.1108/IJRDM-05-2020-0191

Alexander, B. and Kent, A. (2022) 'Change in technology-enabled omnichannel customer experiences in-store.' *Journal of Retailing and Consumer Services*, 65, 102338. https://doi.org/10.1016/j.jretconser.2020.102338

Amed, I. and Berg, A. (2020) *The state of fashion 2021*. Business of Fashion. [Online] [Accessed 9th September 2021] https://www.businessoffashion.com/reports/news-analysis/the-state-of-fashion-2021-industry-report-bof-mckinsey.

Andajani, E. (2015) 'Understanding customer experience management in retailing.' *Procedia-Social and Behavioral Sciences*, 211, pp. 629–633.

Andreini, D., Pedeliento, G., Zarantonello, L. and Solerio, C. (2018) 'A renaissance of brand experience: Advancing the concept through a multi-perspective analysis.' *Journal of Business Research*, 91, pp. 123–133.

Andreu, L., Bigne, E., Chumpitaz, R. and Swaen, V. (2006) 'How does the perceived retail environment influence consumers' emotional experience? Evidence from two retail settings.' *The International Review of Retail, Distribution and Consumer Research*, 16(5), pp. 559–578.

Antéblian, B., Filser, M. and Roederer, C. (2013) 'Consumption experience in retail environments: A literature review.' *Recherche et Applications en Marketing (English Edition)*, 28(3), pp. 82–109.

Arnold, E.J. and Price, L.L. (1993) 'River magic: Extraordinary experience and the extended service encounter.' *Journal of Consumer Research*, 20(1), pp. 24–45.

Arnold, E.J., Price, L.L. and Zinkhan, G. (2002) *Consumers*. New York: McGraw-Hill.

Arnold, M.J. and Reynolds, E. (2003) 'Hedonic shopping motivations.' *Journal of Retailing*, 79(2), pp. 77–95.

Arnold, M.J., Reynolds, K.E., Ponder, N. and Lueg, J.E. (2005) 'Customer delight in a retail context: Investigating delightful and terrible shopping experiences.' *Journal of Business Research*, 58(8), pp. 1132–1145.

Asmare, A. and Zewdie, S. (2022) 'Omnichannel retailing strategy: A systematic review.' *International Review of Retail, Distribution and Consumer Research*, 32(1), pp. 59–79.

Atwal, G. and Williams, A. (2017) 'Luxury brand marketing - the experience is everything,' in Kapferer, J.N., Kernstock, J., Brexendorf, T. and Powell, S. (eds.) *Advances in luxury brand management, Journal of Brand Management: Advanced Collections*. Cham: Palgrave Macmillan, pp. 43–57.

Aurier, P. and Guintcheva, G. (2014) 'Using affect– expectations theory to explain the direction of the impacts of experiential emotions on satisfaction.' *Psychology & Marketing*, 31(10), pp. 900–913.

Avery, J., Steenburgh, T.J., Deighton, J. and Caravella, M. (2012) 'Adding bricks to clicks: Predicting the patterns of cross-channel elasticities over time.' *Journal of Marketing*, 76(3), pp. 96–111.

Avsar, B.Z. (2021) 'Omni-channel trends in COVID-19 pandemic.' *Journal of International Trade, Logistics and Law*, 7(1), pp. 97–104.

Babin, B.J. and Attaway, J.S. (2000) 'Atmospheric affect as a tool for creating value and gaining share of customer.' *Journal of Business Research*, 49, pp. 91–99.

Babin, B.J., Darden, W.R. and Griffin, M. (1994) 'Work and/or fun: Measuring hedonic and utilitarian shopping value.' *Journal of Consumer Research*, 20(4), pp. 644–656.

Babin, B. and Darden, W.R. (1995) 'Consumer self-regulation in a retail environment.' *Journal of Retailing*, 71(1), pp. 47–70.

Babin, B.J., Hardesty, D.M. and Suter, T.A. (2003) 'Color and shopping intentions.' *Journal of Business Research*, 56(7), pp. 541–551.

Bäckström, K. (2011) 'Shopping as leisure: An exploration of manifoldness and dynamics in consumer shopping experiences.' *Journal of Retailing and Consumer Services*, 18(3), pp. 200–209.

Bäckström, K. and Johansson, U. (2006) 'Creating and Consuming Experiences in Retail Store Environments: Comparing Retailer and Consumer Perspectives.' *Journal of Retailing and Consumer Services*, 13(6), pp. 417–430.

Bäckström, K. and Johansson, U. (2017) 'An exploration of consumers' experiences in physical stores: Comparing consumers' and retailers' perspectives in past and present times.' *The International Review of Retail, Distribution and Consumer Research*, 27(3), pp. 241–259.

Badrinarayanan, V., Becerra, E.P., Kim, C-H. and Sreedhar, M. (2012) 'Transference and congruence on purchase intentions in online stores of multi-channel retailers: Initial evidence from the US and South Korea.' *Journal of the Academy of Marketing Science*, 40(4), pp. 539–557.

Bagdare, S. (2013) 'Antecedents of retail customer experience.' *Journal of Marketing and Communication*, 8(3), pp. 45–51.

Bagdare, S. (2015) 'Emotional determinants of retail customer experience.' *International Journal of Marketing and Business Communication*, 4(2), pp. 9–16.

Bagdare, S. (2016) 'Retail customer experience: A research agenda.' *International Journal of Research in Commerce and Management*, 7(4), pp. 55–58.

Bagdare, S. and Jain, R. (2013) 'Measuring retail customer experience.' *International Journal of Retail & Distribution Management*, 41(10), pp. 790–804.

Baier, D. and Rese, S. (2020) 'How to increase multichannel shopping satisfaction? An adapted Kano based stage-gate approach to select new technologies.' *Journal of Retailing and Consumer Services*, 56, pp. 157–163.

Baker, J. (1987) 'The role of the environment in marketing services: The consumer perspective,' in Czepiel, J.A., Congram, C.A. and Shanahan, J. (eds.) *The services challenge: Integrating for competitive advantage*. Chicago, IL: American Marketing Association, pp. 79–84.

Baker, J., Levy, M. and Grewal, D. (1992) 'An experimental approach to making retail store environmental decisions.' *Journal of Retailing*, 68(4), pp. 445–460.

Baker, J., A. Parasuraman, Grewal, D. and Voss, G.B. (2002) 'The influence of multiple store environment cues on perceived merchandise value and patronage intentions.' *Journal of Marketing*, 66(2), pp. 120–141.

Balasubramanian, S., Raghunathan, R. and Mahan, V. (2005) 'Consumers in a multichannel environment: Product utility, process utility and channel choice.' *Journal of Interactive Marketing*, 19(2), pp. 12–30.

Ballantine, P.W., Jack, R. and Parsons, A.G. (2010) 'Atmospheric cues and their effect on the hedonic retail experience.' *International Journal of Retail & Distribution Management*, 38(8), pp. 641–653.

Ballantine, P.W., Parsons, A. and Comeskey, K. (2015) 'A conceptual model of the holistic effects of atmospheric cues in fashion retailing.' *International Journal of Retail & Distribution Management*, 43(6), pp. 503–517.

Ballina, F.J., Valdes, L. and Del Valle, E. (2019) 'The phygital experience in the smart tourism destination.' *International Journal of Tourism Cities*, 5(4), pp. 656–671.

Banik, S. (2021) 'Exploring the involvement-patronage link in the phygital retail experiences.' *Journal of Retailing and Consumer Services*, 62, pp. 1–12.

Barann, B., Betzing, J.H. and Niemann, M. (2020) 'Exploring customers' likeliness to use e-service touchpoints in brick and mortar retail.' *Electronic Markets*. https://doi.org/10.1007/s12525-020-00445-0

Barbosa, J. and Casais, B. (2022) 'The transformative and evolutionary approach of omnichannel in retail companies: Insights from multi-case studies in Portugal.' *International Journal of Retail and Distribution Management*, 50(7), pp. 799–815.

Barwitz, N. and Maas, P. (2018) 'Understanding the Omnichannel customer journey: Determinants of interaction choice.' *Journal of Interactive Marketing*, 43, pp. 116–133.

Batat, W. (2019) 'Phygital customer experience: Definition, characteristics, types, and key success factors,' in Experiential Marketing, 1st Ed. (pp. 207–227). Routledge. https://doi.org/10.4324/9781315232201

Batat, W. (2022) 'What does phygital really mean? A conceptual introduction to the phygital customer experience (PH-CX) framework.' *Journal of Strategic Marketing*, pp. 1–24. https://doi.org/10.1080/0965254X.2022.2059775

Baxendale, S., Macdonald, E.K. and Wilson, H.N. (2015) 'The impact of different touchpoints on brand consideration.' *Journal of Retailing*, 91(2), pp. 235–253.

Beck, N. and Rgyl, D. (2015) 'Categorization of multiple channel retailing in multi-, cross-, and omni- channel retailing for retailers and retailing.' *Journal of Retailing and Consumer Services*, 27, pp. 170–178.

Becker, L. (2018) 'Methodological proposals for the study of consumer experience.' *Qualitative Market Research: An International Journal*, 21(4), pp. 465–490.

Becker, L. and Jaakkola, E. (2020) 'Customer experience: Fundamental premises and implications for research.' *Journal of the Academy of Marketing Science*, 48, pp. 630–648.

Bell, D.R., Gallino, S. and Moreno, A. (2014) 'Showrooms and information provision in omni-channel retail.' *Production and Operations Management*, 24(3), pp. 359–368.

Bell, D.R., Gallino, S. and Moreno, A. (2018) 'Offline showrooms in omnichannel retail: Demand and operational benefits.' *Journal of Management Science*, 64(4), pp. 1629–1651.

Bellizzi, J.A. and Hite, R.E. (1992) 'Environmental color, consumer feelings, and purchase likelihood.' *Psychology & Marketing*, 9(5), pp. 347–363.

Bendoly, E., Blocher, J.D., Bretthauser, K.M., Krishnan, S. and Venkataramanan, M.A. (2005) 'Online/in-store integration and customer retention.' *Journal of Service Research*, 7(4), pp. 313–327.

ben Mimoun, M.S., Lancelot Miltgen, C. and Slama, B. (2022) 'Is the shopper always the king/queen? Study of omnichannel retail technology use and shopping orientations.' *Journal of Retailing and Consumer Services*, Pergamon, 65, 102844. https://doi.org/10.1016/j.jretconser.2021.102844

Berger, A., Schlager, T., Sprott, D. and Herrmann, A. (2018) 'Gamified interactions: Whether, when, and how games facilitate self–Brand connections.' *Journal of the Academy of Marketing Science*, 46(4), pp. 652–673.

Berman, B. and Thelen, S. (2004) 'A guide to developing and managing a well-integrated multichannel retail strategy.' *International Journal of Retail & Distribution Management*, 32(3), pp. 147–156.

Berman, B. and Thelen, S. (2018) 'Planning and implementing an effective omnichannel marketing program.' *International Journal of Retail & Distribution Management*, 46(7), pp. 598–614.

Berry, L.L., Carbone, L.P. and Haeckel, S.H. (2002) 'Managing the total customer experience.' *Sloan Management Review*, 43(3), pp. 85–90.

Bèzes, C. (2016) 'Comparing online and in-store risks in multichannel shopping.' *International Journal of Retail and Distribution Management*, 44(3), pp. 284–300.

Bèzes, C. (2019) 'What kind of in-store smart retailing for an omnichannel real-life experience?' *Recherche et Applications en Marketing*, 34(1), pp. 91–112.

Bhalla, R. (2014) 'The omni-channel customer experience: Driving engagement through digitization.' *Journal of Digital and Social Media Marketing*, 1, pp. 365–372.

Bhattacharya, M. (2015) 'A conceptual framework of RFID adoption in retail using Roger's stage model.' *Business Process Management Journal*, 21(3), pp. 517–540.

Bilgihan, A., Kandampully, J. and Zhang, T.C. (2016) 'Towards a unified customer experience in online shopping environments: Antecedents and outcomes.' *International Journal of Quality and Service Sciences*, 8(1), pp. 102–119.

Biswas, D. (2019) 'Sensory aspects of retailing: Theoretical and practical implications.' *Journal of Retailing*, 95(4), pp. 111–115.

Biswas, D., Labrecque, L.I., Lehmann, D.R. and Markos, E. (2014) 'Making choices while smelling, tasting and listening: The role of sensory (dis) similarity when sequentially sampling products.' *Journal of Marketing*, 78(1), pp. 508–519.

Bitner, J.M. (1992) 'Servicescapes: The impact of physical surroundings on customers and employees.' *Journal of Marketing*, 56(2) pp. 57–71.

Bitner, J.M., Faranda, W.T., Hubbert, A.R. and Zeithaml, V.A. (1997) 'Customer contributions and roles in service delivery.' *International Journal of Service Industry Management*, 8(3), pp. 193–205.

Blakeney, J. (2016) 'What are the benefits of creating an omnichannel brand experience.' *Journal of Brand Strategy*, 5(1), pp. 57–66.

Blázquez, M. (2014) 'Fashion shopping in multichannel retail: The role of technology in enhancing the customer experience.' *International Journal of Electronic Commerce*, 18(4), pp. 97–116.

BoF (2020) *The evolution of omnichannel.* Business of Fashion [Online] [Accessed 9th Sept 2021] https://www.businessoffashion.com/articles/retail/affirm-evolution-omnichannel-retail.

Bolton, R.N., McColl-Kennedy, J.R., Cheung, L., Gallan, A., Orsingher, C., Witell, L. and Zaki, M. (2018) 'Customer experience challenges: Bringing together digital, physical and social realms.' *Journal of Service Management*, 29(5), pp. 776–808.

Bonfanti, A., Vigolo, V., Vannucci, V. and Brunetti, F. (2023) 'Creating memorable shopping experiences to meet phygital customers' needs: Evidence from sporting goods stores.' *International Journal of Retail & Distribution Management*, 15(13), pp. 81–100.

Botschen, G. and Wegerer, P.L. (2017) 'Brand-driven retail format innovation: A conceptual framework.' *International Journal of Retail & Distribution Management*, 45(7/8), pp. 874–891.

Brakus, J.J., Schmitt, B.H. and Zarantonello, L. (2009) 'Brand experience: What is it? How is it measured? Does it affect loyalty?' *Journal of Marketing*, 73(3), pp. 52–68.

Brighenti, A.M. (2010) 'On territorology: Towards a general science of territory.' *Theory, Culture & Society*, 27(1), pp. 52–72.

Briedis, H., Kronschbabl, A., Rodriguez, A. and Ungerman, K. (2020) *Adapting to the next normal in retail: The customer experience imperative.* McKinsey and Company [Online] [Accessed 1st June 2021] https://www.mckinsey.com/industries/retail/our-insights/adapting-to-the-next-normal-in-retail-the-customer-experience-imperative.

Bridges, T. (2021) *How consumer buying patterns could continue to change in 2021.* Verdict [Online] [Accessed 20th August, 2021] https://www.verdict.co.uk/consumer-buying-patterns/

Brocato, E.D., Voorhees, C.M. and Baker, J. (2012) 'Understanding the influence of cues from other customers in the service experience: A scale development and validation.' *Journal of Retailing*, 88(3), pp. 384–398.

Bruce, H.L., Krolikowska, E. and Rooney, T. (2023) 'Guest editorial: Investigating the effect of the physical context on customer experience.' *Journal of Services Marketing*, 37(6), pp. 689–699.

Brun, I., Rajaobelina, L., Ricard, L. and Berthiaume, B. (2017) 'Impact of customer experience on loyalty: A multichannel examination.' *The Service Industries Journal*, 37(5/6), pp. 317–340.

Brynjolfsson, E., Hu, Y. and Rahman, M.S. (2009) 'Battle of the retail channels: How product selection and geography drive cross-channel competition.' *Journal of Management Science*, 55(11), pp. 1755–1765.

Brynjolfsson, E., Hu, Y.J. and Rahman, M.S. (2013) 'Competing in the age of Omnichannel retailing.' *MIT Sloan Management Review*, pp. 1–7. [Online] [Accessed 1st September 2021] https://sloanreview.mit.edu/article/competing-in-the-age-of-omnichannel-retailing/

Bueno, E.V., Weber, T.B.B., Bomfim, L. and Kato, H.T. (2019) 'Measuring customer experience in service: A systematic review.' *The Service Industries Journal*, 39(11/12), pp. 779–798.

Burke, R.R. (2002) 'Technology and the customer interface: What consumers want in the physical and virtual Store.' *Journal of the Academy of Marketing Science*, 30(4), pp. 411–432.

Bustamante, J.C. and Rubio, N. (2017) 'Measuring customer experience in physical retail environments.' *Journal of Service Management*, 28(5), pp. 884–913.

Cachon, G.P. and Lariviere, M.A. (2005) 'Supply chain coordination with revenue-sharing contracts: Strengths and limitations.' *Management Science*, 51(1), pp. 30–44.

Cai, Y-J. and Lo, C.K.Y. (2020) 'Omni-channel management in the new retailing era: A systematic review and future research agenda.' *International Journal of Production Economics*, 229. No page number assigned. https://doi.org/10.1016/j.ijpe.2020.107729

Cao, L. (2014) 'Business model transformation in moving to a cross-channel retail strategy: A case study.' *International Journal of Electronic Commerce*, 18(4), pp. 69–96.

Cao, L. and Li, L. (2015) 'The impact of cross-channel integration on retailers' sales growth.' *Journal of Retailing*, 91(2), pp. 198–216.

Cao, L. and Li, L. (2018) 'Determinants of retailers' cross-channel integration: An innovation diffusion perspective on omni-channel retailing.' *Journal of Interactive Marketing*, 44, pp. 1–16.

Carbone, L.P. and Haeckel, S.H. (1994) 'Engineering customer experiences.' *Marketing Management*, 3(3), pp. 9–19.

Carú, A. and Cova, B. (2003) 'Revisiting consumption experience: A more humble but complete view of the concept.' *Marketing Theory*, 3(2), pp. 267–286.

Chandler, J. and Lusch, R. (2015) 'Service systems: A broadened framework and research agenda on value propositions, engagement, and service experience.' *Journal of Service Research*, 18(1), pp. 6–22.

Chaney, D., Lunardo, R. and Mencarelli, R. (2018) 'Consumption experience: Past, present and future.' *Qualitative Market Research*, 21(4), pp. 402–420.

Chang, Y-W., Hsu, P-Y., Chen, J., Shiau, W-L. and Xu, N. (2023) Utilitarian and/or hedonic shopping – consumer motivation to purchase in smart stores, *Industrial Management & Data Systems*, 123(3), pp. 821–842.

Chang, Y.P. and Li, J. (2022) 'Seamless experience in the context of omnichannel shopping: Scale development and empirical validation.' *Journal of Retailing and Consumer Services*, 64, 102800. https://doi.org/10.1016/j.jretconser.2021.102800

Chatterjee, P. (2006) 'Cross-channel product ordering and payment policies in multichannel retailing: Implications for shopping behavior and retailer profitability.' *Journal of Shopping Center Research*, 13(2), pp. 31–56.

Chatterjee, P. (2010) 'Multiple-channel and cross-channel shopping behavior: Role of consumer shopping orientations.' *Marketing Intelligence & Planning*, 28(1), pp. 9–24.

Chen, C.C. (2012) 'Identifying drivers for adoption intention in RFID service.' *International Journal of Mobile Communications*, 10(3), pp. 231–247.

Chen, Y., Cheung, C.M.K. and Tan, C.W. (2018) 'Omnichannel business research: Opportunities and challenges.' *Decision Support Systems*, 109, pp. 1–4.

Chevtchouk, Y., Veloutsou, C. and Paton, R.A. (2021) 'The experience - economy revisited: An interdisciplinary perspective and research agenda.' *Journal of Product & Brand Management*. In press. DOI 10.1108/JPBM-06-2019-2406.

Childers, T.L., Carr, C, L., Peck, J. and Carson, S. (2001) 'Hedonic and utilitarian motivations for online retail shopping behavior.' *Journal of Retailing*, 77(4), pp. 511–535.

Chiu, H.C., Hsieh, Y.C., Roan, J., Tseng, K.J. and Hsieh, J.K. (2011) 'The challenge for multichannel services: Cross-channel free-riding behavior.' *Electronic Commerce Research and Applications*, 10(2), pp. 268–277.

Chopra, S. (2016) 'How omni-channel can be the future of retailing.' *Decision*, 43(2), pp. 135–144.

Colombi, C., Kim, P. and Wyatt, N. (2018) 'Fashion retailing 'tech-gagement': Engagement fuelled by new technology.' *Research Journal of Textile and Apparel*, 22(4), pp. 390–406.

Cook, G. (2014) 'Customer experience in the omni-channel world and the challenges and opportunities this presents.' *Journal of Direct, Data and Digital Marketing Practice*, 15, pp. 262–266.

Cummins, S., Peltier, J.W. and Dixon, A. (2016) 'Omni-channel research framework in the context of personal selling and sales management: A review and research extensions.' *Journal of Research in Interactive Marketing*, 10(1), pp. 2–16.

Curran, J.M., Meuter, M.L. and Surprenant, C.F. (2003) 'Intentions to use self-service technologies: A confluence of multiple attitudes.' *Journal of Service Research*, 5(3), pp. 209–224.

De Borba, J.L.G., de Magalhaes, M.R., Filgueiras, R.S. and Bouzon, M. (2020) 'Barriers in omnichannel retailing returns: A conceptual framework.' *International Journal of Retail and Distribution Management*, 49(1), pp. 121–143.

De Keyser, A., Lemon, K.N., Keiningham, T. and Klaus, P. (2015) 'A framework for understanding and managing the customer experience.' *MSI Working Paper* No. 15–121. Marketing Science Institute, Cambridge, MA.

Dekimpe, M.G. and Geyskens, I. (2019) 'Retailing research in rapidly changing times: On the danger of being leapfrogged by practice.' *Journal of Retailing*, 95(1), pp. 6–9.

Dekimpe, M.G., Geyskens, I. and Gielens, K. (2020) 'Using technology to bring online convenience to offline shopping.' *Marketing Letters*, 31(1), pp. 25–29.

Dennis, C., Newman, A., Michon, R., Brakus, J.J. and Wright, T.L. (2010) 'The mediating effects of perception and emotion: Digital signage in mall atmospherics.' *Journal of Retailing and Consumer Services*, 17(3), pp. 205–215.

Dewey, J. (1938) *Experience and education.* New York: Free Press.

Donovan, R.J. and Rossiter, J.R. (1982) 'Store atmosphere: An environmental psychology approach.' *Journal of Retailing*, 58, pp. 34–58.

Duhan, P. and Singh, A. (Eds.). (2019) *M-commerce: Experiencing the phygital retail.* CRC Press.

Dutta, S., Kwan, S. and Segev, A. (1998) 'Business transformation in electronic commerce: A study of sectoral and regional trends.' *European Management Journal*, 16(5), pp. 540–551.

Eastlick, M.A., Ratto, C., Lotz, S.L. and Mishra, A. (2012) 'Exploring antecedents of attitude toward co-producing a retail checkout service utilising a self-service technology.' *International Review of Retail Distribution and Consumer Research*, 22(4), pp. 337–364.

Euromonitor (2021) *World market for apparel and footwear.* Passport Euromonitor. [Online] [Accessed 20th August 2021] https://www.euromonitor.com/world-market-for-apparel-and-footwear/report.

Euromonitor (2023) *Shifting channels in luxury and fashion.* Passport Euromonitor [Online] [Accessed 15th September 2023] https://www.euromonitor.com/shifting-channels-in-luxury-and-fashion/report

Falk, T., Schepers, J., Hammerschmidt, M. and Bauer, H.H. (2007) 'Identifying cross-channel dissynergies for multichannel service providers.' *Journal of Service Research*, 10(2), pp. 143–160.

Fernandes, T. and Pedroso, R. (2017) 'The effect of self-checkout quality on customer satisfaction and repatronage in a retail context.' *Service Business*, 11(1), pp. 69–92.

Fernández, N.V., Pérez, M.J.S. and Vázquez-Casielles, R. (2018) 'Webroomers versus showroomers: Are they the same?' *Journal of Business Research*, 92, pp. 300–320.

Fish, I. (2020) *The changing shape of retail in the 2020s.* Drapers. [Online] [Accessed 19th August 2021] https://www.drapersonline.com/companies/the-changing-shape-of-retail-in-the-2020s.

Foroudi, P., Gupta, S., Sivarajah, U. and Broderick, A. (2018) 'Investigating the effects of smart technology on customer dynamics and customer experience.' *Computers in Human Behavior*, 80, pp. 271–282.

Froehle, C.M. and Roth, A.V. (2004) 'New measurement scales for evaluating perceptions of technology-mediated customer service experience.' *Journal of Operations Management*, 22(1), pp. 1–21.

Frow, P. and Payne, A. (2007) 'Toward the 'perfect' customer experience.' *Journal of Brand Management*, 15(2), pp. 89–101.

Fuentes, C. and Svingstedt, A. (2017) 'Mobile phones and the practice of shopping: A study of how young adults use smartphones to shop.' *Journal of Retailing and Consumer Services*, 38, pp. 137–146.

Galipoglu, E., Kotzab, H., Teller, C., Yumurtaci Hüseyinoglu, I.Ö. and Pöppelbuß, J. (2018) 'Omni-channel retailing research - state of the art and intellectual foundation.' *International Journal of Physical Distribution & Logistics Management*, 48(4), pp. 365–390.

Gallino, S. and Moreno, A. (2014) 'Integration of online and offline channels in retail: The impact of sharing reliable inventory availability information.' *Management Science*, 60(6), pp. 1434–1451.

Gao, F. and Su, X. (2017) 'Omnichannel retail operations with buy-online-and-pick-up-in-store.' *Journal of Management Science*, 63(8), pp. 2478–2492.

Gao, W., Fan, H., Li, W. and Wang, H. (2021) 'Crafting the customer experience in omnichannel contexts: The role of channel integration.' *Journal of Business Research*, 126, pp. 12–22.

Garlin, F.V. and Owen, K. (2006) 'Setting the tone with the tune: A meta-analytic review of the effects of background music in retail settings.' *Journal of Business Research*, 59(6), pp. 755–764.

Gartner (2021) *Customer service trends and priorities: Discovering what's top of mind for service and support leaders*. Gartner. [Online] [Accessed 21st July 2021] https://www.gartner.com/en/customer-service-support/insights/service-leaders-priorities.

Gasparin, I., Panina, E., Becker, L., Yrjölä, M., Jaakkola, E. and Pizzutti, C. (2022) 'Challenging the integration imperative: A customer perspective on omnichannel journeys.' *Journal of Retailing and Consumer Services*, 64, p. 102829. https://doi.org/10.1016/j.jretconser.2021.102829

Gauri, D.K., Jindal, R.P., Ratchford, B., Fox, E., Bhatnagar, A., Pandey, A., Navallo, J.R, Fogarty, J., Carr, S. and Howerton, E. (2021) 'Evolution of retail formats: Past, present, and future.' *Journal of Retailing*, 97(1), pp. 42–61.

Gazzola, P., Pavione, E., Pezzetti, R. and Grechi, D. (2020) 'Trends in the fashion industry: The perception of sustainability and circular economy: A gender/generation quantitative approach.' *Sustainability*, 12, pp. 2–19.

Gensler, S., Verhoef, P.C. and Böhm, M. (2012) 'Understanding consumers' multichannel choices across the different stages of the buying process.' *Marketing Letters*, 23(4), pp. 987–1003.

Gentile, C., Spiller, N. and Noci, G. (2007) 'How to sustain the customer experience: An overview of experience components that co-create value with the customer.' *European Management Journal*, 25(5), pp. 395–410.

Gerea, C., Gonzalez-Lopez, F. and Herskovic, V. (2021) 'Omnichannel customer experience and management: An integrative review and research agenda.' *Sustainability*, 13(2824), pp. 1–24.

Gilmore, J.H. and Pine, B.J. (2002) 'Customer experience places: The new offering frontier.' *Strategy & Leadership*, 30(4), pp. 4–11.

GlobalData. (2020) *Global online retailing 2019–2023 with COVID-19 impact*. GlobalData. [Online] [Accessed 20th August 2021] https://retail-globaldata-com.arts.idm.oclc.org/Analysis/details/global-online-retailing-2019-2023-with-covid-19-impact.

Goode, M., Dahl, D. and Moreau, P. (2010) 'The effect of experiential analogies on consumer perceptions and attitudes.' *Journal of Marketing Research*, 47(2), pp. 274–286.

Grace, D. and O'Cass, A. (2004) 'Examining service experiences and post-consumption evaluations.' *Journal of Services Marketing*, 18(6), pp. 450–461.

Grewal, D., Levy, M. and Kumar, V. (2009) 'Customer experience management in retailing: An organizing framework.' *Journal of Retailing*, 85(1) pp. 1–14.

Grewal, D., Roggeveen, A.L. and Nordfält, J. (2017) 'The future of retailing.' *Journal of Retailing*, 93(1), pp. 1–6.

Grewal, D. and Roggeveen, A.L. (2020) 'Understanding retail experiences and customer journey management.' *Journal of Retailing*, 96(1), pp. 3–8.

Grewal, D., Noble, S.M., Roggeveen, A.L. and Nordfält, J. (2020) 'The future of in-store technology.' *Journal of Academy of Marketing Science*, 48(1), pp. 96–113.

Grewal, D., Gauri, D.K., Roggeveen, A.L. and Sethuraman, R. (2021) 'Strategizing retailing in the new technology era.' *Journal of Retailing*, 97(1), pp. 6–12.

Ha, Y. (2020) 'The effects of shoppers' motivation on self-service technology use intention: Moderating effects of the presence of employee.' *Journal of Asian Finance, Economics and Business*, 7(9), pp. 489–497.

Hagberg, J., Sundstrom, J.M, Nicklas, E.Z. (2016) 'The digitalization of retailing: An exploratory framework.' *International Journal of Retail & Distribution Management*, 44(7), pp. 694–712.

Hagberg, J., Jonsson, A. and Egels-Zandén (2017) 'Retail digitalization: Implications for physical stores.' *Journal of Retailing & Consumer Services*, 39, pp. 264–269.

Halsted, C.P. (1993) 'Brightness, luminance and confusion.' *Information Display*, 9, pp. 21–24.

Hänninen, M., Kwan, S.K. and Mitronen, L. (2021) 'From the store to omnichannel retail: Looking back over three decades of research.' *The International Review of Retail, Distribution and Consumer Research*, 31(1), pp. 1–35.

Hansen, R. and Sia, S.K. (2015) 'Hummel's digital transformation toward omnichannel retailing: Key lessons learned.' *MIS Quarterly Executive*, 14(2), pp. 51–66.

Hauser, M., Günther, S.A., Flath, C.M. and Thiesse, F. (2019) 'Towards digital transformation in fashion retailing: A design-orientated IS research study of automated checkout systems.' *Business and Information Systems Engineering*, 61(1), pp. 51–66.

Healy, M.J., Beverland, M.B., Oppewal, H. and Sands, S. (2007) 'Understanding retail experiences - the case for ethnography.' *International Journal of Market Research*, 49(6), pp. 751–778.

Heinonen, K., Strandvik, T., Mickelsson, K., Edvardsson, B., Sundström, E. and Andersson, P. (2010) 'A customer-dominant logic of service.' *Journal of Service Management*, 21(4), pp. 531–548.

Heitz-Spahn, S. (2013) 'Cross-channel free-riding consumer behavior in a multichannel environment: An investigation of shopping motives, socio-demographics and product categories.' *Journal of Retailing and Consumer Services*, 20(6), pp. 570–578.

Helm, S., Kim, S.H. and Van Riper, S. (2020) 'Navigating the "retail apocalypse": A framework of consumer evaluations of the new retail landscape.' *Journal of Retailing and Consumer Services*, 54, pp. 1–9.

Helkkula, A. (2011) 'Characterising the concept of service experience.' *Journal of Service Management*, 15(1), pp. 59–75.

Hepola, J., Karjaluoto, H. and Hintikka, A. (2017) 'The effect of sensory brand experience and involvement on brand equity directly and indirectly through consumer brand engagement.' *Journal of Product & Brand Management*, 26(3), pp. 282–293.

Herhausen, D., Binder, J., Schoegel, M. and Herrmann, A. (2015) 'Integrating bricks with clicks: Retailer-level and channel-level outcomes of online-offline channel integration.' *Journal of Retailing*, 91(2), pp. 309–325.

Hickman, E., Kharouf, H. and Sekhon, H. (2020) 'An omnichannel approach to retailing: Demystifying and identifying the factors influencing an omnichannel experience.' *The International Review of Retail, Distribution and Consumer Research*, 30(3), pp. 266–288.

Hirschman, E.C. and Holbrook, M.B. (1982) 'Hedonic consumption: Emerging concepts, methods and propositions.' *Journal of Marketing*, 46(3), pp. 92–101.

Hoch, S.J. (2002) 'Product experience is seductive.' *Journal of Consumer Research*, 29(3), pp. 448–454.

Hoch, S.J. and Ha, Y-W. (1986) 'Consumer learning: Advertising and the ambiguity of product experience.' *Journal of Consumer Research*, 13(2), pp. 221–233.

Hoepner, A., Ganzer, P.P., Chais, C. and Olea, P.M. (2015) 'Consumer retail experience: A bibliometric study.' *Revista Brasileira de Marketing*, 14(4), pp. 513–528.

Hoffman, K.D. and Turley, L.W. (2002) 'Atmospherics, service encounters and consumer decision making: An integrative perspective.' *Journal of Marketing Theory and Practice*, 10(3), pp. 33–47.

Holbrook, M.B. and Hirschman, E.C. (1982) 'The experiential aspects of consumption: Consumer fantasies, feelings and fun.' *Journal of Consumer Research*, 9(2), pp. 132–140.

Holloway, B.B. and Beatty, S.E. (2008) 'Satisfiers and dissatisfiers in the online environment: A critical incident assessment.' *Journal of Service Research*, 10(4), pp. 347–364.

Holt, D.B. (1995) 'How consumers consume: A typology of consumption practices.' *Journal of Consumer Research*, 22(1), pp. 1–16.

Homburg, C., Jozic, D. and Kuehnl, J. (2017) 'Customer experience management. Towards implementing an evolving marketing concept.' *Journal of Marketing Science*, 45(3), pp. 377–401.

Hossain, T.M.T., Akter, S., Kattiyapornpong, U. and Dwivei, Y.K. (2019) 'Multichannel integration quality: A systematic review and agenda for future research.' *Journal of Retailing and Consumer Services*, 49, pp. 154–163.

Hosseini, S., Merz, M., Roeglinger, M. and Wenninger, A. (2018) 'Mindfully going omni-channel: An economic decision model for evaluating omni-channel strategies.' *Decision Support Systems*, 109, pp. 74–88.

Hoyer, W.D., Kroschke, M., Schmitt, B., Kraume, K. and Shankar, V. (2020) 'Transforming the customer experience through new technologies.' *Journal of Interactive Marketing*, 51, pp. 57–71.

Hsieh, Y.-C., Roan, J., Pant, A., Hsieh, J.-K., Chen, W.-Y., Lee, M. and Chiu, H.-C. (2012) 'All for one but does one strategy work for all? Building consumer loyalty in multichannel distribution.' *Management Service Quality: An International Journal*, 22(3), pp. 310–335.

Hu, T-I. and Tracogna, A. (2020) 'Multichannel customer journeys and their determinants: Evidence from motor insurance.' *Journal of Retailing & Consumer Services*, 54. https://doi.org/10.1016/j.jretconser.2019.102022

Huang, L., Lu, X. and Ba, S. (2016) 'An empirical study of the cross-channel effects between web and mobile shopping channels.' *Journal of Information Management*, 53(2), pp. 265–278.

Hübner, A., Holzapfel, A. and Kuhn, H. (2016) 'Distribution systems in omni-channel retailing.' *Business Research*, 9(2), pp. 255–296.

Hübner, A., Hense, J. and Dethlefs, C. (2022) 'The revival of retail stores via omnichannel operations: A literature review and research framework.' *European Journal of Operational Research*, 302(3), pp. 799–818.

Hultén, B., Broweus, N. and van Dijk, M. (2009) *Sensory marketing*. Basingstoke: Palgrave MacMillan.

Hultén, B. (2012) 'Sensory cues and shoppers' touching behavior: The case of IKEA.' *International Journal of Retail & Distribution Management*, 40(4), pp. 273–289.

Huré, E., Picot-Coupey, K. and Ackermann, C.L. (2017) 'Understanding omni-channel shopping value: A mixed-method study.' *Journal of Retailing & Consumer Services*, 39, pp. 314–330.

Huuhka, A., Laaksonen, M. and Laaksonen, P. (2014) 'The evolution of new systematic forms in retailing and digital business.' *Contribution to International Business, Acta Wasaensia*, 303, pp. 239–249.

Hwang, J. and Seo, S. (2016) 'A critical review of research on customer experience management: Theoretical, methodological and cultural perspectives.' *International Journal of Contemporary Hospitality Management*, 28(10), pp. 2218–2246.

Hwangbo, H., Kim, Y.S. and Cha, K.J. (2017) 'Use of the smart store for persuasive marketing and immersive customer experiences: A case of Korean apparel enterprises.' *Mobile Information Systems*, 2017. https://doi.org/10.1155/2017/4738340

Hyun, H., Park, J., Hawkins, M.A. and Kim, D. (2022) 'How luxury brands build customer-based brand equity through phygital experience.' *Journal of Strategic Marketing*, Ahead of print. https://doi.org/10.1080/0965254X.2022.2052937

Iannilli, V.M. and Spagnoli, A. (2021) 'Phygital retailing in fashion. Experiences, opportunities and innovation trajectories.' *ZoneModa Journal*, 11(1), pp. 43–69. https://doi.org/10.6092/issn.2611-0563/13120

Ieva, M. and Zillani, C. (2018) 'Mapping touchpoint exposure in retailing: Implications for developing an omnichannel customer experience.' *International Journal of Retail & Distribution Management*, 46(3), pp. 304–322.

Iglesias, O., Singh, J. and Batista-Foguet, J. (2011) 'The role of brand experience and affective commitment in determining brand loyalty.' *Journal of Brand Management*, 18, pp. 570–582.

Ilius, L. (2023) *A definition of 'phygital': The space where real and virtual dimensions meet*. Talent Formation. [Online] [Accessed 26th Sept 2023] https://talentformation.com/definition-of-phygital/#:~:text=The%20origin%20of%20'phygital',the%20physical%20and%20digital%20worlds.

Inman, J.J. and Nikolova, H. (2017) 'Shopper-facing retail technology: A retailer adoption decision framework incorporating shopper attitudes and privacy concerns.' *Journal of Retailing*, 93(1), pp. 7–28.

Jaakkola, E., Helkkula, A. and Aarikka-Stenroos, L. (2015) 'Service experience co-creation conceptualisation, implications, and future research directions.' *Journal of Service Management*, 26(2), pp. 182–205.

Jacob, F., Pez, V. and Volle, P. (2023) 'Shifting to phygital experience management with design science: A six-step method to manage customer journeys.' *Journal of Strategic Marketing*, 31(5), pp. 961–982. https://doi.org/10.1080/0965254X.2021.2016894

Jain, R. and Bagdare, S. (2011) 'Music and consumption experience: A review.' *International Journal of Retail & Distribution Management*, 39(4), pp. 289–302.

Jain, R., Aagja, J. and Bagdare, S. (2017) 'Customer experience - a review and research agenda.' *Journal of Service Theory and Practice*, 27(3), pp. 642–662.

Jantzen, F., Fitchett, J., Østergaard, P. and Vetner, M. (2012) 'Just for fun? The emotional regime of experiential consumption.' *Marketing Theory*, 12(2), pp. 137–154.

Jin, B., Kim, G. and Moore, M. (2021) 'Consumer store experience through virtual reality: Its effects on emotional states and perceived store attractiveness.' *Fashion & Textiles*, 8(19). https://doi.org/10.1186/s40691-021-00256-7.

Jo, W., Kim, J.J. and Choi, J. (2020) 'Who are the multichannel shoppers and how can retailers use them? Evidence from the French apparel industry.' *Asia Pacific Journal of Marketing and Logistics*, 33(1), pp. 250–274.

Jocevski, M., Arvidsson, N., Mirangliotta, G., Ghezzi, A. and Mangiaracina, R. (2019) 'Transitioning towards omni-channel retailing strategies: A business model perspective.' *International Journal of Retail & Distribution Management*, 47(2), pp. 78–93.

Jocevski, M. (2020) 'Blurring the lines between physical and digital spaces: Business model innovation in retailing.' *California Management Review*, 63(1), pp. 99–117.

Johnstone, M.-L. and Conroy, D.M. (2006) 'Seeking social experiences within the retail environment.' In Lees, M.C., Davis, T. and Gregory, G. (eds.) *AP - Asia-Pacific advances in consumer research*. Sydney: Association for Consumer Research. pp. 401–407.

Johnstone, M.-L. (2012) 'The servicescape: The social dimension of place.' *Journal of Marketing Management*, 28(11/12), pp. 1399–1418.

Jones, M.A. (1999) 'Entertaining shopping experiences: An exploratory investigation.' *Journal of Retailing and Consumer Services*, 6, pp. 129–139.

Jones, M.A., Reynolds, K.E and Arnold, M.J. (2006) 'Hedonic and utilitarian shopping value: Investigating differential effects on retail outcomes.' *Journal of Business Research*, 59(9), pp. 974–981.

Jones, P., Comfort, D., Clarke-Hill, C. and Hillier, D. (2010) 'Retail experience stores: Experiencing the brand at first hand.' *Marketing Intelligence & Planning*, 28(3), pp. 241–248.

Jones, R.P. and Runyan, C. (2013) 'Brand experience and brand implications in a multi-channel setting.' *The International Review of Retail Distribution and Consumer Research*, 23(3), pp. 265–290.

Joy, A. and Sherry, J.F. (2003) 'Speaking of art as embodied imagination: A multisensory approach to understanding aesthetic experience.' *Journal of Consumer Research*, 30(2), pp. 259–282.

Juaneda-Ayensa, E., Mosquera, A. and Sierra Murillo, Y. (2016) 'Omnichannel customer behavior: Key drivers of technology acceptance and use and their effects on purchase intention.' *Frontiers in Psychology*, 7(1117), pp. 1–11.

Juttner, U., Schaffner, D., Windler, K. and Maklan, S. (2013) 'Customer service experiences developing and applying a sequential incident laddering technique.' *European Journal of Marketing*, 47(5/6), pp. 738–769.

Kang, J.Y.M. (2019) 'What drives omnichannel shopping behaviors? Fashion lifestyle of social-local-mobile consumers.' *Journal of Fashion Marketing and Management: An International Journal*, 23, pp. 224–238.

Kärrholm, M. (2012) *Retailising space: Architecture, retail and the territorialising of public space.* Farnham: Ashgate Publishing.

Kazancoglu, I. and Aydin, H. (2018) 'An investigation of consumers' purchase intentions towards omni-channel shopping.' *International Journal of Retail and Distribution Management*, 46(10), pp. 959–976.

Kim, Y., Sullivan, P. and Forney, J.C. (2007) *Experiential retailing*. New York: Fairchild.

Kim, E., Lin, J.S. and Sung, Y. (2013) 'To app or not to app: Engaging consumers via branded mobile apps.' *Journal of Interactive Advertising*, 13(1), pp. 53–65.

Kim, D., Hyun, H., Park, J. and Hawkins, M. (2022) 'How luxury brands build customer-based brand equity through phygital experience.' *Journal of Strategic Marketing*. https://doi.org/10.10 80/0965254X.2022.2052937

Khan, I. and Rahman, Z. (2015a) 'A review and future directions of brand experience research.' *International Strategic Management Review*, 3, pp. 1–14.

Khan, I. and Rahman, Z. (2015b) 'Brand experience anatomy in retailing: An interpretive structural modelling approach.' *Journal of Retailing and Consumer Services*, 24, pp. 60–69.

Khan, I. and Fatma, M. (2017) 'Antecedents and outcomes of brand experience: An empirical study.' *Journal of Brand Management*, 24, pp. 439–452.

Khan, I., Hollebeek, L.D., Fatma, M., Ul-Islam, J. and Riivits-Arkonsuo, I. (2020) 'Customer experience and commitment in retailing: Does age matter?' *Journal of Retailing and Consumer Services*, 57, pp. 1–9.

Klaus, P. (2020) 'The end of the world as we know it? The influence of online channels on the luxury customer experience.' *Journal of Retailing and Consumer Services*, 57, p. 102248. https://doi.org/10.1016/j.jretconser.2020.102248

Klaus, P. (2021) 'Viewpoint: Phygital – the emperor's new clothes?' *Journal of Strategic Marketing*. [Online] [Accessed 26th September 2023] https://doi.org/10.1080/0965254X.2021.1976252

Klaus, P. and Maklan, S. (2012) 'EXQ: A multiple-item scale for assessing service experience.' *Journal of Service Management*, 23(1), pp. 5–33.

Klaus, P. and Maklan, S. (2013) 'Towards a better measure of customer experience.' *International Journal of Market Research*, 55(2), pp. 227–246.

Knoferle, K.M., Spangenberg, E.R., Herrmann, A. and Landwehr, J.R. (2012) 'It is all in the mix: The interactive effect of music tempo and mode on in-store sales.' *Marketing Letters*, 23(1), pp. 325–337.

Knoferle, K.M., Paus, V.C. and Vossen, A. (2017) 'An upbeat crowd: Fast in-store music alleviates negative effects on high social density on customers' spending.' *Journal of Retailing*, 93(4), pp. 541–549.

Kotler, P. (1973) 'Atmospherics as a marketing tool.' *Journal of Retailing*, 49(4), pp. 48–64.

Krishna, A., Elder, R.S. and Caldara, C. (2010) 'Feminine to smell by masculine to touch? Multisensory congruence and its effects on the aesthetic experience.' *Journal of Consumer Psychology*, 20(4), pp. 410–418.

Krishna, A. (2012) 'An integrative review of sensory marketing: Engaging in the senses to affect perception, judgement and behaviour.' *Journal of Consumer Psychology*, 22(3), pp. 332–351.

Kwon, K.N. and Jain, D. (2009) 'Multichannel shopping through non-traditional retail formats: Behavior with hedonic and utilitarian motivations.' *Journal of Marketing Channels*, 16(2), pp. 149–168.

Kwon, W.-S. and Lennon, S.J. (2009) 'What induces online loyalty? Online versus offline brand images.' *Journal of Business Research*, 62(5), pp. 557–564.

Larke, R., Kilgour, M. and O'Connor, H. (2018) 'Build touchpoints and they will come: Transitioning to omnichannel retailing.' *International Journal of Physical Distribution & Logistics Management*, 48(4), pp. 465–483.

Lawry, C.A. (2023) Futurizing luxury: An activity centric model of phygital luxury experiences, *Journal of Fashion Marketing and Management: An International Journal*, 27(3), pp. 397–417.

Lazaris, C. and Vrechopoulos, A. (2014) 'From multi-channel to 'omnichannel' retailing: Review of the literature and calls for research.' In *Proceedings of the 2nd International Conference on Contemporary Marketing Issues*, (ICCMI), 18–20 June, Athens, Greece.

Lazaris, C., Vrechopoulos, A., Sarantopoulos, P. and Doukidis, G. (2022) 'Additive omnichannel atmospheric cues: The mediating effects of cognitive and affective responses on purchase intention.' *Journal of Retailing and Consumer Services*, Elsevier, 64, p. 102731. https://doi. org/10.1016/j.jretconser.2021.102731

Lee, H.-H. and Kim, J. (2010) 'Investigating dimensionality of multichannel retailer's cross-channel integration practices and effectiveness: Shopping orientation and loyalty Intention.' *Journal of Marketing Channels*, 17(4), pp. 281–312.

Lee, H.-J. (2015) 'Consumer-to-store employee and consumer-to-self-service technology (SST) interactions in a retail setting.' *International Journal of Retail and Distribution Management*, 43(8), pp. 676–692.

Lee, H. and Leonas, K.K. (2018) 'Consumer experiences, the key to surviving in an omnichannel environment: Use of virtual technology.' *Journal of Textile Apparel Technology Management*, 10(3), p. 1–23.

Lee, H. and Lyu, J. (2019) 'Exploring factors which motivate older consumers' self-service technologies (SSTs) adoption.' *International Review of Retail, Distribution and Consumer Research*, 29(2), pp. 218–239.

Lee, W.J. (2020) 'Unravelling consumer responses to omni-channel approach.' *Journal of Theoretical and Applied Electronic Commerce Research*, 15(3), pp. 37–49.

Lee, D-J., Yu, G.B. and Sirgy, J.M. (2023) 'Reflections on phygital experiences: Conceptual boundaries, wellbeing benefits and methodological suggestions.' *Qualitative Market Research: An International Journal* (ahead of print). https://doi.org/10.1108/QMR-05-2023-0067

Lemon, K.N. (2016) 'The art of creating attractive consumer experiences at the right time: Skills marketeers will need to survive and thrive.' *New Skills*, 8(2), pp. 45–49.

Lemon, K.N. and Verhoef, P.C. (2016) 'Understanding customer experience throughout the customer journey.' *Journal of Marketing*, 80(6), pp. 69–96.

Levy, M., Weitz, B. and Grewal, D. (2013) *Retailing Management*, 9th Ed., New York: McGraw-Hill Education.

Lewis, J., Whysall, P. and Foster, C. (2014) 'Drivers and technology-related obstacles in moving to multichannel retailing.' *International Journal of Electronic Commerce*, 18(4), pp. 43–68.

Lin, M-H., Cross, S.N.N. and Childers, T.L. (2018) 'Understanding olfaction and emotions and the moderating role of individual differences.' *European Journal of Marketing*, 52(3/4), pp. 811–836.

Lindstrom, M. (2005) *Brand sense: Build powerful brands through touch, taste, smell, sight and sound*. New York: The Free Press.

Lorente-Martinez, J., Navio-Marco, J. and Rodrigo-Moya, B. (2020) 'Analysis of the adoption of customer facing in-store technologies in retail SMEs.' *Journal of Retailing and Consumer Services*, 57, pp. 1–9.

Lynch, S. and Barnes, L. (2020) 'Omnichannel fashion retailing: Examining the customer decision-making journey.' *Journal of Fashion Marketing and Management: An International Journal*, 24(3), pp. 471–493.

Mahadevan, K. and Joshi, S. (2021) 'Omnichannel retailing: A bibliometric and network visualization analysis.' *Benchmarking: An International Journal* (ahead of print). https://doi.org/10.1108/BIJ-12-2020-0622

Madzharov, A.V., Block, L.G. and Morrin, M. (2015) 'The cool scent of power: Effects of ambient scent on consumer preferences and choice behavior.' *Journal of Marketing*, 79(1), pp. 83–96.

Mahr, D., Stead, S. and Odekerken-Schröder, G. (2019) 'Making sense of customer service experience: A text mining review.' *Journal of Services Marketing*, 33(1), pp. 88–103.

Maklan, S. and Klaus, P. (2011) 'Customer experience: Are we measuring the right things?' *International Journal of Market Research*, 53(6), pp. 771–792.

Marketing Science Institute (MSI) (2022) *2022–2024 research priorities*. [Online] [Accessed 30th July 2023] www.msi.org/wp-content/uploads/2022/10/MSI-2022-24-Research-Priorities-Final.pdf

Martin, B.A.S. (2011) 'A strangers touch: Effects of accidental interpersonal touch on consumer evaluations and shopping time.' *Journal of Consumer Research*, 39(1), pp. 174–184.

Mathwick, C., Malhotra, N. and Rigdon, E. (2001) 'Experiential value: Conceptualization, measurement and application in the catalog and internet shopping environment.' *Journal of Retailing*, 77(1), pp. 39–56.

McGoldrick, P.J. and Collins, N. (2007) 'Multichannel retailing: Profiling the multichannel shopper.' *International Review of Retail, Distribution and Consumer Research*, 17(2), pp. 139–158.

McKinsey (2020) *Fashion's digital transformation: Now or never* [Online] [Accessed 19th August 2021] https://www.mckinsey.com/industries/retail/our-insights/fashions-digital-transformation-now-or-never.

Mehrabian, A. and Russell, J.A. (1974) *An approach to environmental psychology*. Cambridge, MA: MIT Press.

Mele, C., Russo-Spena, T., Tregua, M. and Amitrano, C.C. (2021) 'The millennial customer journey: A phygital mapping of emotional, behavioural, and social experiences.' *Journal of Consumer Marketing*, 38(4), pp. 420–433.

Mele, C., Russo-Spena, T., Marzullo, M. and Di Bernardo, I. (2023) 'The phygital transformation: A systematic review and a research agenda.' *Italian Journal of Marketing*, pp. 323–349. https://doi.org/10.1007/s43039-023-00070-7

Melero, I., Sese, F.J. and Verhoef, P.C. (2016) 'Recasting the customer experience in today's omnichannel environment.' *Universia Business Review*, 50, pp. 18–37.

Melis, K., Campo, K., Breugelmans, E. and Lamey, L. (2015) 'The impact of the multi-channel retail mix on online store choice: Does online experience matter?' *Journal of Retailing*, 91(2) pp. 272–288.

Mende, M. and Noble, S.M. (2019) 'Retail apocalypse or golden opportunity for retail frontline management.' *Journal of Retailing*, 95(2), pp. 84–89.

Meng, H., Sun, Y., Liu, X., Li, Y. and Yang, Y. (2023) 'Antecedents and mediators of experiential retailing consumer behavior.' *International Journal of Retail & Distribution Management*, 51(7), pp. 920–938.

Meuter, M.L., Bitner, M.J., Ostrom, A.L. and Brown, S.W. (2005) 'Choosing among alternative service delivery modes: An investigation of customer trial of self-service technologies.' *Journal of Marketing*, 69(2), pp. 61–83.

Meyer, C. and Schwager, A. (2007) 'Understanding customer experience.' *Harvard Business Review*, 85(2), pp. 116–126.

Mikunda, C. (2007) *Brand lands, hot spots and cool spaces: Welcome to the third place and the total marketing experience*. London: Kogan Page.

Milliman, R.E. (1982) 'Using background music to affect the behavior of supermarket shoppers.' *Journal of Marketing*, 46(3), pp. 86–91.

Mirsch, T., Lehrer, C. and Jung, R. (2016) *Channel integration towards omnichannel management: A literature review*. [Online] [Accessed 15th July 2021] alexandria.unisg.ch/publications/248768.

Mishra, R., Singh, R.K. and Koles, B. (2021) 'Consumer decision-making in Omnichannel retailing: Literature review and future research agenda.' *International Journal of Consumer Studies*, 45(2), pp. 147–174.

Mishra, S., Malhotra, G., Chatterjee, R. and Shukla, Y. (2023) 'Consumer retention through phygital experience in omnichannel retailing: Role of consumer empowerment and satisfaction.' *Journal of Strategic Marketing*, 31(4), pp. 749–766.

Mondal, J. and Chakrabarti, S. (2021) 'Insights and anatomy of brand experience in app-based retailing (eRBX): Critical play of physical evidence and enjoyment.' *Journal of Retailing and Consumer Services*, 60. No page number assigned. https://doi.org/10.1016/j.jretconser.2021.102484

Montoya-Weiss, M.M., Voss, G.B. and Grewal, D. (2003) 'Determinants of online channel use and overall satisfaction with a relational, multichannel service provider.' *Journal of the Academy of Marketing Science*, 31(4), pp. 448–458.

Morin, S., Dubé, L. and Chebat, J.-C. (2007) 'The role of pleasant music in servicescapes: A test of the dual model of environmental perception.' *Journal of Retailing*, 83, pp. 115–130.

Mosquera, A., Olarte-Pascual, C., Ayensa, E.J. and Murillo, Y.S. (2018) 'The role of technology in an omnichannel physical store: Assessing the moderating effect of gender.' *Spanish Journal of Marketing – ESIC*. 22(1), pp. 63–82.

Naylor, G., Kleiser, S.B., Baker, J. and Yorkston, E. (2008) 'Using transformative appeals to enhance the retail experience.' *Journal of Retailing*, 84(1), pp. 49–57.

Neslin, S.A., Grewal, D. and Leghorn, R. (2006) 'Challenges and opportunities in multichannel customer management.' *Journal of Service Research*, 9(2), pp. 95–112.

Neslin, S.A. and Shankar, V. (2009) 'Key issues in multichannel customer management: Current knowledge and future directions.' *Journal of Interactive Marketing*, 23(1), pp. 70–81.

Neslin, S.A. (2022) 'The omnichannel continuum: Integrating online and offline channels along the customer journey.' *Journal of Retailing*, 98(1), pp. 111–132.

Nguyen, A., McClelland, R., Hoang Thuan, N. and Hoang, T.G. (2022) 'Omnichannel marketing: Structured review, synthesis, and future directions.' *The International Review of Retail, Distribution and Consumer Research*, 32(3), pp. 221–265.

Norman, D. (2004) *Emotional design: Why we love (or hate) everyday things*. New York: Basic Books.

Novac, T.P., Hoffman, D.L. and Yung, Y-F. (2000) 'Measuring the customer experience in online environments: A structural modelling approach.' *Marketing Science*, 19(1), pp. 22–42.

O'Dell, T. (2005) 'Experiencescapes: Blurring borders and testing connections,' in O'Dell, T. and Billing, P. (eds.) *Experiencescapes: Tourism, culture, and economy*. Copenhagen Business School Press, Copenhagen, pp. 3–17.

Otto, J.R. and Chung, Q.B. (2000) 'A framework for cyber-enhanced retailing: Integrating ecommerce retailing with brick-and-mortar retailing.' *Electronic Markets*, 10(3), pp. 185–191.

Palmer, A. (2010) 'Customer experience management: A critical review of an emerging idea.' *Journal of Services Marketing*, 24(3), pp. 96–208.

Pangarkar, A., Arora, V. and Shukla, Y. (2022) 'Exploring phygital omnichannel luxury retailing for immersive customer experience: The role of rapport and social engagement.' *Journal of Retailing and Consumer Services*, 68, p. 103001. https://doi.org/10.1016/j.jretconser.2022.103001

Pantano, E. (2016) 'Engaging consumer through the storefront: Evidences from integrating interactive technologies.' *Journal of Retailing and Consumer Services*, 28, pp. 149–154.

Pantano, E. and Priporas, C.V. (2016) 'The effect of mobile retailing on consumers' purchasing experiences: A dynamic perspective.' *Computers in Human Behavior*, 61, pp. 548–555.

Pantano, E., Priporas, C.V. and Dennis, C. (2018) 'A new approach to retailing for successful competition in the new smart scenario.' *International Journal of Retail & Distribution Management*, 46(3), pp. 264–282.

Pantano, E. and Viassone, M. (2015) 'Engaging consumers on new integrated multichannel retail settings: Challenges for retailers.' *Journal of Retailing and Consumer Services*, 25, pp. 106–114.

Pantano, E. and Vannucci, V. (2019) 'Who is innovating? An exploratory research of technologies diffusion in retail industry.' *Journal of Retailing and Consumer Services*, 49, pp. 297–304.

Parasuraman, A. (2000) 'Technology readiness index (Tri): A multiple-item scale to measure readiness to embrace new technologies.' *Journal of Service Research*, 2(4), pp. 307–320.

Parasuraman, A., Zeithaml, V.A. and Malhotra, A. (2005) 'E-S-QUAL: A multiple-item scale for assessing electronic service quality.' *Journal of Service Research*, 7(3), pp. 213–233.

Parise, S., Guinan, P.J. and Kafta, R. (2016) 'Solving the crisis of immediacy: How digital technology can transform the customer experience.' *Business Horizons*, 59(4), pp. 411–420.

Park, S. and Lee, D. (2017) 'An empirical study on consumer online shopping channel choice behavior in omni-channel environment.' *Telematics and Informatics*, 34(8), pp. 1398–1407.

Patricio, L., Fisk, R. and Cunha, J. (2008) 'Designing multi-interface service experiences: The service experience blueprint.' *Journal of Service Research*, 10(4), pp. 318–334.

Paul, J. and Rosenbaum, M. (2020) 'Retailing and consumer services at a tipping point: New conceptual frameworks and theoretical models.' *Journal of Retailing & Consumer Services*, 54, pp. 1–4.

Pauwels, K. and Neslin, S.A. (2015) 'Building with bricks and mortar: The revenue impact of opening physical stores in a multichannel environment.' *Journal of Retailing*, 91(2), pp. 182–197.

Pawar, S. and Sarmah, T. (2015) 'Omni-channel retailing: The opulent blend moving towards a customer driven approach.' *Journal of Arts, Science and Commerce*, 6(3), pp. 1–10.

Payne, A. and Frow, P. (2004) 'The role of multichannel integration in customer relationship management.' *Industrial Marketing Management*, 33(6), pp. 527–538.

Perry, P., Kent, A. and Bonetti, F. (2019) 'The use of mobile technologies in physical stores: The case of fashion retailing.' *In* Piotrowicz, W. and Cuthbertson, R. (eds.) *Exploring omnichannel retailing: Common expectations and diverse realities*. Berlin: Springer, pp. 169–195.

Petermans, A., W. Janssens and K. Van Cleempoel. (2013) 'A holistic framework for conceptualizing customer experiences in retail environments.' *International Journal of Design*, 7(2), pp. 1–18.

Picot-Coupey, K., Huré, E. and Piveteau, L. (2016) 'Channel design to enrich customers' shopping experiences: Synchronizing clicks with bricks in an omni-channel perspective – the Direct Optic case.' *International Journal of Retail & Distribution Management*, 44(3), pp. 336–368.

Piercy, N. (2012) 'Positive and negative cross-channel shopping behavior.' *Marketing Intelligence and Planning*, 30(1), pp. 83–104.

Pine, B.J. and Gilmore, J.H. (1998) 'Welcome to the experience economy.' *Harvard Business Review*, 76(4), pp. 97–105.

Pine, B.J. and Gilmore, J.H. (1999) *The experience economy: Work is theatre and every business a stage*. Boston, MA: Harvard Business School Press.

Pine, B.J. and Gilmore, J.H. (2019) *The experience economy: Competing for customer time, attention, and money*. Updated ed. Boston, MA: Harvard Business School Press.

Pinker, S. (1997) *How the mind works*. New York, NY: Norton.

Piotrowicz, W. and Cuthbertson, R. (2014) 'Introduction to the special issue: Information technology in retail: Toward omnichannel retailing.' *International Journal of Electronic Commerce*, 18(4), pp. 5–16.

Poncin, I. and Mimoun, M.S.B. (2014) 'The Impact of 'e-atmospherics' on physical stores.' *Journal of Retailing and Consumer Services*, 21, pp. 851–859.

Poorrezaei, M., Pich, C., Resnick, S. (2023) 'A framework to improve retail customer experience: A qualitative study exploring the customer journey.' *Qualitative Market Research: An International Journal*. Ahead of print. https://doi.org/10.1108/QMR-07-2022-0120

Prentice, C., Wang, X. and Loureiro, S.M.C. (2019) 'The influence of brand experience and service quality on customer engagement.' *Journal of Retailing and Consumer Services*, 50, pp. 50–59.

Puccinelli, N.M., Goodstein, R.C., Grewal, D., Price, R., Raghubir, P. and Stewart, D. (2009) 'Customer experience management in retailing: Understanding the buying process.' *Journal of Retailing*, 85(1), pp. 15–30.

Pullman, M.E. and Gross, M.A. (2004) 'Ability of experience design elements to elicit emotions and loyalty behaviors.' *Decision Sciences*, 35(3), pp. 551–578.

Pusceddu, G., Moi, L. and Cabiddu, F. (2023) 'Do they see eye to eye? Managing customer experience in phygital high tech retail.' *Management Decision*. Ahead of print. DOI 10.1108/MD-05-2022-0673.

Quach, S., Barari, M., Moudrý, D.V. and Quach, K. (2020) 'Service integration in omnichannel retailing and its impact on customer experience.' *Journal of Retailing and Consumer Services*. Ahead of print. https://doi.org/10.1016/j.jretconser.2020.102267

Quinones, M., Gomez-Suarez, M., Cruz-Roche, I. and Díaz-Martín, A.M. (2023) 'Technology: A strategic imperative for successful retailers.' *International Journal of Retail & Distribution Management*, 51(4), pp. 546–566.

Raconteur (2021a) *The fashion economy*. [Online] [Accessed 13th August 2021] https://www.raconteur.net/report/fashion-economy-2020/.

Raconteur (2021b) *Future of marketing and customer experience*. [Online] [Accessed 6th June 2021] https://www.raconteur.net/report/future-marketing-cx/.

Rangaswamy, A. and van Bruggen, G.H. (2005) 'Opportunities and challenges in multichannel marketing.' *Journal of Interactive Marketing*, 19(2), pp. 5–12.

Rapp, A., Baker, T.L., Bachrach, D.G., Ogilvie, J. and Beitelspacher, L.S. (2015) 'Perceived customer showrooming behavior and the effect on retail salesperson self-efficacy and performance.' *Journal of Retailing*, 91(2), pp. 358–369.

Ratchford, B., Soyal, G., Zentner, A. and Gauri, D.K. (2022) 'Online and offline retailing: What we know and directions for future research.' *Journal of Retailing*, 98, pp. 152–177.

Reinartz, W., Wiegand, N. and Imschloss, M. (2019) 'The impact of digital transformation on the retailing value chain.' *International Journal of Research in Marketing*, 36(3), pp. 350–366.

Renko, S. and Druzijanic, M. (2014) 'Perceived usefulness of innovative technology in retailing: Consumers' and retailers' point of view.' *Journal of Retailing and Consumer Services*, 21(5), pp. 836–843.

Rese, A., Baier, D., Geyer-Schulz, A. and Schreiber, S. (2017) 'How augmented reality apps are accepted by consumers: A comparative analysis using scales and opinions.' *Journal of Retailing*, 85(1), pp. 15–30.

Rey-Moreno, M. and Medina-Molina, C. (2016) 'Omnichannel strategy and the distribution of public services in Spain.' *Journal of Innovation & Knowledge*, 1(1), pp. 36–43.

Reynolds, J. (2000) 'E-commerce: A critical review.' *International Journal of Retail & Distribution Management*, 28(10), pp. 417–444.

Reynolds-McIlnay, R., Morrin, M. and Nordfält, J. (2017) 'How product-environment brightness contrast and product disarray impact consumer choice in retail environments.' *Journal of Retailing*, 93(3), pp. 266–282.

Richins, M.L. (1997) 'Measuring emotions in the consumption experience.' *Journal of Consumer Research*, 24(2), pp. 127–146.

Rigby, D.K. (2011) 'The future of shopping.' *Harvard Business Review*, 89(12), pp. 65–76.

Rodrigues, C., Hultén, B. and Brito, C. (2011) 'Sensorial brand strategies for value creation.' *Innovative Marketing*, 7(2), pp. 40–47.

Rodriguez-Torrico, P., Cabezudo, R.S.J. and San-Martín, S. (2017) 'Tell me what they are like and I will tell you where they buy. An analysis of omnichannel consumer behavior.' *Computers in Human Behavior*, 68, pp. 465–471.

Roggeveen, A.L., Grewal, D. and Schwiger, E.B. (2020) 'The DAST framework for retail atmospherics: The impact of in- and out-of-store retail journey touchpoints on the customer experience.' *Journal of Retailing*, 96(1), pp. 128–137.

Roggeveen, A.L., Nordfält, J. and Grewal, D. (2016) 'Do digital displays enhance sales? Role of retail format and message content.' *Journal of Retailing*, 92(1), pp. 122–131.

Roggeveen, A.L. and Sethuraman, R. (2020) 'Customer-interfacing retail technologies in 2020 and beyond: An integrative framework and research directions.' *Journal of Retailing*, 96(3), pp. 299–309.

Roozen, I. and Katidis, P.I. (2019) 'The importance of the service and shopping customer experience in a retail environment.' *Journal of Relationship Marketing*, 18(4), pp. 247–279.

Rose, S., Clark, M., Samuel, P. and Hair, N. (2012) 'Online customer experience in re-retailing: An empirical model of antecedents and outcomes.' *Journal of Retailing*, 88(2), pp. 308–322.

Rosenbaum, M.S. (2006) 'Exploring the social supportive role of third space in consumers' lives.' *Journal of Service Research*, 9(1), pp. 59–72.

Roy, S.K., Balaji, M.S., Quazi, A. and Quaddus, M. (2018) 'Predictors of customer acceptance of and resistance to smart technologies in the retail sector.' *Journal of Retailing and Consumer Services*, 42, pp. 147–160.

Saari, U. and Mäkinen, S. (2017) 'Measuring brand experiences cross-nationally.' *Journal of Brand Management*, 24(1), pp. 86–104.

Sachdeva, I. and Goel, S. (2015) 'Retail store environment and customer experience: A paradigm.' *Journal of Fashion Marketing and Management: An International Journal*, 19(3), pp. 290–298.

Saghiri, S., Wilding, R., Mena, C. and Bourlakis, M. (2017) 'Toward a three-dimensional framework for omni-channel.' *Journal of Business Research*, 77 pp. 53–67.

Sahu, K.C., Naved Khan, M. and Gupta, K.D. (2021) 'Determinants of webrooming and showrooming behavior: A systematic literature review.' *Journal of Internet Commerce*, 20(2), pp. 1–28.

Salvietti, G., Ziliani, C., Teller, C., Ieva, M. and Ranfagni, S. (2022) 'Omnichannel retailing and post pandemic recovery: Building a research agenda.' *International Journal of Retail and Distribution Management*, 50, pp. 1156–1181.

Samir, M. and Soumia, A. (2020) 'Phygitalization of the customer experience: A qualitative approach.' *International Journal of Marketing, Communication and New Media*, 6, pp. 56–73.

Savastano, M., Bellini, F., D'Ascenzo, F. and De Marco, M. (2019) 'Technology adoption for the integration of online-offline purchasing: Omnichannel strategies in the retail environment.' *International Journal of Retail and Distribution Management*, 47(5), pp. 474–492.

Schmitt, B.H. (1999) 'Experiential marketing.' *Journal of Marketing Management*, 15(1/3), pp. 53–67.

Schmitt, B.H. (2003) *Customer experience management*. Hoboken, NJ: Wiley.

Schmitt, B., Brakus, J.J. and Zarantonello, L. (2015) 'From experiential psychology to consumer experience.' *Journal of Consumer Psychology*, 25(1), pp. 166–171.

Schmitt, B. and Zarantonello, L. (2013) 'Consumer experience and experiential marketing: A critical review,' in Malhotra, N.K. (ed.) *Review of marketing research*. Vol. 10. [Online] [Accessed 15th July 2021] https://doi.org/10.1108/S1548-6435(2013)0000010006.

Schoenbachler, D.D. and Gordon, G.L. (2002) 'Multi-channel shopping: Understanding what drives channel choice.' *Journal of Consumer Marketing*, 19(1), pp. 42–53.

Schramm-Klein, H., Wagner, G., Steinmann, S. and Morschett, D. (2011) 'Cross-channel integration – is it valued by customers?' *The International Review of Retail, Distribution and Consumer Research*, 21(5), pp. 501–511.

Schröder, H. and Zaharia, S. (2008) 'Linking multi-channel customer behavior with shopping motives: An empirical investigation of a German retailer.' *Journal of Retailing and Consumer Services*, 15(6), pp. 452–468.

Shankar, V., Kalyanam, K., Setia, P., Golmohammadi, A., Tirunillai, S., Douglass, T., Hennessey, J., Bull, J.S. and Waddoups, R. (2020) 'How technology is changing retail.' *Journal of Retailing*, 97(1), pp. 13–27.

Shankar, V., Venkatesh, A., Hofacker, C. and Naik, P. (2010) 'Mobile marketing in the retailing environment: Current insights and future research avenues.' *Journal of Interactive Marketing*, 24(2), pp. 111–120.

Sharma, H. and Dutta, N. (2023) 'Omnichannel retailing: Exploring future research avenues in retail marketing and distribution management.' *International Journal of Retail & Distribution Management*, 51(7), pp. 894–919.

Shaw, C. and Ivens, J. (2002) *Building great customer experiences*. London: Palgrave Macmillan.

Shen, X.L., Li, Y.J., Sun, Y. and Wang, N. (2018) 'Channel integration quality, perceived fluency and omnichannel service usage: The moderating roles of internal and external usage experience.' *Decision Support Systems*, 109, pp. 61–73.

Shi, S., Wang, Y., Chen, X. and Zhang, Q. (2020) 'Conceptualisation of omnichannel customer experience and its impact on shopping intention: A mixed-method approach.' *International Journal of Information Management*, 50, pp. 325–336.

Siebert, A., Gopaldas, A., Lindridge, A. and Simões, C. (2020) 'Customer experience journeys: Loyalty loops versus involvement spirals.' *Journal of Marketing*, 84(4), pp. 45–66.

Silva, D.G. and Cachinho, H. (2021) 'Places of phygital shopping experiences? The new supply frontier of business improvement districts in the digital age.' *Sustainability*, 13(23), 13150. https://doi.org/10.3390/su132313150

Soars, B. (2003) 'What every retailer should know about the way into shoppers head.' *International Journal of Retail and Distribution Management*, 31(12), pp. 628–637.

Sopadjieva, E., Dholakia, U.M. and Benjamin, B. (2017) *A study of 46,000 shoppers shows that omnichannel retailing works*, Harvard Business Review. [Online] (Accessed 4th December 2019) hbr. org/2017/01/a-studyof-46000-shoppers-shows-that-omnichannel-retailing-works.

Souiden, N. and Ladhari, R. (2019) 'New trends in retailing and service.' *Journal of Retailing and Consumer Services*, 50, pp. 286–288.

Sousa, R. and Voss, C.A. (2006) 'Service quality in multichannel services employing virtual channels.' *Journal of Service Research*, 8(4), pp. 356–371.

Spangenberg, E.R., Crowley, A.E. and Henderson, P.W. (1996) 'Improving the store environment: Do olfactory cues affect evaluations and behaviours?' *Journal of Marketing*, 60(2), pp. 67–80.

Spence, C., Puccinelli, N.M., Grewal, D. and Roggeveen, A.L. (2014) 'Store atmospherics: A multisensory perspective.' *Psychology & Marketing*, 31(7), pp. 472–488.

Spies, K., Hesse, F. and Loesch, K. (1997) 'Store atmosphere, mood and purchasing behaviour.' *International Journal of Research in Marketing*, 14, pp. 1–17.

Stein, A. and Ramaseshan, B.(2016) 'Towards the identification of customer experience touch point elements.' *Journal of Retailing and Consumer Services*, 30, pp. 8–19.

Stephens, D. (2018) *Retail's innovation problem*. Business of Fashion. [Online] [Accessed 19th August 2021] https://www.businessoffashion.com/opinions/retail/retails-innovation-problem.

Sweeney, J.C. and Soutar, G.N. (2001) 'Consumer perceived value: The developments of a multiple item scale.' *Journal of Retailing*, 77(2), pp. 203–220.

Talukdar, N. and Yu, S. (2021) 'Breaking the psychological distance: The effect of immersive virtual reality on perceived novelty and user satisfaction.' *Journal of Strategic Marketing*. https://doi.org/10.1080/0965254X.2021.1967428

Tasci, A.D.A. and Pizam, A. (2020) 'An expanded nomological network of experiencescape.' *International Journal of Contemporary Hospitality Management*, 32(3), pp. 999–1040.

Tate, M., Hope, B. and Coker, B. (2005) 'The buywell way: Seven essential practices of a highly successful multi-channel e-tailer.' *Australasian Journal of Information Systems*, 12(2), pp. 147–163.

Tauber, E.M. (1995) 'Why do people shop?' *Marketing Management*, 4(2), pp. 58–60.

The Future Laboratory, (2023) *Retail futures 2023*. LS:N Global [Online] [Accessed 15th September 2023] https://www.thefuturelaboratory.com/reports/2023/retail-futures

Thomson, R. (2019) *Fashion's top tech innovations in 2018*. Drapers. [Online] [Accessed 18th July 2019] https://www.drapersonline.com/business-operations/fashions-top-tech-innovations-in-2018/7033627.

Tom Dieck, C.M. and Han, D. (2022) 'The role of immersive technology in Customer Experience Management.' *Journal of Marketing Theory and Practice*, 30(1), pp. 108–119.

Tresidder, R. and Deakin, E.L. (2019) 'Historic buildings and the creation of experiencescapes: Looking to the past for future success.' *Journal of Tourism Futures*, 5(2), pp. 193–201.

Triantafillidou, A., Siomkos, G. and Papafilippaki, E. (2017) 'The effects of retail store characteristics on in-store leisure shopping experience.' *International Journal of Retail & Distribution Management*, 45(10), pp. 1034–1060.

Tueanrat, Y., Papagiannidis, S. and Alamanos, E. (2021) 'A conceptual framework of the antecedents of customer journey satisfaction in omnichannel retailing.' *Journal of Retailing and Consumer Services*, 61. https://doi.org/10.1016/j.jretconser.2021.102550

Turley, L.W. and Milliman, R.E. (2000) 'Atmospheric effects on shopping behavior.' *Journal of Business Research*, 49(2), pp. 193–211.

Tyrväinen, O. and Karjaluoto, H. (2019) 'Omnichannel experience: Towards successful integration in retail.' *Journal of Customer Behavior*, 18(1), pp. 17–34.

Van Rompay, T.J.L., Tanja-Dijkstra, K. and Verhoeven, J.W.M. (2012) 'On store design and consumer motivation: Spatial control and arousal in the retail context.' *Environment and Behaviour*, 44(6), pp. 800–820.

Vargo, S.L. and Lusch, R.F. (2004) 'Evolving to a new dominant logic for marketing.' *Journal of Marketing*, 68(1), pp. 1–17.

Vargo, S.L. and Lusch, R.F. (2008) 'Service-dominant logic: Continuing the evolution.' *Journal of the Academy of Marketing Science*, 36, pp. 1–10.

Vargo, S.L. and Lusch, R.F. (2016) 'Institutions and axioms: An extension and update of service dominant logic.' *Journal of the Academy of Marketing Science*, 44(1), pp. 5–23.

Varshneya, G., Das, G. and Khare, A. (2017) 'Experiential value: A review and future research agenda.' *Marketing Intelligence & Planning*, 35(3), pp. 339–357.

Venkatesh, V. and Davis, F.D. (2000) 'A theoretical extension of the technology acceptance model: Four longitudinal field studies.' *Management Science*, 46(2), pp. 186–204.

Venkatesh, V., Aloysius, J.A, Hoehle, H. and Burton, S. (2017) 'Design and evaluation of auto-ID enabled shopping assistance artifacts in customers' mobile phones: Two retail store laboratory experiments.' *MIS Quarterly: Management Information Systems*, 41(1), pp. 83–113.

Verhoef, P.C. (2021) 'Omni-channel retailing: Some reflections.' *Journal of Strategic Marketing*, 29(7), pp. 608–616.

Verhoef, P.C., Kannan, P.K. and Inman, J.J. (2015) 'From multi-channel to omni-channel retailing: Introduction to the special issue on multi-channel retailing.' *Journal of Retailing*, 91(2), pp. 174–181.

Verhoef, P.C., Lemon, K.N., Parasuraman, A., Roggeveen, A., Tsiros, M. and Schlesinger, L.A. (2009) 'Customer experience creation: Determinants, dynamics and management strategies.' *Journal of Retailing*, 85, pp. 31–41.

Verhoef, P.C., Neslin, S.A. and Vroomen, B. (2007) 'Multichannel customer management: Understanding the research-shopper phenomenon.' *International Journal of Research in Marketing*, 24(2), pp. 129–148.

von Briel, F. (2018) 'The future of omnichannel retail: A four-stage Delphi study.' *Technological Forecasting and Social Change*, 132, pp. 217–229.

Voorhees, C., Fombelle, P., Gregoire, Y., Bone, S., Gustafsson, A., Sousa, R. and Walkowiak, T. (2017) 'Service encounters, experiences and the customer journey: Defining the field and a call to expand our lens.' *Journal of Business Research*, 79, pp. 269–280.

Wagner, G., Schramm-Klein, H. and Steinmann, S. (2013) 'Effects of cross-channel synergies and complementarity in a multichannel e-commerce system: An investigation of the interrelation of e-commerce, m-commerce and IETV-commerce.' *International Review of Retail, Distribution and Consumer Research*, 23(5), pp. 571–581.

Wang, C., Harris, J. and Patterson, P. (2013) 'The roles of habit, self-efficacy and satisfaction in driving continued use of self-service technologies: A longitudinal study.' *Journal of Service Research*, 16(3), pp. 400–414.

Watson, A., Alexander, B. and Salavati, L. (2018) 'The impact of experiential augmented reality applications on fashion purchase intention.' *International Journal of Retail & Distribution Management*, 48(5), pp. 433–451.

Weijters, B., Rangarajan, D., Falk, T. and Schillewaert, N. (2007) 'Determinants and outcomes of customers' use of self-service technology in a retail setting.' *Journal of Service Research*, 10(1), pp. 3–21.

Wiedmann, K-P., Hennigs, N., Klarmannn, C. and Behrens, S. (2013) 'Creating multi-sensory experiences in luxury marketing.' *Marketing Review*, 30(6), pp. 60–69.

Wiener, M., Hoßbach, N. and Saunders, C. (2018) 'Omnichannel businesses in the publishing and retailing industries: Synergies and tensions between coexisting online and offline business models.' *Decision Support Systems*, 109, pp. 15–26.

Willems, K., Brengman, M. and Van de Sanden, S. (2017) 'In-store proximity marketing: Experimenting with digital point-of-sale communication.' *International Journal of Retail & Distribution Management*, 45(7–8), pp. 910–927.

Wolny, J. and Charoensuksai, N. (2014) 'Mapping customer journeys in multichannel decision-making.' *Journal of Direct, Data and Digital Marketing Practice*, 15(4), pp. 317–326.

Wolpert, S. and Roth, A. (2020) 'Development of a classification framework for technology based retail services: A retailers' perspective.' *International Review of Retail, Distribution and Consumer Research*, 30(5), pp. 498–538.

Woodward, M.N. and Holbrook M.B. (2013) 'Dialogue on some concepts, definitions and issues pertaining to "consumption experiences".' *Marketing Theory*, 13(3), pp. 323–344.

Wright, P., McCarthy, J. and Meekison, L. (2003) 'Making sense of experience,' in Blythe, M., Monk, A., Overbeeke, K. and Wright, P. (eds.) *Funology: From usability to enjoyment.* Dordrecht: Kluwer Academic Publishers, pp. 43–53.

Xu, X. and Jackson, J.E. (2019) 'Examining customer channel selection intention in the omnichannel retail environment.' *International Journal of Production Economics*, 208, pp. 434–445.

Yadav, M.S. and Pavlou, P.A. (2020) 'Technology-enabled interactions in digital environments: A conceptual foundation for current and future research.' *Journal of Academy of Marketing Science*, 48, pp. 132–136.

Yakhlef, A. (2015) 'Customer experience within retail environments: An embodied, spatial approach.' *Marketing Theory*, 15(4), pp. 545–564.

Yan, R., Wang, J. and Zhou, B. (2010) 'Channel integration and profit sharing in the dynamics of multi-channel firms.' *Journal of Retailing and Consumer Services*, 17(5), pp. 430–440.

Ye, Y., Lau, K.H. and Teo, L.K.Y. (2018) 'Drivers and barriers of omni-channel retailing in China: A case study of the fashion and apparel industry.' *International Journal of Retail & Distribution Management*, 46(7), pp. 657–689.

Ylilehto, M., Komulainen, H. and Ulkuniemi, P. (2021) 'The critical factors shaping customer shopping experiences within innovative technologies.' *Baltic Journal of Management*, 16(5), pp. 661–680.

Yrjölä, M., Saarijärvi, H. and Nummela, H. (2018a) 'The value propositions of multi-, cross-, and omni-channel retailing.' *International Journal of Retail and Distribution Management*, 46(11/12), pp. 1133–1152.

Yrjölä, M., Spence, M.T. and Saarijärvi, H. (2018b) 'Omni-channel retailing: Propositions, examples and solutions.' *The International Review of Retail, Distribution and Consumer Research*, 30(5), pp. 529–553.

Zhang, J., Farris, P.W., Irvin, J.W., Kushwaha, T., Steenburgh, T.J. and Weitz, B.A. (2010) 'Crafting integrated multichannel retailing strategies.' *Journal of Interactive Marketing*, 24(2), pp. 168–180.

Zhang, J., Xu, Q. and He, Y. (2018) 'Omnichannel retail operations with consumer returns and order cancellation.' *Transportation Research Part E: Logistics and Transportation Review*, 118, pp. 308–324.

Zeithaml, V.A., Parasuraman, A. and Malhotra, A. (2002) 'Service quality delivery through web sites: A critical review of extant knowledge.' *Journal of the Academy of Marketing Science*, 30(4), pp. 362–375.

Zomerdijk, L. and Voss, C. (2010) 'Service design for experience-centric services.' *Journal of Service Research*, 13(1), pp. 67–82.

2

(Re)envisioned future retail customer experience

Bethan Alexander

> There is no physical setting that is not also a social, cultural, and psychological setting.
> (Proshansky, 1978:150)

As Babin et al. (2021) opine, the basis for any prediction is the past. The previous chapter described the progression of retailing and customer experience over four decades to the current point in time. This chapter aims to synthesise those developments in conceptual terms and look to the future. Given the rapidly evolving retailing industry, scholars are recognising the increasing gap between academic research and retail practice, doubting the saliency and alignment of traditional conceptualisations (Roggeveen and Sethuraman, 2018; Dekimpe and Geyskens, 2019; Hänninen et al., 2021) to ongoing developments. Arguably, more nuanced, contemporary and interdisciplinary theorisations are required to help advance new retail and customer experience in meaningful ways (Picot-Coupey et al., 2016; Shi et al., 2019; Chevtchouk et al., 2021; Batat, 2022).

Informed by the work of Deleuze and Guattari (1987), Brighenti (2010, 2014) and Kärrholm (2012), this chapter takes a territorological perspective, widely discussed in various academic disciplines, such as political, biological, geographical, psychological and social and behavioural sciences (see Kärrholm, 2007, 2012; Brighenti, 2010; Warnaby, 2018), to unify the variety of spatial retail contexts discussed in Chapter 1. Specifically, the (re) evaluation of retail space and place in terms of a more fluid spatial 'territory' could be regarded as a new lens through which to offer the conception of the re-envisioned retail customer experience, consistent with the notion of omnichannel retailing.

First, the chapter introduces conceptions of space and place and situates these complex terms within a specific fashion retail context. Next, the conceptual metaphor of territory is discussed and contextualised. Finally, the chapter concludes by discussing the nature of reimagined future retail places and spaces and their characterisation as constituted Experiential Retail Territories (ERTs). This is then contextualised through three significant global drivers shaping fashion retail experience futures: hyper-phygital (i.e. one online and offline continuous experience), hyper-personalised (i.e. human-centric as well as AI-tech-induced experiences) and hyper-responsible (i.e. socially and environmentally sustainable experiences). Each of these pervasive, powerful and often intersecting experiential drivers is discussed using fashion retail examples where relevant, and extended in Part 3 through the case studies.

DOI: 10.4324/9781003378099-3

The meaning of space and place in a retail context

The origins of the term place dates back to the ancient Greek philosophers Plato and Aristotle, yet despite what has become a widespread and interdisciplinary concept (e.g. in philosophy, geography, anthropology, ecology, arts, humanities, social sciences and marketing management), its meaning remains contested (Cresswell, 2015). Until the 1970s and the emergence of humanistic geography, place within spatial science was confined to a location delineated by finitude, boundary, area, volume, function, populations of people and materiality (e.g. Gieryn, 2000; Escobar, 2001). However, since that time, eminent human geographers beginning with, for example, Tuan (1974), Relph (1976) and Buttimer and Seamon (1980) pioneered a re-conceptualisation of place away from 'things in the world' to a way of understanding the world that emphasised experiences, connections and attachments.

A tripartite definition of place was conceived by Agnew (1987) as (1) *location* – most commonly conceived as a fixed point on the surface of the earth; (2) *locale* – referring to the material setting for social relations; and (3) *sense of place* – referring to the subjective and emotional attachment people have to places. In doing so, this seeks to differentiate place from space, as in place being conceived as "space invested with meaning" (Cresswell, 2015:19). Space is generally accepted as a more abstract concept than place; namely, as a "realm without meaning" (Cresswell, 2015:16), detached from materiality and cultural interpretation (Gieryn, 2000). Tuan (1974) likens space to movement and place to pauses, stopping and becoming involved, in his theorisation of place as humanised space (Borghini et al., 2009), which is constructed, understood and imagined (Gieryn, 2000).

However, this duality of meaning related to space and place masks the complexity and often coinciding conception of the terms. Lefebvre (1991), for example, conceived the notion of social spaces that are lived and imbued with meaning, which is arguably similar to definitions of place (e.g. Agnew's (1987) notion of locale) and resonates with philosopher Martin Heidegger's (1993) notion of place as central to cementing the socio-relational dimensions through his lexicon of "Dasein" – being in, and "Dwelling" – to depict a sense of nearness and care. This emphasis on the bond between people and place, value and belonging is similarly developed by Relph (1976) and Pred (1984), who posit that place is not bound by fixed location but rather by their visuality, sense of community, attachment and rootedness that they create, which are never finished but are the result of ongoing processes and practices. This idea of simultaneously being *in* place and doing *through* place is developed by Platt et al. (2021) in their revisiting of Heidegger's (2013) notion of dwelling, which they reframe as an active and emergent process. Collectively grounded in phenomenological thinking, proponents of humanistic approaches to place recognise that "to be human is to be in place" (e.g. Tuan, 1974, 2001; Relph, 1976; Buttimer and Seamon, 1980; Pred, 1984; Sack, 1992; Heidegger, 1993; Casey, 1996; Malpas, 1999, Cresswell, 2015:38).

Within traditional fashion retailing, interchangeable use of the terms space and place has dominated the business lexicon. From physical store operations that focus on doing things to the selling space within, such as 'space allocation' and 'space planning' (Varley and Rafiq, 2014; Goworek and McGoldrick, 2015), to the characterisation of physical stores as 'bricks and mortar' retailing and 'servicescapes' (Bitner, 1992; Sikos et al., 2019; Jocevski, 2020), and the selling 'channels', which refer to the materiality of the place element of traditional conceptualisations of the marketing mix. Indeed, more broadly, within a marketing context the fundamental construct of the marketing mix emphasises 'place' as one of the dimensions of the 4Ps framework (i.e. product, price, place, promotion), relating to geographic location and the physical movement of goods from point of production to point of consumption (conceived by McCarthy and Perrault, 1960). In doing so, they reaffirm traditional theorists of socio-spatial relations, associated with boundaries, parcelisation and enclosure, by taking an arguably reductionist approach to place (Johnstone and Conroy, 2006, 2008; Jessop et al., 2008; Kärrholm, 2012; De Juan-Vigaray and Segui, 2019), while perpetuating the overlap in terms which hinders a more nuanced understanding of place and space.

These rather binary spatial notions of space and place have been contested by several theorists, with conceptions of 'third-place' (Oldenburg, 1989; see also Alexander, 2019), 'third-space' (Lefebvre, 1991, i.e. first space being real space, second space being perceived space and third-space as lived space), 'progressive place' (Massey, 1987) and 're-place' (i.e. reconceptualisation of place beyond physical locales as inseparable aspects of consumers' lives) (Rosenbaum et al., 2017). Massey, for example, argues that places are marked by openness and change rather than boundedness and permanence, which Crewe and Lowe (1995) appertain in their consideration of the heterogeneity of retailing and consumption spaces, specific to fashion. Building on this, Crewe (2013) argues for a recalibrated understanding of fashion consumption practice, process, space and place with the surging collision, coalescence and coexistence of physical and virtual fashion worlds. The transformative effects of digitally mediated technologies on fashion spaces that are increasingly portable demand a reframing and reconfiguration of traditional spatial and relational perspectives (Crewe, 2013). Dominant early narratives of digitally mediated retailing perpetuating social disconnectedness are contested, but, rather, seen to augment socio-relational, interactive, imaginative, immersive, immediate, expansive, sensory, fluid, ubiquitous experience possibilities (Currah, 2002; Lehdonvirta, 2010; Turkle, 2011). Indeed, "spaces are not separately imagined, designed or commodified but, rather, are incorporated into a coalescent spatial landscape" (Crewe, 2013:765). She calls for new theorisations, visions and vocabularies of (fashion) time, space and knowledge, to better reflect the relations between people and places as "elements of a constitutive moving ... fabric that is constantly being spun over and over again" (Thrift, 2011:7, cited in Crewe, 2013). It is in this non-binary and non-bipolar (Crewe, 2013) sense of place that the notion of territory is introduced and ascribed to retail.

Towards retail as Experiential Retail Territories (ERT)

Cheetham et al. (2018:4) posit that, rather than trying to reduce a given place to one dominant narrative, scholars would benefit from celebrating the "complex kaleidoscopic nature of a place". Thus, in keeping with the humanistic approach previously discussed, and taking a more nuanced understanding of place and space, Brighenti (2010:53) argues that territory is "not an absolute concept, but is better conceived as an act or practice rather than an object or physical space" that has both expressive and functional components. This means a territory is a result of human and institutional relations, having both spatial and relational implications, and that territorial boundaries become the object of an ongoing work of enactment, reinforcement, interpretation and negotiation (Brighenti, 2010:62).

This territorological perspective changes the meaning of place as a site of consumption (Kärrholm, 2012), in that instead of restricting territory to material, fixed spatial entities (i.e. servicescapes, retail settings, etc.), it can be considered as having much broader socio-material and relational attributes. Thus, territories are ongoing, open productions that may prove useful to advance towards that "place beyond place" (Massey, 1987:15). According to Malpas (1999, cited by Cresswell, 2015:48), "no place exists except in relation to other places, and every place contains other places that are related within it" – a perspective that encompasses both place and space together. In this regard, the notion of territory represents an important conceptual metaphor to capture the simultaneous proliferation of mobilities and borders (Brighenti, 2014) as fluid, adaptable practices rather than static and immutable structures (Lambach, 2019). Applied to retail, territories become embodied spaces, in which social space and social action are inseparable, and part of a lived experience of people (Cohen, 2007), made, shaped, given meaning and de-and re-territorialised in social and individual action (Paasi, 2003; Elden, 2013).

Retail scholars have tended to focus on the materiality and physicality of the location, as a structural boundaried space, controlled by the retail brand – a place of consumption that consumers had to go to, as opposed to other disciplines that take a broader temporal, spatial, natural and social perspective to place (Johnstone and Conroy, 2006, 2008; Rosenbaum and Massiah, 2011; Rosenbaum et al., 2017). Consumers were perceived as passive agents, their role limited to selecting the goods available in the stores that they relied on for shopping (De Juan-Vigaray and Segui, 2019). This unequal consumption dynamic, which generated a relationship of dependence between consumer and retailer, prevailed for decades (De Juan-Vigaray and Segui, 2019). However, with the proliferation of channels and touchpoints, this traditional notion of the more physical retail place has been displaced, with multi-omnichannel and phygital approaches creating new physical and virtual territories of consumption that blend, merge, morph, collide and change, enabled and enhanced through retail technologies (Crewe, 2013).

Virtually, the emergence of multiple spaces, conceived as 'metaverses' – computer-generated, multi-user, three-dimensional collaborative virtual environments (defined by Stephenson, 1992, cited in Gadalla et al., 2013) – enabled economic and social encounters. In "Metaverse retailing" (Bourlakis et al., 2009:140), the myriad of spaces and the activities connect with other offline and online spaces, thus extending retailer opportunities to improve customer experience, through the co-creation of experience (Papagiannidis and Bourlakis, 2010).

Consequently, retail territories can be non-exclusive, overlapping and intersecting constructs whose shapes, characteristics and experiences are constantly being renegotiated. A shift has occurred from traditional separate, singular channels (places) to a convergence of on- and offline and interstitial *spaces* of retail consumption (Lambach, 2019; Shi et al., 2019). Retail on- and offline territories can be understood as layered, where physical, digital and social realms intersect (Bolton et al., 2018; Alexander and Warnaby, 2023). Moreover, at the interface of this convergence of online and traditional retail forms, new possibilities emerge, such as AR, VR, artificial intelligence (AI) and the internet of things (IoT) (Hoyer et al., 2020; Ylilehto et al., 2021; Calvo and Franco, 2023). This evolution of retailing beyond omnichannel (bound by a functional perspective) is depicted in Figure 2.1, as entering a developmental fourth phase, conceived as ERTs. In doing so the conception concords with recent scholarly recognition that phygitality transcends omnichannel management (Klaus, 2021) and urges retailers to extend beyond

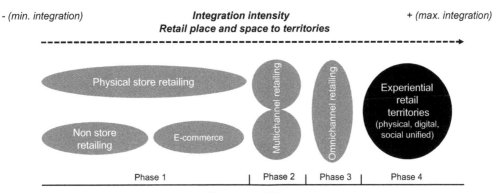

Figure 2.1 Retail futures – ERT unification.

Source: Authors own.

bounded omnichannel logic to fully realise the potential of phygitality for managing CX (e.g. Klaus, 2021; Lecointre-Erickson et al., 2021; Batat, 2022).

The territorial boundaries of online and offline retail will continue to blur, as online becomes an increasingly natural space in people's everyday lives. In this context, retail becomes liminal, shifting from solid to liquid – the solid retail location (place) is virtualised and liquified through e-commerce and social commerce, in which the point of sale moves and becomes hybrid, which closely aligns with Lefebvre's (1991) notion that territory and borders should be viewed as fluid, adaptable practices rather than static, immutable structures (McIntyre, 2013; Belghiti et al., 2018; Alexander and Blazquez Cano, 2019, 2020; Darveau and Cheikh-Ammar, 2021).

Retailing is thus becoming increasingly ephemeral (Boustani, 2020), in which new commerciality is combining phygital and omnichannel retailing within reconfigured territoriality where space is both physical and virtual (Belghiti et al., 2018; De Juan-Vigaray and Segui, 2019; Klaus, 2021; Mele et al., 2021; Batat, 2022). It is in this hybrid space that the notion of retail territory animates Deleuze and Guattari's (1987) and Massey's (1987) belief that territories are always places of passage. Meaning that places are open, hybrid and dynamic, a result of interconnecting flows and mobility, which, in doing so, contests the traditional notions of place as rooted, introspective and immobile (e.g. Harvey, 1996; Lippard, 1997). If territorialisation is better understood as the process of inscribing and imbuing space with meaning and experience (Johnstone and Conroy, 2008; Elden, 2013; McIntyre, 2013; Cresswell, 2015) then in the context of retail, the conventional meaning of place is unshackled from its physical confines (Ballantyne and Nilson, 2017). These (re)conceptualised retail territories are neither reductionist nor determinist, but they are emplaced; that is, they happen somewhere and are ensconced with meaning, value and experience (Gieryn, 2000).

An imagined, more holistic customer experience could be described and characterised using numerous adjectives, including *multiplicity* (of interacting channels), *complexity* (of management processes and structures), *temporality* (continually evolving online and offline presences), *socio-relationality*, *intersectionality* (through channel and touchpoint convergence), *non-linearity* (in the customer purchase journey) and *liminality* (of 'new'

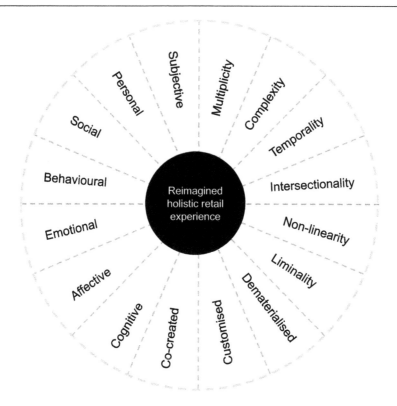

Figure 2.2 Reimagined holistic retail experience characterisation.

Source: Authors own.

in-between spaces, such as, for example, pop-up activities), to create *dematerialised* (beyond the physical), *customised* and *co-created* (between consumer, retailer, others) space, which can engender collective *cognitive*, *affective*, *emotional*, *behavioural* and *social* customer responses to the retailer, which are *personal* and *subjective* and also time- and context-specific, generating hedonic (e.g. immersive) and/or utilitarian (e.g. convenience) customer value (see Figure 2.2). All this arguably combines to create a reimagined holistic retail experience in 'territories' (both online and offline) that potentially enable new customer communities and representations, unbounded by spatial or psychic territorial boundaries (Ballantyne and Nilsson, 2017; Belghiti et al., 2018; Pusceddu et al., 2023).

These amorphous physical and virtual retail environments can create what Moor (2003:41) terms "spaces of proximity" for consumers. Therefore, retail territories arise through processes of producing, maintaining and assigning these myriad spaces with meaning (Kärrholm, 2007, 2008). Notions of digital- or physical-first retailers are displaced by the idea of an integrated retail territory – fully blended (Bolton et al., 2018) and 'holistic' – as conceived in Figure 2.3.

In this model, each circle represents a point on a continuum of convergence, orientated towards physical (to the left) or digital (to the right) spheres with complete coalescence and overlay in the centre. But, importantly, these retail territories are not seen as singular entities but complex colliding, converging and conjunct spatialities and temporalities,

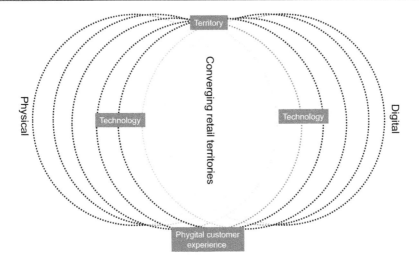

Figure 2.3 Retail territories continuum conceptual schema.
Source: Authors own.

and in this, the nature of the boundaries between these territories assumes importance. The experiential characteristics presented in Figure 2.2 overlay this continuum, with their relative resonance dependent on the retailer's temporal spatial reality. Collectively, they encompass the fluidity, openness and mobility of the retail territories, including the porosity of their boundaries.

ERT milieus

Brighenti (2010:60) notes that boundaries "are a constitutive prerequisite of territory", which can be 'drawn' in various ways. Given the converging and conjunct spatialities in this particular context, one concept that has explanatory utility is Deleuze and Guattari's notion of interior, intermediary, exterior and annexed *milieus*. Deleuze and Guattari state that "milieus pass into one another; they are essentially communicating" (1987:313), the implication being that milieus are not mutually exclusive and they blend into each other. Indeed, the ordering of the descriptions of the different milieus below reflects the expanding of the scalar extent of the nature of the space in question. Thus, the *interior milieu* constitutes the in-store environment, evident in the materiality of store design elements (e.g. fixtures/fittings, etc.) and the visual and other corporate identity symbols that identify the retailer. The *intermediary milieu* constitutes the interface of the store with its immediate environs, thereby creating boundaries, which may be manifest in both material and performative ways. It denotes what Deleuze and Guattari term the 'membranes' that limit and mark the extent of the physical store 'territory'. The *exterior milieu* denotes the wider – usually urban – locale within which the store is located. Finally, the *annexed milieu* combines the materiality of the store with a potentially wider, virtual operation, recognising the increasingly multi-omnichannel and phygital nature of the contemporary retail industry. Thus, retail experience potentially becomes more holistic, not only restricted to the physical territory of the physical store, but also incorporating a related digital experience in other retail channels and touchpoints which could be conceptualised as virtual territories.

Value creation within ERTs

Whilst technology is expected to continue to play a critical role in retail territories and customer experience (Bolton et al., 2018; Hoyer et al., 2020; Gauri et al., 2021), offering retailers new tools with which to create new interacting spatial touchpoints, arguably the fundamentals of retail value creation remain constant (Babin et al., 2021). As previously discussed, satisfying consumers' utilitarian and hedonic shopping value has received varying attention, often in dualism to each other over the years, but these values are regarded as working in synchronicity today, in delivering customer-centric experiences, characterised by either their 'immersive' nature (e.g. entertainment) or their 'convenience' (e.g. immediacy) (Gauri et al., 2021).

It is argued that the physical store remains central in generating both hedonic and utilitarian value for customers (Babin et al., 2021) within this ERT, which transcends channels and encompasses the reimagined characteristics aforementioned on a continuum of change, based on integration intensity. As previous scholars allude (Moisander and Eriksson, 2006) when it comes to digitalisation "it is an ongoing process that should be approached with openness and dynamism to what it might encompass" (Hagberg et al., 2016:696). Not something imposed upon us that sits outside of retailing, but rather reflects what we do and create through use and social interaction, a process of transformation from *within* retailing. In this sense, the conception of ERTs aptly conveys the envisioned future of retailing, wherein "place is a centre of meaning constructed by experience" (Tuan, 1975:152).

The physical territory emerges as an experience-based hub that connects the various touchpoints and facilitates seamless integration, customer experience and value creation. The chapter posits that in the reimagined physical store space, it is not just about what is offered (i.e. a shift from products to experiences; see also Alexander and Kent, 2018; Alexander, 2019), but how it is being offered (in particular facilitated by technology; see also Alexander and Olivares Alvarado, 2017; Alexander and Kent, 2021, 2022), thus challenging the very locus of retailers' value proposition, creation and delivery (Bell et al., 2018; Jocevski, 2020). A focus on deriving value through creating and delivering customer experience will remain a strategic priority for retailers to survive and thrive regardless of inevitable future retail paradigm shifts (Cook, 2014; Babin and Krey, 2020; Batat, 2022).

Future fashion retail customer experience

Chapters 1 and 2 offered a theoretical synthesis of customer experience in retail and proffered a prognosis for its development. Practitioners concur with the strategic imperative of customer experience management for retailers, with a recent report stating, "In the years ahead retail's biggest strength will be that it is experiential" (Wahi and Medeiros, 2023). The successive section brings this chapter to a close by contextualising three strategically important areas of customer experience that are challenging and changing fashion retail customer experience today. These relate to and cohere to the practitioner perspectives in Part 2 and are brought to life in the collection of cases in Part 3.

Hyper-phygital experiences

Recent reports state 27% of global customers (increasing to 36% for Generation Z) choose to mix physical and digital channels while shopping and over two-thirds of customers still purchase at physical stores, with digital experiences forecast to influence up to 70% of sales by 2027 (The Future Laboratory, 2023; Ho, 2023a) (see Figure 2.4).

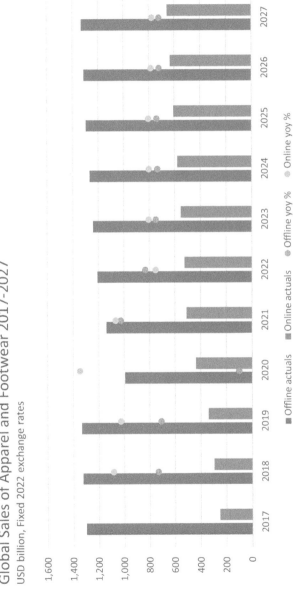

Figure 2.4 Global sales of clothing and footwear, 2017–2027.

Source: Euromonitor (2023a).

In addition, in-store customers who engage with technology are spending up to four times more shopping than those who do not (BoF Team, McKinsey and Co., 2022). Hyper-phygital experiences are therefore not only imperative to fashion consumers purchase journeys but they are growing in importance.

Fashion consumers' continuing demands for seamless integration of online and offline channels have accelerated retailers' digitalisation efforts, which is leading to new physical store openings by e-commerce players and store renovations to improve the hybrid in-store experience (Euromonitor, 2023a). Physical stores are increasingly being reimaged as spaces to showcase the best of the brand and offer immersive experiences that embed and leverage technologies to connect the on- and offline channel and effectuate a seamless customer experience (Euromonitor, 2023a). Global consumers are expecting technology integrations in-store, including entertainment (34%), immersive digital experiences (30%) and digital customer services (28%) (Ho, 2023a). The latest expression of this is 'meta-real' stores, that is, the integration of immersive virtual worlds (metaverses) – where people can connect, share, play games and shop – into physical stores, including elements from people's daily lives (music and films listened to and watched) to generate fully customisable in-store physical and digital content, touchpoints and experience.

Whilst an agreed upon definition of the metaverse remains elusive, Hadi et al. (2023) offer one aligned to CX, described as "a network of digitally mediated spaces that immerse users in shared, real-time experiences". Recent reports highlight the attractiveness of the metaverse opportunity, with it estimated to generate up to £4.7 trillion in value sales globally by 2030, of which £1.8 trillion is attributed to e-commerce, and 64% of consumers are said to be excited about shopping in the metaverse (Elmasry et al., 2022; Walker et al., 2022). Harnessing the metaverse and web3 to sell virtual products in store and driving digital customers towards physical spaces, and vice versa, (Ho, 2023a; Stylus, 2023a), is seen as the ultimate phygital merger, between physical places and virtual spaces, with cross-generational appeal, but especially for digital native and phygital first Generation Z and Alpha consumers (Napoli and Tan, 2023). Moreover, the fashion industry is seen to be at the forefront of metaverse advancement, with many retailers and brands across market levels, from luxury to mainstream, experimenting with it (e.g. Balenciaga, H&M, Zara, Nike, Adidas) (Park and Lim, 2023). Yet despite the hype, experimentation has been restricted to progressive and predominantly large players. It is estimated that 64% of global shoppers want more retail technological innovation, yet with less than 28% retailer adoption rate (Saunter and Medeiros, 2023), the retail challenge is in closing this opportunity gap, to achieve progressive phygital customer experiences.

Academics and practitioners recognise that phygitality is predicted to continue and is a strategic priority (Batat, 2022; Bonfanti et al., 2023; Euromonitor, 2023a; Iannilli and Spagnoli, 2021; The Future Laboratory, 2023; Jacob et al., 2023; Mele et al., 2023), as customers seek the best of the online and offline environments simultaneously, reinforcing a future of complementary, coalescing and converging hybrid spaces and places in generating CX, as constructed and depicted in Figure 2.3 (see earlier section).

There is a need for more nuanced phygital academic research (Batat, 2022; Bonfanti et al., 2023; Tom Dieck and Han, 2022), for example, identifying the intrinsic values, motivations and benefits used in a phygital context and assessing their collective influence on CX and consumer behaviours (Klaus, 2021) and, in turn, how retailers can provide more compelling phygital customer experiences (Batat, 2022; Mele et al., 2023). These will differ according to cultural context, consumer typology, digital readiness (for devices and platforms), technology type and sector. In addition, fashion retail practitioners are compelled to re-envision retail as phygitality, that is, perceiving online and offline as one continuous experience (Batat, 2022; Euromonitor, 2023a; The Future Laboratory, 2023; see also previous section on ERT), to leverage the advantages of both in optimising CX. Retailers need to reconfigure the function of the physical store, away from a linear to a multifunctional hybrid place to satisfy shopper plurality (Alexander and Blazquez Cano, 2019, 2020; Saunter and Medeiros, 2023). This includes experimenting with ways to augment 'IRL and URL' to create fluid in-store experiences through seamless technology integration, e.g. digital interfaces, interactive screens and smart mirrors for personalised recommendations, QR codes, cryptocurrency payments, automated (just walk out) stores, mixed reality AR and VR for virtual product try-on, shoppable store-fronts, etc. (Saunter and Medeiros, 2023) to create intelligent, empathic customer journey experiences (Farringdon, 2023).

The prominence given to hyper-phygital customer experiences relates to the previous section on the ascendance of phygitality and towards retail as ERTs, as an evolution or extension of omnichannel retailing. Readers are encouraged to review these sections simultaneously to formulate their own interpretation and speculation on retail's continual transition. Part 3 and the Zara, Nike, Sunnei and Glossier case studies exemplify and showcase how these fashion, sport and beauty retailers demonstrate best practice in forging a phygital-first customer experience.

Hyper-personalised experiences

Hyper-personalised retail customer experiences may be considered through a human-centric, digital-centric or hybrid lens. This section first explores evolving human-centric customer experiences in-store, before moving onto reviewing digital-centric personalised experiences enabled, accelerated and enhanced through rapidly advancing technologies like AI.

The COVID-19 global pandemic caused a shift in customer values, with greater emphasis on social interaction, recreational experiences and heightened customer service (Bruce et al., 2023; Vilnai-Yavetz et al., 2022). After almost two years of lockdown restrictions that saw the shuttering of stores, consumer footfall to physical stores have rebounded, with demand for novel immersive and personalised experiences resulting in new store openings and revamped retail concepts (Saunter, 2022). With increasing consumer expectations around service, convenience, flexibility and novel experiences, stores have become hyper-physical, extending beyond traditional experiential retail to incorporate unusual locations, visual merchandising, TikTok-friendly aesthetics, unique collaborations and one-of-a-kind experiences to satiate consumer expectations (Yaw-Miller, 2022). Augmenting and elevating physical stores through materiality, design, sensory stimuli and human interaction to offer distinctive in-person, memorable and engaging experiences, at a time when we increasingly spend more time in the digital space, is deemed critical (Bruce et al., 2023; Buller and Scott, 2022; Yaw-Miller, 2022).

Post the pandemic, over 80% of Millennial and Generation Z shoppers say they are willing to change their shopping behaviour if stores are more experiential (Buller and Scott, 2022), with 81% visiting physical stores to disconnect from their 'always on' digital lifestyle (Ho, 2023b). A resounding 82% of consumers expect a multisensory experience when interacting with retailers (Saunter and Medeiros, 2023). As these statistics show, it is posited that retail innovation is less about sales and more about providing "us with enriching, emotional, ethereal and exclusive experiences" (Martin Raymond, co-founder The Future Laboratory in Buller and Scott, 2022).

This notion of hyper-physical stores centred on human-centric relations relates directly with Shepherd's Chapter 5 on creating visceral and human-centric customer experiences as well as Quinn's Chapter 4 that emphasises the importance of building a social community. This is brought to life in Part 3, in the Aesop Sensorium, Tosummer and Anya Hindmarch case studies that exemplify how these retail brands demonstrate best practice in establishing and advancing a human-centric personalised experience based on multi-sensory, visceral, service-orientated and hyper-physical approaches.

In contrast to heightened human-based customer centricity, digital-centric personalised experiences are being accelerated and enhanced through technologies like AI. Over the past decade or so, personalisation has become increasingly important to retailers, but how it is achieved is rapidly changing with advancements in technologies paving the way for more intelligent, empathic customer journey experiences, propelled by AI. It is reported that 66% of customers expect retailers to understand their unique needs and expectations, yet only 32% of companies can convert data into personalised solutions in real time across the purchase journey (The Future Laboratory, 2023). It is inferred that 80% of consumers are more likely to purchase when the online experience is personalised, 60% are more likely to become repeat customers (Medeiros, 2023) and 43% have switched brands due to poor customer service (Wahi and Medeiros, 2023). The compelling opportunity gap coupled with rapid developments in AI, making true personalisation more efficient, effective and scalable (ibid), is gaining both attention and investment by fashion retailers (Calvo and Franco, 2023; Fu et al., 2023; Harreis et al., 2023).

In response to increasing global customer demand for personalised products and services (see Figure 2.5), AI's utility in delivering personalisation is driving retailer adoption of this technology (Euromonitor, 2023b). In fashion specifically, whilst still nascent, generative AI is reshaping the fashion ecosystem, especially customer service and experience, improving business productivity and speed to market (Harreis et al., 2023). Globally, AI is predicted to transform the economy, contributing up to USD 15 trillion (£13 trillion) by 2030 (The Future Laboratory, 2023; Wahi and Medeiros, 2023), and for the fashion industry (clothing, fashion, luxury) specifically, could add between $150 and $275 billion to the sectors' operating profits by 2028 (Harreis et al., 2023).

AI tools that are unlocking personalisation and efficiency are in their thousands and increasing daily, including some well-known ones like ChatGPT, Midjourney and DALL-E. AI's applications in the retail industry include text mining, chatbots, speech and image recognition, data mining and machine learning techniques, bringing benefits across the value chain from identifying trends, product design (and product co-creation), pricing, promotion, customer service management (e.g. tailoring virtual try-on, enhancing virtual assistants or chatbot capabilities), customer purchase journey, retail design process, enhancing visual merchandising, budget allocation, reducing environmental footprint, boosting revenue, while cutting costs and saving time (Euromonitor, 2023b; Fu et al., 2023; Saunter and Medeiros, 2023). In short, it has the potential to make retailing more dynamic, yet its application by retailers is still considered in its infancy (Fu et al., 2023; Harreis et al., 2023; Saunter and Medeiros, 2023).

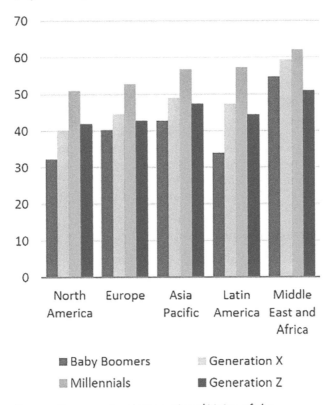

"I Want Products and Services That Are Uniquely Tailored To Me" 2023

% global respondents

- Baby Boomers
- Generation X
- Millennials
- Generation Z

Source: Euromonitor International Voice of the Consumer: Lifestyle Survey, fielded April 2023

Figure 2.5 Customer demand for personalised products and services.
Source: Euromonitor (2023b).

Whilst generative AI has the potential to revolutionalise the retail ecosystem, within digital and phygital commerce and customer experience specifically, its utility includes categorising and generating sales descriptions based on browsing and purchase history and customer feedback, gathering information on customer preferences for personalised recommendations, ChatGPT app integration to provide customers with bespoke recommendations, personalising online consumer journeys and product offers based on individual consumer profiles, tailored virtual product try-on and styling recommendations, enhanced virtual assistants/chatbots and self-service to cater to different consumer enquiries to better support human customer service teams (Harreis et al., 2023; Medeiros, 2023; Wahi and Medeiros, 2023). Predictive customer service will enable retailers to solve customer problems arguably before they are even aware of them (Wahi and Medeiros, 2023). AI is helping to close the gap between consumer needs and retailer decision-making (Euromonitor, 2023b).

It is estimated that global retail adoption of AI will increase from 40% in 2023 to over 80% by 2026, enabling retailers to innovate at speed and generate competitive advantage; however, adoption involves risks and the ethical and privacy considerations that come with implementation is crucial, ensuring equitable harnessing of human intelligence with generative AI intelligence in the creation of customer-centric hyper-personalised experiences (Harreis et al., 2023; Medeiros, 2023). A recent report stated that 49% of global digital Generation Z consumers will share personal preferences with brands online in exchange for personalised experiences (Euromonitor, 2023b), showing customers are willing to trade privacy for elevated experience.

It is forecast that "by 2030, artificial intelligence will become more attuned and better at directing technology to suit specific needs, creating a world of hyper-individualised experiences" (The Future Laboratory, 2023). Arguably, however, it is the hybrid approach that will effectuate future CX – involving harnessing the best of both human and digital capabilities – to deliver optimum hyper-personalised future customer experiences.

Hyper-responsible experiences

The fashion industry has been called out for not being on track to meet its sustainability targets, but rather continuing to contribute directly to the planetary and social crisis of climate change, nature and biodiversity loss, pollution and waste and social injustice, through its dominant economic model based on 'take-make-waste'. This focus on newness, immediacy and disposability has resulted in unsustainable production and consumption practices (Arthur, 2023). Today, fashion consumers buy 60% more but keep their items for just half as long compared to 20 years ago (Saggese, 2023).

Fashion retailers are facing soaring pressure from customers, campaigners and regulators to shift towards a more responsible mindset and improve their environmental and social impact as Environmental, Social and Governance (ESG) reporting becomes enforced in many parts of the world. Global policy initiatives are numerous and constantly evolving, with the majority being led by the Global North. These include the European Green Deal, Strategy for Sustainable and Circular Textiles (EU), the Sustainable Consumption Pledge (EU), Fashion Sustainability and Social Accountability Act (USA) that are collectively progressing a number of proposals that signal significant shifts for responsible practices, related to the 4Rs: reduce, reuse, repair, recycle (Arthur, 2023; Euromonitor, 2023a).

Whilst many retailers have circularity principles embedded into their business from the get-go, it is forcing others to seek ways to reduce their waste and carbon footprint and achieve traceability. Misinformation and greenwashing are ubiquitous across fashion communication, resulting in growing mistrust in what is and is not sustainable (Arthur, 2023). In accord with UNEP's (United Nations Environmental Programme) (Arthur, 2023:11) definition of sustainable fashion communication as "communicating sustainably across the fashion sector" and transitioning towards sustainable narratives of regeneration, equity and care, pioneering retailers are demonstrating tangible engagement through circular store design, activations and experiences, embracing eco-adoption in green energy, material choices, furniture and fixtures, packaging, consumer-facing storytelling, images, messages and collaborations (Ho, 2022; Stylus, 2023b). Implementing green principles of repurposing (e.g. furniture), recycling or upcycling (e.g. materials, products), refurbishment, adaptive reuse designs (i.e. minimal building interventions), near-sourcing for store fit-outs, to the selling of recycled products and offering regenerative services like recycling, repair and resale, to connect with consumers, create better retail designs and experiences and meet sustainability goals (LeRolland, 2023; Stylus, 2023b).

Increasingly, consumer mindsets are shifting towards sustainability and more conscious consumption habits (LeRolland, 2023) (see Figure 2.6). Over 60% of global consumers are concerned about the world's outlook and 70% want to feel part of something bigger than themselves (Euromonitor, 2023a; Saunter and Medeiros, 2023). With this shift towards a more mission-based mindset, with consumers actively seeking alternative ways of accessing product whilst prioritising experiences over actual purchases, retailers have the opportunity to rethink ways in which events, services and retail spaces can be used to build community, drive co-creation, educate and engage whilst demonstrating commitment to their social and environmental responsibility (Saggese, 2023). Global sales from the fashion circular economy is forecast to reach USD 691 billion by 2030, with resale (secondhand) the largest model (USD 476 billion, 2030), followed by rental (USD 167 billion, 2030), repair (USD 32 billion, 2030) and remaking (recycling, USD 16 billion, 2030) (Stylus, 2023b), demonstrating the transition afoot, but also a strong motivation for retailers to integrate and augment these aftercare models into existing retail spaces and service proposition to elevate customer experience.

As a forerunner in creating (re)tail experiences, UK department store Selfridges is planning for half of all transactions to come from resale, rental and repair by 2030. Its Reselfridges programme is used to capture curiosity, excite, educate, immerse and reorientate fashion consumption habits. Worn Again is part of this programme, which

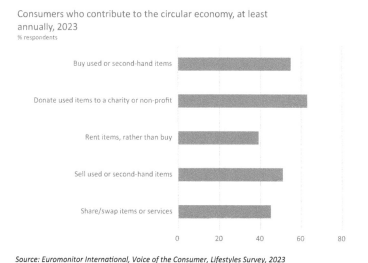

Source: Euromonitor International, Voice of the Consumer, Lifestyles Survey, 2023

Figure 2.6 Consumers who contribute to the circular economy at least annually, 2023.
Source: Euromonitor (2023a).

is a season of secondhand shopping, repairing, swapping, upcycling spaces, dedicated to ideas, collaborations and events (Ho, 2023b, Selfridges.com). Increasingly, retailers are recognising the value in utilising their retail channel and touchpoints to create fun, exciting, interactive and responsible in-store designs, activations and experiences to enhance customer experience whilst communicating their sustainable values (see, for example, Loewe ReCraft store, Golden Goose Renewals, Timberland's The Shed, Rizo x H&M Create in-store rental, Patagonia's Activism Hub) (Ho, 2022, 2023b; Saggese, 2023, Stylus, 2023b). As the spotlight on retailers and their sustainability strategies and actions becomes increasingly acute, creating responsible customer experiences will become progressively imperative.

Hyper-responsible customer experiences are prominent in Part 2 with Quinn's Chapter 4, highlighting the need to embed responsible retail mindsets into retail design, with specific consideration to materiality and circularity. Part 3 (Chapter 7) and the RÆBURN Lab, Ecoalf and Loanhood case studies exemplify and showcase how these fashion retailers, brands and services foster and amplify responsible customer experiences based on sustainable store design and in-store communications.

Expounded by many practitioners and scholars, the retail industry has experienced as much disruption in the past 5 years as it has in the previous 25, fundamentally shifting behaviours and expectations of all stakeholders simultaneously (customers, suppliers, employees and investors) (Begley et al., 2023). As demonstrated in this book, one underlying construct that has been a constant since the 1950s, and has only grown in prominence and relevance amid increasing disruption, is customer experience. Through the coherence of multiple perspectives, and through theory and practice, this volume provides a complete and holistic account of customer experience conception, from inception to present today, through the lens of the fashion industry. Whilst customer experience expressions will inevitably change with the constantly changing 'wheel of retailing' (Hollander, 1960), its basic tenet will undoubtedly remain, that is, that retail creates value by "creating customer experience that is personally gratifying" (Babin et al., 2021:88).

References

Agnew, J. (1987) *Place and politics: The geographical mediation of state and society.* Boston, MA: Allen & Unwin.

Alexander, B. (2019) 'Commerce, culture and experience convergence: Fashion's third places.' *Journal of Services Marketing*, 33(3), pp. 257–272. https://doi.org/10.1108/JSM-04-2018-0116

Alexander, B. and Olivares Alvarado, D. (2017) 'Chapter 8: Convergence of physical and virtual retail spaces: The influence of technology on consumer in-store experience,' in Vecchi, A. (ed.) *The book of advanced fashion technology and operations management.* Hershey, PA: IGI Global, pp. 191–219. https://doi.org/10.4018/978-1-5225-1865-5.ch008

Alexander, B. and Kent, A. (2018) 'Chapter 5: Retail environments,' in Petermans, A. and Kent, A. (eds.) *Retail design.* Routledge Publishing, pp. 62–86. ISBN: 9781472467836.

Alexander, B. and Blazquez Cano, M. (2019) 'Futurising the physical store in the omnichannel retail environment,' in Piotrowicz, W. and Cuthbertson, R. (eds.) *Exploring Omnichannel retailing: Common expectations and diverse realities.* Springer Press. ISBN 978-3-319-98272-4.

Alexander, B. and Blazquez Cano, M. (2020), 'Store of the future: towards a (re)invention and (re) imagination of physical store space in an omnichannel context', *Journal of retailing and consumer services*, Vol. 55, pp.1–12. DOI: https://doi.org/10.1016/j.jretconser.2019.101913

Alexander, B. and Kent, A. (2021) 'Tracking technology diffusion in-store: a fashion retail perspective.' *International Journal of Retail & Distribution Management*, 49(10), pp. 1369–1390. https://doi.org/10.1108/IJRDM-05-2020-0191

Alexander, B. and Kent, A. (2022) 'Change in technology-enabled omnichannel customer experiences in-store.' *Journal of Retailing and Consumer Services*, 65, p. 102338. https://doi.org/10.1016/j.jretconser.2020.102338

Alexander, B. and Warnaby, G. (2023) 'Territorialising retail: An alternative spatiality,' in Nieto Garcia, M., Acuti, D., Sit, J. and Brusset, X. (eds.) *Book of proceedings, 8th Colloquium on European Research in Retailing (CERR)*, 22–23 June, 2023, University of Portsmouth. ISBN: 9781861376787.

Arthur, R. (2023) *The sustainable fashion communication playbook, UNEP and UNF-CCC*. [Online] [Accessed 4th October 2023] https://www.unep.org/resources/publication/sustainable-fashion-communication-playbook

Babin, B.J., Feng, C. and Borges, A. (2021) 'As the wheel turns toward the future of retailing.' *Journal of Marketing Theory and Practice*, 29(1), pp. 78–91.

Babin, B.J. and Krey, N. (2020) 'Meta-analytic evidence on personal shopping value.' *Recherche Et Applications En Marketing*, 35(3), pp. 124–132.

Ballantyne, D. and Nilsson, E. (2017) 'All that is solid melts into air: The servicescape in digital service space.' *Journal of Services Marketing*, 31(3), pp. 226–235.

Batat, W. (2022) 'What does phygital really mean? A conceptual introduction to the phygital customer experience (PH-CX) framework.' *Journal of Strategic Marketing*, pp. 1–24. https://doi.org/10.1080/0965254X.2022.2059775

Begley, S., Coggins, B., Green, C., Hamdan, J., Kuipers, D. and Laizet, F. (2023) *Retail reset: A new playbook for retail leaders*. McKinsey Quarterly. [Online] [Accessed 4th October 2023] https://www.mckinsey.com/industries/retail/our-insights/retail-reset-a-new-playbook-for-retail-leaders

Belghiti, S., Ochs, A., Lemoine, J.F. and Badot, O. (2018) 'The phygital shopping experience: An attempt at conceptualization and empirical investigation,' in Rossi, P. and Krey, N. (eds.) *Marketing transformation: Marketing practice in an ever changing world*. AMSWMC 2017. Developments in Marketing Science: Proceedings of the Academy of Marketing Science. Springer, Cham, pp. 61–74.

Bell, D.R., Gallino, S. and Moreno, A. (2018) 'The store is dead - long live the store.' *MIT Sloan Management Review*, pp. 59–66. [Online] [Accessed 1st September 2021] https://sloanreview.mit.edu/article/the-store-is-dead-long-live-the-store/

Bitner, J.M. (1992) 'Servicescapes: The impact of physical surroundings on customers and employees.' *Journal of Marketing*, 56(2), pp. 57–71.

BoF team and McKinsey & Co. (2022) *The technologies reinventing physical retail*. Business of Fashion. [Online] [Accessed 4th October 2023] https://www.businessoffashion.com/articles/technology/state-of-fashion-technology-report-connected-retail-stores/

Bolton, R.N., McColl-Kennedy, J.R., Cheung, L., Gallan, A., Orsingher, C., Witell, L. and Zaki, M. (2018) 'Customer experience challenges: Bringing together digital, physical and social realms.' *Journal of Service Management*, 29(5), pp. 776–808.

Bonfanti, A., Vigolo, V., Vannucci, V. and Brunetti, F. (2023) 'Creating memorable shopping experiences to meet phygital customers' needs: Evidence from sporting goods stores.' *International Journal of Retail & Distribution Management*, 15(13), pp. 81–100.

Borghini, S., Diamon, N., Kozinets, R.V., McGrath, M.A., Muniz, A.M. and Sherry, J.F. (2009) 'Why are themed brandstores so powerful? Retail brand ideology at American Girl place.' *Journal of Retailing*, 85(3), pp. 363–375.

Bourlakis, M., Papagiannidis, S. and Li, F. (2009) 'Retail spatial evolution: Paving the way from traditional to Metaverse retailing.' *Electronic Commerce Research Journal*, 9(1), pp. 135–148.

Boustani, G. (2020) *Ephemeral retailing: Pop-up stores in a postmodern consumption era*. Abingdon: Routledge Focus.

Brighenti, A.M. (2010) 'On territorology: Towards a general science of territory.' *Theory, Culture & Society*, 27(1), pp. 52–72.

Brighenti, A.M. (2014) 'Mobilizing territories, territorializing mobilities.' *Sociologica*. https://doi.org/10.2383/77043.

Brocato, E.D., Voorhees, C.M. and Baker, J. (2012) Understanding the influence of cues from other customers in the service experience: A scale development and validation.' *Journal of Retailing*, 88(3), pp. 384–398.

Bruce, H.L., Krolikowska, E. and Rooney, T. (2023) 'Guest editorial: Investigating the effect of the physical context on customer experience.' *Journal of Services Marketing*, 37(6), pp. 689–699.

Buller, A. and Scott, S. (2022) *Hyperphysical stores*. LS:N Global. [Online] [Accessed 4th October 2023] https://www.lsnglobal.com/

Buttimer, A. and Seamon, D. (1980) *The human experience of space and place*. New York: St. Martins Press.

Calvo, A.V. and Franco, A.D. (2023) 'The role of artificial intelligence in improving the omnichannel customer experience.' *International Journal of Retailing & Distribution Management*. Ahead of print. https://doi.org/10.1108/IJRDM-12-2022-0493

Casey, E.S. (1996) *The fate of place: A philosophical history*. Berkeley: University of California Press.

Cheetham, F., McEachern, M.G. and Warnaby, G. (2018) 'A kaleidoscopic view of the territorialised consumption of place.' *Marketing Theory*, 18(4), pp. 473–492.

Chevtchouk, Y., Veloutsou, C. and Paton, R.A. (2021) 'The experience – economy revisited: An interdisciplinary perspective and research agenda.' *Journal of Product & Brand Management*. In press. https://doi.org/10.1108/JPBM-06-2019-2406.

Cohen, J.E. (2007) 'Cyberspace as/and space.' *Columbia Law Review*, 107(1), pp. 210–256.

Cook, G. (2014) 'Customer experience in the omni-channel world and the challenges and opportunities this presents.' *Journal of Direct, Data and Digital Marketing Practice*, 15, pp. 262–266.

Cresswell, T. (2015) *Place: An introduction*. 2nd ed. West Sussex: John Wiley & Sons, Blackwell Publishing Ltd.

Crewe, L. (2013) 'When virtual and material worlds collide: Democratic fashion in the digital age.' *Environment and Planning A*, 45, pp. 760–780.

Crewe, L. and Lowe, M. (1995) 'Gap on the map? Towards a geography of consumption and identity.' *Environment and Planning A*, 27, pp. 1877–1898.

Currah, A. (2002) 'Behind the web store: The organisational and spatial evolution of multichannel retailing in Toronto.' *Environment and Planning A*, 34, pp. 1411–1441.

Darveau, J. and Cheikh-Ammar, M. (2021) 'The interplay between liminality and consumption: A systematic literature review with a future research agenda.' *International Journal of Consumer Studies*, 45, pp. 868–888.

De Juan-Vigaray, M.D. and Espinosa Segui, A.I. (2019) 'Retailing, consumers and territory: Trends of an incipient circular model.' *Social Sciences*, 8, pp. 1–15.

Dekimpe, M.G. and Geyskens, I. (2019) 'Retailing research in rapidly changing times: On the danger of being leapfrogged by practice.' *Journal of Retailing*, 95(1), pp. 6–9.

Deleuze, G. and Guattari, F. (1987) *A thousand plateaus: Capitalism and schizophrenia* (trans. Massumi, B). London: The Athlone Press.

Donovan, R.J. and Rossiter, J.R. (1982) 'Store atmosphere: An environmental psychology approach.' *Journal of Retailing*, 58, pp. 34–57.

Elden, S. (2013) *The birth of territory*. Chicago: University of Chicago Press.

Elmasry, T., Hazan, E., Khan, H., Kelly, G., Srivastava, S., Yee, L. and Zemmel, R.W. (2022) *Value creation in the metaverse: The real business of the virtual world*. McKinsey & Company [Online]. https://www.mckinsey.com/capabilities/growth-marketing-and-sales/our-insights/value-creation-in-the-metaverse

Escobar, A. (2001) 'Culture sits in place: Reflections on globalism and subaltern strategies of locali-zation.' *Political Geography*, 20, pp. 139–174.

Euromonitor (2023a) *Shifting channels in luxury and fashion*. Passport Euromonitor [Online] [Accessed 15th September 2023] https://www.euromonitor.com/shifting-channels-in-luxury-and-fashion/report

Euromonitor (2023b) *Top five digital consumer trends in 2023*. Passport Euromonitor [Online] [Accessed 15th September 2023] https://www.euromonitor.com/top-five-digital-consumer-trends-in-2023/report

Farringdon, A. (2023) *Six fashion brands deploying EQ-Commerce strategies*. LS:N Global [Online] [Accessed 3rd October 2023] https://www.lsnglobal.com/

Fu, H-P., Chang, T-H., Lin, S-W., Teng, Y-H. and Huang, Y-Z. (2023) 'Evaluation and adoption of artificial intelligence in the retail industry.' *International Journal of Retail & Distribution Management*, 51(6), pp. 773–790.

Gadalla, E., Keeling, K. and Abosag, I. (2013) 'Metaverse-retail service quality: A future framework for retail service quality in the 3D internet.' *Journal of Marketing Management*, 29(13/14), pp. 1493–1517.

Gauri, D.K., Jindal, R.P., Ratchford, B., Fox, E., Bhatnagar, A., Pandey, A., Navallo, J.R., Fogarty, J., Carr, S. and Howerton, E. (2021) 'Evolution of retail formats: Past, present, and future.' *Journal of Retailing*, 97(1), pp. 42–61.

Gieryn, T.F. (2000) 'A space for place in sociology.' *Annual Review of Sociology*, 26, pp. 463–496.

Goworek, H. and McGoldrick, P. (2015) *Retail marketing management: Principles and practice.* Harlow: Pearson Education Ltd.

Hadi, R., Melumad, S. and Park, E.S. (2023) 'The metaverse: A new digital frontier for consumer behavior.' *Journal of Consumer Psychology*, pp. 1–25 [Online]. https://doi.org/10.1002/jcpy.1356

Hagberg, J., Sundstrom, J.M. and Nicklas, E.Z. (2016) 'The digitalization of retailing: An exploratory framework.' *International Journal of Retail & Distribution Management*, 44(7), pp. 694–712.

Hänninen, M., Kwan, S.K. and Mitronen, L. (2021) 'From the store to omnichannel retail: Looking back over three decades of research.' *The International Review of Retail, Distribution and Consumer Research*, 31(1), pp. 1–35.

Harreis, H., Koullias, T., Roberts, R. and Te, K. (2023) *Generative AI: Unlocking the future of fashion*. McKinsey & Company. [Online] [Accessed 3rd October 2023] https://www.mckinsey.com/industries/retail/our-insights/generative-ai-unlocking-the-future-of-fashion

Harvey, D. (1996) *Justice, nature and the geography of difference*. Cambridge, MA: MIT Press.

Heidegger, M. (1993) *Basic writings: From Being and Time (1927) to the Task of Thinking (1964)*. Krell, D.F. (ed.) San Francisco: Harper Collins Publishers.

Ho, A. (2022) *Case studies: Sustainable store design 2022*. WGSN. [Online] [Accessed 3rd October 2023] https://www.wgsn.com/en

Ho, A. (2023a) *Meta-rich retail strategies 2023*. WGSN. [Online] [Accessed 3rd October 2023] https://www.wgsn.com/en

Ho, A. (2023b) *Offline re-commerce: Shifts & strategies*. WGSN. [Online] [Accessed 3rd October 2023] https://www.wgsn.com/en

Hollander, S.C. (1960) 'The wheel of retailing.' *Journal of Marketing*, 25(1), pp. 37–42. https://doi.org/10.1177/002224296002500106.

Hoyer, W.D., Kroschke, M., Schmitt, B., Kraume, K. and Shankar, V. (2020) 'Transforming the customer experience through new technologies.' *Journal of Interactive Marketing*, 51, pp. 57–71.

Iannilli, V.M. and Spagnoli, A. (2021) 'Phygital retailing in fashion. Experiences, opportunities and innovation trajectories.' *ZoneModa Journal*, 11(1), pp. 43–69.

Jacob, F., Pez, V. and Volle, P. (2023) 'Shifting to phygital experience management with design science: A six-step method to manage customer journeys.' *Journal of Strategic Marketing*, 31(5), pp. 961–982. https://doi.org/10.1080/0965254X.2021.2016894

Jessop, B., Brenner, N. and Jones, M. (2008) 'Theorizing sociospatial relations.' *Environment and Planning D: Society and Space*, 26(3), pp. 389–401.

Jocevski, M. (2020) 'Blurring the lines between physical and digital spaces: Business model innovation in retailing.' *California Management Review*, 63(1), pp. 99–117.

Johnstone, M.-L. and Conroy, D.M. (2006) 'Seeking social experiences within the retail environment,' in Lees, M.C., Davis, T. and Gregory, G. (eds.) *AP - Asia-Pacific advances in consumer research*, Vol. 7. Sydney: Association for Consumer Research. pp. 401–407.

Johnstone, M.-L. and Conroy, D.M. (2008) 'Place attachment: The social dimensions of the retail environment and the need for further exploration,' in Lee, A.Y., Soman, D. and Duluth, M.N (eds.) *NA - Advances in consumer research*, Vol. 35. US: Association for Consumer Research, pp. 381–386.

Kärrholm, M. (2007) 'The materiality of territorial production: A conceptual discussion of territoriality, materiality, and the everyday life of public space.' *Space and Culture*, 10, pp. 437–453.

Kärrholm, M. (2008) 'The territorialisation of a pedestrian precinct in Malmo: Materialities in the commercialisation of public space.' *Urban Studies*, 45(9), pp. 1903–1924.

Kärrholm, M. (2012) *Retailising space: Architecture, retail and the territorialising of public space.* Farnham: Ashgate Publishing.

Klaus, P. (2021) 'Viewpoint: Phygital – The emperor's new clothes?' *Journal of Strategic Marketing*. [Online] [Accessed 26th September 2023] https://doi.org/10.1080/0965254X.2021.1976252

Lambach, D. (2019) 'The territorialization of cyberspace.' *International Studies Review*. [Online] [Accessed 15th July 2021] https://doi.org/10.1093/isr/viz022

Lecointre-Erickson, D., Adil, S., Daucé, B. and Legohérel, P. (2021) 'The role of brick-and-mortar exterior atmospherics in post-COVID era shopping experience: A systematic review and agenda for future research.' *Journal of Strategic Marketing*. https://doi.org/10.1080/0965254X.2021.2016895

Lefebvre, H. (1991) *The production of space.* Oxford: Blackwell.

Lehdonvirta, V. (2010) 'Online spaces have material culture: Goodbye to digital post-materialism and hello to virtual consumption.' *Media, Culture and Society*, 32, pp. 883–889.

LeRolland, M. (2023) Why integrating sustainability in retail is becoming a must. Passport Euromonitor. [Online] [Accessed 4th October 2023] https://www.euromonitor.com/article/why-integrating-sustainability-in-fashion-retail-is-becoming-a-must

Lippard, L. (1997) *The lure of the local: Senses of place in a multicultural society.* New York: The New Press.

Malpas, J.E. (1999) *Place and experience: A philosophical topography.* Cambridge: Cambridge University Press.

Massey, D. (1987) 'A global sense of place,' in Barnes, T. and Gregory, D. (eds.) *Reading human geography*. London: Arnold, pp. 315–323.

McCarthy, J.E. and Perrault, W.D. (1960) *Basic marketing: A managerial approach.* Homewood, IL: Irwin.

McIntyre, C. (2013) 'Physical retail space and place: The historical development of a social psycho-geography of liminal consumption.' In *Proceedings of the 16th Biennial Conference on Historical Analysis and Research in Marketing*, Copenhagen Business School, Denmark, 30 May–2 June. [Online] [Accessed 15th July 2021] https://ojs.library.carleton.ca/index.php/pcharm/article/view/1396

Medeiros, C. (2023) *Generative AI: Retail & shopping futures.* WGSN. [Online] [Accessed 3rd October 2023] https://www.wgsn.com/en

Mele, C., Russo-Spena, T., Tregua, M. and Amitrano, C.C. (2021) 'The millennial customer journey: A phygital mapping of emotional, behavioural, and social experiences.' *Journal of Consumer Marketing*, 38(4), pp. 420–433.

Mele, C., Russo-Spena, T., Marzullo, M. and Di Bernardo, I. (2023) 'The phygital transformation: A systematic review and a research agenda.' *Italian Journal of Marketing*, pp. 323–349. https://doi.org/10.1007/s43039-023-00070-7

Moisander, J. and Eriksson, P. (2006) 'Corporate narratives of information society: Making up the mobile consumer subject.' *Consumption Markets & Culture*, 9(4), pp. 257–275.

Moor, E. (2003) 'Branded spaces: The scope of "new marketing".' *Journal of Consumer Culture*, 3(1), pp. 39–60. https://doi.org/10.1177/1469540503003001929

Napoli, C. and Tan, E. (2023) *Metaverse: Future applications*. WGSN [Online] [Accessed 3rd Oct 2023] https://www.wgsn.com/en

Oldenburg, R. (1989) *The great good place*. New York: Marlowe & Company.

Paasi, A. (2003) 'Territory,' in Agnew, J., Mitchell, K. and Tuathail G-O. (eds.) *A companion to political geography*. Malden, MA: Blackwell, pp. 109–122.

Papagiannidis, S. and Bourlakis, M. (2010) 'Staging the new retail drama: At a Metaverse near!' *Journal of Virtual Worlds Research*, 2(5), pp. 4–17.

Park, H. and Lim, E.E. (2023) 'Fashion and the metaverse: Clarifying the domain and establishing a research agenda.' *Journal of Retailing and Consumer Services*, 74, p. 103413 [Online]. https://doi.org/10.1016/j.jretconser.2023.103413

Picot-Coupey, K., Huré, E. and Piveteau, L. (2016) 'Channel design to enrich customers' shopping experiences: Synchronizing clicks with bricks in an omni-channel perspective – The Direct Optic case.' *International Journal of Retail & Distribution Management*, 44(3), pp. 336–368.

Platt, L., Medway, D. and Steadman, C. (2021) 'Processional walking: Theorising the "place" of movement in notions of dwelling.' *Geographical Research*, 59(1), pp. 106–117.

Pred, A.R. (1984) 'Place as historically contingent process: Structuration and the time-geography of becoming places.' *Annals of the Association of American Geographers*, 74, pp. 279–297.

Proshansky, H.M. (1978) 'The city and self-identity.' *Environment and Behavior*, 10(2), pp. 147–169. https://doi.org/10.1177/0013916578102002

Pusceddu, G., Moi, L. and Cabiddu, F. (2023) 'Do they see eye to eye? Managing customer experience in phygital high tech retail.' *Management Decision*. Ahead of print. https://doi.org/10.1108/MD-05-2022-0673.

Relph, E. (1976) *Place and Placelessness*. London: Pion.

Roggeveen, A.L. and Sethuraman, R. (2018) 'Understanding the JR heritage, publishing in JR, and the evolving retail field.' *Journal of Retailing*, 9(4), pp. 1–4.

Rosenbaum, M.S., Kelleher, C., Friman, M., Kristensson, P. and Scherer, A. (2017) 'Re-placing place in marketing: A resource-exchange place perspective.' *Journal of Business Research*, 79, pp. 281–289.

Rosenbaum, M.S. and Massiah, C. (2011) 'An expanded servicescape perspective.' *Journal of Service Management*, 22(4), pp. 471–490.

Sack, R.D. (1992) *Place, modernity, and the consumer's world: A relationship framework for geographic analysis*. Baltimore, MD: John Hopkins University Press.

Saggese, B. (2023) *Challenging Overconsumption: Shifts & strategies*. WGSN. [Online] [Accessed 4th October 2023] https://www.wgsn.com/mywgsn

Saunter, L. (2022) *Retail forecast 2022*. WGSN. [Online] [Accessed 3rd October 2023] https://www.wgsn.com/mywgsn

Saunter, L. and Medeiros, C. (2023) *Stores in 2024: Experiential and innovative formats*. WGSN. [Online] [Accessed 3rd October 2023] https://www.wgsn.com/mywgsn

Shi, C., Warnaby, G. and Quinn, L. (2019) 'Territorialising brand experience and consumption: Negotiating a role for pop up retailing.' *Journal of Consumer Culture*, 21(2), pp. 359–380.

Sikos, T.T., Kozák, T. and Kovács, A. (2019) 'New retail models in online and offline space.' *Deturope: The Central European Journal of Regional Development and Tourism*, 11(2), pp. 9–28.

Stylus (2023a) *Retail regenerated: Powerhouse predictions for 2023/24*. Stylus. [Online] [Accessed 3rd October 2023] https://campaigns.stylus.com/retailregenerated/

Stylus (2023b) *Circular economy concept stores.* Stylus [Online] [Accessed 3rd October 2023] https://stylus.com/retail-brand-comms/circular-economy-concept-stores-resales-repairs-evaluations.

The Future Laboratory (2023) *Retail futures 2023 report.* LS:N Global. [Online] [Accessed 3rd October] https://www.thefuturelaboratory.com/reports/2023/retail-futures

Thrift, N. (2011) 'Lifeworld Inc—and what to do about it.' *Environment and Planning D: Society and Space*, 29, pp. 5–26.

Tom Dieck, C.M. and Han, D. (2022) 'The role of immersive technology in customer experience management.' *Journal of Marketing Theory and Practice*, 30(1), pp. 108–119.

Tuan, Y.-F. (1974) 'Space and place: Humanistic perspective.' *Progress in Human Geography*, 6, pp. 211–252.

Tuan, Y.-F. (1975) 'Place: An experiential perspective.' *The Geographical Review*, 65(2), pp. 151–165.

Tuan, Y.-F. (2001) *Space and place.* 25th ed. Minneapolis: University of Minnesota Press.

Turkle, S. (2011) *Alone together.* New York: Basic Books.

Varley, R. and Rafiq, M. (2014) *Principles of retailing.* 2nd ed. Basingstoke, Hampshire: Palgrave Macmillan.

Vilnai-Yavetz, I., Gilboa, S. and Mitchell, V. (2022) 'There is no place like my mall': Consumer reactions to the absence of mall experiences.' *Journal of Services Marketing*, 36(4), pp. 563–583.

Wahi, R. and Medeiros, C. (2023) *Retail forecast 2023.* [Online] [Accessed 3rd October 2023] https://www.wgsn.com/en/wgsn/press/press-releases/wgsn-reveals-top-trends-2023-and-beyond

Walker, J., Poile, M. and Smith, J. (2022) *Meta-physical retail market.* LS:N Global. [Online] [Accessed 3rd October 2023] https://www.lsnglobal.com/

Warnaby, G. (2018) 'Taking a territorological perspective on place branding?' *Cities*, 80, pp. 64–66.

Yaw-Miller, D. (2022) *How to open a store in 2022.* Business of Fashion. [Online] [Accessed 4th October 2023] https://www.businessoffashion.com/articles/retail/how-to-open-a-store-in-2022/

Part 2

Practitioner perspectives on retail customer experience

3

Placing people at the heart of customer experience journeys

Christina Herbach

An audience-centric approach

The realm of fashion retail design is an exciting one filled with creative and commercial choices. Key decisions encompass an array of aspects, from the physical store format type and size to the product selection, service offerings and experiential elements, as well as the essential consideration of where, when and how to integrate digital elements and channels. The interpersonal element of the staff's role adds yet another layer of complexity to the process.

This chapter will make the case that the best starting point for designing fashion retail (or any retail design for that matter) is to begin by placing people at the heart of the customer experience.

The section will delve into what it actually means to place people at the centre of the design process. The practice is centred on deeply understanding people's stable underlying identities, needs and desires as well as their more mutable mindsets and missions. This fundamental understanding serves as the foundation upon which all experience design decisions can and should be made.

Ultimately, by immersing oneself in the intricacies of the target audience, the designer ensures that the retail experience fulfils its objectives, whether that be attracting new shoppers, engaging with fans, exhibiting creative prowess or achieving commercial aims. Indeed, true audience comprehension provides a guiding compass, allowing the designer to return to it repeatedly while navigating through choices both major and minute.

Demographics and psychographics: audience basics

Developing an intimate understanding of a retail audience begins with customer research focused on fundamental descriptors – demographics and psychographics.

Demographics encompasses relatively fixed identity traits, such as age, gender and ethnicity. Depending on a retailer's strategy and the cultural context that they are operating in, additional considerations like income level, language, educational background or occupation may also be relevant to explore.

Psychographics, on the other hand, delves into the audience's values, attitudes and lifestyle choices. These traits often transcend demographic boundaries and have the potential to evolve over time. For instance, in the domain of fashion retail, comprehending personal style choices and cultural preferences is of utmost importance.

DOI: 10.4324/9781003378099-5

When exploring psychographics, the VALS (Values, Attitudes and Lifestyles) framework is a popular segmentation model developed by SRI International. It classifies individuals into distinct segments based on their values, attitudes and lifestyles, providing insights into their motivations, behaviours and preferences (Yankelovich and Meer, 2006).

Practically, a wide variety of market research methodologies exist to gather insights on audience demographics and psychographics, ranging from quantitative to qualitative approaches. For instance, commissioning large-scale online surveys or conducting global social media sentiment studies are popular quantitative research approaches. Similarly, facilitating in-store focus groups or conducting virtual, video-based in-home customer diaries are useful qualitative methods to gain valuable insights into how a potential audience relates to a specific retail brand or broad category.

No matter what quantitative and qualitative research methods the retailer choses, Table 3.1 offers a list of demographic and psychographic questions for developing audience empathy. Answering these is the first step in mapping an audience's basic profile.

In addition to the quantitative and qualitative research methods discussed thus far, observation is recommended as an important part of gaining a more holistic insight into an audience. This is because of a well-researched phenomena called the 'attitude-behaviour' gap (Jerolmack and Khan, 2014), wherein there is often a difference between what an individual will say (their attitude) and what they will actually do in an unmonitored real-life situation (their behaviour).

Table 3.1 Demographic and psychographic evaluation questions

Demographics	What is the target audience's age range and gender identity?
	What is their income level and willingness to spend?
	Where do they live and for whom are they typically shopping (themselves vs. family members or others)?
Values	What are the core values and beliefs related to fashion and personal style? Do they prioritise fashion in their lives?
	What social dynamics, environmental causes or ethical considerations influence purchasing decisions?
	What motivates their fashion choices – self-expression, comfort or social status?
Attitudes	How do they feel about the role of fashion in expressing their individuality or personal style?
	What are their perceptions of different fashion brands in terms of quality, sustainability or social responsibility?
	How do they perceive the relationship between price and value when making purchasing decisions?
	Are there any intrinsic traits to the audience such as an appetite for adventure vs. security or humour vs. elegance?
Lifestyles	What are their typical daily activities, hobbies or interests, and how do they influence their shopping behaviours?
	How do they balance work, leisure and personal life, and how does that impact their shopping habits?
	Who or what inspires their fashion choices? Are there any specific fashion trends or subcultures they are drawn to?
	What are their preferred styles and fashion aesthetics?

Therefore, in addition to classic research techniques, it can be incredibly illuminating to spend time as a secret shopper, observing how people navigate and interact with existing physical retail spaces. Similar observations can be gleaned in online channels through studying website heatmaps, which show the density of interactions and dwell time on particular parts of a desktop or mobile site, as well as the flows through the site's digital architecture.

To develop a deeper understanding of an audience via observation, consider the following questions in a physical store scenario: What type of people are walking down the street? How are they dressed and are they carrying competitor's shopping bags? Who enters the store and who walks past? Once in the store, what displays do people stop to examine and what do they ignore? Are they interacting with staff or more focused on their smartphones? Who's buying which products?

In a digital environment scenario, a designer would consider the virtual equivalents: Where is web traffic coming from – organic search, paid ads, social media, influencer blogs and/or newsletter campaigns? Which Hero images are clicked on the most often? Which pages have the longest dwell versus which tend to produce a bounced visitor? What is the average time it takes for someone to transact and how many online baskets are abandoned or revisited?

Mindsets and missions: an advanced understanding

Demographics and psychographics are a powerful starting point and the foundational elements of mapping an audience, but alone they are not enough to design a retail fashion experience that truly understands and prioritises the people at the centre. This is because a given brand's audience is not static or monolithic. Rather, it is made of many different individuals, who, despite having many values and preferences in common, also have many differences. Even one individual within a broader audience segment will have different desires and needs depending on the context, day and even hour. This is where mindsets and missions come in.

A mindset is the mental attitude, outlook or disposition that a particular audience member happens to be experiencing when they begin their journey with the retailer. For example, an individual shopper might be in an optimistic, leisurely and excitable state of mind. A contrasting mindset might be the individual who is feeling rushed, uncertain and discouraged at not yet having found the perfect item.

Missions are often related to mindsets, but are a distinct concept. A mission is the purpose or end goal that a particular retail audience person has set out on when they begin their journey with the retailer. For example, an individual might be on a straightforward, focused and informed mission to replace their favourite pair of Levi jeans. A very different mission would be one in which an individual isn't looking for anything in particular at all, but rather simply browsing online while waiting inline, or simply enjoying the sights and social experience of shopping during a holiday season.

Both missions and mindsets can vary significantly, even within the same individual on the same day. Some determinants of mission and mindset might include timing and setting. For example, mindsets can be impacted by internal and external factors such as personal stress levels or simply the weather. Missions at the same retailer might vary by the time of year. During the December holiday season, for example, the same person might be in a mad dash to find a party dress versus in the first weeks of the year, they could be browsing the latest workout clothing to motivate a New Year fitness regime.

Similarly, while demographic statistics like annual income remain constant, an individual might reign in spending on non-essentials towards the end of the month and before the next pay-check comes in – and that same person might spend more lavishly on a new outfit after being awarded a generous bonus or tax return.

Variability in missions and mindsets doesn't have to mean complete unpredictability. In the following section a useful framework for the three broad missions and mindsets that can guide the design of a retail experience are explored: the Seeker, the Scout and the Sightseer. This framework can be used by retail experience designers to ensure they are considering the experience of on- and offline journeys through a range of scenarios, and optimising for the most common or compelling use cases (Figure 3.1).

The Seeker

The Seeker is the first of the three broad types of audience members. This shopper has a very clear idea of what they need and is motivated to find it quickly and efficiently. They tend to be very informed about the category (e.g. denim or beauty, etc.) either having done their research or having previously purchased the same type of product. Seekers may be on a tight schedule or have a specific task in mind. For these reasons, Seekers may prefer the seamless convenience of shopping online and home delivery, but they may also pop to the shop or use click and collect options to make their lives easier.

Mindset: "I hope they have exactly what I need!"
Core Needs: Convenience, availability and reliability

Three core shopper types tend to occur across fashion retailing, which can help designers create experiences suited across missions and mindsets

The Seeker

Informed and often in a hurry, they make a beeline to exactly what they need and want

The Scout

Exploring their options, they're looking to make an intentional choice between options

The Sightseer

Rich in time and open-minded, they seek general entertainment and inspiration

Figure 3.1 Mindsets and Missions: Three core shopper types.

Source: Author's own, based on FITCH (2020).

Example missions

- "It's my partner's birthday and I promised to buy them that new shirt they loved. I really hope they still have a medium size in light blue!"
- "I lost my favourite Prada wallet last night in the taxi, and now I need a new one to store my replacement IDs and credit cards".
- "I've just used up the last of my go-to waterproof mascara, and I need a replacement tube. I'll stock up and grab two".

Retailers who want to appeal to 'Seekers' don't need to carry every option available, but they need to be reliably stocked with plenty of inventory and deep ranges for the top-selling products.

For Seekers, the practical and physical layout of the shopping experience is really important. Retailers that serve Seekers need to ensure that their space, whether online or in-store, is well-organised with clear, concise signage, intuitive layouts and signage. They also need to offer fast and efficient checkout options to minimise wait times and make the shopping experience as seamless as possible (Figure 3.2).

Amazon is an excellent example of a retailer that appeals primarily to Seekers. The online experience, with its one-click cart, and the physical Amazon Go shops are designed with frictionless efficiency in mind. In-store, bold fonts on signage and bright lighting make it easy for shoppers to find what they need. The website provides numerous ways to search for items and quickly repurchase past orders, offering an entirely self-serve experience. Customers pull up the app, load their baskets and proceed to checkout, as if they have just visited an immersive vending machine.

Uniqlo also stands out as another great example of a fashion retailer catering to Seekers. The stores offer a wide range of basics in various colourways for the whole family,

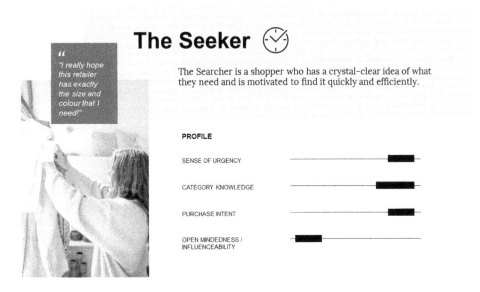

Figure 3.2 The Seeker.

Source: Authors own, based on FITCH (2020).

and loyalists often return to replace their favourite affordable cashmere sweaters or puffy jackets when they wear out. Uniqlo's self-checkout system is renowned for its technological innovation and ease of use. Customers simply place their items to purchase in the designated area, and radio frequency identification (RFID) tags automatically identify each item and calculate the total amount, eliminating the need to scan a barcode ever again.

The Scout

The Scout is a shopper who is in exploration and evaluation mode. They are considering their options and seeking to learn more about the category, whether that be scouting out the best cosmetic products for their skin type or researching the latest high-tech cycling gear. They don't have one specific item or solution in mind. While Scouts tend to have an occasion or general need they want filled, they are open to new possibilities.

Mindset: "I need some help and time to make my decision. Let's see what's available".
Core Needs: Guidance, variety and reassurance

Example missions

- "I need a thoughtful gift for a partner's birthday party. I'm thinking of a new shirt or maybe a cashmere sweater".
- "My Prada handbag is starting to look worn out and there is a hole in the lining. I want to explore the latest season's styles, then choose a new one to buy".
- "My favourite mascara has just been discontinued! I'm on the hunt to find something that's a similar colour and style – ideally one that's vegan".

Retailers who want to appeal to 'Scouts' need to create an engaging and visually appealing store environment that sparks their curiosity and invites experimentation and trial. Often these are retailers that stock a wide range of third party brands, such as a department store. If they are a single-brand retailer, they will tend to offer a wide range of product assortment.

For Scouts, the human element of shopping is important, with retail staff serving as a guide, muse or trusted adviser, whether in-person or via online chat either with a virtual assistant or with a bot. In-store demonstrations, free samples, pleasant changing rooms and QR codes where shoppers can read more are ways to help more self-serve Scouts. Similarly, a hassle-free return policy can help encourage Scouts to take risks and try new things (Figure 3.3).

Nike is an excellent example of a fashion retailer that designs an omnichannel ecosystem well designed for Scouts. In particular, the brand's urban flagship locations showcase products for this type of customer to trial and test, such as basketball half-courts with adjustable hoops and digital video screens, an enclosed soccer trial area and treadmills. On their own, Scouts can freely navigate at their own pace – or they can schedule appointments with dedicated store staff, ranging from 'coaches' who can help recommend items based on running preferences and stylists that run a customisation shoe bar where shoppers can fully personalise a pair of Nike Air Force 1s. Similarly, Nike's website offers a full range of buying guides, from finding your glove size to the best sneakers for dancing. The free Nike run app has training programmes for everything from an easy 5k to a full marathon – with recommended shoes for each (see also Chapter 6 for the Nike case study).

The Scout

> "I need some help and time to make my decision. Let's see what's available."

The Scout is a shopper in exploration and evaluation mode. They are considering their options and seeking to learn more.

PROFILE

SENSE OF URGENCY

CATEGORY KNOWLEDGE

PURCHASE INTENT

OPEN MINDEDNESS / INFLUENCEABILITY

Figure 3.3 The Scout.

Source: Authors own, based on FITCH (2020).

Sephora is another example of a beauty retailer that caters particularly well to Scouts. Walking into the physical store, a shopper is presented with a wonderland of beauty, skincare and cosmetic products from various brands to explore and evaluate. Expert assistance is on hand in the form of beauty advisers who are trained to provide personalised guidance into different brands, ingredients and application techniques. For those who prefer self-service, Sephora has abundant in-store trial stations and a generous sampling policy, and online community reviews and ratings are also a resource for making informed decisions.

The Sightseer

The Sightseer is a shopper motivated by open-ended discovery and the thrill of finding something unexpected and unique. They are the most open-minded and curious of the three mindsets – and least committed to purchase, without a specific need or task in mind. The mission and mindset of a Sightseer also tend to be the most social. They might see a day out shopping as much about having fun with friends or spending quality time with family as it is about actually coming home with a new wardrobe.

Mindset: "I'm looking for some fresh inspiration! What's new and intriguing?"
Core Needs: Inspiration, newness and revitalisation

Example missions

- "I'm tired of always buying the same type of shirt and sweater for my partner every year.. I'm curious what inspiration I can find to spice this year up".
- "I'm planning to attend a big New Year's Eve party and I want to look my best with a new designer purse … or shoes or necklace. I'd love to see what's the latest".

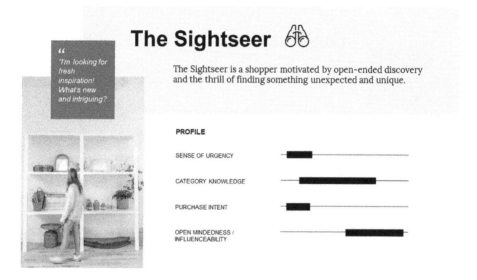

The Sightseer 👓

"I'm looking for fresh inspiration! What's new and intriguing?

The Sightseer is a shopper motivated by open-ended discovery and the thrill of finding something unexpected and unique.

PROFILE

SENSE OF URGENCY

CATEGORY KNOWLEDGE

PURCHASE INTENT

OPEN MINDEDNESS / INFLUENCEABILITY

Figure 3.4 The Sightseer.
Source: Authors own, based on FITCH (2020).

- "I'm about to start an important new job and I want to refresh my professional look and treat myself ... I'm looking for inspiration on how to be more put together".

Retailers who want to appeal to Sightseers often seek to create an immersive store environment that engages all the senses and captures the imagination. They often showcase the latest trends and styles and offer personalised advice. As a general rule of thumb, luxury brands are more likely to fall into this category. By definition, luxury goods tend not to be an immediate need, aren't frequently replaced and may require more contemplation and trial before making the purchase (Figure 3.4).

In fashion retailing, **Selfridges** is the Sightseer's dream. The UK-based department store is a dream-like wonderland; starting from the elaborate wrap-around window displays to the ever-changing corner-shop pop-up there is always something new to see and try. The many restaurants and activities in the store, such as the skateboarding rink, encourage people to return often, even if they don't intend to make an immediate clothing purchase.

From an online perspective, **TikTok** as an integrated shopping platform is well designed for open-ended discovery and exploration. The algorithm presents users with an endless stream of short videos, allowing Sightseers to continuously encounter new and intriguing content and stay up-to-date with the latest trends and discover unique ideas by exploring the popular content on the platform. It is an ideal place to find inspiration – and make impulse purchases – based on users' preferences and engagement patterns to curate a personalised For You Page.

Mindsets and missions: existing on a spectrum

Audience's mindsets and missions exist on a variety of spectrums, and, by understanding their groupings, we can craft spaces and experiences that are ideally suited to each. One way to visualise the spectrum is shown in Figure 3.5.

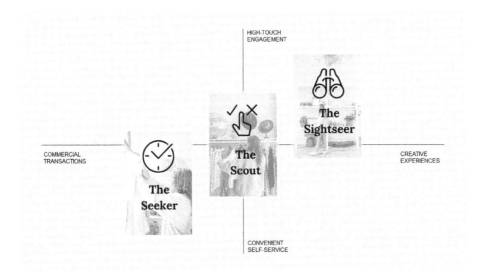

Figure 3.5 Three core shopper types mapped to retail experience.

Source: Authors own, based on FITCH (2020).

In this figure, the *X*-axis represents the primary goal of the fashion retail space. On the left side, the focus is on creating spaces (both physical and digital) that are more geared towards straightforward commercial transactions. On the right side of the *X*-axis are retail spaces that serve more as an experiential retailing or brand-building channel than a pure sales channel. The *Y*-axis shows the level of interaction and service provided by the retailer. At the bottom of the chart are retail spaces which are self-serve and low-touch from a customer service perspective. At the top of the axis are high-touch, even white-glove service interactions.

Layering on the Seeker, Scout and Sightseer framework demonstrates how retailers can design for different mindsets and missions. In the bottom left are retail spaces that are most suited to Seekers, who have a specific need and are typically looking to make a quick purchase with little support from a staff member or digital tools. Conversely, the top right for retail spaces are best suited to Sightseers, who are seeking inspiration, demonstrations and immersive experiences over an immediate purchase. The Scout tends to be found near the middle, striking a balance between commercial and creative goals, with a need for some (but not extensive) assistance.

Retail formats: designing for multiple missions

By understanding demographics, psychographics, mindsets and missions, and through the use of the Seeker, Scout, Sightseer framework, it should become clear that not all audience members need the same thing, in the same moment or place. This, in turn, is why retail experience designers often seek to create a spectrum of retail spaces, both on- and offline, that can cater to distinct needs.

For example, a local shopper that is looking to 'get in and get out' quickly, picking up a new Nike sports bra, might prefer a hyper-convenient self-checkout station or 'buy again' feature in the mobile app. While a tourist on holiday might prefer being assisted by an

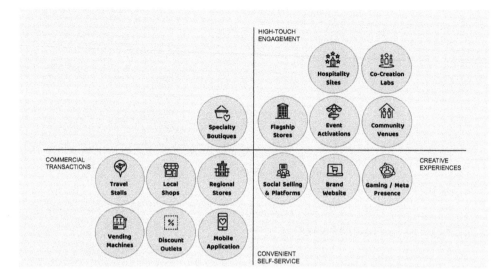

Figure 3.6 Map of 15 common retail formats.
Source: Authors own (2023).

associate who can thoughtfully wrap the new yoga kit they purchased and email them a convenient gift receipt. Some retail spaces can accommodate a spectrum of audience profiles; however, it is typically a mistake to try and have one retail concept be everything to everyone.

Therefore, most retailers must choose the best store format type for audience missions and mindsets they are hoping to serve – in that specific location or need state. Ultimately, there are nearly as many different types of retail formats as there are retailers, but it can be helpful to think of formats as falling into broad categories. Figure 3.6 is a depiction of 15 different types of retail formats, organised again on the two axes. From left to right, bottom to top, they are as follows:

1 **Vending Machines:** Automated machines that dispense beauty, small clothing and accessories, offering convenience and accessibility in high-traffic locations.
2 **Discount Outlets:** Stores that sell branded fashion merchandise at significantly reduced prices, attracting bargain-seeking shoppers and clearing excess inventory.
3 **Mobile Applications:** Mobile phone-based applications that offer a range of typically functional services from browsing new collections to placing orders and generating return labels or QR codes.
4 **Travel Retail Stalls:** Temporary or permanent retail spaces in airports or transportation hubs, catering to travellers with a selection of fashion items and accessories.
5 **Local Shops:** Small-format shops typically located in residential neighbourhoods, focusing on personalised service and catering to the local community's preferences.
6 **Regional Stores:** Fashion retail outlets with a broader presence than local stores, covering a specific region with a wider range of service and product offerings.
7 **Social Selling and Platforms:** Web-based marketplaces (e.g. Amazon or Instagram Shops) where brands, vendors and influencers demonstrate, promote and sell products.

8 **Brand Website:** An online website, accessible across devices, where customers can independently browse and order from a wide range of products and services, as well as explore more immersive, entertainment and educational content.

9 **Gaming and Meta presence:** Virtual in-game or in-world experiences and stores where customers can explore, interact with and even purchase physical and virtual merchandise.

10 **Specialty Boutiques:** Niche stores offering unique and curated selections of clothing and accessories, often focusing on a particular style, designer or theme.

11 **Flagship Stores:** Prominent and large-scale fashion stores, usually located in major cities, serving as a retailer's primary retail presence and showcasing their full range of products.

12 **Event Activations:** Fashion retail experiences created around events or occasions, such as music festivals and sporting events that offer limited-edition collections.

13 **Community Venues:** Fashion retail spaces that collaborate with local communities or host events and workshops, fostering a sense of belonging and engagement.

14 **Hospitality and Hotels:** Restaurants, bars and hotel establishments, where guests can more fully experience the full extent of a fashion brand's lifestyle offering.

15 **Co-Creation Labs:** Innovative fashion retail formats where customers can actively participate in the design process or customise their clothing.

Straight-forward, self-serve retail formats such as vending machines, discount outlets and the majority of retailer's mobile apps are in the lower left. These formats are focused on serving the Seeker with ultimate convenience and minimal friction.

In the top right are the more elaborate retail formats such as community venues and co-creation Labs. These formats are focused on serving the needs of Sightseers who are looking for stimulation and fresh inspiration.

In the middle sit physical formats such as regional stores and flagships as well as digital formats such as brand-owned websites and third party selling platforms. These types of formats tend to be created with Scouts in mind, as they carry a wide range of merchandise options and have knowledgeable influencers and assistants at hand.

More sophisticated retailers tend to have evolved a diverse range of different physical and digital format types. This allows them to tap into broad audience groups, across their many different life missions and evolving mindsets. The following section brings to life this diverse channel and format strategy with two examples: the fashion clothing and athleisure brand Lululemon and the global furniture and home fashion retailer IKEA.

Example 1: Lululemon

As of 2023, athleisure and yoga lifestyle retailer Lululemon has experimented with at least ten of the different retail format types shown in Figure 3.6. This is true of their fashion retail presence globally, but interestingly the brand also strategically uses different types of retail spaces within even the same locale, such as in New York City (NYC).

Starting from the bottom left and progressing towards the top right of Figure 3.6, the following list shows some of the different retail formats Lululemon uses to serve the brand's audience, from the Seeker to the Scout to the Sightseer:

- **Vending Machines.** In 2018, Lululemon rolled out Run Stop Shop automated vending machines to serve as an oasis for runners to refuel, repair and gear up in the lead-up to the NYC marathon. These machines stocked things like hair ties, tampons, sunscreens and even energy gels as a convenient way to reach Seekers mid exercise, with items that meet their immediate needs.
- **Mobile Applications:** As of 2023, the Lululemon app is largely a convenience play that enables customers to browse from the comfort of anywhere, quickly purchase and track deliveries. Additional functionality includes creating and sharing wish lists and generating membership QR code passes which make in-store shopping easier as well.
- **Event Activation.** Over the years, Lululemon has strategically used pop-up shops. These are a flexible way to meet yogis and other wellness influencers at key events and during peak seasons. For example, Lululemon launched 70 pop-up spaces during the 2020 December holidays as a way to provide an enhanced presence, particularly for Seekers and Scouts.
- **Local Shops.** The backbone of the LuluLemon format strategy is local stores; from the Upper East Side in NYC to Marylebone in London, these stores have a smaller footprint and more curated localised range. Localisation goes beyond product range to take the form of partnerships with local fitness influencers who host run clubs and yoga sessions in these shops.
- **Specialty Boutiques.** When launching new product lines, Lululemon has supplemented its local stores with specialty boutiques – sometimes even right across the road from each other. For example, in NYC's Soho in 2016 there was a Men's only specialty boutique. In contrast to the typical interior, this shop was outfitted with rich leather features and offered an on-site tailor specialised in adjusting men's running shorts and business casual slacks.
- **Brand Website.** The Lululemon website is a comprehensive, yet primarily functional home base for the brand online. It has portals for all shoppers' most common needs, from shopping the full range of athleisure fashion and accessories to exploring hybrid digital and physical workout classes in partnership with Peloton.
- **Flagship Stores.** Lululemon has several large-scale flagships in urban centres around the world. The NYC 5th Ave location receives a high percentage of tourist traffic, and so has a city concierge expert who can advise visitors on fitness-related tourism, from the best place to get a green juice to where to book hot yoga classes. There are even free to use in-store mediation pods for those seeking a temporary reprieve from the city's hustle and bustle.
- **Gaming/Meta Presence.** In 2020, Lululemon acquired Mirror, an in-home fitness company that manufactures full-body, wall-mounted screens that live stream live on-demand as well as personalised workout classes from home. This format allows Lululemon to diversify channels into in-home selling and the sale of digital membership as much as physical goods.
- **Community Venue.** Opened in 2015, Hub Seventeen is another key part of Lululemon's diverse NYC store format strategy. The location is dedicated to the community, with co-working spaces and frequent exercise classes. In the evenings, the space plays host to a variety of events from quarterly talk series and intimate dinner parties to film screenings and poetry readings. The space does not sell merchandise but focuses almost exclusively on offering brand-building experiences.

- **Co-Creation Labs**. NYC and Vancouver are home to speciality LuluLemon Labs. This format is described as "a centre of creativity for functional and experimental design that taps into the culture, trends and technology of the people and place it celebrates" (Harris, 2016) The LAB stocks experimental capsule collections that appeal specifically to urbanites (mostly black items with a few whites and neutrals) In addition, the space is part design and fabrication studio, creating limited-edition and bespoke items in collaboration with fans.

Example 2: IKEA

Like Lululemon, IKEA has also experimented with a wide range of retail formats. The following list shows how the affordable yet stylish homewares brand flexes its offer across distinctly designed spaces to address different mindsets and missions.

- **Vending Machines**. IKEA has experimented with different vending solutions in high-traffic transport hubs, such as Swiss train stations. These space-saving, high-turnover formats tend to be hyper-localised, and offer everything from ice cream bars to everyday essentials like pens and notebooks for commuters.
- **Mobile Application**. The IKEA mobile app is the brand's most convenient online home. It's designed to be a space where customers can browse thousands of products, and either purchase online or scan products while walking through the store (which conveniently allows users to skip the checkout line). Wish lists, order tracking, receipt organisation and return generation are all key parts of the app offer.
- **Local Shops**. Some of IKEA's local stores take the form of planning studios in cities like NYC and London. These spaces are conceived of as more intimate brand theatres with a focus on small space living. They offer urbanites 1:1 home planning consultations with interior designers and planners to mock up kitchen and other solutions within modular demo spaces.
- **Regional Stores**. IKEA's most classic and common store format associated with the brand. As expected, these stores sit closest to the centre of the format mapping diagram and aim to serve Scouts through the famous model rooms where customers can compare and contrast the full range of products, from sitting on the firmness of different mattress types to feeling the range of upholstery options.
- **Brand Website**. IKEA's website, which is tailored to each specific region, is a more extended and inspirational space as compared to the mobile app. It invites shoppers to explore by product type or by room and features fresh inspiration that is curated both by the in-house team and via featured user-generated content on Instagram. There are also tips on IKEA 'hacks' and trend pieces on how to live more sustainably.
- **Gaming/Meta Presence**. In 2020, IKEA Taiwan capitalised on the Animal Crossing craze by recreating its catalogue in-game, providing a link between IKEA -themed islands to its own online store. This format was a playful way for the brand to tap into a zeitgeist and connect with potential customers in a playful and relevant way.
- **Specialty Boutique**. IKEA also frequently experiments with retail concepts through a variety of specialty boutiques. For example, the 'Home of Tomorrow' was an urban concept in Poland that converted a 100-year-old apartment to showcase sustainable design solutions and to educate visitors how to introduce environmentally friendly

solutions into their homes. Such specific executions facilitate exploration of non-core categories such as house plants.

- **Community Venue.** The venue concept 'IKEA House' is the brand's version of a community hub. The space doesn't sell furniture but rather is much more experiential, offering classic dishes such as Swedish Meatballs in an upscale restaurant setting. Offering frequent educational classes and events catering to home fashion DIYers.
- **Hotels and Hospitality.** In the brand's home country of Sweden, IKEA has launched a hotel concept, pushing into an even more experimental format. The space is designed for gatherings and getaways – whether customers are visiting with their families or taking a corporate retreat. Strategically, the space is a great way to test and showcase products in situ, which guests can purchase during or after their visit.

An audience-centric approach summary

Starting from a macro view, this section has explored the importance of understanding an audience through the lens of demographics, psychographics, mindsets and missions, and through the use of the Seeker, Scout, Sightseer framework. Through this exercise, most retail fashion brands find that their audience has a diverse set of needs, which vary based on time and location.

There is no 'one-size-fits-all' fashion retail. Hence we see successful retail brands such as Lululemon and IKEA deploy such a wide range of digital and physical spaces. The map of 15 common retail formats can be used as a starting point for imagining a responsive and flexible approach to crafting a channel and format strategy; however, each retailer will need to design the specific formats that are best suited to their audience.

The following section dives deeper into the art of experience design within a given space. This will offer a more specific set of frameworks and strategies for crafting a compelling customer experience journey through one of these retail spaces.

Compelling customer journeys

A retail customer journey can be defined as the end-to-end path that consumers travel from initial awareness of the brand through to post-purchase engagement (see also Chapter 1). In the most comprehensive sense, this encompasses each touchpoint across the retailer's channels, every interaction with staff and the diverse range of emotions experienced by customers throughout their shopping expedition. As a baseline, good customer experiences are characterised by an understanding of customers' expectations and the successful delivery of those expectations.

Customer journey as conversion funnel

The classic customer journey has long been thought of as a 'conversion funnel'. The funnel metaphor refers to the one-way path through which some proportion of the customer base descends (while other customers may fall out of the funnel at each different stage, for example, because the retailer is not part of their consideration set or because they are not retained for future sales) (Figure 3.7).

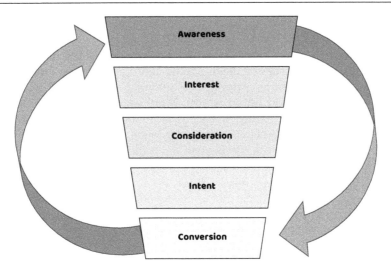

Figure 3.7 The customer journey as a classic conversion funnel.
Source: Authors own, based on Jansen and Schuster (2011).

Typically, a conversion funnel has the following five stages:

1   **Awareness:** A 'conversion funnel' journey begins with a customer becoming aware of the brand, product or service. This stage involves capturing the customer's attention, generating interest and sparking curiosity. A brand's advertising and marketing budget is typically spent on filling this top part of the funnel – particularly for new brands where potential customers may not have yet heard of the company.
2   **Interest:** Once customers are aware of a brand or offering, they move into the interest stage. Here, they actively seek more information, research and evaluate options. They may engage with content, visit a website or compare products. The aim is to nurture their interest, address their needs and provide relevant information to keep them engaged.
3   **Consideration:** In the consideration stage, customers have narrowed down their options and are evaluating specific products or services. They compare features, pricing, reviews and other factors to make a decision. This is a critical stage where businesses need to differentiate themselves and provide persuasive arguments to convince customers to choose their offering.
4   **Intent:** Once customers have considered their options, they enter the intent stage. At this point, they have a strong intention or desire to make a purchase or take a specific action. They may add items to a shopping cart, sign up for a trial or initiate the checkout process. The goal is to facilitate the conversion and make it as seamless and frictionless as possible.
5   **Conversion:** The final stage of the conversion funnel is the conversion itself. This can vary depending on the specific goal of the funnel, such as a purchase. The conversion stage is the ultimate goal of the funnel, where customers complete the intended action and become customers or qualified leads.

This classic 'conversion funnel' approach to thinking about customer journeys can be a helpful jumping off point, but as a framework it has major limitations. For example, if a retailer is to be successful today, the customer's journey should not simply end with the conversion stage. Instead, fashion retailers should continue to engage and retain customers, creating a loop that inspires customers to become loyal to the brand and influence others to enjoy and explore the brand as well. More importantly, the classic conversion funnel is a relatively narrow-minded and extractive model based on gaining something from the audience at each stage, from attention through to their purchase. In this telling, the journey is seen almost exclusively through the commercial lens of the company. It is not truly about the customer's experience.

In today's reality, great retail relationships are multi-dimensional, unfolding over many touchpoints, from social media and online forums to in-store and brand-sponsored events. Knowledge and affection and loyalty are built over time, as a give and take between both the audience and the retailer. Therefore, the classic conversion funnel needs to be updated in order to craft a truly compelling journey that better resonates with people today.

Creating a more compelling customer journey

As Pine and Gilmore (1999) have explored in their work on the Experience Economy, audience-centric experiences revolve around creating drama and infusing entertainment, awe, education and self-expression into the experience. Fashion retailers that design great customer journeys elicit these types of elevated emotions. They don't just meet expectations; they anticipate unstated needs and unarticulated desires. Prioritising the audience involves elevating them and even transforming the way they are perceived.

In the previous section, the discussion focused on having a deep understanding and appreciation for who the audience is and what they need. Armed with that deep understanding, great fashion retail brands then go about transforming their 'audience' members into the protagonists or 'Heroes' of the story.

Customer journey as Hero's journey

One way to reimagine the idea of the customer journey is to take inspiration from the broader culture of experience design and storytelling. The Hero's journey, first articulated by Joseph Campbell et al. (2003), is one of the most famous attempts to create a framework for compelling stories and journeys, and one that fashion retail and customer experience designers can draw ample inspiration from.

In the book, *The Hero with a Thousand Faces* (Campbell et al., 2003), the authors set out the fundamental story structure which explains and underpins countless myths, legends and heroic tales across global cultures. Specifically, they make the case that a compelling journey encompasses a consistent series of stages and archetypal elements. Figure 3.8 is a visual representation of Campbell et al.'s framework, showing each stage in the Hero's journey.

There are several benefits of using the Hero's journey. The first is that it is more customer-centric. By thinking about the retail customer experience as a holistic story, the brand consciously elevates the individual from merely being a passive consumer

Figure 3.8 A simplified Hero's Journey.

Source: Authors own, based on Vogler (2007).

Table 3.2 From conversion funnel to Hero's journey

From the conversion funnel approach	To the Hero's journey approach
How might we increase our digital and physical impressions and make more people aware of the product?	How might we awaken a sense of adventure, excitement or empowerment in our audience members?
How might we get the customer to view this brand as more relevant or distinctive than the competition?	How might we invite the audience into the process of discovery, exploration and learning?
How might we get the customer to consider purchasing this brand now?	How might we help our audience to overcome a challenge they are facing?
How might we direct as many customers as possible to convert at the desired price point?	How can we help our audience to arrive at the end of their journey feeling more confident, content and infused with a little bit of magic?

caught in a funnel to an active protagonist. It takes the view of the audience as more than just a consumer or shopper, and positions them as a holistic person and guest in the brand's universe.

Second, using the Hero's journey encourages a shift in mindset from the retailer's goal being the simple sale of product to the solution to an individual's need or desire. Thinking broadly about the desired end state and not simply the narrow solution helps foster a more authentic and long-term relationship between the brand and the individual. It also encourages more creative, innovative and adaptive thinking over time.

To demonstrate how a customer experience designer might evolve their design approach from an extractive, funnel approach towards an interactive Hero's journey approach, Table 3.2 reframes several strategic questions.

Having introduced the framework, the following section explains the stages of the simplified Hero's journey and how each stage can usefully map to a fashion retail experience:

1   **The Call to Adventure:** In the classic telling of the story, a Hero begins their journey in the ordinary, familiar world, but they are soon called or invited to something greater. There may be some kind of problem or the Hero may simply be fed up with the status quo, and so they embark on a journey or quest that will lead to growth or purpose. A literal Hero's journey example would be Harry Potter receiving letters by owl or Luke Skywalker triggering R2-D2's message from Princess Leia.

   In the realm of fashion retail, an individual similarly first engages with a brand because they need or desire something greater in their life. This might be a practical need for a pair of shoes, an aspirational desire to indulge oneself or to signal social status, or it might be due to social or environmental motivations.

   For retailers, the Call to Adventure is the first opportunity to invite and entice their audiences. Whether done through an enticing shop window, a splashy landing page or a well-timed push notification, a successful call will intrigue, invite and excite a potential shopper with possibility. In particular, fashion retailers often invoke this call during major seasonal or social moments of change, when shoppers are most open to embarking on an exploration of the new.

2   **Meeting the Mentor:** The next moment in the simplified Hero's journey is encountering a mentor figure who provides guidance, wisdom and support, empowering the protagonist to tackle the challenges ahead. Again, to provide literal Hero's journey examples, this might be the role Dumbledore plays in mentoring Harry Potter or the training Yoda gives to Luke Skywalker.

   In the retail customer's journey, the mentor can be thought of as the provision of trusted advice to helpful information, guidance and confidence to the customer. Again, this might be literal in the sense of a sales associate welcoming a shopper, providing orienting directions through the store or asking how they can help. It might also be more subtle, simply in the sense of providing a warm confidence-building welcome and reassuring presence should questions arise. Digitally, the mentor might take the form of a chatbot on a retailer's owned website or a trusted influencer on social media who helps followers navigate complex shopping tasks such as decorating a new home or preparing for life milestones like a wedding or new baby.

3   **Tests, Allies and Enemies:** Progressing through the stages of the framework, the next step for the Hero are a series of tests and encounters with Allies who assist them, and adversaries that test their skills, resolve and determination. This is the building action, the small wins and challenges along the path to success. In the examples of Harry Potter and Luke Skywalker alike, they encounter minor threats, make new friends, learning and honing their skills along the way.

   In a fashion retail setting, tests might take the form of literal trials – testing different colours of beauty products in-store or using an augmented reality (AR) feature using an app or filter on social media. In-store fitting rooms, online size guides and at home trial programmes are all forms of tests for the shopper. Some items may suit, while others do not or are out of budget.

   Few retail experiences are entirely devoid of 'enemies'; the strategic retail experience designer will aim to mitigate them. For example, providing entertainment and stimulation during long checkout lines or offering email notifications if an item is found to be out of stock. Allies can also be found in the form of positive reviews, recommendations and helpful signage – as well as helpful in-store and online assistants. These friends of the retail journey are the individuals and technical solutions that recommend the eyeglass shape for an individual's face or prescribe a new routine for a tricky skincare question.

4   **Ordeal and Transformation:** The fourth step in the simplified Hero's journey is the facing of a transformative ordeal, often representing their ultimate test or commitment. After overcoming the ordeal, the Hero achieves their reward or gains a significant insight, power or treasure that will aid them in fulfilling their quest.

In the case of a fashion retail journey, the Ordeal and Transformation can be thought of as the purchase decision and process associated with acquiring the item. Ideally, this is not actually a traumatic ordeal in the same vein as Harry Potter facing Dumbledore or Luke Skywalker defeating Darth Vader. Rather, it can be seen as a way to reframe purchase from a simple commercial transaction to more of a transformation, which ultimately helps the individual shopper solve the challenge that initiated their adventure. This is the moment of reward, fulfilment and satisfaction.

Specifically, fashion retailers can heighten the moment of transformation by emphasising the positive impact that the purchase will have. It is providing the confidence that the shopper will look incredible in their new suit or that the new lipstick they have chosen is bold and gorgeously suited to their skin tone. In addition to the physical acquisition, this is the moment for retailers to help a shopper manifest their higher-order social and emotional needs. Ideally, the moment of transformation is not one simply of extracting sales, but of generously exchanging value.

5   **Return Home:** Finally, the simplified Hero's journey ends with a return to the ordinary world, where the protagonist brings back the elixir, wisdom or bounty they have gained from their journey. This is a moment that can also extend to and benefit the Hero's family or community or bring about positive change. The Return Home is Harry Potter and Luke Skywalker not only saving their respective worlds but also finding a sense of belonging, acceptance and self-mastery.

In the realm of fashion retail, this is the stage where the shopper integrates the product or service into their daily life and adapts to using it and experiencing its benefits. Often there is a direct personal enjoyment in wearing a new fashionable item, but often it is just as important to enjoy the social status, camaraderie and compliments it confers. In a successful journey, the individual ends up stronger (or more confident and successful) than when they started – and equipped with knowledge or a gift to share with others. If the customer has had a compelling experience, they then become loyal brand advocates, sparking word of mouth and positive reviews.

Example of the Hero's journey in fashion retail

To bring the concept of the Hero's journey in the context of retail design to life, take the following example of the global fashion, beauty and homewares retailer Anthropologie. The brand talks about their audiences in the following way:

Our customers are creative people, who want to be and look like themselves. They have a sense of adventure about what they wear, and take a thoughtful, personal approach to interior décor and the harmony of home. Although personal style is important to them, they're not governed by trends. We listen to our customers and look to our community for inspiration and feedback – the intention is to exceed their every expectation, in unexpected ways.

URBN (2023)

In the eyes of the Anthropologie brand, their shopper audience is a Hero in the guise of a creative explorer, and the five stages of the journey are each designed to evoke and engage with this type of mindset and mission.

Anthropologie's 'Call to Adventure' begins outside the store – with creative store window displays. This is an intentional first act in the creation of the customer experience, as the company employs dedicated teams of designers and crafters to create seasonally resonant art installations as window displays that serve to stop a passerby. Other sensory cues, from a signature candle scent and specific musical playlists, are layered onto the experience in order to draw the shopper in (Anthropologie, 2022).

Digitally, the 'Call to Adventure' is translated on the brand's website with typically large glossy Hero images on the landing page that invite a web shopper to explore new collections with enticing, editorial styling. For example, rather than featuring the functional benefits of a new set of tableware, the collection is framed in terms of how hosting can bring you happiness and how the shopper can make dinner guests feel at home.

The 'Meet the Mentor' stage of the customer journey takes place upon entering the store, which typically happens in the guise of a proactive greeting from a sales associate who orients the shopper with the store layout, offering to help answer any questions or offer style suggestions that run the gamut from designing a stylish home, crafting a gathering or completing the perfect outfit.

The digital equivalent is the UX wayfinding, with specific seasonal holiday and occasion shops (e.g. the BHLDN weddings section). Frequently refreshed Instagram and Pinterest accounts further bring the brand to life in the context of shopper's needs and desires.

Similarly, Anthropologie incorporates many strategic Allies to help shoppers ace shopping trials and banish typical shopping enemies. One example is the offer of the personal styling appointments which can be made via the brand's website, for individual fashion, home decor or wedding styling. Being an integrated omnichannel retailer, Anthropologie offers these in three formats: 1:1 in-store, virtually via Zoom or asynchronously via chatting and inspiration sharing over email. The 'At Home with Anthropologie' section also offers a range of guides from fabric care to furniture measuring guides.

In-store, shoppers can similarly find Allies in sales associates if they are on a specific mission – or they can allow themselves to meander the intentionally designed bazaar-like displays and tables if they are sightseeing. Each table arrangement is cross merchandised with products in a context that might include candles, beauty products, clothing, accessories and home decor – each arranged thematically, such as gardening or raw denim. Most displays invite trial, whether flipping through books or spritzing perfume samples. Allies are found in the form of descriptive notes and baskets to help the explorer collect and carry their items (Anthropologie, 2022).

The fourth stage of the Hero's journey, the Ordeal and Transformation, happens upon checkout and, if relevant, the scheduling of delivery. Both off- and online, this is a moment when the brand works to make a personalised connection with the individual shopper. In person, the transaction is not just a checkout and bagging process, but the offer of gift wrapping and providing small tokens of appreciation such as crafted, decorated pom poms to further personalisation before gifting. Online, pressure is relieved by having a 'Save Later' option as opposed to only 'Buy Now' and there are two options for the inclusion of both pre-done and DIY gift wrapping.

During the final stage of the journey, the Return Home, Anthropologie designs the customer experience with intention. The brand uses customer data to send targeted newsletter content about early access to new arrivals, sales, exclusive content and local events with the aim to draw customers deeper into their world. The global loyalty programme AnthroPerks rewards loyal shoppers with free shipping, early access to the newest collections and birthday treats.

Universal journey ingredients

As with developing a format and channel strategy, each fashion retailer's specific customer experience journey should be uniquely designed to bring their brand story to life. As we have seen for Anthropologie, their Hero is a creative explorer. For a brand such as Nike, their Hero might be the confident athlete. For Ralph Lauren, the Hero might be a timeless aesthete. There are, however, some consistent core principles that can guide customer experience designers in their craft, regardless of brand specifics.

These principles include shaping a narrative arc across space and time, reducing unnecessary pain points, crafting memorable peak points and injecting just the right quantity of intentional friction. The following sections define and explore each principle in turn.

Shaping the narrative arc

Regardless of the journey specifics, the narrative arc of a customer's Hero story must inevitably play out over some period of time and some set of spaces, either physical or digital. Furthermore, throughout the journey, the audience will have a baseline expectation of how the experience and story will unfold.

These expectations are usually an amalgam, formed by sum of all their past experiences – not only with the specific retailer's brand but from experiences navigating retail spaces and shopping more generally. Even before entering a specific store or landing on a website, an individual will have a baseline expectation of how long the shopping journey might take – and how challenging or enjoyable they expect certain aspects to be, from trying on clothing to queuing to checkout. Figure 3.9 demonstrates the ebbs and flows of a typical customer journey. A retailer is meeting expectations if they are tracking along the baseline. The audience is neither pleased nor disappointed.

How a fashion retailer chooses to map out the journey will depend not only on the brand's creative direction, but also upon category norms, customer expectations and commercial realities. Take, for example, two ends of the retail jewellery spectrum, engagement rings and costume jewellery. An engagement ring shopper is likely to do research both online and in-person across many different sources and to take several months to make a final decision. A costume jewellery shopper, on the other hand, may make an impulse decision to buy a new set of fashion rings at the Zara checkout counter.

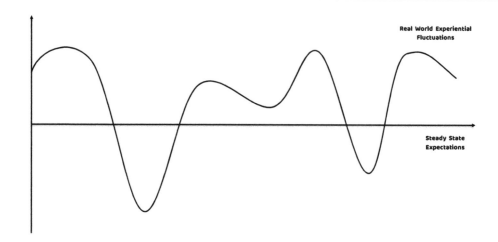

Figure 3.9 An example of customer journey vs. expectation.
Source: Authors own.

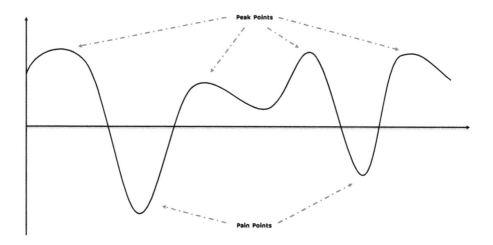

Figure 3.10 Customer journeys with peak and pain points.
Source: Authors own.

Peak points

Meeting expectations throughout a customer journey is not necessarily a bad thing – but it is unremarkable and in reality rarely happens. Instead, a more likely customer journey will be filled with various peak and pain points – moments when the actual experience of the customer's journey differs from their expectation of it. Figure 3.10 depicts the peak and pain points of an illustrative customer journey.

A peak point refers to a specific moment or experience during the journey that stands out as exceptionally positive, memorable or impactful for the customer. It is a high point that evokes strong positive emotions and leaves a lasting impression, contributing to overall satisfaction and possibly longer-term loyalty.

At its most modest, a peak point is a moment of delight or a small but pleasant surprise. On the other end of the spectrum, a monumental peak point can invoke awe or even create a life-long memory. Whether small or large, peak points play a crucial role in creating a compelling and delightful customer experience.

Table 3.3 shows an illustrative list of peak points in the context of visiting a fashion department store. The examples are given throughout the stages of a heroic audience journey mapped above.

When designing a narrative arch with either modest or monumental peak points, there are a few general rules of thumb for retailers to keep in mind. First, it is important to spread out the excitement and surprise of peaks, and, second, it's advisable to try ending on a peak point given that endings tend to be one of the most memorable parts of the customer experience.

Table 3.3 Fashion retailers can create peak points throughout the journey

Journey stage	A modest peak	A monumental peak
The Call to Adventure	A brightly coloured, enticing new window display catches the eye of a passerby on the street	A live demonstration of hand embroidery on custom wedding gowns is featured in the corner-shop window, with QR codes to meet the maker and learn about the art of embroidery
Meeting the Mentor	A store associate proactively asks if there is anything that they might be able to help with today	A personalised wedding stylist meets a bride-to-be and her mother with glasses of champagne before taking them into a private salon to try on a curated selection of the brand's best dresses
Tests, Allies and Enemies	The customer finds themselves drawn into the thoroughfare of the shop, with abundant displays that appeal to the senses. QR codes and handwritten notes provide helpful context and suggest staff favourites	The personal stylist is able to accommodate a specific request to incorporate lace detailing from the mother's bridal gown into the new dress, and an on-staff tailor is able to take measurements right away for a rushed turnaround time
Ordeal and Transformation	After sampling several perfumes and cosmetics the customer selects their favourite items. They are able to quickly navigate the seamless self-checkout with no queue	After suggesting a matching tie bar for the groom, the stylist arranges to have it complimentary engraved with a personalised message. Everything will be hand delivered in a few weeks, while the payment process is handled easily and efficiently on site
Return Home and Integration	The customer reflects on their positive experience and vows to make the retailer their top choice for future beauty purchases	The customer's partner wears their new tie bar on the day of the wedding. Guests compliment the exquisite tailoring of the couple's clothes and the engraved message becomes a wedding day photo highlight

It might be tempting to think that the best customer experience is simply an unending string of peak points, but that is not necessarily the case. As the Hero's journey indicates, drama, anticipation and fulfilment come from building a varying narrative arc of different moments. Spreading out moments of delight can create more distinction in a journey and prevent overwhelm.

Similarly, variety is an essential part of peak points. If an individual receives a complimentary glass of champagne or a free perfume sample every time they visit, the peak will diminish over time until it becomes merely part of the baseline expectation. Similarly, customers tend to disproportionately remember the last moment of an interaction or experience. If possible, customer experience designers should seek to end the journey on a high.

Pain points

A **pain point** refers to a moment or stage in the customer's experience where they encounter an issue, problem or challenge that causes them frustration, dissatisfaction or inconvenience.

Table 3.4 offers an illustrative example of pain points both small and large in the context of visiting a fashion department store. The examples are given throughout the stages of a heroic audience journey.

As with the journey's peak points, there are a few nuances to keep in mind when it comes to pain points. First, it is important to consider the severity of the pain. Despite the temptation to eliminate all pain from a customer journey, the reality is that there are many pain points which are not possible to solve – as well as those that would require a disproportionately large and costly intervention. In fact, not every pain point actually needs to be eliminated.

For example, a fast fashion retailer might assess the wait time for the store's fitting room. If the wait is more than ten minutes on average, the retailer would need to consider investing in a greater number of fitting rooms and employees in order to not irk customers and lose potential sales. On the other hand, a two-minute wait time is only a small inconvenience, and it might be just the right amount of time for a retailer to strategically encourage people to browse an accessories display while in line.

In online channels, the equivalent analysis might be done on shipping delivery times. While today's customers generally expect speedy shipping, same-day delivery might not be needed in the majority of cases or might be a service for which those customers truly in a rush would be willing to pay for in addition.

The second thing to keep in mind regarding pain points is that they are highly context dependent based on the audience's expectations and perceptions. What constitutes a pain point for one shopper might actually be another shopper's peak. For example, at a mass market retailer such as Zara or Uniqlo, some customers will prefer to use self-checkout, speeding through the process. Another customer, however, may find catching up with their long-standing checkout person to be a highlight of the afternoon.

Before investing in eliminating every perceived pain point, a strategic experience designer will seek to understand the implications across the audience profiles, dependent upon the various missions that the brand is seeking to serve.

Table 3.4 Fashion retailers can suffer from pain points throughout the journey

Journey stage	A minor pain	A mega pain
The Call to Adventure	The department store's window displays are outdated and starting to gather dust. The customer is unsure if the latest season will be in stock and has to venture in to ask	The store lacks parking options and so the customer has to park far away in the summer heat. Then the entrance is unintuitive and hard to find, leaving them to try several sides before figuring it out
Meeting the Mentor	The customer has a simple question, but has to wait, for a relatively long and unclear amount of time, before being serviced by the store associate	Despite having come to the store specifically to talk through an issue with an associate, there are none available – or worse yet they lack product knowledge and are unable to help
Tests, Allies and Enemies	The customer finally finds and settles on which item they want, only to realise the item is not the right fit or has some small imperfection	In addition to not having any in-person help, the store is a visual mess, with disorganised shelves and no wayfinding signage. The customer becomes lost
Ordeal and Transformation	The customer decides to purchase, but finds the returns and the checkout line have been merged, the wait is over 30 minutes and they worry the whole time they will be late to their next appointment	The customer, not able to find the item they want, settles on a poorer substitute and tries to checkout, but the self-service payment process keeps timing out and is riddled with glitches
Return Home and Integration	The customer reflects on their pain point-filled experience with the retailer and resolves not to shop with the brand again	The customer is filled with frustration. They are not able to get through to anyone helpful at the call centre and so they leave an angry one star review online and tell all of their friends to avoid the retailer

Positive friction

Positive friction is a term used to describe obstacles or challenges that are intentionally designed into a customer experience. The term is often associated with digital interaction design for practical purposes such as customer security or to validate important actions such as the transfer of money (Spano, 2022).

In a fashion retail setting, positive friction are any intentional design choices which slow down or encourage greater interaction or concentration from the audience. Depending on the stage of the journey, such positive friction might cause a brief delay that heightens the sense of anticipation or accomplishment. On the other hand, positive friction can reduce the sense of being rushed, and foster a greater sense of trust, assurance or care between the retailer and the individual.

For example, in recent years jewellery companies such as Pandora, Tous and Swarovski have moved away from keeping items locked away in glass vitrines in favour of open displays and drawers where customers can try on pieces themselves. Positive friction is nonetheless reintroduced into the shopping experience when sales associates will suggest that you sit and wait at the 'beauty bar' while they bring out the correct sizes and colours on display trays.

In another example, high-end department stores such as Nordstrom find it valuable to offer personalised styling consultations and alterations services, which can be time-consuming to book and attend, but ultimately give customers confidence in their purchases and a sense of being cared for.

Ultimately, the goal for fashion retailers should not be to strive for a perfectly seamless journey with no pain points and endless peak points. Instead, the aim is to create a more meaningful and memorable journey fit for the Hero of the story that each audience member feels themselves to be.

Conclusions and reflections for crafting compelling customer journeys

The first part of this chapter introduced the concept of understanding customer mindsets and missions in the context of fashion retailing, specifically focusing on the Seeker, the Scout and the Sightseer. These mindsets can be represented on two spectrums: the primary goal of the fashion retail space and the level of interaction and service provided by the retailer. By mapping these mindsets and missions, retailers can design spaces and experiences that cater to the specific needs and preferences of each audience group.

The recommendation is for fashion retailers to adopt a diversified approach to store formats. By offering a range of different retail formats, each tailored to different audience mindsets and missions, retailers can effectively serve a broader audience and cater to their various life missions and evolving mindsets. By combining both digital and physical experiences, retailers can create a more comprehensive and engaging shopping journey, leading to increased customer satisfaction and loyalty.

In addition, crafting a compelling customer journey in the retail context requires understanding the end-to-end path that consumers traverse from initial awareness to post-purchase engagement. The traditional conversion funnel approach, while helpful, has limitations as it assumes there is only one real destination – purchasing from the retailer.

Instead, this chapter argues that a more effective approach is to shift towards the Hero's Journey framework, which focuses on elevating the customer to the role of the protagonist in their own story. The Hero's Journey involves several stages that align with the customer experience in fashion retail. The Call to Adventure corresponds to the customer becoming aware of the brand and its offerings, while Meeting the Mentor involves providing guidance and support to customers during their journey. Tests, Allies and Enemies represent the challenges and interactions customers face as they explore and evaluate products, while the Ordeal and Transformation stage corresponds to the actual purchase decision and the positive impact it has on the customer. Finally, the Return Home stage involves integrating the product into the customer's daily life and fostering ongoing loyalty.

To create more compelling customer journeys, retailers should focus on infusing emotions like entertainment, awe and self-expression into the experience. By prioritising the audience and making them feel like heroes, retailers can exceed their expectations and build authentic relationships. Embracing the idea of peak and pain points in the journey can help create memorable moments that leave a lasting impression on the customers.

Successful fashion retailers create customer experiences that align with their brand identity and target audience. They design their journey to evoke emotions, entice and excite customers from the moment they hear that Call to Adventure.

In conclusion, adopting the Hero's Journey approach and creating emotionally engaging experiences can transform the customer journey from a transactional process into a transformative adventure. By understanding and exceeding customer expectations, infusing emotions and designing for peak points and positive friction, fashion retailers can create compelling and authentic customer journeys that lead to long-term success. As the retail landscape continues to evolve, embracing these principles will be essential for retail brands to stand out and foster loyal customer relationships in a competitive market.

Chapter Questions

1   Reflect on the three core shopper types, the Scout, the Seeker and the Sightseer. In what ways might their mindsets, missions and ultimately their shopping goals be complementary versus conflicting? Which fashion retailers can you think of that have found effective ways to dual or triple track the experience journey to serve multiple groups at a time?

2   Consider the Fifteen Common Retail Formats framework. Which formats do you think are most important to fashion retailers today? Can you think of newer or more innovative formats that belong on this chart? What does the role of brand positioning and price point mean for the types of formats that are chosen (e.g. a luxury versus a value brand)?

3   In this chapter, the Hero's Journey is posited as a new framework for thinking about crafting compelling customer experiences. Which fashion retailers embody this journey best today? Which stages of the journey do you think have the potential for the greatest impact?

4   Finally, consider the narrative arc of a customer journey and the way peak points, pain points and positive friction are interwoven into the experience. In what ways do digital and physical channels behave differently in this regard? If online touchpoints are most often used for convenience, when does it make sense to integrate friction? If offline stores are most compelling for immersive inspiration, where does it make sense to reduce friction?

References

Anthropologie (2022) *The art of anthropologie*. New York: Rizzoli International Publications.

Campbell, J., Cousineau, P. and Brown, S.L. (2003) *The hero's journey: Joseph Campell on his life and work*. Novato, CA: New World Library.

FITCH (2020) *Welcome to the Brand.com Dream*. [Online] Medium. [Accessed 2nd October 2023] https://fitchdesign.medium.com/welcome-to-the-brand-com-dream-b1859f520e7d

Harris, A. (2016) *Lululemon Lab: Activewear brand's fashion-focused incubator sets up shop in Gastown*. Vancouver Sun. [Online] [Accessed 2nd October 2023] https://vancouver-sun.com/life/fashion-beauty/lululemon-lab-activewear-brands-fashion-focused-incubator-sets-up-shop-in-gastown

Jansen, B.J. and Schuster, S. (2011) 'Bidding on the buying funnel for sponsored search and keyword advertising.' *Journal of Electronic Commerce Research*, 12(1), pp. 1–18.

Jerolmack, C. and Khan, S. (2014) 'Talk is cheap ethnography and the attitudinal fallacy.' *Sociological Methods & Research*, 43(2), pp. 178–209.

Pine, J.B. and Gilmore, J.H. (2011) *The experience economy.* Revised ed. Boston, MA: Harvard Business School Press.

Spano, S. (2022) *Positive friction: How you can use it to create better experiences.* The Interaction Design Foundation. [Online] [Accessed 2nd October 2023] https://www.interaction-design.org/literature/article/positive-friction-how-you-can-use-it-to-create-better-experiences.

URBN (2023) *Our story: Anthropologie.* [Online] [Accessed 2nd October 2023] https://www.anthropologie.com/help/our-story

Vogler, C. (2007) *The writer's journey: Mythic structure for writers.* 3rd ed. Studio City, CA: Michael Wiese Productions.

Yankelovich, D. and Meer, D. (2006) *Rediscovering market segmentation.* Harvard Business Review, pp. 1–11. [Online] [Accessed 2nd October 2023] https://hbr.org/2006/02/rediscovering-market-segmentation

4

Designing harmonised customer experiences for brand environments

Andrew Quinn

Contextualising retail store design and its importance

Retail store design plays a pivotal role in the success and overall customer experience (CX) of a retail business. It serves as the tangible manifestation of a brand's identity, creating a visually captivating and emotionally resonant environment that engages and entices its audience. A well-designed retail store has the power to leave a lasting impression on its audience, influencing their perception of the brand and their likelihood to make purchases both impulsively and in the future.

One of the key aspects of retail store design is its ability to establish a strong visual brand identity. Through carefully considered aesthetics, including interior layout, architectural elements and visual storytelling, a store can communicate its unique value proposition, personality and brand values. The design elements work harmoniously to reflect the brand's essence, whether it's conveying luxury, affordability, eco-consciousness or any other defining cultural characteristic. This cohesive branding promotes brand loyalty, as shoppers develop an emotional connection and sense of trust with the retailer.

An intelligently designed store optimises the customer journey, facilitating effortless navigation and product discovery. The layout should be intuitive, guiding customers through various sections and encouraging exploration for self-discovery. Thoughtful placement of product displays, seasonal campaign storytelling and signage can enhance product visibility, draw attention to key products and guide consumers towards desired areas or focal product ranges.

Retail store design serves as a vital tool for differentiation in a highly competitive marketplace. In an era where online shopping continues to gain popularity, physical stores must offer unique and immersive experiences that digital-only platforms cannot replicate – a tactile envelope of brand presence. Innovative design concepts, interactive theatre, sensorial landscapes and engaging technologies can captivate customers and create memorable moments that keep them coming back to the brand through other channels.

A well-designed store becomes a destination, not just for purchase, but also for the experiences it offers. It becomes a social epicentre, a source of inspiration and a community space – a place where you can truly connect with the brand, its services and what it stands for. It's an opportunity to engage, sense and learn more about a brand and discover shared values – ultimately creating a reason to come back.

For the lasting success of the store and the brand's perception in the eyes of the consumer, the store will harness the right balance of the power of the physical, digital as well as social opportunities that its presence offers.

DOI: 10.4324/9781003378099-6

Introduction to the Attention, Connection, Attachment (ACA) framework by Seen Studios, London, UK

As an agency, Seen Studios[1] approaches any retail design brief with an in-house strategic framework referred to as 'Attention, Connection, Attachment' (ACA).

Our strategic ACA framework evaluates our insight and demographic research to design a harmonious customer journey leveraging physical, social and digital channel opportunities and, most importantly, build a balance that creates the most human-centric result for its audience to resonate with.

To build a solid foundation, an agency must gather background research and data available to them. This can range from client-supplied brand collateral, previously identified target audience research as well as the brand's ethos and values. Following an audit of available resources, agencies may take stock and identify any opportunities for the brand's forward vision and see how their retail store offer can help support these goals. Further secondary and primary research can be supplemented to aid a more current insight into desired audience types and needs through questionnaires, insight reports and interviews.

Following initial research, as an agency, we pose ourselves evergreen questions to allow for this framework to evolve with retail trends over time and be a timeless strategic tool to identify opportunities to design to and with. Below is a summary of what we ask ourselves with examples that may evolve given current retail trends.

Attention – *are you relevant?*
For example: How do we create an 'always on' space that responds to our audience's challenges and motivations?
Connection – *are you engaging?*
For example: How can local communities inspire how we design environments that pique curiosity?
Attachment – *are you supportive?*
For example: How would our retail space serve as a collaborative platform to further local communities and support their off-site experience?

Posing these questions and narratives for each of a brand's physical, digital and social channels allows us to address where opportunities lie for creating fully harmonised retail offerings. Each ACA aspect is considered to have lasting effects and gives purpose to the store's offer.

Through our research, we have found that long-lasting success for a retail brand will be sustained when the right balance between channels (physical, digital, social) is achieved. For example, some brands may be more digitally focused or more socially (i.e. social media) focused due to their product type or offer, but by taking a well-balanced approach in leveraging other channels, the overall offer for the audience will feel more humanised and appealing with a deeper meaning. The same may be said for a typically digital-only e-commerce brand, for example, by leveraging a physical pop-up shop coupled with community-driven programming, the audience finds new ways to resonate and engage with the brand – enhancing their previous perceptions.

The need for harmonious integration of physical space, digital content platforms and social involvement

Retail brand audiences and consumers live in an ever-evolving age where the digital world has become second nature to their day-to-day lives. Shopping is accessible at the touch of a screen, the sound of their voice or even automatically ordered through artificial intelligence (AI) trusted software. As a collective, humans are constantly stimulated by visual noises in competition for our attention. The landscape of brands and technology around us consistently tailors itself to the latest trend or algorithm that tells us what we want – on demand. As humans, we crave real emotion. Emotion that stands out from the day-to-day repetitive routine. As we navigate the digital world, we seek to find moments of curiosity and deeper value that we can connect with, human-centric touches that feel far more real than an algorithm or advert. To help achieve this human-centric approach, a retail store can balance how a retailer's physical, digital and social channels co-exist with one another – with the ultimate view of building a deeper human connection with the audience.

> 56% of consumers say they want seamless communications across physical and digital channels.
>
> (Wunderman Thompson, 2023)

For retail, the need for a harmonious integration of physical space, digital content platforms and social involvement in-store design has become crucial for long-lasting success. The audience should always feel like they are connecting to the same brand, regardless of which channel they engage with at any one time. The rapid advancement of technology and the widespread use of digital platforms has transformed the way audiences engage with brands and make purchasing decisions. To thrive in this evolving landscape, retail stores must embrace the convergence of physical and digital realms, seamlessly blending the two to create an immersive and engaging shopping experience that the audience feels is in tandem with e-commerce and their social channels.

The integration of digital content platforms within the physical store enables brands to provide a seamless omnichannel experience. By connecting online and offline channels and touchpoints, customers can seamlessly transition between browsing products on a brand's website or mobile app and experiencing them in person at the store, the experience of which should be as fluid as possible for the audience, with both channels speaking in the same tone of voice and appearing in the same visual language. Retailers can leverage technologies like QR codes, mobile payments, RFID (radio frequency identification) and bespoke recommendations to bridge the gap between the physical and digital worlds, making the shopping journey convenient, personalised and cohesive. This not only magnifies the shopping experience through added communication channels, but can provide the customer with more choices at their fingertips. From product storytelling to colourway options, the customer will be given the choice to shop their way – be it in-store or online. This integration fosters customer loyalty and satisfaction as shoppers experience a seamless and consistent brand experience across different touchpoints. (See also Chapters 1 and 6 on omnichannel retailing and phygital CX.)

Social media plays a significant role in bridging the physical and digital realms of retail. Retailers can create opportunities for customers to engage with the store and its products on social media platforms through user-generated content, hashtags, contests and sharing incentives. By encouraging customers to share their experiences online, retailers amplify their brand reach, foster online communities and curate user-generated content that can influence potential expanded audiences. This integration of social media extends the store's influence beyond its physical space, creating a digital presence that complements and enhances the overall retail experience.

Social involvement is another critical component in the harmonised store design – one that has long-lasting emotional value. Retailers can create spaces within the store that encourage social interaction and community engagement. This could involve incorporating social dwelling spaces, hosting events or partnering with local influencers, makers or organisations. By facilitating social involvement, stores become more than just transactional spaces; they become cultural hubs for meaningful connections and shared experiences between a brand and the local community. Audiences feel a sense of belonging and are more likely to return to stores that provide a vibrant and community-oriented atmosphere that resonates with their values and purpose.

Retail brands are shifting to looking for community audiences rather than shoppers, audiences that will look at the brand's channels as an ecosystem for eventual transaction rather than for immediate needs (Raymond, 2023).

In this sense, traditional store performance metrics are being usurped. A store is no longer seen as a space, measured simply in sales per square metre, but, rather, emotion and experience per square metre is gaining saliency. With the ease of online shopping platforms, and how to navigate customers to other shopping channels, other metrics have come into consideration for success. Metrics such as dwell time, repeat visits, specific product or information engagement and online visits can now indicate a brand's retail success. With continuous advancements in retail technology to gather data, from beacon technology, RFID, mobile identity tracing, heatmap tracing and footfall counters to name a few, better and more reliable data is quantifying results for retailers. This coupled with overall sales results gives retailers a better understanding of how experiences are increasing positive brand perceptions.

By beginning to understand how these channels can work together and what strategic opportunities they may provide – the 'ACA' framework allows us to have a purpose behind each channel, a purpose that is tangible with the brand's audience and values. How do we physically, digitally and socially win our audience's undivided *attention* to the retail store, allow them to *connect* to the brand in an engaging way and allow for a social involvement that gives authentic *attachment* to the brand and echoes the common emotional ground in values between the brand and its target audience? We aim to answer these questions next.

A retail store design – considerations and practice

The following sections focus on key considerations when undertaking a retail store design for a lasting purpose. As an agency, Seen Studios will identify opportunities for new retail store concepts by posing the right strategic questions from the ACA framework. How will the retail store be relevant? How will it engage its audience? And how will it support its audience's needs?

By asking these evergreen questions, purposeful concepts may be instigated to give the store design meaning and value. Environment aesthetics and well-presented products in a store can be successful alone – however, for retail store designs that may resonate further with their audience – a deeper meaning is often required.

The below considerations, coupled with the right store ACA framework purpose, can help build a solid foundation for a purpose-led store design. Putting some of these considerations into practice, case studies will highlight how we or others do this.

Audience considerations

Global vs. local communities

For a retail store design, considering the preferences and expectations of the target audience is crucial for success. However, the question arises: should retailers focus on catering to the local community or adopt a more global approach? The following section explores the importance of both local and global audience communities in retail store design. It delves into the factors that influence these communities and discusses strategies that can help retailers strike the right balance to create a captivating retail experience.

Understanding the local audience community

- **Cultural relevance**

    Each local community possesses its own unique cultural nuances, traditions and preferences. Understanding and incorporating these elements into store design can create a sense of familiarity and resonate with the local audience.
- **Community identity**

    Local audience communities often have a strong sense of identity and pride. Brands that tap into this identity can foster a stronger connection with the community. Creating a store environment that reflects the community's values, history or landmarks can evoke a sense of belonging and loyalty among local audiences – something to resonate with on a human and personal level, allowing the audience to see that the brand recognises and values their localised qualities.
- **Tailored experiences**

    By understanding the specific needs and desires of the local audience, retailers can tailor their store design to offer personalised experiences. A brand may have globally led experiences throughout all their stores – but how do these experiences adapt and flex to a more local audience? What can locally help build a bridge to community relevancy?

Embracing the global audience community

- **Brand consistency**

    For retailers with a global presence, maintaining a consistent brand image across various locations is vital. Global audience communities expect a familiar experience when they encounter a brand. A cohesive store design that reflects the brand's core values, visual identity and CX helps build trust and recognition.

- **Accessibility and adaptability**

  Global audience communities encompass diverse demographics, cultures, preferences and motivations. Retailers need to design their stores with a broad customer base in mind. Spaces that are accessible, inclusive and adaptable to diverse cultural and regional needs can attract and engage a wide range of customers.

- **Trend and innovation focus**

  In a globalised retail landscape, trends and innovations spread rapidly. Retailers must stay attuned to global fashion, technology and design trends to remain competitive. Incorporating innovative concepts into store design can attract a global audience seeking novel and forward-thinking experiences. Similarly, different territories shop differently and have different values – global brands that recognise this will leverage better results from understanding different territory audience shopping patterns.

Go 'Glocal' – striking the right balance

- **Research and data analysis**

  Understanding the local and global audience communities requires comprehensive research and data analysis. This includes studying local demographics, preferences and behaviours, as well as global market trends and customer insights. This information can guide retailers in making informed decisions about store design elements.

- **Localisation with global touches**

  Combining localised elements with global influences (i.e. glocalising) can create a unique store experience that resonates with both local and global customers. For example, a retailer may infuse traditional cultural elements into a modern store design or incorporate international design inspirations while maintaining a strong local connection through graphic communication, local craft or materials.

- **Flexibility and adaptation**

  Retailers should aim for store designs that allow for flexibility and adaptation. Spaces that can be easily modified to reflect local nuances or accommodate global trends ensure a store remains relevant and engaging to both local and global audience communities over time, regardless of current trends or desires.

A successful retailer recognises the value of understanding and embracing the local community's preferences and culture while maintaining a consistent brand image globally. By striking the right balance between local and global influences, retailers can create captivating retail experiences that resonate with customers near and far. Adapting to the dynamic demands of the target audience communities ensures that retail stores remain relevant, engaging and successful in an ever-evolving market. Audiences will want to recognise one brand, but also feel like through their own personal travel they may experience something new from the brand from region to region – always changing the pace and surprising them with different outlooks. Brands may leverage their 'glocal' balance through various means, from store aesthetics, materials and graphical storytelling to product selection.

The following Nike case study demonstrates how a brand has adapted its product offering to meet the local demands of its location and developed to influence the offer of global store formats. A key example of a brand that creates stores aesthetic unique to their location and inspired by the site or surrounding area and culture is Aesop.[2] Each Aesop store is very different, yet can be globally recognisable in their design approach; this gives the audience an opportunity to see something new from the brand with different location visits (see also Chapter 8, Aesop case study).

Identifying audience needs and building a social community

Retail brand communities have specific needs and expectations when it comes to their retail experience. To develop a strong and engaged community, retail brands should focus on delivering a varying balance of the following seven key elements in their retail experience depending on the type of brand:

- Authenticity
    Communities and audiences value authenticity and seek genuine emotional connections with the brand. They want to feel that the brand understands and respects their values, aspirations and needs. Authenticity can be demonstrated through transparent communication, consistent brand messaging and a commitment to delivering on promises. Clear brand values in messaging or tone of voice will help communicate between brand and the audience.
- Personalisation
    Communities and audiences appreciate personalised experiences that make them feel seen and understood. Brands can achieve personalisation by leveraging customer-approved data to tailor product recommendations, promotions, communications and brand activations. This level of personalisation helps community members feel valued and strengthens their connection with the brand. Brands who leverage an engaging app or online platform will help to create a data ecosystem that will dictate personalised moments in-store.
- Meaningful engagement
    Communities and audiences desire meaningful engagement with the brand and other community members. This can be achieved through interactive and engaging experiences and initiatives such as workshops, events and activations that encourage participation and a sense of belonging. Brands can also facilitate community engagement by providing platforms for members to share their experiences, ideas and feedback.
- Exclusive in-store benefits
    Offering exclusive benefits to retail brand community members reinforces their loyalty and commitment. These benefits can include early access to new or exclusive member products, special discounts, experiential member events or access to limited-edition items. Providing community members with unique advantages creates a sense of exclusivity as well as belonging.
- Education and inspiration
    Brand communities appreciate brands that go beyond product offerings and provide educational and inspirational content and storytelling. This can be in the form of informative opinion blogs posts, tutorials, styling inspiration and key opinion leader talks. By providing valuable content, brands position themselves as trusted sources of knowledge and inspiration. Brands can be a point of 'paying it forward'

and coaching or educating the next generation – this can have long-lasting brand value.

- **Two-way communication**

  Brand communities want to feel heard, with the opportunity to engage in meaningful conversations with the brand. Brands should actively listen to community feedback, respond to enquiries and comments and seek input from community members. Two-way communication encourages a sense of co-creation and inclusivity within the community. Brands can host panel talks for opinions to be heard and quantified – in turn becoming data useful for shaping how the store should evolve for its community.

- **Social responsibility**

  Communities increasingly prioritise brands that demonstrate social and environmental responsibility. Brands that actively engage in sustainability initiatives, support charitable causes or promote ethical practices resonate deeply with community members. Demonstrating a commitment to social responsibility strengthens the bond between the brand and its community. By fulfilling these needs within the retail experience, retail brands can create a thriving and loyal community. Cultivating a strong brand community not only enhances customer loyalty and advocacy but also provides valuable insights and feedback that can drive continuous improvement and innovation within the brand.

One of the key approaches to engaging with the local community is through *partnerships and collaborations*. A fashion brand can collaborate with local designers, artists, makers, influencers or organisations to create unique and impactful initiatives. For example, hosting a collaborative fashion show or exhibition featuring local talent can generate excitement and showcase the brand's commitment to supporting the local creative community. A brand can serve as a platform for giving smaller businesses, under-represented groups or forward-thinking innovators, makers and artists a voice for a wider audience. Brands can allow their social reach or physical footprint to become the steppingstone for social improvement – and, when done in an authentic and honest way, can give a much more sustainable long-lasting impression for the wider audience – that brands are there for future good, and not only for profit.

In addition to partnerships, hosting *events or pop-up activations* can create a sense of exclusivity and anticipation within the local community. These events can offer exclusive viewings of the brand's upcoming collections, provide exclusive discounts or promotions or even host experiences such as styling sessions or workshops in partnership with focal groups and key opinion leaders. By inviting local influencers, community leaders and customers to these events, the brand can create hype and generate word-of-mouth marketing. These pre-launch events not only engage the local community but also serve as opportunities to collect feedback, understand customer preferences and refine the in-store experience before the official opening.

The Nike case study below is a holistic approach to a global campaign, through the lens of a city and its own communities – through campaign-led content and in-store experiences. A key example of glocalisation in practice, a global brand bringing a global campaign to a localised level and partnering with local communities is Nike Join Forces.[3]

Case Study – Nike Join Forces, London, 2022

Join Forces was a global campaign by Nike, celebrating the 40th anniversary of the iconic Air Force 1 as well as dance as a cultural movement and sport that has influenced products, brands and culture over the years. This campaign was a global offering, tailored to key dance-influenced epicentres in both the US and Europe, including New York, Los Angeles, Memphis, Paris and London. To celebrate dance in London and Air Force 1, Seen Studios teamed up with Nike to bring this global campaign to a London audience.

Seen Studios was briefed to turn the ground floor of Nike Town London into a fully functioning dance studio. As part of the project scope, Seen Studios directed and produced the London-based campaign content, the in-store retail design and the programming of the retail experience over the campaign's month-long duration. As part of the Nike app's member experience scheme, this series of events was designed to educate, motivate, inspire and reward the Nike member.

To ground the global campaign with the local London community, Seen Studios sought to create and capture content with authentic relevancy and style. Conducting local partnership research that resonated in parallel with the campaign's dance culture ethos, a series of London-based dance groups were identified as collaborators and the protagonists of this content. Dance Crews: Aim Collective,[4] The Movement Factory[5] and Bami Kuteyi of Twerk after Work[6] participated in the campaign, capturing the friendships, talent and energy of the dancers, as well as the new Nike Air Force 1 Collection. Content was captured and purpose-led by supporting London-based groups and bringing them to the forefront of the campaign.[7] The photoshoot and content capture were filmed and shot taking over the rooftop of Peckham Levels[8] – an iconic London venue for arts and culture. The content went on to be used on Nike's web and social channels, on billboards throughout London and on in-store digital screens during the four-week-long programme of experiences.

The physical store played host to a series of consecutive events over the space of four weeks with local dance crews. The space was designed with flexibility in mind, ensuring it was both a day-to-day retail zone and an experiential activation zone when required. Mirrored digital walls featured immersive content and simultaneously switched to a large dance mirror to look back on, floor artworks brought the branding to life, moveable tiered seating created a dynamic landscape and strategically curved walls doubled up as both features of the space and tools for wayfinding, guiding Nike members into specific activation zones on event days.

Further contributing to the experience, interactive features were sprinkled throughout the space, from the live-painted mural wall with a London-centric narrative, by commissioning local talent in Hackney-based artist, Joy Yamusangie,[9] to the TikTok podium,[10] fitted with phone holders and routine walk-throughs from the dance crews, allowing visitors to record their own dance moves and share on social channels.

In between classes and performances, members were welcomed in across the weekends with a series of activations. From tooth gems and hair braiding to Air Force 1 customisation sessions in the Nike Town Makers Studio, the space boasted a range of experiential retail for all ages. Food and drink were also provided to members across the weekend, partnering with the likes of Juicy Jerk[11] from Tooting and The Treats Club[12] from Hackney, London.

A collaboration between an array of talent and creatives, this project was a celebration of both the London dance scene and the potential that lies within retail spaces. This was a retail store installation that had the London community in mind, from the content capture of local groups and organisations to putting them at the forefront of the campaign and experiences in-store.

This project is a good example of how we apply the ACA framework; putting a focus on ensuring a global campaign was locally authentic and experiences were led and championed by community groups – all while speaking to the relevancy of the campaign's movement with the product – Nike Air Force 1.

Applying and assessing the ACA approach highlights and contextualises this further:

Attention: How is Nike Join Forces *relevant*? The campaign and experiences were brought to London, but most importantly – for Londoners or for London's dancing community. The content felt bespoke and true to the audience primarily viewing it.

Connection: How is Nike Join Forces *engaging*? Through its relevant content, the range of in-store experiences allowed audience members to take part in several ways that suited them – from dance battles, dance classes and TikTok creations down to hair braiding and nail art – there was something to suit a wide cultural audience.

Attachment: *How is Nike Join Forces supportive?* At the heart of the collaborations and partnerships were local communities and how a global brand championed them. From the dance crews to the food and drinks suppliers – elevating London communities was integrated throughout. This created a clear authentic impression with the audience and further helped to anchor Nike and Air Force 1 products with London culture – allowing for a two-way conversation between audience and brand.

Integrating physical and digital retail channels

Importance of seamless integration between physical and digital purchasing

Research shows that most Generation Z consumers don't think in terms of traditional channel boundaries, and they increasingly evaluate brands and retailers on the seamlessness of their experience (Briedis et al., 2021).

In today's digitally interconnected world, the expectations of consumers have evolved, demanding seamless experiences that transcend the boundaries of physical and digital platforms. The rapid expansion of e-commerce and the ubiquitous presence of smartphones have reshaped consumer behaviour, prompting brands to adopt an *omnichannel* approach that seamlessly integrates their physical and digital channels. The significance of a well-integrated omnichannel experience cannot be overstated, as it not only enhances customer satisfaction and ease of use but also drives customer loyalty and is more likely to boost future sales.

A key advantage of a well-integrated omnichannel experience lies in its capacity to deliver consistent and personalised interactions across diverse touchpoints. By seamlessly connecting the physical and digital realms, brands can offer their in-store audience a cohesive journey that caters to their individual preferences, needs and behaviours. For example, a customer might browse products online, review customer feedback and compare prices, only to decide to visit a physical store for a hands-on experience before making a purchase. With a well-integrated omnichannel experience, customers can transition effortlessly between these channels without any disruptions, ensuring a seamless and hassle-free journey.

An omnichannel approach empowers brands to leverage the unique strengths of each platform, resulting in a more comprehensive and enriched CX when used appropriately. Physical stores provide customers with the opportunity to engage with products first-hand, enabling them to touch, feel and receive personalised assistance from knowledgeable staff – an inherently human-centric approach. In contrast, digital platforms offer convenience, accessibility and the freedom to research products and complete purchases anytime and anywhere, in a self-serve way. By integrating these platforms, brands can harness the power of both worlds, seamlessly merging the sensory and tactile experiences of physical stores and products with the convenience and content-information-rich nature of digital platforms, catering to the diverse preferences and shopping behaviours of their target audiences.

A well-integrated omnichannel experience enables brands to harness the potential of data and analytics to gain profound insights into customer behaviour and preferences. By capturing and analysing data from various touchpoints, including online browsing patterns, purchase history and in-store interactions, brands can develop a holistic understanding of their customers. This data-driven approach empowers brands to personalise their marketing efforts, recommend relevant products and deliver targeted messages across channels. For instance, a customer who recently purchased a pair of shoes online may receive personalised recommendations for complimentary accessories when visiting a physical store. By leveraging data, brands can create highly relevant and timely interactions that deeply resonate with customers, ultimately enhancing their overall experience. From a retailer point of view, it allows them to use marketing budgets in a more specific and tailored way, manage inventory and product options throughout their retail estate and understand better pricing models.

With 65% of consumers stating that more personalisation is crucial to their purchase intent, retailers should embrace AI[13] to supercharge product discovery. "The next generation of consumers will expect a highly personalised shopping experience where products find them instead of the other way around" (Bivigou et al., 2023).

Furthermore, a well-integrated omnichannel experience has a substantial impact on customer loyalty and retention. When customers can seamlessly switch between physical and digital channels, while consistently enjoying positive experiences, they develop a sense of trust and familiarity with the brand. This fosters customer loyalty and encourages repeat purchases. Additionally, a well-integrated omnichannel strategy enables brands to implement loyalty programmes that span across channels, rewarding customers for their engagement and creating incentives to foster an ongoing relationship with the brand. By nurturing loyalty and promoting continuous engagement, brands can cultivate a community of dedicated advocates who are more likely to recommend the brand to others, amplifying its reach and influence.

From a sales perspective, a well-integrated omnichannel experience has the potential to drive substantial revenue growth.

> Omnichannel customers shop 1.7 times more than shoppers who use a single channel.
> (McKinsey and Company, 2022)

This statistic is a clear statement that customers who engage with a brand through omnichannel tend to spend more. By providing a seamless and convenient shopping experience across channels, brands can capture sales at various touchpoints, whether through in-store purchases, online transactions or mobile applications. By facilitating these multiple pathways to purchase and removing friction points, brands can maximise their sales potential and capitalise on customer demand.

Lastly, a well-integrated omnichannel experience positions a brand as a trailblazer within the industry, exemplifying its adaptability, innovation and unwavering commitment to meeting customer needs. By skilfully navigating the ever-evolving landscape of consumer behaviour and technology, brands demonstrate their expertise and thought leadership, solidifying their position as frontrunners within the industry. A key example of a brand that has leveraged the seamless nature of their channels is Burberry's 'Open Spaces' store in Shenzhen, China, which focused on social retail, and harmonised their physical, digital and social channels to engage with their audience.[14]

In summary, a well-integrated omnichannel experience transcends the boundaries of physical and digital platforms, delivering exceptional customer journeys. By seamlessly connecting diverse touchpoints, harnessing data insights, nurturing customer loyalty, driving sales and showcasing adaptability, brands can create a captivating and comprehensive experience that delights customers, fuels growth and establishes their leadership within the industry (see also Parts 1 and 3, specifically Chapters 1–3 and 6).

Engaging communication and storytelling

Storytelling holds an unparalleled significance for conveying a brand's vision and campaign or product details. It is through stories that an audience can continue to learn, nurture their curiosity and make sense of the surroundings. Stories enable people to navigate the complexities of society, pushing the boundaries of their own humanity. They serve as a means of entertainment, allowing people to escape the repetitions and mundanity of everyday life. At its finest, storytelling becomes an act of co-creation, inviting the power of the audience's imagination to fill the gaps and pauses intentionally left by the storyteller.

From a brand perspective, storytelling forms the foundation of campaigns in their purest essence. However, audiences sometimes place excessive emphasis on physical builds and products. Audiences must remember that it is their shared human experiences that emotionally connect them. When the underlying meaning and purpose behind a retail space's narrative – often left unspoken – is rooted in the collective experiences of living in today's world, audiences foster genuine connections between them. They activate the dopamine rush of genuine human interaction and the bonds that unite them. They facilitate a physical response in a physical world.

Emotion, driven by an awareness of the social challenges that motivate and inspire the audience, should guide brand stories in the retail space, transcending mere product innovation. It is the seamless integration of brand storytelling and product storytelling that forges a truly immersive and emotionally resonant connection with the audience. The retail space transforms into a destination that goes beyond the transactional nature of commerce. This holistic approach engages not only the intellect but also the emotions and senses, leaving an indelible mark in the memories of the audience.

There are different mediums for delivering product and brand storytelling – from large campaign graphics and content videos to point-of-sale storytelling. Below is a starting foundation of diverse types of storytelling outputs.

- **Visual Merchandising**
  Visual merchandising conveys narratives and aesthetics associated with products, brands or almost any other influence that is engaging to the audience to pique their interest. It can work on a distance-from-product basis – from a window or large theatrical installations that draw the audience in from afar to in-store moments that bring a change of pace to the retail landscape and more often permanent fixtures. These moments can highlight and promote key new products to simply create intrigue and fascination. A key example of engaging window visual merchandise in retail can often be seen by Selfridges, London[15] – where the window displays tell cohesive stories centred around a range of narratives, from product and campaign-inspired stories to sustainable initiatives to drive awareness as well as seasonally inspired window designs. Meanwhile, some brands work with window theatre to draw attention; brands like Gentle Monster[16] have become synonymous with in-store theatre with their approach to visual displays – always capturing the imagination of their audience, treating every retail store as a unique gallery of immersive conceptual storytelling.

- **Large campaign graphics and content screens**
  Large eye-catching screens, lightboxes and projections can not only work as navigational tools to draw customers through a given space, but also bring immersive dynamic content to life in-store. These can often be easily swapped out for different imagery or content reels that tell different narratives, from product campaigns to brand initiatives.

- **Point-of-sale information and graphics**
  At a smaller level and situated closer to product, print graphics or digital displays can give further information on the product and campaign as well as price and promotions. These can help contextualise the product within its surrounding world to give the viewer an opportunity to learn about its details and story through well-presented copy and imagery.

- **Product innovation storytelling**
  Innovation storytelling can work alongside digital touchpoints and/or print copy imagery – however, it also has a level of visual intrigue and theatre. It may be a dissected element of clothing, footwear or digital device where the viewer is encouraged to see all the different layers and details that the product comprises of – thus highlighting the quality, craft and innovation of the brand. For example, in any of Nike's House of Innovation[17] stores, key hero visual merchandising is showcased throughout – spotlighting iconic product in a range of innovative ways with the intent to highlight

the quality of the product to the audience – embellishing on details from thread, lace, comfort layers, lightweight fabrics amongst many more.

- **Live craft and making**

  Depending on the type of retailer and the craft that may go into the product, brands may want to showcase a live making session where the audience can appreciate the time and expertise that goes into making the products. In many cases, this may be to encourage and show that the products are handmade but also to allow the audience to see the level of skill that goes into making them. This not only encourages further in-store dwell time but helps to justify price points in certain products. A live atelier or specialist maker can have a level of showmanship to learn from, encouraging future purchase (see Chapter 8, Anya Hindmarch case study). One example Seen Studios designed and produced with client Bally saw a crafts shoemaker in-store at their London flagship store, where a repair, resoling, polishing and fixing service was offered as well as a shoe dissecting demonstration to highlight craft and details (see Figure 4.1) – this allowed the audience to watch on and see the level of skill that goes into the products, but also encouraged reuse and repair of existing products for a better circular approach.

- **QR codes to Web**

  In-store QR codes are a simple way to bridge the gap between in-store communication and leveraging online marketing or e-commerce product details as well as navigating an audience to a brand's website. This can be an effective tool to allow for an added level of information when visual noise in-store can become over-stimulating. A key example of this can be seen with Burberry's 'Open Spaces'[18] store in Shenzhen, China, where the customer is able to seamlessly scan product and find out more information and content from their mobile device.

Figure 4.1 Live Atelier, Bally, London.
Photograph by Seen Studios.

- **Augmented reality (AR) and the metaverse**

  AR can be a playful and immersive overlay to the physical landscape – allowing a brand to tell elaborate stories that are either too costly for brick-and-mortar physical builds or simply fictional escapes to transform and gamify a store's envelope to new territories of aesthetic. The opportunity with this type of storytelling can transcend the retail store's demise and be taken to iconic landmarks to tell stories. A successful example of this is French luxury house Louis Vuitton during their 2023 collaboration (LV×YK) with artist Yayoi Kusama,[19] where not only were globally iconic retail shops adorned in Kusama's iconic polka dots, but globally recognised landmarks, from the Eiffel Tower to Statue of Liberty, were the foundation for AR possibilities to immerse further. Phone technology allowed these landmarks to be recognised using Snapchat filters to trigger the polka dots to be overlaid through the lens of a phone – bringing a fashion brand's artistic collaboration to the everyday world.

  > The campaign was created using Snap's Landmarker Lenses, which are able to detect geographically specific architectural landmarks and portray realistic-looking digital overlays on top of them.
  >
  > (Schulz, 2023)

  While AR may help build a bridge between physical and immersive digital overlays, the metaverse further extends these possibilities. The metaverse can enable gamification where the retail store's virtual environment can escape the physical altogether or it can blend offline and online by amplifying the phygital experience. Brands are experimenting with ways in which the metaverse can reach new and wider audiences, not just by attracting them in-store or to a website, but by going to them and inviting them to shop in a way that most resonates. For example, in 2021, Balenciaga collaborated with Epic Games[20] game 'Fortnite', where they launched a digital fashion line that could be purchased for the games characters as a 'skin'. This in turn influenced physical product in-store and drove a new audience to the brand's physical retail offer.

  > With Balenciaga joining the world of Fortnite to celebrate digital fashion, both brands are also debuting a limited run collab of physical apparel exclusively available in select Balenciaga stores.
  >
  > (Epic Games, 2021)

  With brands today striving to recruit Generation Z advocates, experimental metaverse retail will continue to explore how storytelling can unfold on the platform. The metaverse physical and online effects are still in infancy, yet the future of the space may become a two-way conversation and influence what physical landscapes could start appearing, enabling brands to achieve truly seamless, immersive channel integration (see also Chapter 2, hyper-phygital experiences section).

- **Customer service**

  While many storytelling layers, initiatives and mediums can be elaborative and information heavy, a human-centric approach cannot be overlooked. Good customer knowledge of brand, product and service will continue to serve as a cornerstone to many retailer's stores. In an age where new technologies and innovations are exciting to many, human interaction will ground and balance an experience in-store for many audiences.

While storytelling is key for information, telling a consistent story across channels is also key for the audience. Establishing and maintaining a consistent brand identity across all channels and touchpoints is a critical imperative in delivering a cohesive and memorable CX. The unwavering uniformity in brand messaging, visual identity and tone of voice reinforces brand recognition, cultivates trust and nurtures a profound emotional connection with customers. Whether it is through physical retail outlets, websites, social media platforms or advertising campaigns, upholding a consistent brand identity ensures that consumers encounter a harmonised and authentic representation of the brand – ultimately building trust in what the audience sees through familiarity.

Multi-purpose store landscape

The retail store can be a destination not only for purchase but, arguably, more importantly, for experience. More brands are looking for dynamic spaces that can shift with their product and audience needs – thus requiring the physical landscape to be flexible and adaptable. Some key reasons why flexibility and adaptability in retail store design are crucial to meet its evolutionary purpose are as follows.

- **Evolving customer needs**

    Customer needs and expectations are constantly evolving. Brands must be able to respond to these changes by adapting their store design and layout accordingly. Flexibility in store design allows for easy reconfiguration of spaces, enabling retailers to introduce new product categories, accommodate changing customer preferences and create engaging experiences that align with evolving consumer trends – from live activations to community workshops.
- **Seasonal and promotional changes**

    Retailers often need to adapt their stores to align with seasonal or promotional changes. Whether it's creating campaign or concept-driven displays or implementing special seasonal promotions, having a flexible store design enables brands to quickly and easily update the store's look and feel. By providing a fresh and relevant shopping experience, brands can capitalise on seasonal trends and create a sense of excitement and urgency amongst its audience – changing the pace of their different visits.
- **Store traffic and flow**

    The layout and design of a retail store should facilitate smooth customer traffic flow to assist with the shopping experience. However, customer traffic patterns may change over time due to various factors such as shifts in demographics or changes in nearby infrastructure. A flexible store design enables brands to adjust the layout to optimise the flow of customers, improve accessibility and ensure a positive shopping experience. This adaptability ensures that the store can effectively handle fluctuations in customer footfall and meet the changing demands of seasonal in-store drivers.
- **Futureproofing**

    By designing retail stores with flexibility and adaptability in mind, brands futureproof their physical spaces. This means that the store can be easily modified or expanded as the brand grows or as new opportunities arise. Whether it's accommodating new product lines, expanding the store footprint or incorporating new technologies, a flexible store design ensures that the brand can adapt to changing market conditions and seize future opportunities.

An example of a brand harnessing the adaptability of a studio space and store design for futureproofing, evolution and reuse of past fixtures is RÆBURN,[21] which until December 2023, had a studio space in Hackney (RÆBURN Lab). The space evoked the remade philosophy of Creative Director Christopher Raeburn. Raeburn started the brand as a collaborative, regenerative design studio where daily design meets responsible production, alongside regular events, tours, discussions and workshops. Speaking of his studio space:

> Everything's flexible. You can move all the rails. Most things are on wheels. We've got screens. You can change everything out. I'd like to think it's then, you know, an agile space that if you can go back say two weeks in a row, it will look different. And I think that's really important for retail today.
>
> (Raeburn interview, 2023) (See also Chapter 7, RÆBURN Lab case study)

Materiality and circularity in retail design

Changing our system and model

> In our current economy, we take materials from the Earth, make products from them, and eventually throw them away as waste – the process is linear. In a circular economy, by contrast, we stop waste being produced in the first place.
>
> (Ellen McArthur Foundation, 2023b)

Within our current and historic climate of overconsumption and global pollution, organisations such as the Ellen McArthur Foundation[22] are spearheading drives to help develop businesses, academia, policy makers and institutions to design and adopt circular thinking for the future. The foundation is not only encouraging brands and economies to react but is acting as an educator in ways to do so.

> Today, in industries like fashion, food and plastics packaging, products and systems are designed in such a way that most materials are destined for landfill, incineration or leaked into natural environments. We have never produced more clothes – nor worn them less, while a third of all food produced goes to waste. It's not just the materials that are wasted but embedded energy, resources, labour, and creativity are lost too.
>
> (Ellen McArthur Foundation, 2023a)

A circular economy will take some time, but the foundation is acting as a resource for information, for guidance and ultimately a navigational partner to designing in a way that doesn't just guide brands on product materials and spaces but the ways and processes in which both are made and designed – highlighted below:

> The application of intent: the process through which we create the material, spatial, visual and experiential environments in a world made ever more malleable by advances in technology and materials, and increasingly vulnerable to the effects of unleashed global development.
>
> (Ellen McArthur Foundation, 2023a)

The foundational three principles of a circular economy are:

- *Eliminate waste and pollution*
- *Circulate products and materials (at their highest level)*
- *Regenerate nature*

By designing and producing with these principles at the inception of product and spaces, brands and agencies can begin to transition to a more circular approach. This is the long-term goal for many brands, representing a continuum of change, ranging from retailers who are pioneering circular systems to others who are making small incremental advances. Many have begun to adopt some initiatives that may be more sustainable rather than fully circular en route.

Organisations like B Corp[23] have begun to assess and verify how brands and agencies stand out for their standards in how they affect people and the environment.

> Certified B Corporations, or B Corps, are companies verified by B Lab to meet high standards of social and environmental performance, transparency and accountability.
>
> (B Corporation, 2023)

To be certified B Corp, businesses are assessed through a rigorous process to quantify how they perform against social and environmental effects as a result of their processes, products and services. Through a points system where companies need to reach a minimum to certify – they are assessed against many factors, from how many, how often employees use a certain type of transport to get to their workplace to what they do to contribute to the social community. A full transparent review analyses how the company performs. This in turn has built lasting effects for job satisfaction and company performance.

> Compared to traditional businesses, our 2021 data shows that B Corps have a faster growth in turnover (27% vs 5%) and employee headcount (14% vs 1%), greater levels of employee retention, engagement and diversity, higher levels of innovation and are more successful in securing equity finance (70% vs 56%).
>
> (B Corporation, 2023)

In turn, brands are now increasingly demanding that retail design agencies have a B Corp certification to qualify for working on future projects – which in turn begins to affect how retail store designs are treated and processed.

Sustainable retail practices and initiatives for consideration

In the era of increasing environmental consciousness, retailers have a significant opportunity to harness a circular and sustainable mindset when designing and building their stores. By adopting sustainable practices throughout the store design and construction process, brands can reduce their environmental footprint, promote resource efficiency and align with the growing demand for more sustainable and/or circular retail experiences. Some key ways in which retailers can embrace circularity and sustainability in-store design are as follows.

- Material selection

    Brands can prioritise the use of eco-friendly and sustainable materials in physical store construction. This does not just have to be materials that can be recycled but materials that are low-impact. By choosing more sustainable low-impact materials, brands minimise the energy consumption of other more harmful processed materials and the environmental impact of their store build.

- Energy efficiency

    Retail stores can be designed to maximise energy efficiency by incorporating features such as LED lighting, motion sensors and energy-efficient HVAC (heating, ventilation and air conditioning) systems. Additionally, utilising natural light opportunities where possible can reduce the need for artificial lighting. By implementing energy-saving measures, brands can reduce their energy consumption, lower greenhouse gas emissions and lower operating costs. Build standards such as BREEAM,[24] amongst others, ensure and require companies measure the environmental effects of builds during their lifecycle and keep to a regulated standard.

- Lifecycle considerations

    When designing stores, retailers should consider the lifecycle of the materials and fixtures they choose. Designing modular fixtures and furniture allows for easy disassembly and reuse when renovations or relocations are required from store to store. Additionally, incorporating flexible layouts that can be easily modified or adapted as needs change reduces the need for complete store rebuilds.

- Afterlife opportunities

    Can the designs of fixtures and materials where possible be repurposed or reinvented? Can they be donated for a second use rather than be discarded into landfill? Could a donation scheme for local groups, schools or community platforms find a new purpose for them? Evaluating and asking the questions at the inception of a design will help drive a longer-lasting purpose for store designs.

- Education and engagement

    Retailers can educate and engage audiences on sustainability through their store design. This can include displaying information about sustainable practices, showcasing eco-friendly products and offering incentives for customers to adopt sustainable behaviours. By raising awareness and providing sustainable alternatives, brands can empower customers to make more conscious choices. A good example of engaging and transparent information can be seen by New York fashion brand Coach with their Coachtopia[25] offer where circularity is at the forefront – and products are created from manufacturing offcut waste and old stock. In-store, any product can be scanned and the customer can trace its origin to understand its past life.

- Choice of retail site

    Agencies can encourage retailers to take on leases or build into existing energy-efficient sites rather than investing in new sites – taking on a reuse, reinvent, repurpose mindset even further.

- Accessibility and carbon footprint

    Accessing materials for a store design's location is a key focus to reduce carbon footprints. Agencies and brands should look for sustainable and/or circular solutions but also minimise travel distances to acquire them. Creating design toolkits for store concepts where materials or like-for-like locally sourced alternatives can be achieved will allow greater scope for finding more eco-friendly solutions.

- Materialist empowerment

  Design agencies and retailers can be the platform in which to elevate non-commercial makers and materialists that have put time into researching circular and sustainable material methods. These materials or methods can have implications when it comes to budget restrictions, but, by early consideration and lead time planning, can be incorporated successfully. Agencies and retailers can champion the research and work that materialists have done and look to build on their innovation and promote them for a more commercial future.

- 5Rs – Reducing, reusing, refurbishing, repairing and recycling

  When designing stores, agencies and retailers can consider any or a combination of the 5Rs as a guiding principle for a more sustainable and responsible design approach and even dictate store concepts as a whole. Below is an example of a brand that channels this ethos in their product and in their retail environments.

Case Study – Marine Serre, Selfridges Corner Shop, London, 2023

Since their debut collection in 2016, French fashion brand Marine Serre has designed collections that fuse classic French couture and sports-inspired garments; 50% of their collections comprise upcycled materials including deadstock, while the other half is made from innovative fabrics such as biodegradable yarns and recycled fibres. At the end of 2022, Marine's commitment to championing sustainability and fashion innovation saw the British Fashion Council honour her as a Leader of Change in the Environment category.

In 2023, Marine Serre designed and launched a pop-up store at the iconic Selfridges Corner Shop, London. The pop-up was inspired by everything that Marine Serre stands for – the reuse, reinvention and repair of products and deadstock, breathing new life into otherwise disregarded throwaway items of processed material.

> In designing The Corner Shop installation, I wanted visitors to have the opportunity to explore how we place the Marine Serre house holistically within the environment. Our goal is to explore new possibilities for the future. To love is to repair.
>
> (Marine Serre, 2023)

The pop-up was filled with a mix of both salvaged vintage and contemporary hired-in retail furniture (see Figures 4.2 and 4.3). The furniture and the space played host to a series of workshops throughout the duration – all with the view to educate Marine's ethos to a wider audience. With the chance to 'regenerate' T-shirts using patchworks of the brand's core materials, participate in a screen-printing experience and transform people's clothes with Moon-shaped customisation – a motif and pattern adorned by the brand in their collections.

Figure 4.2 Marine Serre Selfridges Corner Shop.
Photograph by Tim Charles.

Circularity, for us is the ability to recycle, and to 'regenerate' materials that already exist, defining our modus operandi in reducing waste by reintegrating the end-of-life products into a cyclical process that ensure transparency and adaptability of our resources. Upcycled and recycled materials are at the centre of our design process.

(Marine Serre, 2023)

This pop-up echoed the brand's values of regeneration and a radical commitment to circularity while bringing in an educational mindset to its audience, to let them take part and understand the value in upcycling and circularity.

Applying and assessing this pop-up through the ACA approach highlights and contextualises the key takeaways that gave the pop-up rich purpose:

Attention: How was this pop-up *relevant*? Following Selfridges 'Project Earth' target to achieve net-zero carbon across the business by 2040, there is an increasing demand

Figure 4.3 Marine Serre Selfridges Corner Shop.

Photograph by Tim Charles.

for sustainably led brands to be championed. The Corner Shop is a focal area in Selfridges' store in which to do so for maximum footfall and exposure.

Connection: How is it *engaging?* The pop-up was focused on an 'atelier' experience – playing host to a series of workshops and services. Over the duration of the pop-up, customers were able to regenerate T-shirts made from the brand's core materials and take part in educational workshops. Two iconic dresses from the brand's SS23 Hardcore Couture collection were available on a made-to-order service and created in the Marine Serre Atelier.

Attachment: How is Marine Serre *supportive?* The immersive pop-up not only regenerated clothes and its own fixtures but educated the customer in its ethos. The brand's approach to fashion and its experiences clearly resonates with an audience that understands the need for change in fashion consumption mindsets (see also Chapters 2 and 7 on responsible CX).

The importance of materialists and circular makers

As the fashion industry faces increasing scrutiny for its environmental impact, as previously discussed, retailers have a responsibility to adopt sustainable practices throughout their operations, including the design and construction of their retail stores. By prioritising sustainable, circular materials and supporting materialists and their research, fashion retailers can reduce their carbon footprint, promote responsible consumption and contribute to the shift towards a more sustainable industry.

There is ongoing work being done by passionate, purpose-led researchers and materialists with a view to building for a sustainable future without the overconsumption of mass-produced harmful materials. These materialists and researchers require funding and support – much of their work is often self-funded, inevitably resulting in steady progress but without the infrastructure to support large-scale builds for a more commercial approach.

Materialists and circular makers utilise a wide range of ways in which to use less, re-use, waste less and biodegrade where they can. Highlighted below are different types of materialists that have been used in some of Seen Studios' retail spatial projects.

Biomaterialists

In the context of the design industry, a biomaterialist is an individual who focuses on incorporating naturally derived materials or even living organisms into the design process. Biomaterials are substances derived from living organisms or engineered to mimic biological structures and properties. They offer unique possibilities for sustainable and innovative design solutions with a view to not harm the environment and even improve it.

By incorporating biomaterials into the design industry, a biomaterialist aims to create more sustainable and environmentally conscious products. They strive to reduce the reliance on non-renewable resources, minimise waste generation and explore new possibilities for biodegradable or compostable materials. An example of a biomaterialist with whom Seen Studios has collaborated on a retail design project for Bally, New York, and whose research and work has begun to pave the way for better materials and understanding on biomaking is Tessa Silva.[26]

Silva's focal body of work, titled 'Feminised Protein' (see Figure 4.4), is a study into the use of milk proteins as a material for the handcrafted production of fine objects. The project has been in development since 2015 and is a material investigation into the use of surplus milk sourced from a raw organic dairy farm in Sussex – skimmed milk being a by-product of the butter making process. The farm has a very small herd that are individually named, grass fed and milked considerably less than the average dairy cow.

> Milk and milk products have helped shape cultures and western civilisation as we know it, with some of the earliest human artefacts including vessels containing residues of cow's milk. Working predominantly with a unique, but historically originated, formula of surplus milk to create a sculpting and manufacturing material free from synthetics, Tessa utilises a valuable raw material that would otherwise be wasted.
>
> (Tessa Silva, 2023)

Figure 4.4 Feminised Protein by Tessa Silva.

Photograph by Tessa Silva.

Waste-less materialists

Waste within the manufacture and production industry is often inevitable in the currently predominant linear economy. One way select materialists are looking to tackle this issue is to give purpose to the wasted material. Repurposing, refabricating and reforming it into a new use which can be commercially viable. Below is a retail design project Seen Studios designed for luxury Swiss fashion brand Bally that highlights how a waste-less type of material thinking can be integrated into store design.

Case Study – Bally, London, 2021

Following Bally's launch of their Bally Haus[27] concept store in Milan, 2019, Seen Studios was approached to bring a local narrative to their concept for their store opening in London's Regent Street.[28] Seen Studios approached the challenge in a simple yet timeless way – for a luxury consumer who values brand heritage, honouring Bally Haus' pillars of art, architecture and craftmanship.

The launch saw us design a range of furniture and midfloor fixtures (see Figure 4.5), to tell the Bally Haus concept story through a London lens. A prevalent design concept centres around London clay and the geological foundations the city sits upon, from the bricks which built the city, the stability which allowed tunnelling for the London Underground and the formation of the banks of the river Thames, the seam of clay beneath London has been essential to the city's development and therefore the conceptual design.

Figure 4.5 Bally Haus London.
Photograph by Guy Archard.

As a focal part of the design, we collaborated with London-based materialist James Shaw.[29] Shaw's work considers the resources around us challenging the notion of 'waste' – often using waste plastics from South London plastic factories among other waste materials. Visual merchandise detailing integrated Shaw's materiality, hand extruded from recycled high-density polyethylene and polypropylene (see Figure 4.6).

Continuing this celebration of innovation, the entrance table is designed to be easily resurfaced, encouraging future collaborations with other sustainable materialist artists

Figure 4.6 Bally Haus London.

Photograph by Guy Archard.

and makers. Seen to work as an ever-changing element, this design feature provides the ability to continuously reinvent the artistic aspect of the store rather than fully replace it.

Applying and assessing this concept store through our ACA approach highlights and contextualises the key takeaways that gave the store rich purpose:

Attention: How was Bally London *relevant*? Although not obvious at first, the store concept is inspired by the city it is built upon. The view for the midfloor fixtures was to draw the eye in their sculptural and unique nature – creating intrigue to unearth their story.

Connection: How is Bally London *engaging*? The store was also designed to house the Bally Art Haus Exhibition series, acting as a cultural hub to explore local talent and innovation in materialism. Described by the CEO of Bally, Bally Art Haus "hopes to fulfil new post-pandemic needs with multi-functional space that engages local artists to give second life to repurposed materials – offering new ways to see old things – while providing an experiential environment that embraces the excitement of discovery" (Girotto, 2021).

Attachment: How is Bally London *supportive*? The store supported local talent and makers and educated its audience on their work. In October 2021, the store exhibited London-based artist Zuza Mangham's[30] sculptural pieces, which explore the connection between crafts and new methods of making, reflecting Bally's longstanding commitment to craftmanship and design innovation.

Agencies and retailers can begin by involving materialist thinking like this from a project's beginnings and building a timeline and budget that can help promote this sustainable way of thinking – which will, in return, enrich store's storytelling, evoke lasting value from a consumer's perspective and be a better approach for the environment. For further information on materialists, material innovation, audience types and other initiatives, see Seen Studios Sustainability Issue, Volume 1.[31]

Seen Studios conceptual process

Case study – Bally Haus, New York 2021

Seen Studios partnered with Bally to design their US Bally Haus Flagship[32] concept in New York's vibrant Meatpacking District (see Figure 4.7). This project provided an exciting opportunity to transcend the traditional purposes of retail in both function and aesthetics, layering the district's industrial heritage with the culture of the contemporary within the concept. Seen Studios' insight and design team developed a concept for the brick-and-mortar store that was distinctively Bally by resonating with the brand's influences in art, nature and their Swiss origins, whilst also celebrating the local area.

Seen Studios' creative narrative was inspired by the angular lines of Manhattan's grid, which uniquely pivots in the Meatpacking District, when cast in the light of the famous 'Manhattan-henge' a few weeks before and after the summer solstice where the sun sets

Figure 4.7 Bally New York.
Photograph by Tom Sibley.

perfectly at the end of the streets of Chelsea – ultimately lining the Meatpacking red brick streets in hard light and enriching the warm hues.

The interior design mimics the spatial unison of the neighbourhood, with light natural textures on the one side and earthy clay tones on the other (see Figure 4.8) – purposely replicating the Italian nature of Bally Haus Milan and the brickwork of Meatpacking's working past.

Functionality and flexibility were the forefront of Seen Studios' and Bally's design goals, developing a visual language that offers spatial elasticity to easily adapt to Bally's various products, services and community events. A multi-functional space, modular fixtures and furniture are seen throughout, such as oak shelves (see Figure 4.9) that are easily removed, becoming interchangeable based upon the store's needs.

Transforming selling into entertaining, many fixtures lend themselves to in-house cultural events such as film screenings and exhibitions. Since opening, the space has housed events and experiences such as the launch of the Bally Hike[33] collection, proving that the design goals for the space were achieved. This is best described by Nicolas Girotto, CEO of Bally, as he calls the store a "multi-functional boutique in a dynamic lifestyle hub … featuring tailor made experiences for our customers, with the physical integrating with the digital through omnichannel services that put convenience and engagement at the core of our retail strategy" (2021).

Complementing Bally's early post-pandemic strategy, throughout the space an emphasis was put on their digital infrastructure. Placing visitors in the centre of unique digital content, at the entrance of the store stands an immersive digital screen that wraps the walls

Figure 4.8 Bally New York.

Photograph by Tom Sibley.

Figure 4.9 Bally New York.

Photograph by Andrew Quinn.

and ceiling (see Figure 4.10) – designed to engage and promote the brand's campaigns and storytelling as well as work as a canvas for digital artists. To the rear of the store, a full wall-to-wall LED screen draws customers through the space and is complemented by smaller screens throughout. This generates a frictionless phygital customer journey, providing new ways of engagement. Smaller touchpoints encourage customers to interact with Bally products that are not physically displayed in the store – not all products are on the shopfloor, but all can be accessed through RFID-triggered screens which bring up different available colourways, campaign content and product storytelling.

Figure 4.10 Bally New York.

Photograph by Tom Sibley.

Seen Studios introduced a pop-up space to the front of the store – to host a total takeover, from campaign-led installations and visual merchandise, to local artist takeovers – it was designed to be a blank canvas that could reinvent itself for its evolving purpose.

It was also crucial for Seen Studios to express Bally's values of combining nature with the contemporary throughout the store. We ensured that the approach to materialism was innovative, circular and quintessentially Bally, using sustainable materials and materialists from Tessa Silva to Paper factor[34] (see Figures 4.11 and 4.12).

Figure 4.11 Bally New York.

Photograph by Andrew Quinn.

Figure 4.12 Bally New York.

Photograph by Andrew Quinn.

Serving as a holistic brand anchor, Bally NY's visually contrasting interior creates a dynamic destination through its multi-functional layout and experiential touchpoints, offering a seamless, ever-evolving consumer journey. Applying and assessing this concept store through our ACA approach highlights and contextualises the key takeaways that gave the store rich purpose:

Attention: How was Bally NYC *relevant*? The store wasn't just for product purchase but played as a host for its audience. It was created to be adaptive with the possibility to remove or relocate most fixtures – allowing it to become a host for talks, presentations, artist displays amongst other activations.

Connection: How is Bally NYV *engaging*? The store could host different artists or internal pop-ups to help ensure the audience could see something new upon their various visits. For the shopping experience, digital touchpoints allowed for added storytelling and ease of product information.

Attachment: How was Bally NYC *supportive*? The store promoted sustainable material solutions throughout, with store staff well educated in the design background – customers were given the chance to learn more through human-centric customer service – well-balanced with the digital landscape implemented throughout.

Conclusions and reflections for harmonious CX integration

As a retail design agency, Seen Studios is constantly evolving the way they work and see projects. The agency believes that approaching any project with a human-centric mindset is key for creating lasting value – especially as the world continues to advance digitally, socially and environmentally.

By understanding the audience and addressing ways in which to gather the right data, the store can become a shape-shifting space that caters to its community's needs and demands. People need to be put at the heart of the retail environment and be made to feel like their opinions and values matter – that the brand is listening and responding. Values and emotional connections are at the core of a retailer's future success – and when a retailer reacts, communicates and engages in the right way for the audience – the audience feels part of a community and not merely a customer.

In designing future stores, agencies must consider who they are for now and who they may become during the store's lifetime. Using Seen Studios' ACA framework can help with framing the right questions to answer when designing for a purpose-led approach.

Most agencies and retailers are at the beginning of an economic reset and reassessment of the way that product, services and retail stores can be built with a greater focus on the circular economy. Through organisations, third sector initiatives and government regulations, retailers and agencies must continue to pave the way for better processes and, in turn, educate the wider audience to follow suit through their eco-consciousness.

While this chapter has looked at Seen Studios' ACA approach and current retail practices, assessing its purpose with evergreen questions, we wonder, what will the relevancy, engagement and support of retail stores be in the future? To this end, we finish by offering some questions for reflection and future consideration: What will future retail experiences, spatial design and narratives entail? How will the future store reward the audience? Will it think for itself? Will it think for you? Will it grow and decompose? Will it sell emotion as well as product? Will it sell products at all or only experiences? Will it be physical? Will it become one channel? Will it be fully circular? Will it have a social purpose?

While some questions and store narratives may drastically change in time, what will not change is that the store will always require relevancy, and it will need to engage and support its audience to stand a better chance at long-term success.

Chapter questions

1   Apply Seen Studios' strategic ACA framework – 'Attention, Connection, Attachment' – to a fashion retailer of your choice in order to propose a creative retail concept that harmoniously connects its physical, social and digital channels and that resonates with its target audience. Once applied, reflect on the framework's utility and what, if anything, you might add to it.

2   Select *one* retail store consideration from those discussed in the chapter (e.g. global vs. local communities, flexibility and adaptation, identifying audience needs and building a social community, integrating physical and digital channels, engaging communication and storytelling and multi-purpose store landscape) and *one* fashion retailer of choice (which differ to those discussed in the chapter) to research and discuss their current strengths and weaknesses in this aspect (consideration), and propose areas for improvement to enhance the customer experience.

3   The chapter highlights the imperative to design retail spaces and experiences according to circular economy principles and offers a list of sustainable practices and considerations. Imagine you are the retail creative team responsible for creating the circular store strategy for a fashion retailer you are familiar with. Work through each consideration to identify the changes required to transition towards sustainable retail practices. This requires you to audit what the retailer's current practices are in order to propose a roadmap for change.

4   Taking forward the rhetorical questions posed at the end of the chapter, you are asked to futurise fashion retail spaces, places and experiences. Specifically choose, consider and discuss *three* of the questions: What will future retail experiences, spatial design and narratives entail? How will the future store reward the audience? Will the store think for itself? Will the store think for you? Will the store grow and decompose? Will the store sell emotion as well as product? Will the store sell products at all or only experiences? Will the store be physical or will it become one channel? Will the store be fully circular? Will the store have a social purpose?

Notes

 1 Seen Studios, https://seen-studios.com/.
 2 Aesop, https://www.aesop.com/uk/r/store-experience/.
 3 Nike Join Forces, https://seen-studios.com/allprojects/nike-br-a-campaign-for-nike-capturing-londons-finest-dance-crews.
 4 AIM Collective, https://www.instagram.com/aimcollective.ig/.
 5 The Movement Factory, https://www.instagram.com/themovementfactory/?hl=en.
 6 Twerk After Work, https://www.bambamboogie.com/.
 7 Juanita Richards Campaign Photography, https://juanitarichards.com/nike-3/.
 8 Peckham Levels, https://peckhamlevels.org/.
 9 Joy Yamusangie, https://joyyamusangie.com/.
10 TikTok podium & event imagery, https://seen-studios.com/allprojects/nike-br-own-the-floor.
11 Juicy Jerk, https://www.blackownedlondon.com/juici-jerk/.
12 The Treats Club, https://thetreatsclub.com/.
13 LS:N Global, https://www.lsnglobal.com/big-ideas/article/29541/world-retail-congress-2023-resilient-retail-futures.
14 Burberry Open Spaces, https://uk.burberry.com/c/burberry-open-spaces-shenzhen/#a-window-into-our-world.

15 Selfridges & Co, www.selfridges.com.
16 Gentle Monster, www.gentlemonster.com/int/store.
17 Nike House of Innovation, www.nike.com/gb/house-of-innovation.
18 Burberry Open Spaces, https://uk.burberry.com/c/burberry-open-spaces-shenzhen/#a-window-into-our-world.
19 Vogue Business, https://www.voguebusiness.com/technology/louis-vuittons-latest-ar-project-covering-landmarks-in-dots.
20 Epic Games, https://www.epicgames.com/site/en-US/news/balenciaga-brings-high-fashion-to-fortnite.
21 Raeburn Lab, https://www.raeburndesign.co.uk/pages/raeburn-lab.
22 Ellen McArthur Foundation, https://ellenmacarthurfoundation.org/.
23 B Corp, https://www.bcorporation.net/en-us/.
24 BREEAM, https://bregroup.com/.
25 Coachtopia, https://uk.coach.com/shop/coachtopia.
26 Tessa Silva, https://www.tessasilva.com/chalk-cheese.
27 Bally Haus, Milan, https://cmk-architects.com/projects/bally-montenapoleone-milan/.
28 Bally Flagship, London, https://www.frameweb.com/project/bally-flagship-london.
29 James Shaw, https://jamesmichaelshaw.co.uk/.
30 Zuza Mengham, https://www.zuzamengham.com/about.
31 Seen Studios Sustainability Issue, https://issuu.com/seenstudios/docs/sustainability_issue_draft_7?fr=xIAEoAT3_NTU1.
32 Bally New York, https://seen-studios.com/allprojects/bally-nyc.
33 Bally Hike, https://retail-focus.co.uk/bally-hike-concept-bridges-the-light-reflections-and-distortions-that-nature-has-on-our-cities-and-landscapes/.
34 Paper Factor, http://paperfactor.com/en/main#cover.

References

B Corporation (2023) *B Corporation certification.* [Online] [Accessed 3rd October 2023] https://bcorporation.uk/b-corp-certification/?gclid=CjwKCAjwyNSoBhA9EiwA5aYlb-Dd0hdWR320OQCrnRzOy8yC9-debAoyb72IHQh9jIs0GZO-crdrZBoCjGgQAvD_BwE

Bivigou, P., Deol, S., Hastings, D., Indeka, M. and Rhodes, E. (2023) *Artificial Intelligence.* LS:N Global. [Online] [Accessed 3rd October 2023] https://www.lsnglobal.com/AI/article/29568/stat-the-next-generation-of-consumers-expect-retailers-to-harness-tech-innovation

Briedis, H., Gregg, B. Heidenreich, K. and Liu, W-W. (2021) *Omnichannel: The path to value.* Mckinsey & Company. [Online] [Accessed 3rd October 2023] https://www.mckinsey.com/capabilities/growth-marketing-and-sales/our-insights/the-survival-guide-to-omnichannel-and-the-path-to-value

Ellen McArthur Foundation (2023a) *Circular design: Turning ambition into action.* [Online] [Accessed 3rd October 2023] https://ellenmacarthurfoundation.org/topics/circular-design/overview

Ellen McArthur Foundation (2023b) *What is a circular economy?* [Online] [Accessed 3rd October 2023] https://ellenmacarthurfoundation.org/topics/circular-economy-introduction/overview

Epic Games (2021) *Epic games.* [Online] [Accessed 3rd October 2023] https://www.epicgames.com/site/en-US/news/balenciaga-brings-high-fashion-to-fortnite

Girotto, N. (2021) *Bally CEO* [Interview with Seen Studios].

Marine Serre (2023) Marine Serre. [Online] [Accessed 3rd October 2023] https://www.marineserre.com/en-uk/core/values

Mckinsey & Company (2022) *What is omnichannel marketing?* [Online] [Accessed 3rd October 2023] https://www.mckinsey.com/featured-insights/mckinsey-explainers/what-is-omnichannel-marketing

Raeburn, C. (2023) *Creative Director* [Interview with Seen Studios] 2023.

Raymond, M. (2023) *Future ready retail.* LS:N Global. [Online] [Accessed 4th October 2023] https://www.lsnglobal.com/viewpoints/article/29157/future-ready-retail

Schulz, M. (2023) *Louis Vuitton's latest AR project? Covering landmarks in dots*. Vogue Business. [Online] [Accessed 4th October 2023] https://www.voguebusiness.com/technology/louis-vuittons-latest-ar-project-covering-landmarks-in-dots

Tessa Silva (2023) *Tessa Silva*. [Online] [Accessed 4th October 2023] https://www.tessasilva.com/chalk-cheese

Wunderman Thompson (2023) *The future shopper report 2023*. [Online] [Accessed 4th October 2023] https://www.mmaglobal.com/files/casestudies/the-future-shopper-report-2023.pdf.

5

Creating visceral and human-centric customer experiences

Kate Shepherd

Contextualising visceral and human-centric store design

This section introduces the notion of visceral and human-centric store design, tracing the origins of human-centred design and explaining why physical and emotive customer experiences (CX) are becoming increasingly popular in today's digitally dominated world.

Globally, we are witnessing a rise in the design of visceral retail experiences that are designed to evoke and instil an emotive, sensory connection between customers and brands. Particularly so, within fashion retailing, a sector known for being ahead of the change curve in terms of innovation and so closely connected to emotional desires (Diderich, 2022).

In a world so dominated by endless digital scrolling and screen time, the allure of real and physical immersive experiences has never been greater (Baron, 2023a). As consumers rediscover their love of experiential shopping and physical stores, brands are responding by upgrading the CX and delivering the ultimate expression of immersive destination retail, which celebrates the essence of physicality (see also Chapter 8 case studies on visceral CX).

In a report entitled 'The Age of Re-enchantment', Wunderman Thompson Intelligence (2023) defines re-enchantment as fulfilling a craving for feelings of wonder and awe, an appetite for joy and fun and an openness to thrills and adventure. Suggesting that we yearn to feel something, in part, because in becoming adults, we lose our sense of child-like wonder over time and the world becomes less magical. But it's also a much-needed counter to the times we live in. We live in a rational, explained world, and one in which we are harried and anxious, with little time to pause and pursue these sensations (Wunderman Thompson Intelligence, 2023).

Spaces that offer a sense of surprise and delight, that provide the ultimate in escapism and theatrical exploration, that are designed with an emotion-led approach that celebrates the role of tactility and community reveal what is possible. Blurring the boundaries between retail, hospitality, culture and entertainment, these new era retail destinations provide an exciting real-world opportunity in an age where we often prioritise digital connectivity (Baron, 2023a).

> Whether a brand's target audience favours surrealistic retail spaces or transcendent wellness experiences, nature-based amazement or multiverse activations, there are myriad ways for companies and designers to collaborate to more sensorially stimulating, spatially intriguing ends.
>
> (Frame, 2023a)

DOI: 10.4324/9781003378099-7

Visionary brands such as Nike, Sony and Samsung are taking this idea to the extreme and creating both permanent and temporary retail and brand experiences that harness all that the latest AR (augmented reality) and VR (virtual reality) technologies offer to create physical experiences that evoke unique emotional and visceral responses (Wunderman Thompson Intelligence, 2022). Realising that the overall sensorial experience has a valuable role to play, they are experimenting with tactility, sound and olfactory elements and employing a kaleidoscopic colour palette that's designed to clearly stand out. For example, the Samsung Galaxy Unpacked Experience on Regent Street in London (2022) employed a host of surreal and awe-inspiring storytelling techniques, designed to take visitors on an immersive technology adventure and demonstrate the capabilities of their latest product innovations (Barker, 2022).

Emotional connections

Good design connects emotionally.

(Job, 2022)

Having witnessed a huge shift in consumer lifestyles, mindsets and goals as a result of the global pandemic, when designing CX it's never been more important for brands and retailers to consider the emotional desires of consumers, as well as their practical needs (WGSN, 2022). Consumers are showing an increasing appetite and desire for retail experiences that evoke intense emotions. This is particularly true of younger generations whereby "61% of Gen Z and Millennials want brands to evoke intense emotions" (Wunderman Thompson Intelligence, 2023, p.20).

Speaking to *Wallpaper* magazine about his vision for the Nike House of Innovation store in Paris, the Chief Design Officer for Nike, John Hoke, stated:

My sense of immersion today and tomorrow about doing a couple of things well. You have to stir the emotions, and I think you do that by captivating and engaging all the senses. I like to say that one of the things we do really well is to design for goosebumps – what I mean by that is when you come across something that literally raises the hair on your neck, captures your emotion and makes your body say 'pay attention'.

(Keh, 2022)

The impact of this heightened attention towards designing to evoke emotional responses and connections is twofold. First, from a design perspective, the retail design process has evolved and expanded in scope, with a much larger emphasis on the initial phases of consumer insights and contextual research. Enabling retail designers to carefully choreograph every step of the customer journey to ensure the experience achieves the intended emotional impact. Embracing the interplay of thoughtful planning, deep consumer insight and understanding, and pioneering creativity, whereby every element, from the space layout to the sensory cues, is tuned in to the human needs, habits and emotions. In short, retail designers are considering not only how each step of the customer journey and experience looks, but how it feels. Second, from a commercial perspective, aside from the practical key performance indicators (KPIs), brands and retailers are now beginning to layer in emotional indicators too, measuring the emotional response that people have when they visit their store or brand experience (Wunderman Thompson Intelligence, 2023).

Taking a human-centric approach to retail design

This move towards the creation of visceral retail experiences demands a human-centric approach to retail design. According to the global design consultancy IDEO, renowned for their pioneering development in the application of design thinking and user research, a human-centric approach is one that focuses on the needs and perspectives of human beings. It is based on the belief that humans are the most important consideration in any situation and that their needs should be given priority.

> Human-centered design is a creative approach to problem-solving that starts with people and ends with innovative solutions that are tailor-made to suit their needs
>
> (Kelley, 2001)

Human-centred design has its origins at the intersection of numerous fields including engineering, psychology, anthropology and the arts (Kelley, 2001). As an approach to creative problem-solving in technical and business fields its origins are often traced to the 1950s. The concept of human-centric design was informally introduced by the American industrial designer Henry Dreyfuss. In his 1955 book *Designing for People*, Dreyfuss explains that industrial design can evolve by beginning and ending with people. He stresses the importance of habits, physical dimensions and psychological impulses. In 1958, Professor John Arnold founded the Stanford University design programme which formally proposed the idea that engineering design should be human-centred (Fast Company, 2022).

Over time, the creative approach to problem-solving in business has seen a wider adoption of human-centric methodologies in the built environment. Human-centric retail design is an approach to designing retail environments that prioritises the needs, comfort and overall experience of the customer.

> The broader one's understanding of the human experience, the better design we will have.
>
> (Steve Jobs, cited in Peek, 2023)

The origins of human-centric retail design can be traced back to the rise of consumerism in the 19th century. The Industrial Revolution brought about mass production, which led to an increase in the variety and quantity of goods available. This growth in consumer goods necessitated a new kind of retail environment: the department store. These early department stores, like Le Bon Marché in Paris, which opened in 1852, were designed with the CX in mind. Wide aisles, clear signage and beautiful displays were all designed to entice customers and make shopping a pleasurable experience (Barr, 1986).

Today, we're witnessing a fundamental shift towards a human-centric approach to retail design (Kelley, 2001). According to Deloitte, Human Centric Retail™ requires companies to "rapidly sense, adapt, and evolve solutions to human needs, configure to enable granular interactions with the brand, and build a culture of empathy" (Deloitte, 2019).

In their report entitled Retail Reset, the design practice The Future Collective describes how we are entering the era of humanised retail, whereby the consumer is at the very heart of the story and the store design is centred on and inspired by human needs, emotions and experiences. More so than ever before, this approach to retail design calls for an approach that is deeply rooted in strategic thinking and consumer empathy, blending insightful strategy and creative ingenuity (Shepherd and Parry, 2020).

It's not digital first, or physical first, it's people first.
(Kate Shepherd, co-founder, Retail Reset Report, The Future Collective, 2020)

The notion of humanised retail focuses on placing the needs of people at the centre of everything and providing the ultimate levels of service, elevating service strategies, empowering staff and harnessing the latest technological capabilities, particularly in artificial intelligence (AI), to provide more personal, tailored and convenient CX.

> The humanisation of retail is about the acceptance that it's no longer about big or small, local or global; it's about where we all meet in the middle. Ultimately it's all about customer service.
> (Matt Parry, co-founder, Retail Reset Report, The Future Collective, 2020)

In summary, there is agreement amongst experts in retail and CX design that a people-centric approach is key. And the most impactful and effective concepts are those that focus on the creation of sensorial CX that engage the senses (see also Part 1, Chapter 2, section on hyper-personalised experiences).

Sensational retail: engaging the senses in retail spaces to enhance CX

This section explores the rise of sensorial CX in fashion retailing. Considering the various types of emotions that can be evoked and how each of the senses have a role to play in enhancing the overall brand experience. In our post-pandemic world, it's only natural that our desire for physical experiences and human connection has grown stronger than ever (Shepherd, 2021). People are now drawn to deeply immersive and sensorial experiences that are difficult to emulate online, seeking shared experiences that are to be enjoyed in the here-and-now.

Brands and retailers, particularly in the beauty and fashion sectors, are experimenting with the creation of enriching brand experiences that awaken the senses and genuinely reward people for their visit. We are seeing the emergence of more enlightened and introspective brand experiences, designed to purposefully slow the pace down, encouraging people to switch off from digital distractions and enjoy the experience (Shepherd, 2021).

Describing the vision behind the luxury retail concept called 'The Village' on the Cadogan Estate in London (2021), which blends permanent and pop-up stores together with hospitality offerings, Anya Hindmarch suggests:

> I very much believe in bricks and mortar retail but also believe that physical retail needs to offer something that cannot be replicated digitally. This is what The Village is all about, these are 'miss them or they are gone' experiences.
> (Shearsmith, 2022). (See also Chapter 8, Anya Hindmarch case study)

The emotional currency of the brand experience is crucial. According to the *Harvard Business Review* (Magids and Zorfas, 2015), connecting emotionally across the brand experience generates 52% more customer value. Within this review, it is stated that several research studies concluded that emotional experiences imprint better in our memory, therefore in-real-life brand experiences must embed products and services in a way that evokes strong and long-lasting emotional responses.

In 1973, business professor Philip Kotler coined the term *atmospherics* for the practice of designing store environments to project a specific image and induce certain behaviours. In an article for the *Journal of Retailing*, he wrote, "In some cases, the place, more specifically the atmosphere of the place, is more influential than the product itself in the purchase decision. In some cases, the atmosphere is the primary product" (Anderson, 2022).

Placing an emphasis on the creation of brand experiences to be enjoyed in the here-and-now opens up a whole host of new ideas, new materials and new approaches. It also encourages designers to consider how to evoke an emotional connection and appeal to all of our senses. Sensational retail can take many forms and channel different emotions. Next, we explore some of the key emotions brands can harness.

Joyful encounters

Joy is the emotion most people want to feel more of, and 49% of people say they would even be more likely to purchase from a brand that brings them a sense of joy.

89% of people see fun as a necessity that keeps them going in tough times, while 83% seek out experiences that bring them joy and happiness.

(Wunderman Thompson Intelligence, 2023)

The first years of this decade have heralded a particularly disruptive period in human history. The return to a 'new normal' following the COVID-19 pandemic was quickly disrupted by the outbreak of war in Ukraine, ushering in a fresh series of crises in food and energy – triggering problems that decades of progress had sought to solve (World Economic Forum, 2023). Our world now appears to lurch from one crisis to the next – with no time to take a breath and adjust after each one before another rolls in (Accenture, 2022). Collins Dictionary announced its word of the year for 2022 as "permacrisis", defined as an extended period of instability and insecurity (Baron, 2023b).

Amid such turbulent economic, social, political and environmental times it may seem counterintuitive that people are seeking out opportunities for fun and playfulness. Yet the appetite for joyful and uplifting experiences is increasingly evident. Driven by the idea of creating a sense of wonderment in the physical world, retail designers are experimenting with new approaches and techniques to create joyful and unexpected encounters (Accenture, 2022).

Never before have we been in such need of brands with optimism and soul. We crave brands that will lift our spirits and spark an emotional connection. Hopeful brands with warmth and positivity will lead the way forward.

(Parry, 2023)

Capitalising on what the trend prediction consultancy Stylus refers to as the Economy of Delight (Baron, 2023a) a growing number of leisure and hospitality brands are offering people a much-needed dose of fun, joy and escapism. This is particularly manifesting in physical exhibitions and cultural spaces such as the Sony INTO-SIGHT exhibition at London Design Festival (2022) and the Parables of Happiness exhibition by Yinka Ilori at the Design Museum (2022), which over-index on colour, pattern, sound, lighting and other state-of-the-art technologies to evoke surprise, delight and even awe.

Equally, a growing number of luxury brands are discarding stuffy, outdated concepts of heritage, minimalism and gloss to reveal a much more playful side to their brand personality. For example, the Marni pop-up in Galeries Lafayette, Paris (2022), with a kaleidoscopic colour palette, and the 60s-inspired Paris pop-up (2022) from the French luxury brand Sonia Rykiel each created quirky, eccentric and nostalgic concepts that are purposefully designed to raise a smile.

It could be argued that the best approaches are also often the simplest, cleverly tapping into natural human behaviour traits to appeal to our childlike curiosity and intuitive desire to touch and play.

Even within the luxury sector, a new brand experience landscape is unfolding that is both unexpected and accessible to all. For example, the iconic fashion house Louis Vuitton has transformed their brand associations in recent years, largely as a result of their wholehearted embracing of a playful and joyful approach to retail experience design. Similarly, the luxury fashion house Jacquemus has risen in brand awareness, recognition and public consciousness as a result of their subversive, playful retail experiences. Reflecting the founder Simon Porte Jacquemus' belief in providing customers with an experiential journey into the brand's story, many are temporary immersive takeovers in notable department stores. Examples include Le Bleu in Selfridges, London, whereby he created a surrealist interpretation of his own bathroom and the Jacquemus Obsession takeover within Galeries Lafayette, Paris, which provided customers with an opportunity to dive into the world of Jacquemus, exploring the brand's unique aesthetic and playful references to everyday items throughout the store.

The designer Yinka llori has risen to fame by adopting an exuberant and joyful approach to design, collaborating with the Design Museum, London, to create The Parables for Happiness (2022/2023) and partnering with Lego to develop the "Launderette of Dreams", an installation in London that reimagines a common community space as a children's playground. Forming part of the brand's "Rebuild the World campaign," the installation, located on Bethnal Green Road, features Ilori's vibrant colours and geometric shapes, alongside over 200,000 Lego bricks for structural and play purposes. The space includes features such as hopscotch floors, a giant Lego mural and a toy-dispensing vending machine. Ilori drew inspiration from his childhood memories at his local launderette, highlighting the significant role these spaces play in community building. Children from Ilori's former school were also invited into the design process, contributing ideas to shape the Launderette of Dreams (Rima, 2021).

> Like Yinka, children are brimming with amazing ideas for how to rebuild the world around them for the better and use play to transform the mundane into a magical experience. Their creative optimism inspires us every day, and we hope the Launderette of Dreams shows how fun and playful the world around us can be when approached with a bit of childlike imagination and joy.
>
> (Alero Akuya, Vice President of Global Brand Development,
> LEGO Group, cited in Rima, 2021)

Taking the idea of portable fashion retailing to the extreme, the New York leather goods brand Coach opened a pop-up store on a Boeing 747-230B aircraft in a shopping mall in Malacca, Malaysia. The brand painstakingly created its first concept store and café housed in a jumbo jet at the Freeport A'Famosa Outlet village. As well as the detailed fit out using retro colourways and prints, the store features a Coach Airways collection specially developed for the project. Speaking with *Forbes*, Tapestry's Southeast Asia and Oceania general manager Campbell O'Shea said that the opening was a space "where customers can explore and interact, reflecting the brand's continued efforts to craft one-of-a-kind experiences" (Rozario, 2023).

Awe-inspiring experiences

A tool for human survival centuries ago. Awe is necessary for future growth. As a collective emotion, awe helps the self shrink and the world expand. Awe will become a great connector in a time of fragmentation.

(WGSN, 2022)

There are many different interpretations of the meaning and purpose of awe in consumer experience. According to Yang Ba, researcher at University of California, Berkeley, "While we're feeling small in an awe moment, we are feeling connected to more people or feeling closer to others. That's awe's purpose, or at least one of its purposes" (WGSN, 2022). Furthermore, University of Michigan psychologist Ethan Kross defines awe as "the wonder we feel when we encounter something powerful that we can't easily explain". A mix of both fear and wonder, it is an emotion that has been discarded in recent years as during the pandemic and the subsequent global economic crisis, people traded awe-inspiring moments for stability, survival and certainty (WGSN, 2022).

Noting the rise of awe in retail design and brand experiences, the trend prediction consultancy WGSN (2022) suggests that awe brings people together and leaves people inspired, explaining that scientists believe that awe may have helped our evolutionary ancestors survive in the face of uncertain environments that demanded group cooperation. A tool for human survival centuries ago, awe is necessary for future growth, particularly if trying to build back better from the extremely challenging times we have lived through in recent years. In a recent report entitled 'The Age of Re-Enchantment' Wunderman Thompson Intelligence suggests that "89% [of people] say awe-inspiring experiences make them feel good" (2023). They go on to cite the seminal book *Awe: The Transformative Power of Everyday Wonder* (2023), wherein psychology professor Dacher Keltner explains: "When we experience awe, regions of the brain that are associated with the excesses of the ego, including self-criticism, anxiety, and even depression, quiet down".

In a bid to create awe-inspiring experiences on the high street, we're witnessing luxury fashion brands create flagship concepts that are becoming landmark destinations in key cities across the world. Expanding their role beyond sales and support, these new global landmarks are designed to provide meaningful access for all, from accessible to absolute luxury consumers. Live demonstrations of the possibilities of future engagement, these spaces push the limits of retail in the most captivating ways (Shepherd and Mitchell, 2023).

One of the most notable examples of this shift is Tiffany and Co's 'Landmark' store on Fifth Avenue in New York (2023). Designed by the architect Peter Marino, the renovation is the first significant change to the store since it opened in 1940. The iconic luxury jewellery brand describes this store as a "world-class museum" rather than a shopping destination, with ten floors devoted to celebrating the past, present and future of the House's 186-year history (Bailey, 2023).

Symbolic of a new era for Tiffany and Co., the Landmark is much more than a jewellery store – it is a cultural hub with an exquisite showcase of architecture and superior hospitality, as well as cutting-edge art and design. Anthony Ledru, President and Chief Executive Officer, Tiffany and Co. (Bailey, 2023)

Opening up their entire brand universe in jaw-dropping style, Christian Dior's flagship store in Paris offers customers the opportunity to explore every facet of their brand within an experience that combines a store, museum, restaurant and apartment for overnight stays. Located in the spiritual home of Dior, 30 Avenue Montaigne in Paris, the store reopened to the public in 2022, 75 years after Monsieur Dior presented his first collection there. All the collections are available, in addition to a garden, pastry bar and restaurant. On the fourth floor, a luxury suite offers overnight guests the keys to 30 Montaigne, whereby they are granted access to the store 24/7 (Serafin, 2022).

The adjacent museum, La Galerie Dior, is a totally separate entity from the store, designed by interior architect Nathalie Crinière and covering 1,577 sq m across four floors; it is the biggest space for a permanent fashion collection in Paris. It displays numerous dresses and other items from the Dior archives, which are changed every three months (Serafin, 2022).

One of the most exciting aspects of the 30 Montaigne project is that it is a journey through the inner essence of the brand, expressed through the architecture, interior design and experience of each space. It's not one idea throughout, but rather, a walk through spaces that tell a story, that keeps the customer engaged and emotionally connected with Dior from start to finish.
Peter Marino, Architect, Dior, 30 Montaigne, Paris (Serafin, 2022)

Serendipity and surprise

What's gone is the moment of happenstance, chance and all the other works that can only be described with magical language. Leaving room for the spontaneous and unplanned is the number one thing that people miss about IRL [in real life] encounters.
(The Immunized Consumer report, HighSnobiety, 2021)

According to the above-mentioned report by HighSnobiety, what people missed the most about real-life experience during the pandemic is the spontaneity of live encounters. What we cherished about offline was its randomness and one of the fundamental reasons that we enjoy shopping in-store is the natural sense of discovery it imbues. As we move firmly into a post-pandemic world, it seems that our desire for the unexpected continues to grow.

In a world increasingly focused on speed and efficiency, consumers have an appetite for an injection of mystery, surprise and serendipity into their lives. But research by Wunderman Thompson Intelligence (2023) suggests that brands are not doing enough to deliver on this: "A massive 70% say they can't remember the last time a brand did something that excited them". There is huge potential for brands to offer a welcome respite from efficiency and predictability by building in moments of serendipity and the unexpected: "74% of our respondents say they enjoy an element of mystery and surprise in the things they do". This unlocks pockets of opportunity for brands to deliver an escape from the everyday.

Providing the perfect antidote to the often linear journeys that people experience on-line, physical brand experiences are becoming increasingly focused on serendipity and surprise. They are inspired by ever-changing concept stores by the likes of Dover Street Market and Wolf and Badger in London and Merci in Paris, which provide a sense of beautiful abundance. They reinvent the way that they lay out their stores and present their offers with chance and discovery in mind.

Forward-thinking department stores such as Selfridges in London are becoming the editor and curator of their product range – reimagining their offer to appeal to shoppers who seek the thrill of discovery, yet also have a growing need to simplify an overwhelm-ing amount of choice. Similarly, the Showfields department store in New York is very imaginative in their product offer and range, embracing direct-to-consumer e-brands, rising stars and new players. Describing themselves as "the most interesting store in the world", the House of Showfields is intent on catering to shoppers' fast-evolving wishes, creating an enticing customer journey from start to finish (Danziger, 2019).

Also, exemplifying this shift towards a more agile and experimental approach to store design and merchandising, the Neighborhood Goods department store in Texas is made up entirely of pop-up shops, offering menswear, womenswear and homewares from both local start-ups and established brands. The goal of the store is to create a dynamic sales floor, where about 15 brands at a time create their own experiences, each shining a light on their products and overall worldview (Danziger, 2020).

In a bid to celebrate the art of discovery and exploration in cities worldwide, Burberry has launched a campaign named 'Burberry Streets' whereby the luxury fashion brand will host a series of brand takeovers in key cities worldwide. The event merges the brand's forward-thinking vision with its rich heritage, bringing modern British luxury to life in new and innovative ways, offering immersive experiences, installations and events that unfold throughout each city (Eberhardt, 2023).

In summary, against this complex and anxiety-fuelled backdrop it's perhaps no sur-prise that 'escapism' and transportative experiences and sensory engagement are now popular themes in spatial and retail design (Frame, 2023b). As a result, when we consider the design of CX within fashion retailing, there is the potential to consider the design concept from a multisensorial perspective.

Physical sensoriums

The new retail experience will make greater use of sight, sound and smell. Materials will be used to convey tactility; sound will create opportunities both for escape and to be present; while smell can be used as a strong reminder of place.

(Kate Machtiger, founder of Extra Terrestrial – Future 100,
Wunderman Thompson Intelligence, 2021)

Lindstrom (2005) states that our emotions are linked to the information gathered through the senses. He introduced the concept of sensory branding that stimulates and enhances consumers' imagination and perception, creating emotional ties between the brand and consumer. Sensory stimuli can motivate consumers' purchasing behaviour, spark their interest and allow emotional responses to dominate their rational thinking (Lindstrom, 2005; Alexander and Nobbs, 2016).

Thinking beyond the visual senses provides a rich canvas for retail design to explore. We're witnessing an imaginative exploration of the often forgotten elements of sound, smell, tactility and touch, along with the creation of physical brand experiences that feel carefully choreographed and considered (Frame, 2022).

Next, each sense is considered in turn, and how they can impact the overall CX within fashion retailing.

Olfactory immersion

> Our capacity to remember our sensory experiences is 1% of what we touch, 2% of what we hear, 5% of what we see, 15% of what we taste and 35% of what we smell..
>
> (The Rockefeller University, 2004)

Our sense of smell is the strongest of the five senses. Olfaction is the most ancient and evolved of our senses and, from a retail design perspective, it can play a key role in creating memorable experiences and driving sales (Mood Media, 2023).

Our emotions and memories are housed on the same side of the brain where scents are processed, forging a deep-seated connection between fragrance, emotion and recall. As adults, we are capable of distinguishing an astounding 10,000 different odours, our bodies continually renewing scent neurons to keep our olfactory systems sharp and responsive (Walsh, 2014). Unlike our other senses, the journey of scent is immediate, bypassing central processing to touch multiple parts of the brain at once (Keenan, 2021).

About 75% of our daily emotions are triggered by smell and, because of this, people are 100 times more likely to remember something they smell over something they hear, see or touch (Mood Media, 2023). Visual recall of images tends to fade to around 50% after three months. In contrast, humans can remember smells with 65% accuracy even after a year (Keenan, 2021). This powerful recall ability allows brands and retailers to form emotional bonds with customers through purposeful scents, including the following benefits:

- *Linking memory and emotion:* Memorable scents encourage customers to recall a store.
- *Communicating value and driving sales:* Customers are inclined to spend more in a store that smells good.
- *Building brand loyalty and image:* The right scent featured in a store builds a powerful, long-lasting association with it and communicates the brand identity.

Scent retailing involves the careful selection and placement of fragrances at key customer touchpoints, creating a potent, enduring association with a store and conveying a brand identity. Two studies carried out by Rutgers University researchers (Morrin, 2003) set out to see if ambient scent could improve memory for branded products and, interestingly, the results were the same. They found that ambient scent used by retailers in their stores, including those reminiscent of walks through fields of plants and flowers, especially lavender and vanilla, improved shoppers' memories of both familiar and unfamiliar brands (Frame, 2023b). A similar study by Nike showed that customers were 84% more likely to buy shoes in a scented environment versus a non-scented environment. They were also willing to pay 10% to 20% more in scented environments for products they wanted (Keenan, 2021).

The persuasive influence of scents goes beyond simple purchasing decisions. They have been empirically demonstrated to entice customers to linger longer in retail spaces, enhancing their browsing experience. In addition, smell positively influences the perceived quality of goods, fostering a sense of warmth and familiarity that resonates with customers (Sanfilippo, 2023).

Thematic scenting has become a key facet of sensory experiences within retail environments, with carefully curated fragrances enhancing the ambience of a space and enhancing the specific products displayed (Herz, 2009). For example, Bloomingdale's infuses its swimwear department with the tropical scent of coconut and its infant clothing section with the comforting smell of baby powder (Sanfilippo, 2023).

Many brands have crafted a signature fragrance that is employed as a subtle yet influential ambient scent in stores. The key lies in ensuring the aroma accurately embodies their brand, store and product offerings, creating an unforgettable sensory experience for consumers. For example, at the end of 2022, Fendi reopened its renovated boutique in the Dubai Mall with a style reminiscent of the brand's Roman headquarters, Palazzo della Civiltà Italiana. It is built on two floors with three main rooms, each of them inspired by a gemstone. They created a scent designed exclusively for each room, which is designed to emotionally match the design – lines, colours, lighting, music, patterns and materials – of each area (Business of Fashion, 2023).

As the fragrance industry moves towards more sustainable practices, there is a notable shift towards the development of sustainable scent identities, using biotechnology and new extraction methods to reuse waste products. One example was in 2020, when Benetton presented its "B-Green" project – a new environmentally friendly store format which was characterised by the use of innovative, recycled materials, with the transformation of the shop windows into digital displays and an increased focus on energy efficiency. Integra Fragrances developed a special scent identity called Visionary Spirit, which is environmentally conscious. It is vegan, created using natural ingredients from ethical and responsible sources, raw materials obtained by upcycling natural, biological waste as well as essential oils extracted from plants with antimicrobial properties (Business of Fashion, 2023).

Within retail experiences, it's interesting to consider how turning down the volume on other sensory cues can heighten others; for example, the perfume brand Curionoir's flagship in Auckland is both dark and immersive by design – it limits the senses of sight and touch while heightening olfaction (Wilson, 2022). Similarly, the Australian skincare brand Aesop has introduced new infusion chamber style 'Sensorium' rooms where shoppers are invited to infuse a piece of clothing with an Aesop scent. To create a sense of exclusivity, the room is only revealed if store assistants consider the visitor a 'fragrance fanatic' (Baron, 2023a) (see also Chapter 8 for the Aesop case study).

Auditory experiences

In the dynamic world of fashion retail, sound is an often-underestimated tool that can profoundly shape consumer experiences. It's not simply about the auditory element; it's about the immersive soundscape that can evoke emotions, inspire purchases and create memorable experiences.

At the heart of sensorial retail, sound occupies a unique position. It is omnipresent, yet subtle, forming an ambient background that often goes unnoticed. Its absence can leave a space feeling empty or disconnected, while its careful curation can create an engaging atmosphere that aligns with a brand's identity and value. In retail design, the strategic application of sound can help narrate a brand's story and deliver a cohesive, sensory experience. From the gentle hum of activity that suggests a lively and welcoming environment, to the carefully selected playlist that reflects a brand's personality, sound can be leveraged to express a brand's identity and foster a deep connection with customers.

The use of sound within a retail environment can also elevate the associations of the brand with their overall proposition, often subliminally from a CX perspective. For example, within the Hunter flagship store on Regent Street in London (2014) within each of the fitting rooms the gentle sound of birdsong can be heard, reminding people of their connections with nature, even on a busy bustling street in the heart of the city. Similarly, ON running in New York (2021) infuses their fitting rooms with the sound and smell of the Swiss Alps, psychologically transporting people far away as they try on their products.

Furthermore, sound can direct and influence consumer behaviour. Research has shown that the tempo, volume and type of in-store music can impact shopping speed, time spent in-store and even purchasing decisions. For example, in 1982, researcher Robert Milliman also found that "the tempo of instrumental background music can significantly influence both the pace of in-store traffic flow and the daily gross sales volume purchased by customers" (Anderson, 2022). Therefore, it's crucial for designers and marketing directors to understand the psychological and behavioural implications of sound and use it as a strategic tool in retail spaces.

The rise of technology has opened up a new frontier in the use of sound. Retailers now possess the capability to create potent sonic experiences that transcend mere music, harnessing innovative audio technologies, creating and implementing bespoke soundscapes broadcasted via a multichannel audio system, generating a sound environment that engulfs shoppers entirely. This kind of immersive audio allows retailers to tailor experiences to distinct zones within the store. For example, the progressive and sustainability-focused fashion brand Pangaia's pop-up store at The Grove in Los Angeles (2022) provided a multisensory experience that fused together audio and visual cues that fostered a deeper connection with nature and the brand's ethos. Through the use of Spatial audio software, they created sonic landscapes that teased out the different sounds of a forest based on in-depth research into the area's local species and weather. Visitors were transported to a lush forest inspired by the coastal coniferous woodland biomes of Northern California. The soundscape evolved as the day went on to mimic the natural progression of the forest. As an added layer of the sensory experience, the landscape was further brought to life through smells of greenery, wet soil and moss, a custom blend created to smell like the forest (Alexis, 2022).

In conclusion, sound is a powerful element in sensorial retail experiences. As retailers and designers, there's a golden opportunity to craft engaging, emotionally resonant soundscapes that can enhance brand perception, increase customer engagement and ultimately drive sales.

Tactile sensoriums

Touch and tactility is the third most important sense in delivering experience and it could be argued that in the past it has often been overlooked as there are not many examples of store design concepts that focus on how touch and tactility will enhance the overall experience, beyond the product itself.

We first began to witness this trend gaining momentum within interior design in our homes. A key trend in interior design is associated with the use of textures, materials and finishes that are as pleasing to touch as they are to look at, creating what the interior design expert Michelle Ogundehin describes as "surfaces that thrill our fingertips and tempt our toes" (2019).

During the London Design Festival in 2020, British designer Tom Dixon transformed his headquarters in Coal Drops Yard, London, into a multisensory lab. Playfully titled 'Touchy Smelly Feely Noisy Tasty', the installation took visitors on a journey through the senses in a series of talks and workshops, designed to heighten each of the senses in turn. In the 'Touchy Feely' arch in the shop, Tom Dixon's interior architecture facility, Design Research Studio, partnered with men's care brand Harry's to create a razor bar that drew on the sensory tactility of shaving (Stanley, 2020).

Following the wave of touch-free/contactless retail elements brought about by the pandemic, we are witnessing a rise in retail environments that *Frame* magazine playfully describes as "museums of touch" whereby tactility, materiality and light play leading roles (Frame, 2023b). Here, these store concepts are constructed from materials that are designed to invite touch and exploration. Taking this idea to the very extreme, fashion brand Balenciaga transformed its Mount Street store in London. Embracing a maximalist aesthetic, the brand enveloped the interior space in vibrant pink faux fur to introduce its Le Cagole collection. The entire interior, including temporary metal fixtures, walls and floors, was wrapped in vibrant fur, creating a cohesive and visually captivating experience for all who entered (Parkes, 2022a).

Inviting tactile sensory engagement and encouraging visitors to lounge, browse and feel at home, the design of the Jacquemus boutiques in London and Paris is a testament to the transformative power of design where the material is not an afterthought but the guide. Drawing from the brand's origins in the south of France, the design studio AMO aimed to capture the atmosphere of Jacquemus' native Provence through the materiality of the spaces (Pintos, 2022).

Illustrating how the allure of texture and tactility can also be applied architecturally to the fascia of the store, the glowing facade of the Dior Femme store, the Place Vendôme mall in Lusail, Qatar, stands 72 feet tall (22 metres tall) with undulating fins. Paying homage to the textile construction used throughout the fashion brand's garments, the design studio Aranda\Lasch describes the concept as

Inspired by how the brand's designers, starting with Monsieur Dior, use pleating to turn something soft into something geometric, we strove to transform the softness, movement, and luminous qualities of fabric into architectural materials. Like the pleats in a Dior dress swaying with the movement of the body, the facade tries to capture a fleeting moment with an architecture of unexpected lightness.

(Eberhardt, 2023)

As brands and retailers continue to consider how to differentiate their CX it's likely that we will see further innovation in this area in the near future, exploring ways to embed scent, sound and tactility into retail strategies to increase engagement.

Restorative retailing: placing well-being at the heart of CX

This section considers the rise of restorative retailing, as the worlds of fashion and well-being continue to converge. Placing a particular focus on the rise of biophilic design principles within fashion retailing, exploring how the CX is evolving to meet consumers' desire for experiences that are slow and considered.

Here we also consider how fashion retailers are adapting to the need to support the mental health of their customers, highlighting innovative advances in CX designed to boost mood and provide a safe space for open conversations and support.

The shift towards holistic wellness retailing

The Global Wellness Institute predicts the wellness economy to reach nearly USD 7 trillion in 2025 (2023). Health and wellness has been a top consumer priority in recent years, and, as a result of the pandemic, its value is even greater.

The perimeters of wellness continue to expand, as our perceptions and understanding evolve at a rapid rate. There is potential to embed health and wellness-centric thinking into every aspect of retail – from the environment and customer journey to the product and service offer. Brands and retailers are recognising that there is a clear opportunity to create retail experiences that redefine the concept of 'retail therapy' – transforming it for a new era of emotion-centric and mood-boosting retail.

> Today's shoppers crave out-of-home, in-person experiences as a form of self-care. For these consumers, experiences beat products.
>
> (Retail Dive, 2023)

The rise of 'care culture'

> People will seek products, services and environments that help them take better care of each other, themselves and their belongings, and they will adopt flexi lifestyles to prioritise this.
>
> (WGSN, 2022)

The global pandemic and economic crisis that followed naturally brought the importance of care within our communities into sharp focus and a whole host of new consumer needs, behaviours and priorities have emerged. Caring for ourselves, our communities and our planet is sparking design innovation throughout the world as brands and retailers of every size and scale seek to promote a nurturing sense of well-being and inclusivity. Within their report *Switching to Survival Mode* (Shepherd, 2020) The Future Collective highlights those brands and retailers who, since the global pandemic, have shifted their focus towards helping consumers in more supportive ways, demonstrating how meaningful and authentic action is becoming a core brand differentiator. Highlights within this report detail how progressive brands such as Nike, Starbucks and John Lewis are placing inclusivity and ethics at the very heart of their offer. Launching community-centric services and fostering and nurturing caring communities whereby kindness is truly king.

We are witnessing a growing number of brands and retailers launching simple products and solutions that empower people to make a positive difference in people's lives.

Equally, a host of new retail design initiatives from high street retailers such as Boots and Holland and Barrett are providing services once only offered by the medical profession, along with experiences originally reserved for spas and hospitality. All this is serving to normalise subjects once regarded as taboo, and open up conversations geared towards the greater good.

Restorative experiences

Having lived through one of the most challenging times in recent years, it's perhaps not surprising that our desire for calming, restorative experiences is greater than ever before. A growing number of brands are creating an inner-city oasis with spa-inspired palettes of neutrals and curved walls and softened shapes that create cocoon-like experiences, evoking the feeling of protection and warmth.

For example, offering shoppers much-needed soothing solace, the ToSummer flagship in Beijing, designed by F.O.G. Architecture, experiments with aesthetic opposites to build a 'modern cave' for aromatherapy. Juxtaposing what the designers describe as "warmth and calmness, coarseness and delicacy, hardness and softness, control and intuition, natural and artificial", ToSummer's first physical shop fully draws consumers in through the senses. "We chose not to directly create the natural appearance of caves but, instead, present the characteristic elements of material textures to inspire the sensory experience" (Parkes, 2021) (see also Chapter 8 for the ToSummer case study).

Slowing it down

The need for slower retail experiences, with limited distractions, feels especially relevant as we adjust to our frenetic post-pandemic lives. We're noting a rise in retail experiences that are designed to intentionally slow the pace down and encourage consumers to shop in a more mindful and considered way.

For example, offering an antidote to the often chaotic in-store beauty shopping experience, Say Architects has given life to the Chinese beauty brand STEPS' first physical store in Hangzhou (see Figure 5.1). The creative journey started with a simple question: "Why should the purchase of beauty products be confined to the bustling, influencer-driven retail spaces, rather than a serene space that allows customers to relish the selection and purchasing process, much like choosing a book?" (Shuangyu, 2021).

With a nostalgic nod to simpler times, when shopping was a more relaxed experience, before the rise of e-commerce, Say Architects aimed to recapture this spirit in their design and slow the pace down for shoppers. Helping customers to find a moment of tranquillity, the design embraces a 'Beauty Book Layout' concept, with comfort, softness, elegance and slowness being the central themes (Shuangyu, 2021).

Contemplation spaces

Contemplation spaces and stores offer moments of quiet respite, deliberately creating store experiences that provide space for reflection. Key examples include The reMarkable store in Oslo (see Figure 5.2), described by the designer Snøhetta as "a better place to think". The Norwegian tech company provides a holistic retail experience that carefully

Figure 5.1 STEPS, Hangzhou.

Source: Reprinted by permission of ©say architects and ©Wang Minjie (photographer).

Figure 5.2 The reMarkable Store, Oslo.

Source: Reprinted by permission Snøhetta and ©Calle Huth (photographer).

blends the analogue and digital sphere. In the store, reMarkable's latest product range can be experienced in an environment that allows visitors to delve into a universe that fosters focused thinking (Andreas, 2021).

Biophilic retreats

According to the World Health Organization, over 50% of the world's population lives in urban areas and that number is expected to rise to 7 in 10 by 2050 (2023). For decades, researchers have demonstrated that incorporating elements of nature into commercial environments can have a positive impact on consumer attitudes and activities (Frame, 2023c). The environments we surround ourselves with have the power to nurture, inspire and help us flourish.

Today, there is a conscious shift towards the creation of healthier, more sustainable retail environments. In particular, there is a rise in the well-being properties associated with the principles of biophilic design. As a term, 'biophilia' comes from Greek and means a love of nature. Biophilic designs therefore are those that connect people to nature and natural processes, helping people act in more productive ways.

The term was popularised in the 1980s by an American biologist named Edward Wilson (1990), whose concern was that increasing urbanisation was leaving people disconnected from the natural world. In his book *Biophilia*, he argues that humans have an innate and evolutionary based affinity with nature and defined the term as referring to the connections that human beings subconsciously seek in the rest of life.

It is widely acknowledged that bringing biophilia into urban spaces can induce positive feelings. According to a paper that was published in the *Urban Forestry and Urban Greening Journal*, integrating green spaces into retail spaces attracts more potential customers, who appreciate the opportunity to shop in a soothing environment (Frame, 2023a).

> We are witnessing an uptick in the wellbeing properties associated with the principles of biophilic design. Urban flagships, malls and stores are featuring lush planting, greenscaping and organic forms and textures to help consumers stay connected to nature.
>
> (Shepherd, 2021)

Most recently, a growing number of fashion retailers are introducing biophilic design principles into their store designs. For example, the dominant feature of the multi-brand menswear boutique Leam in Rome is a large, verdant indoor garden installation encased in a cubical metal framework. Visitors can walk inside it or perch on marble blocks just outside. Similarly, Atelier Miss Lu, Shanghai, is filled with nature – plants and trees emerge from the ceiling, walls and floor. Examples such as these appear to be becoming increasingly untamed, as retailers fully embrace the beauty of nature in-store. No longer about just welcoming greenery in, biophilic design now is let nature run wild (Frame, 2023a). Designers including Shanghai-based studio Spacemen are now incorporating overgrown nature into retail interiors. The studio's store design for luxury leather brand Braun Büffel's Malaysian flagship store included a giant tree-like structure covered in moss, which dominates the middle of the store. It bursts from the floor and through the ceiling, alluding to "how it would grow out of a beaker in a mad scientist's lab towards natural light" (Spacemen founder Edward Tan, cited in Englefield, 2023).

Biophilic design principles are also being introduced to larger spaces, including department stores and shopping malls. For example, Aim Architecture has revamped the atrium of the Xintiandi shopping mall in Shanghai as a 'garden plaza'. It now features plants suspended from terraced balconies, masses of natural light and wooden benches (Frearson, 2021).

Adopting a similar approach, The Hyundai Seoul in South Korea has developed a retail concept that fully embraces nature, offering city dwellers a place to shop and wind down amidst lush greenery. As a result, the department store has dedicated almost half of its space to indoor landscaping, most notably Sounds Forest, a triple-height indoor park dotted with 30 trees, flower plants and grasses to meet up or relax in between shopping sprees. The standalone structure housing The Hyundai Seoul has been designed to allow natural light to permeate all floors above ground, reinforcing the sense of being in touch with nature. Another major feature which boldly signals the theme is the large Waterfall Garden on the ground floor, featuring a 12-metre (39 ft.) waterfall (Morris, 2022).

Another compelling and dynamic example of the shift towards the creation of green malls can be found in Shanghai's arts district, one of the world's busiest cities. Designed by Heatherwick Studio, 1000 Trees is an extraordinary construction featuring 1,000 structural columns throughout, which not only form a series of outdoor terraces, but also double as plinths for the thousands of trees and plants that cascade down its multiple levels. Thomas Heatherwick has said this breaks down the monolithic scale of a typical retail development into a multitude of human-scale spaces. This is echoed by Lisa Finlay, partner and Heatherwick Studio's group lead on the project: "We wanted to create a place that brings together nature, commerce and wellbeing" (Frame, 2023c).

We are also witnessing a growing number of brands and retailers recognising the potential to introduce greenery to the rooftops of the retail space. On a small scale, concepts such as FREITAG in Shanghai with its rooftop garden are leading the way (see Figure 5.3). Whereas on a much larger scale, in Singapore, the city state which has been a pioneer of green architecture in Asia, the City Hall district's Funan Mall has undergone extensive redevelopment that includes the addition of a rooftop urban farm, a cycling track and a seven-storey-high green wall.

However, the creation and maintenance of biophilic spaces can be expensive. Indoor plants require constant care, which entails heat regulation, proper exposure to light and a well-built irrigation system. Therefore, an increasingly popular option, which coincides with the rising prevalence of emerging technologies, is to mimic the outdoors within the confines of a retail environment (Frame, 2022).

Simulating nature

Many retailers are bringing simulated nature into their stores. A beautiful example of this direction can be seen in Glossier's Capitol Hill store in Seattle, USA, with its references to the Pacific Northwest's landscapes, focusing particularly on the world of fungi. A central Alice in Wonderland-esque moss and mushroom covered installation is mirrored by fern-coloured seating that mimics natural topographics found in Seattle, a city renowned for its forests and lakes.

In a dynamic shift, a number of interiors commissioned by various retailers throughout the world are embracing a fresh narrative where technology and nature are intertwined. This shift is captured in the striking displays of 3D-printed coral structures within the

Wow marketplace in Madrid, an artful design by External Reference. Another compelling example is Jacob Egeberg's aluminium-skinned sculpture at Rains in Paris, where a rocky formation symbolises the interplay between nature and the detritus of our contemporary lifestyle, connecting the interior of the rainwear lifestyle brand to its surroundings. The glossy finish of the geologic shape, which incorporates modern iconography in a tech-meets-nature tussle, reflects the ever-changing light from the aperture above (Frame, 2022).

Mental health and well-being hubs

> More than 1 billion people worldwide have a form of mental disorder.
> (World Health Organization, 2023)

Mental health is a global crisis and younger generations in particular are believed to be more stressed, self-conscious and anxious than at any time in our history (Keltner, 2023). According to Wunderman Thompson Intelligence, "More than half of Generation Z and parents with children under 18 tell us they are too stressed with daily life to think about seeking experiences that are all about fun" (2023).

The global economic crisis is a key source of anxiety as concerns loom large in many people's minds. A survey by the British Association for Counselling and Psychotherapy revealed that 66% of therapists in the UK said that the cost-of-living crisis is impacting people's mental health but, despite their increasing need for help, 47% reported patients cancelling their sessions because they could no longer afford them (Accenture, 2022). Equally, the COVID-19 pandemic exposed millions to the impacts of illness, grief, isolation and sensory deprivation (Wunderman Thompson Intelligence, 2023). The way people are thinking about their health and well-being is evolving, moving beyond the physical to encompass mental, emotional, spiritual and social health. The relentless pursuit of self-improvement is giving way to self-transformation and healing, with the pandemic having acted as a catalyst for personal growth. Every business is arguably now a health business (Shepherd, 2021).

> 76% of people say that mental health and physical health are equally important. This reprioritisation means that every brand needs to ideate how to integrate wellness into 2023's products, services, experiences, campaigns and more.
> (TrendWatching, 2023)

Against this backdrop it's understandable that supporting mental and emotional health has become a particular focus for brands and retailers of every size and scale. The subsequent sections explore the different ways that retailers are helping to support their customers, using their physical retail environments and CX in ways previously never experienced.

Accessible therapy

In a bid to provide mental health support to their customers, enlightened brands are seeking to dispel the stigma and normalise the conversation surrounding mental health and encouraging people to talk about how they are feeling, providing non-judgemental safe spaces and sparking conversations about subjects that were previously thought of as taboo.

Figure 5.3 FREITAG, Shanghai.
Source: Reprinted by permission of FREITAG Media.

For example, the founders of SoulCycle have recently opened a social wellness club dedicated to fostering meaningful relationships called Peoplehood in New York (2023). During 60-minute guided conversations called Gathers, participants practise active listening. Each session includes an intention, thought-provoking prompts, de-stressing breathwork and feel-good music. Describing the inspiration behind the concept, the founder Elizabeth Cutler states: "In a world that's more digitally connected than ever, there's a human connection crisis and studies show healthy relationships are the number one way to improve our overall physical and mental health.... Peoplehood is not therapy, but it's certainly therapeutic and intended to complement people's portfolio of physical, mental and social health practices" (Whitby, 2023).

On the UK high street we have also witnessed CX such as Self Space open in Manchester and London (Jeffries, 2019), geared towards the provision of on-demand mental health and well-being therapy. Similarly, but on a temporary pop-up basis, Gymshark opened the doors to a pop-up barbershop, named Deload in London (2022). An innovative mental health initiative platform that encouraged young people to focus on their mental as well as their physical well-being, providing content, stories and advice from well-being experts and medical professionals, described as a 'non-judgemental safe space' for men to open up, offload and have a chat with professional mental health-trained barbers, while receiving a free trim. Deload's intention was to foster open dialogue, allowing for the sharing of thoughts and emotions often kept hidden. Deload hosted a series of panel discussions with representatives from Calm, Lions Barbers and Curfew Grooming.

With the aim to catalyse conversations that may otherwise feel challenging, these discussions also served as a platform to spread awareness of CALM's lifesaving work, especially crucial given that 84% of men in the UK are said to suppress their emotions (Fish, 2022).

Wellness hubs

Throughout the world, many of the most notable department stores are beginning to augment and enhance their offer to encompass well-being destinations and hubs. For example, in Paris, Galeries Lafayette has launched La Wellness Galerie, where private, extraordinary-looking 'care space' bubble chambers deliver treatments, including cryotherapy and nutritional coaching (Weil, 2022).

Similarly, the British luxury department store Selfridges launched The Feel Good Bar, a new permanent well-being destination at Selfridges London in 2022, dedicated to the discovery of feeling good. The bar is a place for visitors to explore more than 250 of the latest and best products in well-being innovation, ranging from gut health to hormones, the ultimate hangover cures and sleep hacking. The destination is anchored by a new energy-lifting bar concept brought by JENKI, introducing a menu of matcha and alternative drinks that reimagine drinking culture (Clark, 2022).

> The pandemic has placed wellbeing in the spotlight and accelerated the evolution of the wellbeing ecosystem. As a result, wellbeing is becoming ever more holistic and tech driven. People are re-evaluating what feeling good actually means and embracing new ideas. We want to help our customers to live brighter by offering experiences and solutions in a way that is non-conventional and future-thinking.
> (Sebastian Manes, Executive Buying and Merchandising Director at Selfridges, cited in Clark, 2022)

Further expanding their venture into health and well-being retailing, Selfridges launched a collaboration with Sensiks in 2022, unveiling a novel concept in immersive retail experience: the Psychedelic Store Therapy. This manifestation of self-care practices and innovative well-being was part of the store's 'Superself' series. The sensory reality pods, offering a unique blend of custom fragrances, infrared light, heat and sound, orchestrated a ten-minute voyage, almost psychedelic in its intensity, honouring the contemporary resurgence of psychedelic culture.

Similarly, on a larger scale, Pixel Artworks and Outernet, the immersive venue in London, unveiled an extraordinary experience called 'Room to Breathe'. Supported by Pixel Artworks, this 15-minute mindfulness session allowed visitors to explore stress management and regain control over daily pressures. Within a serene environment accompanied by soothing music by Matt Wilcock, participants immersed themselves in breathwork techniques (see Figure 5.4). This free experience not only provided relief but also contributed to breaking the stigma surrounding mental health. Pixel Artworks and Outernet successfully transported attendees to a realm of tranquillity where the power of breath was harnessed and cherished (Barker, 2022).

The notion of well-being is also remodelling the future of malls. As wellness takes centre stage in future-facing retail concepts, new expressions of biophilia and community-driven design are transforming malls and mixed-use developments (Frame, 2023c).

People today are seeking more than just functional retail. With health and wellness now among the top design priorities in the built environment, shoppers desire commercial spaces that promote emotional, physical and social benefits too. This perspective is driving malls and mixed-use developments forward, as seen by rising numbers of ambitious, sprawling retail projects that find subtle yet immersive ways to tap into the USD 1.5 trillion global wellness economy, blurring the lines between commerce and community (Frame, 2023c).

To alleviate shopping fatigue and activate a sense of community, Clou Architects 'planted' an immersive jungle garden inside Qingdao's Future City Mall, which provides space for both respite and socialising (see Figure 5.5). When designing the fourth-floor atrium, Clou Architects looked to the natural world to create an alluring public forum.

Figure 5.4 Room to Breathe, Pixel Artworks and Outernet, London.
Source: Reprinted by permission of Pixel Artworks.

Figure 5.5 Future City Mall, Qingdao, China.

Source: Reprinted by permission of © Clou Architects.

The idea was to craft a community hub by energising the retail and dining areas, drawing people to the upper levels. The solution lay in planting a jungle-like garden, which creates a striking visual contrast with the bright red chosen as the interior's dominant colour (Shuangyu, 2022).

Much of this is in response to the steady decline of retail malls globally, which picked up pace amid the pandemic. In the US, Placer.ai found that foot traffic in shopping malls continued to fall from 2019 to 2022, with a 7% drop for indoor malls and a 9% decrease for outlet malls. It follows that nature connectedness and social elements are breathing new life into otherwise ailing retail formats, striking the right balance between stimulating and restorative features (Frame, 2023c).

In summary, there is clearly a great deal of potential for CX and retail environments to be designed with the well-being of people front of mind. It's likely that we will witness further innovation in the near future, as retail designers experiment with ways to create spaces that have a positive impact on those who visit, emotionally and physically.

Conclusions and reflections for human-centric experiences

Adopting a human-centric approach to retail design and CX ignites a great deal of innovative conceptual thinking.

This chapter has highlighted many inspirational examples and it's interesting to note that, from a global perspective, brands and retailers in Asia are currently leading the way. Particularly in their adoption of the principles of biophilic design. Equally, it's clear that the creation of visceral and human-centric CX has been adopted the most by luxury brands and retailers, suggesting that in the near future we may well see similar approaches begin to trickle down into the mass market.

Another observation within this chapter is that many of the most progressive approaches are currently found within beauty retailing, providing a rich source of inspiration for fashion brands to follow suit in the future.

Whether building upon and elevating the CX within an existing destination, or creating an entirely new experience proposition, brands and retailers must think imaginatively to compete in today's complex and competitive fashion retailing landscape. In terms of retail formats, both temporary and permanent concepts will need to have greater levels of agility, to enable concepts to flex, change and evolve over time. Thinking far beyond the traditional four walls of the store, portable or touring brand experiences are likely to rise in popularity in the near future, appealing to the consumer's appetite for joyful and awe-inspiring moments of unexpected surprise and serendipity.

The blending of retail formats with hospitality is likely to further strengthen as a key means of fostering and nurturing emotional and human-to-human connection in physical bricks-and-mortar fashion retailing experiences. It's also likely that we will continue to see a blurring of the lines between retail store, art gallery and culture house, as fashion retailers continue to experiment at the intersection of commerce and culture.

The skills and experience that retail designers and strategists require to create truly outstanding CX in fashion retailing extend beyond spatial design to encompass an understanding of human psychology too. In the future, there will be a need to co-create and collaborate together with experts in consumer psychology and also those who understand the very latest advances in technologies.

From a technological perspective, we are likely to continue to see a valuable coalescence of physical and digital CX in fashion retailing, combining interactive displays, virtual and AR, alongside analogue, tactile and hands-on product trial (see Chapter 1 on the ascendance of phygitality and Chapter 6 for phygital case studies).

> New types of activities, often powered by technology, should spark an additional €60 billion to €120 billion in sales by 2030, from sources such as the metaverse and brand-related media content.
>
> (D'Arpizio et al., 2023)

Immersive technology is driving retail towards new frontiers at speed. Mixed reality, sensory technologies and high-impact visuals are engaging the consumer like never before (Wunderman Thompson Intelligence, 2023).

In this chapter we have focused on the physical CX in-store. It would be interesting to apply the same themes and consider how digital CX are evolving to become more visceral and human-centric too. In particular, exploring how global fashion retailers are introducing CX within the metaverse and evaluating where these digital experiences are currently falling short and what the future opportunities are for brands to explore.

Perhaps one of the most important technological advances to explore within this context isAI. The era of augmentation, often termed as industry 5.0, will disrupt the market at a much faster pace. AI will play a significant role in augmenting CX and traditional service models (Parry, 2023).

(See also Chapter 2 on hyper-personalised experiences.)

> There is a $275 billion generative AI opportunity for luxury. The coming months will likely see a surge in AI integration across more facets of the luxury sector, heralding an era that respects the tradition of craftsmanship while embracing the boundless possibilities of digital artistry. The fashion world is poised for an exciting transformation.
> (The Future of Generative AI Report, cited in *Jing Daily*, 2023)

As the world becomes more reliant on technology, retailers must find the perfect balance between art and science, leveraging AI's benefits in the most valuable way, while not losing sight of the human touch. A clear opportunity for further research would be to consider how AI can be embraced to enable visceral and human-centric experiences to become even further elevated.

Chapter questions

1   Reflect on the design of customer experiences that are designed to purposefully evoke an emotional response and connection, joyful experiences, awe-inspiring encounters and serendipity and discovery.

- What kind of emotion do you think is the most effective and relevant to fashion retailing, and why?
- Which fashion brands do you think should explore this route, and why?
- Is this move towards the creation of joyful experiences simply a reflection of the challenging times we are living in or an approach that will continue to be popular for years to come? Consider and discuss.
- What role do you believe technology should play in the design of fashion retailing environments that evoke an emotional connection?

2   Reflect on the creation of customer experiences that are designed to engage all of the senses, in particular, smell, sound and touch.

- Which sense do you personally feel has the greatest impact on your overall experience in-store? Why is that?
- Which fashion retailers can you think of that have found innovative and effective ways to engage the senses within the retail experience? Provide examples and evidence to support.
- How does the size and scale of the store impact on how much the experience can engage the senses?
- How does the location of the store/retail experience impact on the approach to customer experience design? For example, rural high street versus inner city.

3   Consider the design of customer experiences that are restorative.

- Do you agree that the design of a fashion retailing experience can have an impact on your mood and overall sense of well-being? Discuss and support your perspectives.
- Do you consider the adoption of biophilic design principles in retail design to be a fad or a trend, or an enduring shift that will last for the long-term? Why?
- How important do you believe that designing for inclusivity and difference will be in fashion retailing in the years to come? Support with evidence.

References

Accenture. (2022) *Life trends report*. [Online] [Accessed 10th October 2023] https://www.accenture.com/us-en/insights/song/accenture-life-trends

Alexander, B. and Nobbs, K. (2016) 'Chapter 17: Multi-sensory fashion retail experiences: The impact of sound, smell, sight and touch on consumer-based brand equity,' in Vecchi, A. and Buckley, C. (eds.) *Handbook of research on global fashion management and merchandising*. IGI Global, pp. 420–443. ISBN 9781522501107.

Alexis, C. (2022) *Pangaia opens its first physical store in Los Angeles at The Grove*. Fashion Network. [Online] [Accessed 10th October 2023] https://www.fashionnetwork.com/news/Pangaia-opens-its-first-physical-store-in-los-angeles-at-the-grove,1438507.html

Anderson, T. (2022) *Immersive audio transforms the retail experience at the speed of sound*. Total Retail. [Online] [Accessed 10th October 2023] https://www.mytotalretail.com/article/immersive-audio-transforms-the-retail-experience-at-the-speed-of-sound/

Andreas. (2021) *Oslo: Remarkable pop-up store*. [Online] [Accessed 10th October 2023] https://superfuture.com/2021/05/new-shops/oslo-remarkable-pop-up-store/

Bailey, J. (2023) *Tiffany & Co: The most famous luxury retail space in the world is about to reopen its doors*. Grazia Magazine. [Online] [Accessed 10th October 2023] https://graziamagazine.com/articles/tiffany-and-co-fifth-avenue-boutique-reopening/

Barker, S. (2022) *This immersive mindfulness experience wants to give Londoners some 'Room To Breathe'*. Secret London. [Online] [Accessed 10th October 2023] https://secretldn.com/room-to-breathe/

Baron, K. (2023a) *Brand spaces*. Stylus. [Online] [Accessed 10th October 2023] https://stylus.com/retail-brand-comms/brand-spaces-2023-24-9-key-trends

Baron, K. (2023b) *Predictions for a Permacrisis: Brand strategies and big ideas for 2023*. Forbes. [Online] [Accessed 10th October 2023] https://www.forbes.com/sites/katiebaron/2023/01/03/predictions-for-a-permacrisis-brand-strategies--big-ideas-for-2023/

Barr, V. and Broudy, C. (1986) *Designing to sell*. New York: McGraw-Hill.

Business of Fashion (2023) *How in-store fragrances positively impact brand value*. [Online] [Accessed 10th October 2023] https://www.businessoffashion.com/articles/retail/how-in-store-fragrances-impact-brand-value-integra-fragrances-lorenzo-cotti-interview/#:~:text=A%20positive%20mood%20can%20increase,and%20communication%20tool%20for%20brands.

Clark, T. (2022) *Selfridges launches new destinations to supercharge sex and sleep wellbeing*. Retail Focus. [Online] [Accessed 10th October 2023] https://retail-focus.co.uk/selfridges-launches-new-destinations-to-supercharge-sex-and-sleep-wellbeing/#:~:text=The%20long%2Dterm%20addition%20of,with%20greater%20clarity%20and%20transparency.

D'Arpizio, C., Levato, F., Prete, F. and Montgolfier, J. (2023) *Renaissance in uncertainty: Luxury builds on its rebound*. Bain & Company. [Online] [Accessed 10th October 2023] https://www.bain.com/insights/renaissance-in-uncertainty-luxury-builds-on-its-rebound/

Danziger, P.N. (2019) *Showfields imagines A new kind of department store combining retail with theater*. Forbes. [Online] [Accessed 10th October 2023] https://www.forbes.com/sites/pamdanziger/2019/09/20/showfields-imagines-a-new-kind-of-department-store-combining-retail-with-theater/?sh=3af4aa826f1b

Danziger, P.N. (2020) *Neighborhood goods proves its new department store model works, as Macy's And JCPenney Flounder*. Forbes. [Online] [Accessed 10th October 2023] https://www.forbes.com/sites/pamdanziger/2020/07/05/neighborhood-goods-proves-its-new-department-store-model-works-as-macys-and-jcpenney-flounder/

Deloitte. (2019) *The retail renaissance: The birth of human centric retail report*. [Online] [Accessed 10th October 2023] https://www.deloittedigital.com/content/dam/deloittedigital/us/documents/offerings/offerings-20190118-cm-pdf.pdf

Diderich, J. (2022) *Experience matters: As metaverse looms, retailers get immersive.* WWD. [Online] [Accessed 10th October 2023] https://wwd.com/business-news/retail/retail-immersive-experiences-metaverse-nike-samaritaine-selfridges-1235167472/

Dreyfuss, H. (1955/2012) *Designing for people.* New York: Simon & Schuster.

Eberhardt, E. (2023) *Aranda\Lasch creates glowing facade with undulating fins for Dior in Qatar.* Dezeen. [Online] [Accessed 10th October 2023] https://www.dezeen.com/2023/10/16/aranda-lasch-glowing-facade-undulating-fins-dior/

Englefield, J. (2023) *Biophilic design informs "otherworldly" moss-covered installation at luxury bag store.* Dezeen. [Online] [Accessed 10th October 2023] https://www.dezeen.com/2023/01/19/biophilic-design-moss-installation-bag-store-braun-buffel/

Fast Company. (2022) *What is human-centered design?* [Online] [Accessed 10th October 2023] https://www.fastcompany.com/90772846/human-centered-design#:~:text=Human%2Dcentered%20design%20offers%20a,problem%2Dsolving%20and%20product%20development.

Fish, I. (2022) *Gymshark opens 'safe space' barbershop.* Drapers. [Online] [Accessed 10th October 2023] https://www.drapersonline.com/news/gymshark-opens-safe-space-barbershop

Frame. (2022) *The next space,* Issue 148. The Netherlands: Frame Publishers.

Frame. (2023a) *Is fake nature better than no nature in retail spaces?* [Online] [Accessed 10th October 2023] https://frameweb.com/article/retail/is-fake-nature-better-than-no-nature-in-retail-spaces

Frame. (2023b) *What's 'Sensory Reality', and why is it key to carving out care-forward spaces?* [Online] [Accessed 10th October 2023] https://frameweb.com/article/whats-sensory-reality-and-why-is-it-key-to-carving-out-care-forward-spaces

Frame. (2023c) *How wellbeing is remodelling the malls of the future.* [Online] [Accessed 10th October 2023] https://frameweb.com/article/retail/how-wellbeing-is-remodelling-the-malls-of-the-future

Frame. (2023d) *Freitag leads in transparent retail design. It's new Shanghai store proves why.* [Online] [Accessed 10th October 2023] https://frameweb.com/article/retail/freitag-leads-in-transparent-retail-design-its-new-shanghai-store-proves-why

Frearson, A. (2021) *AIM Architecture turns shopping mall atrium into plant-filled plaza.* Dezeen. [Online] [Accessed 10th October 2023] https://www.dezeen.com/2021/05/03/aim-architecture-xintiandi-shopping-mall-atrium-plants/

Global Wellness Institute. (2023) *Wellness economy statistics and facts.* [Online] [Accessed 10th October 2023] https://globalwellnessinstitute.org/press-room/statistics-and-facts/

Herz, R.S. (2009) *The emotional, cognitive, and biological basics of olfaction.* New York: Routledge.

HighSnobiety (2021) *The immunized consumer report.* [Online] [Accessed 10th October 2023] https://www.highsnobiety.com/p/hype-generation-quarantine/

Jeffries, S. (2019) *Can going to therapy become as straightforward as going to the gym?* The Guardian. [Online] [Accessed 10th October 2023] https://www.theguardian.com/lifeandstyle/2019/apr/15/can-going-to-therapy-become-as-straightforward-as-going-to-the-gym

Jing Daily. (2023) *The future of generative AI report.* [Online] [Accessed 10th October 2023] https://jingdaily.com/downloads/how-luxury-brands-stay-ahead-with-new-technologies-planning-for-the-future/

Job, H. (2022) *SPACE 10: What is good design?* Talk at design for better event, part of London Design Festival, London.

Keenan, M. (2021) *How scent marketing works for retail businesses.* Shopify. [Online] [Accessed 10th October 2023] https://www.shopify.com/uk/retail/scent-marketing

Kelley, T. (2001) *The art of innovation (IDEO).* New York: Harper Collins Business.

Keltner, D. (2023) *Awe: The transformative power of everyday wonder.* London: Penguin.

Keh, P. (2022) *Nike's chief design officer John Hoke on the future of retail design.* Wallpaper. [Online] [Accessed 10th October] https://www.wallpaper.com/fashion/nike-house-of-innovation-002-paris-john-hoke-interview

Lindstrom, M. (2005) *Brand senses.* New York: Free Press.

Magids, S. and Zorfas, A. (2015) *The new science of customer emotions.* Harvard Business Review. [Online] [Accessed 10th October 2023] https://hbr.org/2015/11/the-new-science-of-customer-emotions#:~:text=Although%20customers%20exhibit%20increasing%20connection,who%20are%20just%20highly%20satisfied

Mood Media (2023) *Scent marketing research.* [Online] [Accessed 10 October 2023] https://us.moodmedia.com/scent/scent-research/

Morrin, M. (2003) *Does it make sense to use scents to enhance brand memory? Research with Rutgers.* Sage Journals. [Online] [Accessed 10th October] https://journals.sagepub.com/doi/abs/10.1509/jmkr.40.1.10.19128

Morris, A. (2022) *Burdifilek creates "zen-like ambience" in Seoul shopping mall.* Dezeen. [Online] [Accessed 10th October] https://www.dezeen.com/2022/05/17/burdifilek-hyundai-seoul-shopping-centre-interior/

Ogundehin, M. (2019) *Tactility, imperfection and a pale flush of colour: Interior design trends for 2019.* Dezeen. [Online] [Accessed 10th October 2023] https://www.dezeen.com/2019/01/11/interior-design-trend-report-2019-michelle-ogundehin-soft-scandi/

Parkes, J. (2021) *FOG Architecture creates "modern cave" for ToSummer's Beijing store.* Dezeen. [Online] [Accessed 10th October 2023] https://www.dezeen.com/2021/06/23/fog-architecture-tosummer-store-beijing-china/

Parkes, J. (2022a) *Balenciaga wraps London store in pink faux fur to celebrate its Le Cagole "it-bag".* Dezeen. [Online] [Accessed 10th October 2023] https://www.dezeen.com/2022/04/28/balenciaga-store-pink-faux-fur-celebrate-le-cagole-it-bag/

Parkes, J. (2022b) *Jacquemus creates surrealist interpretation of his own bathroom for Selfridges pop-up.* Dezeen. [Online] [Accessed 10th October 2023] https://www.dezeen.com/2022/05/11/jacquemus-le-bleu-selfridges-retail-interiors/

Parry, M. (2023) *Industry 5.0: The age of augmentation.* The Future Collective. [Online] [Accessed 10th October 2023] https://future-collective.co.uk/forethought/industry-50-the-human-centric-revolution

Peek, S. (2023) *Steve jobs biography.* Business News Daily. [Online] [Accessed 10th October 2023] https://www.businessnewsdaily.com/4195-business-profile-steve-jobs.html

Pintos, P. (2022) *Jacquemus store selfridges London / AMO.* Arch Daily. [Online] [Accessed 10th October 2023] https://www.archdaily.com/990391/jacquemus-store-selfridges-london-amo

Retail Dive. (2023) *Understanding today's consumer and increasing their spend in 2023.* [Online] [Accessed 10th October 2023] https://www.retaildive.com/spons/understanding-todays-consumer-and-increasing-their-spend-in-2023/639680/

Rima, S.A. (2021) *Yinka Ilori builds colourful Lego launderette in east London for kids to play in.* Dezeen. [Online] [Accessed 10th October 2023] https://www.dezeen.com/2021/10/28/yinka-ilori-lego-launderette-of-dreams-east-london/

Rozario, K. (2023) *Coach airways may be a short-lived but valuable flight of fancy.* Forbes. [Online] [Accessed 10th October 2023] https://www.forbes.com/sites/kevinrozario/2023/07/30/coach-airways-may-be-a-short-lived-but-valuable-flight-of-fancy/?sh=3d48ccc1111f

Sanfilippo, M. (2023) *The smells that make shoppers spend more.* Business News Daily. [Online] [Accessed 10th October 2023] https://www.businessnewsdaily.com/3469-smells-shoppers-spend-more.html

Serafin, A. (2022) *Past meets present: Inside 30 Avenue Montaigne, Dior's new look Parisian flagship.* Wallpaper Magazine. [Online] [Accessed 10th October 2023] https://www.wallpaper.com/fashion/dior-30-avenue-montaigne-paris-store-museum

Shuangyu, H. (2021) *Steps flagship store / say architects.* Arch Daily. [Online] [Accessed 10th October 2023] https://www.archdaily.com/971548/steps-flagship-store-say-architects

Shuangyu, H. (2022). *Qingdao future city / CLOU architects.* Arch Daily. [Online] [Accessed 10th October 2023] https://www.archdaily.com/996616/qingdao-future-city-clou-architects#:~:text=

A%2520circular%2520bridge%2520on%2520the,customers%2520to%2520linger%2520an
d%2520explore

Shepherd, K. (2020) *Switching to survival mode*. The Future Collective. Subscription only report, publicly unavailable.

Shepherd, K. (2021) *Design for Better report*. The Future Collective. Subscription only report, publicly unavailable.

Shepherd, K. (2021) *Perishable moments*. The Future Collective. [Online] [Accessed 10th October 2023] https://future-collective.co.uk/forethought/perishable-moments

Shepherd, K. and Mitchell, C. (2023) *Reframing Luxury report*. The Future Collective. [Online] [Accessed 10th October 2023] https://future-collective.co.uk/forethought/reframingluxury

Shepherd, K. and Parry, M. (2020) *Retail reset report*. The Future Collective. Subscription only report, publicly unavailable.

Shearsmith, T. (2022) *The Interview: Anya Hindmarch, The Industry*. Fashion. [Online] [Accessed 10th October 2023] https://www.theindustry.fashion/the-interview-anya-hindmarch/

Stanley, J. (2020) *Tom Dixon Announces "OCTAGON" Exhibition at London Headquarters*. Hypebeast. [Online] [Accessed 10th October 2023] https://hypebeast.com/2020/8/tom-dixon-octagon-exhibition-london-design-festival-details

Superfuture. (2021) *Oslo, The remarkable pop-up store*. [Online] [Accessed 10th October 2023] https://superfuture.com/2021/05/new-shops/oslo-remarkable-pop-up-store/#:~:text=Set%20in%20a%20clean%20and,of%20blue%20and%20concrete%20flooring.

The Rockefeller University. (2004) *Smell study*. [Online] [Accessed 10 October 2023] https://www.rockefeller.edu/research/vosshall-laboratory/current-projects/completed-projects/166747-smell-study/

TrendWatching. (2023) *Trend check report*. [Online] [Accessed 10th October 2023] https://www.trendwatching.com/2023-trend-check

Walsh, B. (2014) *Your nose can smell at least 1 Trillion scents*. Time Magazine. [Online] [Accessed 10th October 2023] https://time.com/32091/nose-trillion-scents/

Weil, J. (2022) *Galeries Lafayette opens mega wellness department*. WWD. [Online] [Accessed 10th October 2023] https://wwd.com/beauty-industry-news/beauty-features/galeries-lafayette-retail-opens-mega-wellness-department-1235248273/

Whitby, M. (2023) *SoulCycle founders launch Peoplehood social wellness club dedicated to fostering meaningful relationships*. Health Club Management. [Online] [Accessed 10th October 2023] https://www.healthclubmanagement.co.uk/health-club-management-news/SoulCycle-founders-launch-Peoplehood-social-wellness-club-dedicated-to-fostering-meaningful-relationships/350940

WGSN. (2022) *Future consumer 2024*. [Online] [Accessed 10th October 2023] https://mlp.wgsn.com/future-consumer-2024-download-en.html?utm_campaign=pspct

Wilson, C. (2022) *Sensory overload: Curio Noir opens flagship store in Auckland*. Wallpaper. [Online] [Accessed 10th October 2023] https://www.wallpaper.com/lifestyle/perfume-brand-curio-noir-opens-flagship-store-in-auckland

Wilson, E.O. (1990) *Biophilia*. Cambridge, MA: Harvard University Press.

World Economic Forum. (2023) *Global risks report*. [Online] [Accessed 10th October 2023] https://www.weforum.org/reports/global-risks-report-2023/

World Health Organization. (2023) *Urban health*. [Online] [Accessed 10th October 2023] https://www.who.int/health-topics/urban-health#tab=tab_1

Wunderman Thompson Intelligence (2021) *Future 100 report*. [Online] [Accessed 10th October 2023] https://www.wundermanthompson.com/insight/the-future-100-2021

Wunderman Thompson Intelligence (2022) *Future 100 report*. [Online] [Accessed 10th October 2023] https://www.wundermanthompson.com/insight/the-future-100-2022

Wunderman Thompson Intelligence. (2023) *The age of re-enchantment*. [Online] [Accessed 10th October 2023] https://www.wundermanthompson.com/insight/the-age-of-re-enchantment

Part 3

Retailer perspectives on retail customer experience

Global case studies showcasing customer experience excellence

Phygital customer experiences

6.1 Nike: exploring the relationship between DTC retail strategy and technology-enhanced customer experience

Rosemary Varley

Learning objectives

On completion of this case study, learners should be able to:

1   Identify the relevance of a DTC (direct-to-consumer) retail strategy for Nike in the era of omnichannel and multiple touchpoints for a brand.
2   Analyse the factors that contribute to Nike retaining competitive advantage by offering the best retail experience in its sector.
3   Evaluate technology-induced customer experiences (CX) in the case of Nike's (physical, digital and virtual) retail spaces.
4   Analyse the strategic fit between Nike's CX strategy and the technologies used to underpin it.
5   Identify the benefits and risks of a DTC retail strategy and assess its relationship to enhanced CX as a strategic imperative.

Introduction

Nike is a company that formidably demonstrates the power of branding. Listed as the most valuable brand in the global clothing and footwear sector (Euromonitor, 2023), and with one of the most recognised logos in the world, the company barely needs an introduction. Founded as a designer of running shoes, Nike's company report (Nike, 2022a:1) cites their business activity now as "the design, development and worldwide marketing of athletic footwear, apparel, equipment, accessories and services", while acknowledging that a large proportion of Nike footwear and clothes "are worn for casual or leisure purposes". Whether a Nike product is worn for sports participation or not, the company has never lost sight of product performance being one of the brand's central tenets and with that customer centricity as core to everything the brand does.

DOI: 10.4324/9781003378099-9

Although Nike does not manufacture any of the vast quantities of product that it sells, the company relies on a network of contracted suppliers to maintain the flow of the high-quality and innovative products that Nike designs. In 2022 Nike was supplied by 120 footwear factories and 270 clothing factories (Nike, 2022a). In both categories five factories accounted for well over half of all Nike-branded goods produced, demonstrating the importance of supplier networks and relationships to the business.

Relationships have also been important in Nike's retailing activities. Although the brand has a global network of its own stores (901 in 2022 according to the Nike company report), historically Nike has used partnerships with an extensive network of retailers who are essentially their wholesale customers, to bring the brand to a worldwide audience. Nike has four geographic operational reporting sections: North America; Europe, Middle East and Africa (EMEA); Greater China; and Asia Pacific and Latin America (APLA), demonstrating the market reach of the brand (Nike, 2022a).

Nike has contributed to, and skilfully ridden, the waves of global market growth over the last two decades in both the sneaker and the athleisure markets. Heading off powerful rivals (such as adidas, Puma, Lululemon, Under Armour, ASICS and more recently On and Chinese brands Anta and Li Ning), Nike dominates the hypercompetitive but lucrative athletic footwear and clothing market. Hero products such as the Pegasus and Air Zoom running lines and the Jordon basketball lines help to carve centrality in their product categories. Nike cites three important aspects of competitive advantage in its industry sector. The first competitive factor is the blend of product attributes (quality, performance, reliability, style, design innovation, and price/value). The second competitive factor is effective sourcing and retail distribution (including attractive merchandising and presentation across in-store and digital platforms). The third competitive factor, significantly for this case study, is consumer connection, engagement and affinity for their brands and products (Nike, 2022a). Nike recognises CX to be central to maintaining brand engagement, in the expounding of their competitive capability based on "marketing, promotion and digital experiences; social media interaction; customer support and service; and identification with prominent and influential athletes" (Nike, 2022a:5).

Just as Nike has had product innovation at its heart, innovative retail environments have been critical in the reinforcing of the Nike brand. The NikeTown flagships that opened throughout the 1990s set a new bar in retail brandscape, with their interactive and emotive spaces surrounding the different sports areas. The use of dramatic lighting, loud music and museum-like displays were a lesson in store atmospherics and visual merchandising. Augmented customer-centric services such as links to running groups and personalisation stations added to the excitement of the store and brand, which filtered down into the network of more mainstream retailers and Nike's own outlet stores. In response to criticisms of the stores being too masculine, Nike softened their store design approaches, dropped the 'Town' part of the store name and put more resources into niche outlets including those orientated to the women's and premium performance markets. In 2014 Nike opened its first Nike Women retail outlet in Newport Beach, California, followed by stores in Shanghai, and London the year after. Around this time Nike also opened a small number of NikeLab concept stores, housing innovative, technical and limited-edition ranges, aimed at the performance athlete. These niche stores were precursors to some of the more recent retail concepts discussed later in the case.

For the last five years Nike has been intensifying a transformative retail strategy to grow its DTC sales through the brand's own retail space, both physical and online, while

Table 6.1.1 Nike sales revenues, 2016–2022

Year	Sales revenue (Nike brand $bn)	% DTC
2016	30,507	26
2017	32,233	28
2018	34,485	30
2019	37,218	32
2020	35,568	35
2021	42,293	39
2022	44,436	42

Source: Nike 10K Reports 2016–2022.

decreasing its involvement with a dispersed retail network of third-party wholesale outlets. In 2017 Chief Executive Mike Parker shocked the sportswear industry when he announced Nike was set to refocus its wholesale strategy on just 40 partners from around 30,000 distributors (Sherman, 2019). The ambition was to work only with those retailers who were able and willing to devote unique spaces to Nike within their stores (Sherman, 2019) and provide superior CX, quality service and storytelling that differentiate the brand (Danziger, 2018). As Iannilli and Spagnoli (2021) note, selling is no longer just about goods and services, but includes participation and co-creation, activities, responsibilities and experiences. They go on to say retailers have moved from being containers of goods and information on brands and products, to being complex spaces capable of extended representation of brands while communicating identity, personality and values to consumers, a place to create emotional, narrative and experiential relationships linked to the brand image (Iannilli and Spagnoli, 2021), exactly the kind of spaces Nike creates in their own retail outlets.

More recently Nike has focused strategic retail development into digital space and the integration of retail touchpoints in a move towards omnichannel retail. Being a store-dependent brand, Nike suffered from the effects of the Covid-19 shutdowns across the globe; however, the popularity of home exercise and the shift to online sales provided mitigation, and by early 2023 Nike's sales performance was back on an upward trajectory. Table 6.1.1 shows the sales revenue of Nike (2016–2022) and the proportion of DTC sales.

Nike's Triple Double Strategy

Although the move towards an increasing proportion of DTC sales had started earlier, it was in mid-2017 that Nike articulated their Consumer Direct Offense to external stakeholders. This bold undertaking consisted of a "Triple Double Strategy", two times product innovation, two times speed to market and two times direct connections with consumers (Sherman, 2019). A central aspect of the direct connections with consumers' part of Nike's Triple Double Strategy was focused on NCX (Nike Customer Experience). "It is through the NCX that the company is feeding its 2X Innovation and 2X Speed initiatives" (Danziger, 2018).

Nike did not get to its dominant global position without focusing on CX well before anyone shortened it to CX. Understanding what performance athlete customers need and what athleisure customers want, both in product and in the surrounding servicescape

(Bitner, 1992), is what has driven Nike as a brand. The Triple Double Strategy simply articulated this in a modern way and helped to give energy and drive to what was a bold move towards DTC. Gauri et al. (2021) suggest that DTC gives brands the opportunity to showcase themselves in the best possible light and create better CX. Nike's ambition is to evolve their retail network so that only those retail partners who can deliver a CX that matches that of their own retail outlets are part of it. Nike refers to these retail partners as "differentiated retailers" (Danziger, 2018).

As a market leader and multichannel retailer, it is no surprise that Nike has embraced evolving retail technology, and as a consumer-centric brand Nike has developed many consumer touchpoints. Ieva and Ziliani (2018) refer to touchpoints as the verbal or non-verbal incidents a consumer perceives and consciously relates to a given firm or brand, and they are increasingly digital, reflecting the changing communication channels and routes to the brand used by Nike's customers. In 2017 Nike launched a new app, activated when customers connect online, within a Nike store or in a 'differentiated partner' store. This app has become a central pillar of NCX. By 2018 over 100 million Nike customers had signed up for the app, and by 2021 that number had increased to 300 million (Johnston, 2021).

Nike's app ecosystem

The main attraction of the app for customers is the NikePlus rewards programme, which allows members to access exclusive products, free shipping and 30-day wear tests. In addition, members have priority access to special events. The Nike app also provides a direct route to a network of Nike's employed athlete/brand advocates for advice and it generates personalised workouts. To encourage customer commitment both to their own fitness and to the Nike brand, members build awards based on their spending and fitness app usage, which, using AI algorithms, unlock further exclusive products and services, including VIP experiences and personalised discounts (Danziger, 2018). The app also recommends workouts and spectator sporting events, based on the members' own interests (CCW, 2019). The app provides valuable customer data for Nike, allowing the company to get insight on shopping habits and product preferences. This data also facilitates further personalisation of the CX (Danziger, 2018). The app has proved to be extremely popular with customers, with NikePlus members spending three times more in the app than non-members on Nike.com and Nike reporting that its NCX platform as driving virtually 100% growth in 2018 (Danziger, 2018). Since then, NCX has evolved into an ecosystem of apps (Johnston, n.d.) accessed with the one-member login. These include Nike Run Club, Nike Training Club, Nike App, SNKRS and on Nike.com.

The Nike Fit app is another example of the use of technology to provide a unique CX to Nike customers. Using pictures of customers' feet taken on their smartphones, the Nike Fit app recommends the best shoe size for every style of Nike shoes, based on a combination of computer vision, data science, machine learning, artificial intelligence and recommendation algorithms (CCW, 2019). According to Alexander and Kent (2022) retailers that experiment with technologies to enhance CX in the omnichannel context are likely be more successful. The Nike app brings Nike to phygital retail, because it integrates digital and physical brand space enabling a customer journey that involves overlapping moments and touchpoints (Mele et al., 2021) to achieve the goal of direct connection with consumers within the context of an omnichannel CX.

Nike's store format ecosystem

At the same time as developing the new Nike app, the company was also putting significant resources into developing new, smaller and more tailored physical store formats. Opened in July 2018 The Nike Live store in Melrose, Los Angeles, US, was designed to operate more like a fashion store, with a fast turnaround of styles. Instead of the traditional Nike 30–45-day stock change, 15% of clothing styles and 25% of footwear were changed every two weeks, keeping the offer fresh, informed by customer sales data (Danziger, 2018). Also, in 2018, the House of Innovation store opened in Shanghai, China, which is a new experiential physical retail concept, with space customised to the location of the store. The layout includes an arena for changing product displays and installations, and a Centre Court area where presentations and workshops can be accommodated (Danziger, 2018). After the disruption caused by Covid-19, Nike has responded to the growing concern about children's physical and mental well-being, which have been affected by low levels of sports participation and exercise. Nike's PLAYLab concept, which is housed within the Oxford Circus, London (UK), store provides a safe and fun social space, with a view to encouraging young people to develop their own ideas for physical games (Adegeest, 2022). These experimental retail concepts provide an opportunity to gather consumer research on the impact of new CX in physical space.

The technology-induced CX model

CX is a multidimensional construct (Alexander and Kent, 2022). As consumers increase the range of different touchpoints in their individual customer journeys, so their experiences may be affected by emotional, cognitive, behavioural and social factors (Mele et al., 2021; Grewel and Roggeveen, 2020). Reflecting these factors, Alexander and Kent (2022) developed a Technology-Induced Customer Experience In-Store Model. Primarily focused on in-store experiences, this model nevertheless can be applied to Nike's simultaneous development of mobile and physical touchpoints, and their CX in the omnichannel Nike DTC ecosystem. The model centres on a range of retail technologies, some of which lean towards the utilitarian experience, driving speed, convenience and efficiency (aligning to behavioural and cognitive factors) while others relate more closely to hedonic experiences, associated with enjoyment, playfulness, excitement and immersion. The conceptual framework also indicates that satisfactory experiences of both types are dependent on a good strategic fit between a brand's channel and experience strategy and the technologies used.

Nike's virtual CX: Nikeland, digital goods and crafting community

In 2021 Nike introduced Nikeland, which is a virtual world experience (metaverse), facilitated by the ecosystem of the gaming platform Roblox (Marr, 2022; Carter, 2023). Inspired by Nike's own headquarters, Nikeland brings a range of experiences to visitors, such as virtual products to clothe their avatars and the opportunity to buy NFT (non-fungible token) virtual products, attend events (such as guest experiences by sporting heroes) and take part in games to win rewards and prizes. The virtual social space includes a digital showroom where users can buy garments and create their own Nike-branded accessories (Carter, 2023). Through this platform Nike is also incorporating the phygital retail experience in a fun way; Nike's New York store has an augmented reality (AR) experience, which connects with a Snapchat feature that allows customers to dress in clothing from the Nikeland virtual product library (Carter, 2023). Another AR experience, launched in 2022, uses QR codes readable by any smartphone, to unlock seminal brand stories and 3D brand assets stored in virtual boxes (Melnick, 2022).

In 2021 Nike acquired RTFKT, a digital design studio, to access competence in the production of virtual clothing and footwear, resulting in the launch of .SWOOSH, "a web3-enabled platform that champions athletes and serves the future of sport by creating a new, inclusive digital community and experience and a home for Nike virtual creations" (Nike, 2022b) followed by the release of its own collection of virtual sneakers in 2023. Avoiding technical descriptors such as NFT, and crypto project in its marketing communications about the launch (Joseph, 2023), it is clear that Nike believes its customers care about brand experiences and not the technologies that bring them. Four of the virtual sneaker designs, out of 106,000 released, were co-created with .SWOOSH community members (Lutz, 2023). Available only through the .SWOOSH platform, and stored inside a digital sneaker box, the virtual sneakers were available to purchase at the accessible price of $19.82, a reference to the year Nike's Air Force 1 style was launched). They were delivered as a 3D file that can be exported to other compatible platforms such as a game. The .SWOOSH site advises how brand fans can access further drops of products and experiences including taking part in community challenges and earning prizes (Joseph, 2023).

Nike's use of brand-engaging technology is summarised well by Marr (2022): "Nike has always been at the forefront of digital transformation ... [leveraging] technologies to remain relevant and on the cultural cutting edge". This leading position however needs continual investment and regular organisational self-reflection to ensure Nike maintains capability in a rapidly changing landscape. The continuous development of Nike's customer-facing personnel allows them to blend their own sports engagement with customer service technology to deliver the customer-centric omnichannel experience that Nike is seeking (CCW, 2019). At the board level too, recent changes support the focus on CX. In 2020 Heidi O'Neill was appointed President of Consumer and Marketplace, building on her previous position as President of Nike Direct. This position allows holistic leadership in the direct business globally, including stores, e-commerce and apps. In the same year global technology and digital transformation was incorporated into the Chief Operating Officer role, currently filled by Andrew Campion, to ensure integration with the other operational areas (demand and supply management, manufacturing, distribution and logistics sustainability, workplace design and connectivity, and procurement). These two positions ensure that CX and the operations that support it are recognised at the main board level (Nike, 2022).

Conclusion

Nike is a formidable force in sports fashion footwear and clothing, reinforcing its leading retail position by embracing consumer centricity, omnichannel and the best CX in its Triple Double Strategy. A brand with the reputation and credibility of Nike needs to ensure that customer engagement at any point, in any retail or media channel, supports the expectation that brand leadership promises. Nike has always been at the forefront of using technology in retail space to provide an exciting CX and, more recently, an even higher level of personalised experience (NCX). The company is also moving with their brand community into virtual retail experiences. However, having the best retail experience as a competitive advantage, while carrying the legacy of a global network of retail partners, is a major challenge to Nike. Cutting out smaller players that failed to make the grade of differentiated partner, despite having been loyal to Nike through the brand's historic growth to global giant, was not a popular move and could be considered as symptomatic of the ruthlessness of powerful brands. For Nike, however, more emphasis on DTC is a strategy where the benefits are considered to outweigh the risks (Morris, 2023) and the omnichannel approach enables brands to pivot between physical, digital and virtual space to adapt to external challenges, such as lockdowns.

> Empowered consumers won't wait for brands to catch up. Nor will product market-ers wait for their retail partners either ... if retailers don't step up to provide superior customer experiences, quality service and storytelling for the brands they carry, then companies and their customers will walk, jog or run away....
>
> (Danziger, 2018)

Retailing is a business where, as the adage goes, the only constant is change. In the pandemic years, sports fashion retailers were saddled with huge inventory build-ups as stores closed, and Nike needed to reignite some of its wholesale retail partnerships to shift excess inventory (Miller and Chen, 2023). The launch of Nike's .SWOOSH didn't go without technical glitches and headlines such as "If NFT's Are Passé, Nobody Told Nike" (Bain, 2023) suggest that what was envisaged three years ago to be an exciting new way to deliver coveted personalised goods to sneakerheads could well be a novelty that fades. Can brands like Nike continue to hold the interest of young consumers by endless drops of rehashed Nike brand creations, and, if so, how do those consumers want to experience that interest? The fast-paced growth of the sneaker market is reported to be running out of steam (Miller, 2023). So, will the resources needed to maintain the NCX the board of directors envisaged in the Triple Double Strategy continue to be available to Nike and should the shift to DTC continue?

Case questions

1 Identify how Nike reaches consumers, referring to retail routes to market and touchpoints.
2 Discuss the strategic implications for Nike of sustaining a competitive advantage in providing the best retail experience, as described by Iannilli and Spagnoli (2021).
3 Discuss the ways in which technology-enhanced customer experiences (Alexander and Kent, 2022) underpin Nike's emphasis on customer experience (NCX) within the Triple Double Strategy.
4 Referring to Alexander and Kent's (2022) Technology-Induced Customer Experience In-Store Model, analyse to what extent does Nike have a good strategic fit between its channel and experience strategy and the customer-facing technologies that Nike uses.
5 Analyse how a DTC retail transformation supports the strategic imperative of customer experience at Nike.

References

Adegeest, D-A. (2022) *Niketown London's PLAYlab gets children involved in experiential sports.* Fashion United. [Online] [Accessed 6 June 2023] https://fashionunited.uk/news/fashion/niketown-london-s-playlab-gets-children-involved-in-experiential-sports/2022010360371

Alexander, B. and Kent, A. (2022) 'Change in technology-enabled omnichannel customer experiences in-store.' *Journal of Retailing and Consumer Services*, 65, p. 102338.

Bain, M. (2023) *If NFTs are Passe, Nobody told Nike.* The Business of Fashion. [Online] [Accessed 10 June 2023] https://www.businessoffashion.com/briefings/technology/if-nfts-are-passe-nobody-told-nike/

Bitner, M.J. (1992) 'Servicescapes: The impact of physical surroundings on customers and employees.' *Journal of Marketing*, 56, pp. 57–71.

Carter, R. (2023) *What is Nike's metaverse? An introduction to Nikeland.* XR Today, 13 March. [Online] [Accessed 5 June 2023] https://www.xrtoday.com/mixed-reality/what-is-nikes-metaverse-an-introduction-to-nikeland/

CCW (2019) *How Nike combines customer centricity with brand reputation to stay on top.* Customer Contact Week, 10 July. [Online] [Accessed 6 June 2023] https://www.customercontactweekdigital.com/customer-insights-analytics/articles/how-nike-combines-customer-centricity-with-brand-reputation-to-stay-on-top

Danziger, P.N. (2018) *Nike's new consumer experience distribution strategy hits the ground running.* Forbes, 1 December. [Online] [Accessed 2 June 2023] https://www.forbes.com/sites/pamdanziger/2018/12/01/nikes-new-consumer-experience-distribution-strategy-hits-the-ground-running/

Euromonitor (2023) *Nike Inc in apparel and footwear, global company profile.* Euromonitor May. [Online] [Accessed 6 May 2023] https://www.euromonitor.com/apparel-and-footwear

Gauri, D.K., Rupinder, P.J., Ratchford, B., Fox, E., Bhatnagar, A., Pandey, A., Navallo, J.R., Fogarty, J., Carr, S. and Howerton, E. (2021) 'Evolution of retail formats.' *Journal of Retailing*, 97(1) pp. 42–61.

Grewal, D., Noble, S.M., Roggeveen, A.L. and Nordfalt, J. (2020) 'The future of in-store technology.' *Journal of the Academy of Marketing Science*, 48(1), pp. 96–113. https://doi.org/10.1007/s11747-019-00697-z

Iannilli, V.M. and Spagnoli, A. (2021) 'Phygital retailing in fashion: Experiences, opportunities and innovation trajectories.' *ZoneModa Journal*, 11(1), pp. 43–69.

Ieva, M. and Ziliani, C. (2018) 'Mapping touchpoint exposure in retailing: Implications for developing an omnichannel customer experience.' *International Journal of Retail and Distribution Management*, 46(3), pp. 304–322.

Johnston, L. (no date) *Nike's record quarter fueled By 300 million members and their consumer insights.* Consumer Goods Technology. [Online] [Accessed 5 June 2023] https://consumergoods.com/nikes-record-quarter-fueled-300-million-members-and-their-consumer-insights#

Joseph, S. (2023) *After Nike's virtual sneaker drop, NFT cynicism is making way for intrigue among marketers.* Digiday, 22 May. [Online] [Accessed 6 June 2023] https://digiday.com/marketing/after-nikes-virtual-sneaker-drop-nft-cynicism-is-making-way-for-intrigue-among-marketers/

Lutz, S. (2023) *Nike unveils First.Swoosh NFTT digital sneaker drop.* Decrypt, 18 April. [Online] [Accessed 5 June 2023] https://decrypt.co/137011/nike-unveils-first-swoosh-nft-collection-for-members

Marr, B. (2022) *The amazing ways Nike is using the metaverse, Web3 and NFTs.* Forbes, 1 June. [Online] [Accessed 5 June 2023] https://www.forbes.com/sites/bernardmarr/2022/06/01/the-amazing-ways-nike-is-using-the-metaverse-web3-and-nfts/?sh=684b3ac256e9

Mele, C., Russo-Spena, T., Tregua, M. and Amitrano, C-C. (2021) 'The millennial customer journey: A phygital mapping of emotional, behavioural, and social experiences.' *Journal of Consumer Marketing*, 38(4), pp. 420–433.

Melnick, K. (2022) *Nike celebrates 50 years with in-store AR experience*. VR Scout, 24 August. [Online] [Accessed 5 June 2023] https://vrscout.com/news/nike-celebrates-50-years-with-in-store-ar-experience/

Miller, D-Y. (2023) *Hyper growth is over for sneakers. What's next?* The Business of Fashion, 4 January. [Online] [Accessed 5 June 2023] https://www.businessoffashion.com/articles/retail/despite-setbacks-nike-is-scoring-with-direct-to-consumer-offense/

Miller, D-Y. and Chen, C. (2023) *What a winning strategy looks like in today's sneaker market*. The Business of Fashion, 22 March. [Online] [Accessed 10 April 2023] https://www.businessoffashion.com/articles/retail/what-a-winning-strategy-looks-like-in-todays-sneaker-market/

Morris, M. (2023) *How to build a profitable DTC brand case study*. The Business of Fashion, January. [Online] [Accessed 6 June 2023] https://www.businessoffashion.com/case-studies/direct-to-consumer/how-to-build-profitable-dtc-brand-marine-layer-trinny-london-meundies/

Nike (2022a) *Nike Form 10-K report*. [Online] [Accessed 5 June 2023] https://s1.q4cdn.com/806093406/files/doc_downloads/2022/399556(1)_27_Nike-Inc._NPS_Combo_Form-10-K_WR.pdf

Nike (2022b) *Nike Launches.Swoosh, A new digital community and experience*. Nike Press Release, 14 November. [Online] [Accessed 5 June 2023] https://about.nike.com/en/newsroom/releases/nike-launches-swoosh-a-new-digital-community-and-experience

Sherman, L. (2019) *Despite setbacks, Nike is scoring with direct-to-consumer 'Offense'*. The Business of Fashion, 9 January. [Online] [Accessed 10 April 2023] https://www.businessoffashion.com/articles/retail/despite-setbacks-nike-is-scoring-with-direct-to-consumer-offense/

Further resources

Barcelona Store Tour Video
https://www.youtube.com/watch?v=0g4eV8LN6Nw
Nike Paris House of Innovation
https://www.youtube.com/watch?v=jqK86qGv8Y0
Nike Digital Retail Experience
https://www.youtube.com/watch?v=xD5e-aFYDKU
Nike Adapting to Technology! Nike Digital Transformation
https://www.youtube.com/watch?v=v4SVQP4K0Wc

Definitions

Servicescape: A concept that explores the relationship between physical environments and their impact on service delivery and perception, both for customers and for retail employees. This term broadly refers to the selling environment and processes that the consumer experiences in connection with purchasing.

Brandscape: Brandscape refers to brand-consumer relationships within the entirety of the relevant product/market landscape, and includes emotional and cultural meanings attached to brands and the creation of their identity.

DTC: DTC refers to brands connecting directly with consumers through their own digital and in some cases, temporary and/or permanent physical retail spaces; omitting third-party retailers, and taking a 'digital first' approach to operations to build global, digitally connected customer bases.

6.2   Zara: pioneering a phygital experience in the mainstream fashion sector

Rocío Elízaga and Patricia SanMiguel

Learning objectives

On completion of this case study, learners should be able to:

1   Understand the diverse nature of omnichannel customer journeys (CJs), with specific reference to Zara.
2   Analyse the benefits and barriers associated with phygital customer experiences (CX).
3   Assess the use of Zara's retail technology in augmenting their customer shopping experience
4   Analyse the positive impact of mobile apps on the phygital CX.
5   Propose future practices for fashion retailers with the aim to optimise phygital retail experiences.

Introduction

When Amancio Ortega opened the first Zara shop in Northern Spain in 1975, he did so convinced that the key to success was to provide quick responses to his customers' fast-changing fashion needs. This business principle remains Zara's fundamental strategy: to connect design, production and manufacturing in response to consumer needs (Arnold and D'Andrea, 2003). Zara is one of seven retail brands that now make up the Inditex Group, which was founded in 1985, the other brands in the group being Zara Home, Massimo Dutti, Pull&Bear, Bershka, Oysho and Stradivarius.

In the 17 years following Zara's launch, Ortega opened more than 1,000 new shops, culminating in an initial public offering (IPO) on 23 May 2001, coinciding with the opening of Inditex's extensive new headquarters in Arteixo (La Coruña) Spain. The funds raised through this IPO provided the fuel for a rapid evolution that saw Inditex grow to operate 6,477 shops in more than 200 markets across the seven brands. In 2022, its global sales revenues totalled €32.5 billion, with an industry-leading gross profit margin of 57.4% (Inditex Annual Report, 2022).

Today, Zara has more than 2,310 stores worldwide (including Zara and Zara Home) and is the flagship brand of Inditex, representing more than 70% of group total revenue (Inditex Annual Report, 2022). Zara has a brand value worth more than USD 18 billion and is ranked third in the top ten most valuable brands in the mass market global fashion sector, after Nike and Shein (Kantar, 2023). Zara sits among the players with the largest global share (around 2%) of the highly fragmented mainstream fashion market, only matched by its competitors Uniqlo, H&M and Nike (Statista, 2023b). While Inditex competes with local retailers in most of its markets, industry commentators tend to agree that Zara's closest comparable global competitors are H&M, Uniqlo and Gap.

With a significant bounceback from the pandemic, sales in the global fashion market increased by 21% overall in 2021–2022 (Amed et al., 2023), but forecasts suggest that the mainstream sector is now struggling with minimal sales growth. With the European market contracting, McKinsey's forecast for 2023 suggests global sales in mass market fashion will flatten to between –2 and +3% growth (Amed et al., 2023). Against this background Zara's annual sales also increased by 21% in 2022 (Inditex Annual Report, 2022), indicating its performance is on a par with the global market in general.

Zara began its digitalisation process by introducing online sales in several markets including Spain, the UK, Portugal, Italy and Germany in 2010. Soon after this Zara installed the first self-service checkouts in selected outlets with the aim of making in-store shopping easier. In spite of massive temporary store closures the global pandemic boosted Zara's online sales, achieving over 50% growth during the 2019–2022 period (Statista, 2023a). This online sales acceleration led to the extension and further implementation of its digital strategy during this time, with the plan to focus on the online channel, reducing the number of physical stores and implementing in-store technology in order to merge the physical and digital channels (Jopson, 2023).

Today, fashion companies recognise that offering an excellent CX is essential. Zara considers CX to be one of the pillars of its business model and therefore aims to enhance it in a strategic way (Jopson, 2023). This case study will allow the reader to learn about the innovative tools and the technological features that the company is implementing with the objective of retail integration to optimise the Zara CX.

Zara's advances towards phygitalisation

The fashion industry has gradually embraced consumer-facing technologies within the retail sector, driving towards a greater integration of physical and digital systems. With the progressive blending of the physical and digital dimensions, omnichannel strategy – where all channels are integrated, resulting in a seamless CX (Iannilli and Spagnoli, 2021) – is turning into a phygital one in light of contemporary consumer dynamics. An augmented scenario is emerging in retail environments as a result of the expansion and integration of channels, the proliferation of brand messages and narratives and the expansion of services to meet customers' expectations. Zara's customer-centric commercial approach provides an excellent example of the phygital experience.

The brand has been specifically working on enhancing CX as one of the main pillars of their business strategy (Inditex Annual Report, 2022), bridging the gap between the physical and the digital (Pangarkar et al., 2022) especially present in their recent flagship stores' openings. Under the Inditex 'go big' store strategy Zara's store portfolio is being altered by the closing of smaller underperforming stores (Jopson, 2023) and doubling the size of flagship stores in key locations. In 2022, Zara opened new, larger flagship stores in Plaza de España, Madrid (April), followed by London (October) and Valencia (December), and then in 2023 with Paris (April) and Rotterdam (September). These stores present Zara's new retail concept, larger premises to include spaces allocated to specific collections such as lingerie, beauty and athletic wear and a customer-centric store environment. Technology is at the service of the customer with the aim to improve CX, for example, through self-checkout counters where customers can finalise their purchase without the need to interact with sales associates. Zara also uses VR (virtual reality) and AR (augmented reality) technology installed on iPads in the beauty area (see Figure 6.2.1) that enhance the experience of consumers testing cosmetic products.

Figure 6.2.1 Zara beauty area. Plaza de España store, Madrid.
Source: Reprinted by permission of Inditex.

Integration of the physical store and the Zara app, a cornerstone of the phygital experience, is achieved through various digital services and store technologies. The app enables customers to:

- Scan and purchase store items with Pay&Go (see Figure 6.2.2). This allows the entire purchase to be made through the Zara app. By using 'Store Mode' consumers are able to scan the garments, generating a QR code after the purchase with which the customer can de-tag the garments in the 'Pay&Go' corners and pack their items (see Figure 6.2.3).
- Reserve fitting rooms to avoid waiting times (see Figures 6.2.4 and 6.2.5).
- Use tools for online browsing through 'Store Mode', which allows customers to check the available inventory, and offers the opportunity to search and locate items in the selected store (see Figure 6.2.6).
- Purchase online (through the app) and pick up in two hours if items are available at the selected store (see Figure 6.2.7).

Furthermore, the smart parcel terminal for online orders permits the collection and return of online orders – initiated through Zara's e-commerce or the Zara app – (see Figures 6.2.8 and 6.2.9) as well as provides a disposal point for donating unwanted items.

The stores act as mini-warehouses in a growing role within online sales processing where channel integration facilitates the CJ. Today, shopping for fashion is much more than purchasing products; consumers, especially digital natives, are looking

Figure 6.2.2 Zara Pay&Go. Plaza de España store, Madrid.

Source: Reprinted by permission of Inditex.

Figure 6.2.3 Zara Pay&Go self-serve. Plaza de España store, Madrid.

Source: Reprinted by permission of Inditex.

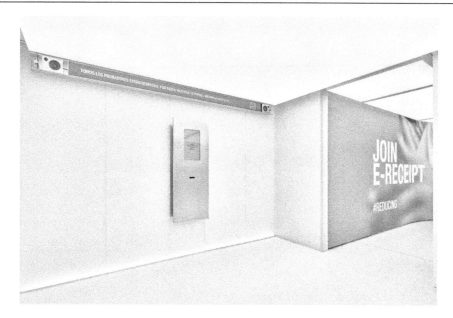

Figure 6.2.4 Zara fitting room. Plaza de España store, Madrid.

Source: Reprinted by permission of Inditex.

STORE EXPERIENCES (4)

Figure 6.2.5 Zara app fitting room.

Source: Reprinted by permission of Inditex.

STORE EXPERIENCES (4)

SEARCH

Figure 6.2.6 Zara app search and locate items.

Source: Reprinted by permission of Inditex.

STORE EXPERIENCES (4)

START

Figure 6.2.7 Zara app online pick-up point.

Source: Reprinted by permission of Inditex.

Figure 6.2.8 Zara online pick-up point. Plaza de España store, Madrid.
Source: Reprinted by permission of Inditex.

Figure 6.2.9 Zara return drop-off point. Plaza de España store, Madrid.
Source: Reprinted by permission of Inditex.

for memorable experiences and a frictionless shopping process (Bueno et al., 2019). In addition, the diversity of personal digital devices available to consumers means that they are in contact with fashion brands through multiple online and offline channels and platforms (Zhao and Deng, 2020). In the context of blurred boundaries between digital and physical contexts, all interactions throughout the shopping cycle make up the CJ, a loop influenced by multiple touchpoints and social interactions. CJs are represented as non-linear processes "punctuated by dynamics such as feedback loops, channel switching and dropouts" (Kranzbühler et al., 2018: 447). Marta Ortega (the current Chairperson of Inditex) is convinced of the importance of integrating channels through a phygital experience: "(…) and my focus is always improving shopping experience, both in the physical stores and online, and maximising integration between the two" (Ellison, 2023).

Zara and the CX journey

In their paper on phygital mapping Mele et al. (2021) identified four essential moments in the CJ: connect, explore, buy and use. In each of these phases the consumer performs particular actions, and experiences a series of emotions and interactions that shape their CX (see Mele et al., 2021: 429, Customer Journey Map).

Connect phase

The connect phase refers to the customer's intention to engage or stay engaged with value propositions. Zara's customers have multiple ways to connect with the brand: social media allows them to keep up to date with the latest trends and news, including collaborations and capsule collections, as well as connect through UGC (user generated content). Physical stores showcase the latest arrivals, encouraging customers to interact with sales associates and the multiple available technological features and services described above. Thanks to geolocalisation, on arrival customers are able to navigate the store layout through Store Mode (see Figures 6.2.10 and 6.2.11) locating collections and detecting locations for products placed in the app shopping basket (see Figure 6.2.12). For Zara's customers, the app has become a key point of connection with the brand, which they use not only in the purchase phase, but throughout the entire CJ.

Explore phase

In the explore phase customers want to learn more and seize further control of their decision-making processes. They may recognise a knowledge or competence gap, and therefore seek alternatives to explore and compare, and organise helpful search information. Customers may become open to being influenced by different sources of content that inspire them to make their choice. In this sense, the seamless integration of Zara's selling channels, especially e-commerce and the Zara app, enhances the exploration momentum. For this reason, the Zara app is a good ally for frequent customers. Both app and e-commerce allow consumers to seize further control of their decision-making process, checking item availability, sizes and colours, both online and in physical stores, thanks to the Shopping Basket Store Mode (see Figure 6.2.13). Enabled services in the app facilitate further exploration of product features before purchase.

Figure 6.2.10 Zara QR Store Mode.

Source: Reprinted by permission of Inditex.

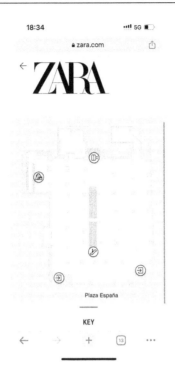

Figure 6.2.11 Zara floor Map Store Mode.
Source: Reprinted by permission of Inditex.

Buy phase

Once customers make their purchase decision, the buy phase comes into play. When individuals reach the final stage of their decision, any additional information, whether discovered online or offline, may alter their opinions about purchasing a certain item. Enabled services at the store, e-commerce features and channel integration are critical to deploy a satisfactory buying process. The Zara buying experience is seamlessly integrated: the purchase is initiated either through online channels (e-commerce and Zara app) or in the physical store. Parcel delivery can be arranged for designated stores, at home or at an alternative collection point. Click&Collect pick-up point dispensers and parcel drop-off points are excellent examples of a seamless and smooth CX at the buying phase. The purchase initiated through an offline channel (physical store) can be finished at self-checkout counters – incorporating the purchase receipt into the app – or the whole buying process could be made through the app via the Pay&Go corners. The use of RFID (radio-frequency identification) – the microchip technology that streamlines orders, stock and distribution – is another factor that helps to make the sale through any channel an integrated experience.

Figure 6.2.12 Zara Shopping Basket Store Mode.

Source: Reprinted by permission of Inditex.

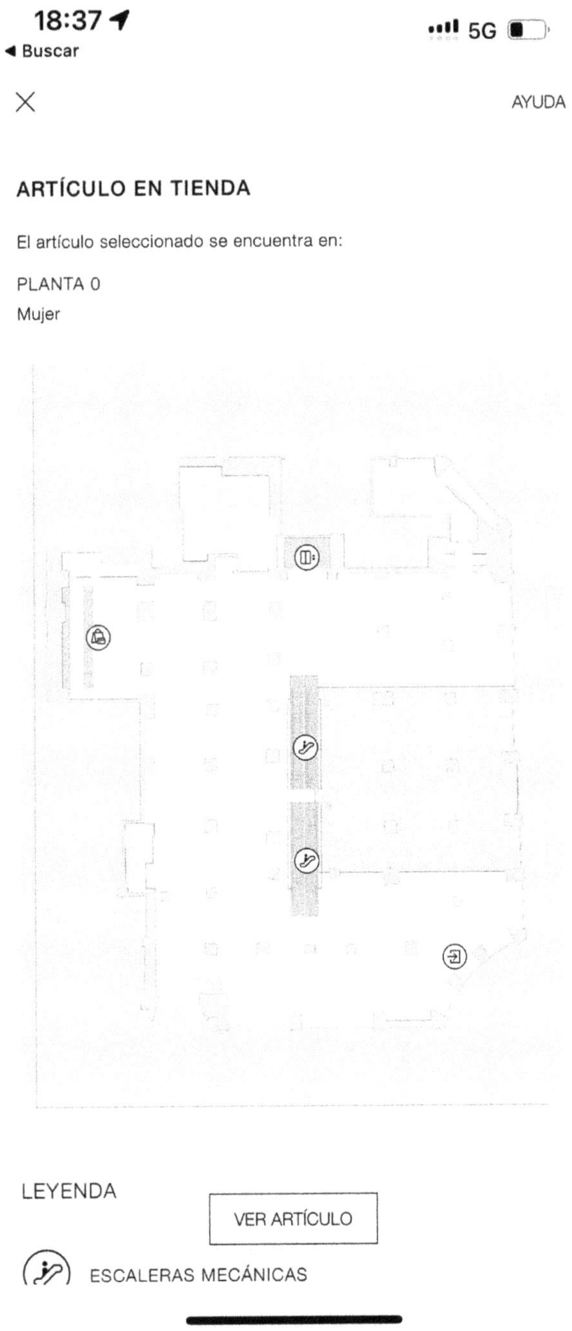

18:37 ✈
◀ Buscar

▬ıll 5G 🔋

✕

AYUDA

ARTÍCULO EN TIENDA

El artículo seleccionado se encuentra en:

PLANTA 0
Mujer

LEYENDA

VER ARTÍCULO

ESCALERAS MECÁNICAS

Figure 6.2.13 Zara Shopping Basket Store Mode.

Source: Reprinted by permission of Inditex.

Use phase

Customers gain confidence in the use phase on whether and how their expectations are met. The Zara app attempts to improve CX via convenience, speed and efficiency of the user experience; however, some apparent frictions need to be resolved to improve useability. For example, easier navigation in the app is needed to select Store Mode and the corresponding services offered, and the Pay&Go service in the store needs to be completed with a sales assistant; otherwise, it is not intuitive for the customer (Villaécija, 2020). To this end, sales assistants are trained to remain at the customer's disposal, contributing to the efficiency of the user experience.

The phygital experience ultimately occurs when shops are able to integrate digital technological resources with the in-store experience, whilst managing information, customer relationships, desires, aspirations and opinions in the form of 'big data' (Iannilli and Spagnoli, 2021; Mele el al. 2021). The use of RFID has enabled Zara to manage inventory better, ship more from stores and drive full-price sales, fostering a good integration amongst channels (Jopson, 2023). Incorporating this technology since 2014, RFID allows the unique identification of each garment through radio-frequency waves that are recorded on a chip inside the security tag. This provides Zara with greater agility in distribution and greater precision in the management of garments. At the beginning of the RFID implementation, the information transparency provided was only available to staff, but the subsequent application of this technology to the Zara website and app has allowed a fully integrated management of the stock at the physical and online level (Rodriguez, 2020). Furthermore, RFID offers a series of advantages in terms of logistics: better quality customer service, fast and accurate replenishment of collections in-store, increased security control, precision and agility in the reception of garments and the location of garments within the physical store (Ellison, 2023), all of which result in better channel integration.

Zara's efforts to implement a phygital strategy through its sales channels are aligned with the objective of satisfying customer needs as the core of its commercial strategy. Millennials and Generation Z are the consumers who currently demand this type of phygital experience (Mele et al., 2021). They need to be able to get in touch with a brand digitally in a quick and easy way; they like to master the buying process from start to finish without interruptions; they prefer flexibility in the purchase process, easy payments and fast shipping; and they prefer frictionless, hassle-free returns and exchanges (Siregar et al., 2023).

The integration of the physical and digital world perceived by customers in the physical store and in the app is the result of a holistic effort to encompass strategy, data, organisational structure and processes (Mele et al., 2021). Inditex explains in its Annual Report (2022) that this is achieved through the Inditex Open Platform (IOP). IOP is a 'living' digital platform which continually incorporates new functionalities to offer an integrated experience, allowing customers to make their purchases as they choose: physically, virtually or mixing with both ease and transparency. The IOP underpins the CX functionalities of Store Mode, Pay&Go and Self-Checkouts. The brand expects to launch a new security technology in 2024 that will eliminate the need for hard tags, which will further facilitate interaction with products and improve the purchasing process. The new system will progressively deepen the digitalisation of stores and their integration with online platforms in the coming years (Inditex Annual Report, 2022).

Conclusion

After the pandemic that brought economic instability and uncertainty to the fashion industry, Zara has reaffirmed its customer-centric approach, focusing its efforts and innovations on continuous improvement of the CX. As a well-established player in the global mainstream fashion market, Zara is strengthening CX as a key pillar of its brand strategy, along with fashion, sustainability and people (Inditex Annual Report, 2022). Improving CX focuses on optimising the integration of physical and online channels by offering a phygital experience. Aware of the demands from Millennials and Generation Z for seamless experiences, Zara aims to achieve a frictionless and smooth CJ, alongside the four essential moments within it: connect, explore, buy and use. Zara shows innovative best practice in leveraging phygital retailing via the Zara app which transforms the integration of the physical and digital world as perceived by the customer, especially in the new, larger flagship stores. The use of RFID technology which achieves single stock unit management has crucially enabled an omnichannel strategy, by making product information accessible to customers and thereby resulting in a better phygital experience. Although Zara has spent millions on digital solutions to achieve strategic objectives, the brand must maintain this level of investment to keep ahead of competition. Ongoing investment in tech solutions to uphold their leading position in the mainstream fashion retail sector is likely to continue into the future.

Case questions

1   Using Mele et al.'s (2021) concept of the four stages within a customer journey (connect, explore, buy and use) and information provided in this case, construct a map of the potential shopping journeys a Zara customer could make using all the different channels and retail technology that Zara provides (store, website, app, social media) to demonstrate the complexity of contemporary omnichannel retail.

2   Analyse how the phygital technologies described in this case contribute to an augmented customer experience (CX). Apply Mele et al.'s (2021) ideas on phygital mapping (including actions, emotions and social interactions) to guide your analysis.

3   Use your own observational research to evaluate the extent of phygital operations within different Zara product categories: (e.g. women, men, kids, home and beauty). To what extent are the channels (store, web, app, social media) integrated to achieve the best customer experience? Identify any instances where full channel integration is not achieved? What additional technologies would you recommend Zara adopt to achieve a consistent phygital customer experience across all categories and in all stores?

4   Selecting a fashion retailer of your own choice, apply the customer journey map model (connect, explore, buy and use) to analyse to what extent they generate an integrated customer experience. Make critical recommendations based on your analysis.

5   What strategic direction(s) should Marta Ortega follow to ensure Zara's phygital retail approach continues to deliver excellent customer experience over the next three years?

References

Amed, I., Berg, A. and Balchandani, A. (2023) *The state of fashion report 2023*. BoF and McKinsey. [Online] [Accessed 6th February 2023] https://www.businessoffashion.com/reports/news-analysis/the-state-of-fashion-2023-industry-report-bof-mckinsey/

Bascur, C. and Rusu, C. (2020) 'Customer experience in retail: A systematic literature review.' *Applied Sciences*, 10(21), p. 7644.

Bueno, E.V., Weber, T.B.B., Bomfim, E.L. and Kato, H.T. (2019) 'Measuring customer experience in service: A systematic review.' *The Service Industries Journal*, 39(11–12), pp. 779–798.

Arnold, D. and D' Andrea, G. (2003) *Zara*. [Online] [Accessed 11th April 2023] https://hbsp.harvard.edu/product/503050-PDF-ENG

Ellison, J. (2023) *The Zara woman: An exclusive interview with Marta Ortega Pérez*. Financial Times. [Online] [Accessed 1st October 2023] https://www.ft.com/content/f5e10605-3c9d-4517-86f5-2e7570bf16f0

Iannilli, V.M. and Spagnoli, A. (2021) 'Phygital retailing in fashion. Experiences, opportunities and innovation trajectories.' *ZoneModa Journal*, 11(1). https://doi.org/10.6092/issn.2611-0563/13120

Inditex (2022) *Annual report – FY2022 results*. [Online] [Accessed 8th May 2023] https://www.inditex.com/itxcomweb/en/press/news-detail?contentId=3dbc9f5d-2f00-46d2-bd45-8bb2ab945261

Jopson, B. (2023) Zara owner bets on big stores to keep sales space growing. *Financial Times*. [Online] [Accessed 13 September 2023] https://www.ft.com/content/5364bea4-4f97-49ba-88fb-845d3b648b96

Kantar (2023) *Kantar BrandZ most valuable global brands 2023*. [Online] [Accessed 18th September 2023] https://www.kantar.com/campaigns/brandz/global

Kranzbühler, A.M., Kleijnen, M.H., Morgan, R.E. and Teerling, M. (2018) 'The multilevel nature of customer experience research: An integrative review and research agenda.' *International Journal of Management Reviews*, 20(2), pp. 433–456.

Mele, C., Russo-Spena, T., Tregua, M. and Amitrano, C.C. (2021) 'The millennial customer journey: A Phygital mapping of emotional, behavioural, and social experiences.' *Journal of Consumer Marketing*, 38(4), pp. 420–433. https://doi.org/10.1108/JCM-03-2020-3701

Pangarkar, A., Arora, V. and Shukla, Y. (2022) 'Exploring phygital omnichannel luxury retailing for immersive customer experience: The role of rapport and social engagement.' *Journal of Retailing and Consumer Services*, 68. https://doi.org/10.1016/j.jretconser.2022.103001

Rodriguez, O. (2020) *RFID: The technology that allows Zara to know where each of its garments are*. El Independiente [Online] [Accessed 4th July 2023] https://www.elindependiente.com/economia/2020/07/04/rfid-la-tecnologia-que-permite-a-zara-saber-donde-esta-cada-una-de-sus-prendas/

Siregar, Y., Kent, A., Peirson-Smith, A.F. and Guan, C. (2023). Disrupting the fashion retail journey: Social media and GenZ's fashion consumption. *International Journal of Retail and Distribution Management*, 51(7), p. 862875. https://doi.org/10.1108/IJRDM-01-2022

Statista (2023a) *Zara.com: E-Commerce net sales from 2014 to 2022*. [Online] [Accessed 19th September 2023] https://www.statista.com/forecasts/1218316/zara-revenue-development-ecommercedb

Statista (2023b) *Worldwide Apparel – Statista market insights*. [Online] [Accessed 12th September 2023] https://www.statista.com/outlook/cmo/apparel/worldwide

Villaécija, R. (2020) *Así es la nueva aplicación de Zara que permite desde hoy navegar por las tiendas y hasta reservar probador*. [Online] [Accessed 3rd September 2023] https://www.elmundo.es/economia/ahorro-y-consumo/2020/09/14/5f5f8926fdddfff0528b45cb.html

Zhao, W.Y. and Deng, N. (2020) 'Examining the channel choice of experience-oriented customers in omni-channel retailing.' *International Journal of Information Systems in the Service Sector*, 12(1), pp. 16–27. https://doi.org/10.4018/IJISSS.2020010102

Definitions

Customer Experience (CX): sum of all online and offline interactions that a customer has with a brand, which can create advantage over competitors (Bascur and Rusu, 2020).

Phygital experience: when retailers integrate digital technological resources with the in-store experience, whilst managing information and customer relationships.

Radio-frequency identification (RFID): technology used to underpin omnichannel and phygital experience strategies. RFID allows the unique identification of each garment through radio-frequency waves that are recorded on a chip inside a security tag. This provides greater agility in distribution and greater precision in the management of garments across selling channels.

6.3   Sunnei: harnessing mediatisation to fuel a multidimensional customer experience

Valeria Iannilli and Alessandra Spagnoli

Learning objectives

On completion of this case study, learners should be able to:

1   Understand how mediatisation and digital media influence the fashion customer experience (CX).
2   Understand the importance of customer orientation (both cognitive and emotional) in building CX.
3   Evaluate the multidimensional aspects of CX as encompassed within Sunnei's relational experiential platform.
4   Explore community-building strategies implemented by a niche fashion brand.

Introduction

Brand background

Sunnei is a digitally native Italian fashion brand based in Milan, Italy, founded in 2014 by Loris Messina and Simone Rizzo. The founders define themselves as a 'creative collective' and a 'movement', specifying that Sunnei is a project that goes beyond fashion and is 'linked to art, culture and experimentation' (Sunnei interview, 2023). The brand was born from the founders' desire to create an independent menswear streetwear brand capable of becoming a point of reference for Milan's creative and cultural communities, including artists, DJs and art directors: people attentive to fashion but not overtly fashionable. The duo's original aesthetic influences came from the Italian sartorial tradition of the 1970s, with a focus on functional items from the male wardrobe, such as shirts, blazers, bomber jackets and suits, and its influence with various artistic and cultural cues, from New York streetwear to music, photography and digital media. Subsequently, the brand expanded its product categories, introducing in 2018 womenswear and accessories – with a genderless style – and, in 2021, its first collection of furniture, evolving into a comprehensive lifestyle brand (Sunnei, 2023).

In September 2020, Vanguards Group acquired a majority stake in the company with an investment of €6 million (Tagwalk, 2020; Williams, 2020; Salibian, 2021b). Before the investment, Sunnei had ten employees, an annual turnover of just over €1 million and a limited number of suppliers. Today, it has 45 employees, partners with more than 20 suppliers and over 100 third-party retailers. Sunnei was forecast to break even in 2023, with estimated revenues of c. €10 million (Leitch, 2023; Salibian, 2023).

Sunnei's brand identity, positioning and distribution strategy

Sunnei is among the earliest hyper-digital brands and immediately showed its vocation as a 'media brand' (Hjarvard, 2008; Becker, 2023; Leitch, 2023). From the get-go, it harnessed social platforms, particularly Instagram, which contributed significantly to brand growth and enabled it to build a strong identity that shunned traditional brand-consumer relationships in favour of a more co-created and inclusive approach.

The brand's DNA can be described "as a clash between streetwear and haute fashion, infused with an awkward sense of cool" (Eytan, 2017), "colourful at first glance, witty at its core" and capable of mixing "irony and sophistication" (Sunnei, 2023). The thoughtful product portfolio and highly experimental communication strategy convey the brand's strong and recognisable identity in its mixture of seemingly opposite attributes. Sunnei offers items that resonate with the playful and active attitude of its consumers; for example, the Do What You Want (DWYW) line, which started with the launch of a basic T-shirt and then developed into an entire collection, including a selection of monochromatic pieces customisable with black or white iron-on Sunnei logos (Brain, 2020) and, more recently, the series of limited T-shirts bearing imaginative nomenclatures referring to roles played in the fashion industry, including the play on words 'Joe Boffer'[1] (Salibian, 2022). Similarly, the unconventional marketing and communication strategy, managed directly by the founders (Eytan, 2017), has always focused on the use of social networks, with the primary objective of communicating the brand's mood and vision on everyday life (Tom Greyhound, 2018) before product and e-commerce-related content.

Regarding positioning, Sunnei is considered a niche brand in the high-end streetwear scene that, despite being rooted in the Italian cultural and creative substratum, is perceived as an international brand. Indeed, early appreciation came from the Japanese and South Korean markets, and, today, South Korea, Italy and the US are listed as top-performing countries, with China and the UK burgeoning (Salibian, 2023). Currently, 75% of Sunnei's total sales are generated from the wholesale channel (Salibian, 2023), with presence in more than 100 retailer partners, including LuisaViaRoma, La Samaritaine, Ssense, Boon the Shop and GR8 (Williams, 2020; Leitch, 2023). In addition to e-commerce, Sunnei has a flagship store in Via Vela in Milan, initially serving as the brand's headquarters (Salibian, 2023). With the Vanguards Group acquisition, the Milan store will be the starting point of a new retail model that involves moving beyond the traditional business-to-business (B2B) model by focusing on the direct-to-consumer experience (B2C). Sunnei aims to enhance the e-commerce platform and create new destination points in target cities (Tagwalk, 2020) by merging the offline and online channels. Figure 6.3.1 presents a summary of the brand's timeline.

Sunnei is characterised as a brand talking a 'multidisciplinary language', adopting a fluid approach (Leitch, 2023) and being innovation-oriented. It aims to "create a new

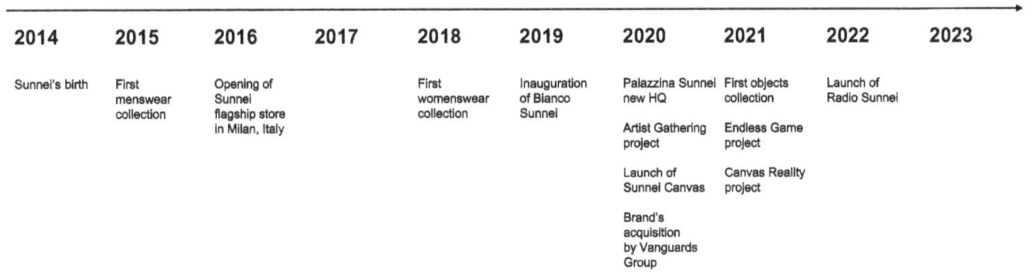

2014	2015	2016	2017	2018	2019	2020	2021	2022	2023
Sunnei's birth	First menswear collection	Opening of Sunnei flagship store in Milan, Italy		First womenswear collection	Inauguration of Bianco Sunnei	Palazzina Sunnei new HQ	First objects collection	Launch of Radio Sunnei	
						Artist Gathering project	Endless Game project		
						Launch of Sunnei Canvas	Canvas Reality project		
						Brand's acquisition by Vanguards Group			

Figure 6.3.1 Sunnei's timeline.

Source: Author's own.

generation space in Milan that does not only live by fashion but by all the energies that [it] feeds daily such as music, photography, cinema and contemporary art" (Bertola and Linfante, 2015: 313). Because of this, Sunnei could be defined as a multidisciplinary platform, that is, a media brand platform delivering fashion, cultural and creative content together with a mix of clothing, music and design (Sunnei, 2023) through all the levers that determine its positioning strategy: from collection development to communication and distribution channel strategy.

Sunnei has created a multidimensional CX (Schmitt, 1999; Verhoef et al., 2009), integrating physical and virtual touchpoints connected to fashion, cultural and creative production that it nurtures with its community. The brand's different consumer experience activations intersect the social, territorial, artistic and musical experimentation contexts.

This case study allows readers to dive into the strategies that Sunnei adopts to nurture an effective multidimensional CX, by harnessing mediatisation and digital media and to explore the impacts of these strategies in building an active, cohesive community which resonates with the brand's values.

Fashion mediatisation and the impact of digital media

Sunnei is increasingly transforming into a 'media brand' (Becker, 2023; Leitch, 2023), producing cultural, creative and artistic content together with clothing, accessories and design objects by exploiting many unconventional physical and digital media. This transformation is part of a broader phenomenon that Rocamora (2017) calls the 'mediatization of fashion'.

Digital media have revolutionised how companies build and implement their marketing strategies (Haenlein et al., 2020; Wongkitrungrueng, Dehouche and Assarut, 2020; Zhou et al., 2022) and the rapid proliferation of social media has strongly impacted user behaviour and perceptions (Kumar et al., 2016; Schivinski and Dabrowski, 2016). Digitally created content is part of their content marketing toolkit and is a distinct element of integrated marketing communication and brand strategy, whereby live streaming has become a leading entertainment choice for consumers (Wang, 2021), gamification an opportunity to co-create brand experiences (Nobre and Ferreira, 2017) and digital brand narratives an occasion to promote global, multimodal visibility (Mouratidou, 2022).

While the convergence of new media creates new contexts for relationships, participation and cooperation, and companies benefit from increased social interaction and engagement (Shen et al., 2021), the 'mediatization of fashion' (Rocamora, 2017) leads to a new way of 'doing fashion through media', using fashion to generate and implement new media and digital tools. Doing fashion through media means shortening the distance between consumers and brands, and acting directly with them. It also means producing specific user generated content (UGC), and integrating or adapting it to be conveyed on the various platforms, including Facebook, Instagram, Snapchat, TikTok, Line in Japan, WeChat in China and KakaoTalk in Korea. The reverse is also enabled, that is, mediatisation changes aspects of the physical environment to fit the digital space. In physical retail, technology augments the spatial set-up through digital screens, touchscreens, smart furniture and fitting rooms, while at the same time providing content to share or interact with on social media.

Sunnei as a community, relational experiential platform

From the outset, Sunnei has been focused on constructing experiential spaces that foster effective interaction between the brand and their consumer, consumer and product, and consumer and other contexts. A conception of experience that goes beyond spectacularisation as an end in itself (Pine and Gilmore, 1999; Rogers, Vrotsos and Schmitt, 2003) but rather is oriented towards a CX that focuses on the person and their experience, sensations, feelings, cognitive performance, memory, social relations and actions (Fuat Firat, Dholakia and Venkatesh, 1995; Schmitt, 1999; Cova and Cova, 2002; LaSalle and Britton, 2003; Resciniti, 2005).

In line with this approach, Sunnei seeks to engender a brand community, by offering a raft of initiatives, events and narratives, both physical and virtual, capable of providing all the cultural, cognitive and emotional tools to make each person a co-creator of their own Sunnei experience (Edvardsson, Tronvoll and Gruber, 2011; Grönroos and Ravald, 2011; Pareigis, Echeverri and Edvardsson, 2012).

Sunnei is thus not configured as a traditional fashion brand but as a 'creative collective' (Venezia, 2022), an 'experiential platform' comprising 'diffuse elements' (Carù and Cova, 2003; Resciniti, 2005) that are the result of co-creation processes with their community with whom they share values, attitudes and an experimental approach to fashion. Sunnei's CX is articulated through a series of brand activities and expressions – that are the 'diffuse elements' of the 'experiential platform' – which, on the one hand, emphasise the relationship and exchange with their community and, on the other hand, consolidate the brand's role as "an incubator of creativity, interpersonal relationships and alternative products" (Sunnei, 2023).

CX as a multidimensional construct

From a CX standpoint, Sunnei creates a series of immersive and engaging experiences. Each expression recognises the active role of the consumer in the co-creation process with the brand (Ramaswamy, 2009), which, in turn, activates extraordinary (LaSalle and Britton, 2003) and/or memorable experiential responses (Pine and Gilmore, 1999).

CX can be defined as a "multidimensional construct focusing on a customer's cognitive, emotional, behavioural, sensorial, and social responses to a firm's offerings during the customer's entire purchase journey" (Verhoef et al., 2009; Lemon and Verhoef, 2016: 71). This holistic perspective highlights the individual nature of the CX, emphasising that each customer's experience is unique and personal (Gentile, Spiller and Noci, 2007) and that "the experience is created not only by those elements which the retailer can control (e.g., service interface, retail atmosphere, assortment, price), but also by elements that are outside of the retailer's control (e.g., influence of others)" (Verhoef et al., 2009: 32). The CX is thus a personal consumer response that influences several dimensions:

- *Cognitive dimension* – the way the consumer thinks, reasons and responds cognitively to brand stimuli;
- *Emotional dimension* – the emotional perceptions and feelings aroused by the messages sent by the brand;
- *Behavioural dimension* – the reactions, in terms of actions and behaviours, to the stimuli sent by the brand through its touchpoints;

- *Sensory dimension* – the stimulation of the senses through visual, olfactory, tactile, gustatory or auditory stimuli;
- *Social dimension* – the influence of the external environment (online or offline), contact with other consumers and the system of social norms that influence consumer perception.

Figure 6.3.2 illustrates the relationships between the theoretical bases discussed above. Specifically, it shows how the mediatisation of fashion is grounded in the notion of the brand as an experiential platform comprising diffuse elements, which, in turn, are expressed through the multidimensionality of CX.

The multidimensional CX of Sunnei is presented next, highlighting how the different dimensions can be recognised within the 'diffuse elements' that the brand, as an experiential platform, makes available to its community.

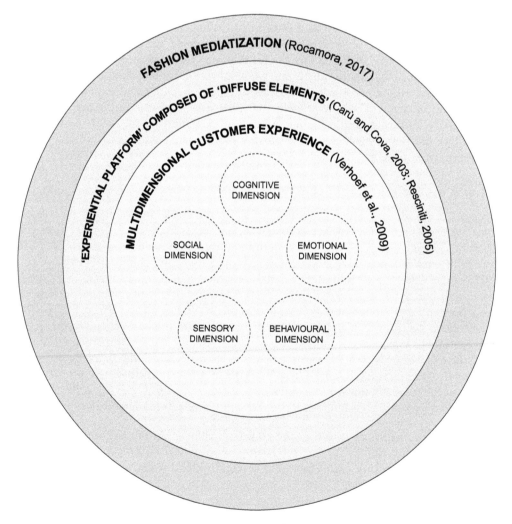

Figure 6.3.2 The interplay between mediatisation, experiential platform and CX dimensions.

Bianco Sunnei

Bianco Sunnei is a project of urban regeneration, bringing together fashion, territory, culture, art and community. Located in the northeast of Milan, in the Rubattino green area, a portion of the Parco dell'Acqua overpass underwent a cultural transformation by the reclamation of 4,000 square metres, leading to a dramatic modification of the venue. Inaugurated in 2019 as a set for Sunnei's SS20 show, it was subsequently transformed into a permanent, participatory, inclusive, cultural open-air art gallery hosting projects and events (Salibian, 2019), which serves to enrich the lived experiences of those who encounter it (Holbrook and Hirschman, 1982; Csikszentmihalyi, 1997; Pine and Gilmore, 1999). In doing so, it showcases how Sunnei takes a people-centric and community approach to its activations.

Artists Gathering

The Artists Gathering Project was launched on Instagram in March 2020, during the global pandemic lockdown. The project involved the Sunnei community of Milanese artists freely streaming their musical and artistic performances. Initially, the project adopted an open and flexible schedule for the inputs and stimuli of the community itself and, later, was consolidated into a more comprehensive international network and structured format (Brain, 2020; LUISAVIAROMA, 2020). The main objective of the Artists Gathering was to open the brand's channels to the community and to offer a collective space for individual free expression at a challenging time, when people were physically socially restricted.

The project represents Sunnei's experimentation with stimulating consumers' active participation in its events and initiatives. For Sunnei, the Instagram platform is a part of the CX, a place to interface with its consumers, share projects, bring the community together for collaboration directly with the founders and make appointments (physical or virtual) to participate in the brand's various initiatives.

Sunnei Canvas

Sunnei Canvas is arguably the brand's most renowned project, emphasising its vocation as a 'media brand'. Sunnei Canvas, which launched in July 2020 during Milan's Digital Fashion Week, was a virtual reality (VR)-enhanced digital platform designed to fully customise the namesake Canvas SS21 collection – a selection of its signature white garments (Blanks, 2020; Salamone, 2020). The platform was released in collaboration with Milan-based digital agency PEZZO DI STUDIO, which specialises in 3D fashion modelling and personalisation. Sunnei created digital twins (Lim, Zheng and Chen, 2020; Kamble et al., 2022) to generate CX, by combining its product design, distribution channels, sustainable production and communication strategies in a single digital action and interface (Iannilli and Linfante, 2022). The project was launched through two connected channels targeting different audiences: the digital customisation platform targeted B2B partners and, in parallel, an ironic and unconventional video targeted consumers (B2C), presenting the collection through human-like avatars wearing the Canvas collection (Turra, 2020).

Sunnei Canvas offers its partners (retailers and consumers) a unique experience in which technology becomes an enabler capable of activating previously nonexistent shared and collaborative experiential contexts. The Canvas project over a period of two years evolved from a customisation platform (outlined above) to the Endless Game (related to the Canvas FW21 collection), a gamified entertainment-based experience designed to engage its community, based on providing fun, rewards, competition, social interactions and personalisation (Nobre and Ferreira, 2017; Hwang and Choi, 2020). Its final iteration was into a hybrid experience called Canvas Reality (related to the SS22 collection), which blended the real-life (IRL) and digital channels and touchpoints, in the pursuit of customisation and CX (Davalli, 2021). Situated within Palazzina Sunnei, the brand's headquarters, the project showcased multi-sensory physical installations of its Canvas collection, adjacent to interactive digital screens that enabled people to virtually try on the garments, resulting in a more immersive CX (Salibian, 2021a; Tancorre, 2021). At the time of writing, Sunnei Canvas is unavailable, yet its iterations over two years demonstrates Sunnei's commitment to co-created, community-based CX improvement and evolution.

Radio Sunnei

Radio Sunnei was conceived in 2022 as a 24/7 listening and viewing platform and is available on https://Sunnei.radio/ and Spotify. The platform offers seamless streaming of music and videos, with different daily programmes and an hour of live DJ sessions twice monthly. The radio station aims to not only provide Sunnei's listeners with a range of live-streamed music but also promote up-and-coming musicians and bands by offering engaging talk shows and interviews with music industry aficionados. At the same time, listeners can share their favourite music tracks, triggering real-time co-creation processes. In this way, the user is connected, engaged, participating and interactive (Al-Emadi and Ben Yahia, 2020). Such a strategy increases customers' perceived value (utilitarian, hedonic and symbolic value) and brand engagement (Sashi, 2012).

Table 6.3.1 shows how Sunnei's mediatisation strategy applies the CX dimensions – cognitive, emotional, behavioural, sensorial and social – (Verhoef et al., 2009) across its different activations and how different value co-creation processes between brand and consumer are activated within the CX to enhance community building.

Table 6.3.1 Application of mediatisation, experiential platform (community building) and CX dimensions to Sunnei

Sunnei experiences	Mediatisation strategies	Community-building processes	CX dimensions
Bianco Sunnei	Open platform	Sharing values	Cognitive, emotional, sensorial, social
Artists Gathering	Interactivity, live streaming, UGC	Producing content Sharing content Community interaction	Emotional, social
Sunnei Canvas	Interactivity, gamified entertainment, multi-channel	Sharing values, community interaction	Cognitive, emotional, behavioural
Radio Sunnei	Live streaming, UGC, open platform, multi-channel		Emotional, behavioural, social

Conclusion

Sunnei exemplifies how a niche brand with an international reach has managed to build a solid and loyal community in a relatively short time by leveraging its ability to produce and distribute content related to fashion, art, music and design through multiple physical and digital channels and to involve the audience in the co-production and dissemination of this content. Acting as an experiential and relational platform, Sunnei has adopted a consumer-centric approach to experience by relying on the multiple dimensions of the experience.

As founders Rizzo and Messina state, "the flexibility in stretching strategies has always proved to be an asset for the brand, which has been a forerunner in Milan in experimenting with collections, presentations and distribution formats" (Salibian, 2023). Being a digital-first, customer-driven and non-trend-driven brand (Williams, 2020) has allowed Sunnei to respond to the expectations of its community and to have the necessary flexibility and aptitude for innovation to experiment with forms and formats of service and consumer experience.

Today, Sunnei is in the process of scaling up, presenting both an opportunity and a challenge for the brand. Given its carefully crafted community-based origins that have proven successful to date, how will Sunnei manage to grow its community without alienating its core audience and remaining authentic and consistent with its experimental 'media brand' vocation? What new multidimensional CX could be offered while remaining consistent and open to innovation and change?

Case questions

1   This case study explores the different and multiple dimensions of Sunnei's customer experience (CX). Focusing on the holistic and multidimensional approach to experience, discuss what it means to adopt a consumer-oriented approach and why it is effective in building compelling CX.

2   Sunnei is ready to scale following the Vanguards Group investment, but such acquisition comes with both benefits and risks. Sunnei's founders recognise two main challenges: maintaining the consistency of the consumer experience and not weakening the connection with its community. Discuss these two challenges and provide insights into strategies to maintain a consistent customer experience (CX).

3   Sunnei currently prioritises its digital channels over its physical store. What experiential strategies could Sunnei adopt in the future to harness and integrate the physical with the digital channels and touchpoints in its activations?

4   For fashion brands, the concept of 'mediatisation' is burgeoning. Discuss the impact of mediatisation on the customer experience (CX), following the example of a small to medium-sized fashion brand of your choice, and how could retail and communication strategies be shaped by and for media.

Notes

1   https://sunnei.it/blogs/news/joe-boffer.

References

Al-Emadi, F.A. and Ben Yahia, I. (2020) 'Ordinary celebrities related criteria to harvest fame and influence on social media.' *Journal of Research in Interactive Marketing*, 14(2), pp. 195–213. https://doi.org/10.1108/JRIM-02-2018-0031

Becker, M. (2023) *Loris Messina and Simone Rizzo cultivate the SUNNEI state of mind*. Document Journal, 27 February. [Online] [Accessed 5th April 2023] https://www.documentjournal.com/2023/02/sunnei-fall-winter-2023-milan-fashion-week-loris-messina-simone-rizzo-crowdsurfing-runway/

Bertola, P. and Linfante, V. (2015) *Il nuovo vocabolario della moda italiana*. Firenze: Mandragora. [Online] [Accessed 4th April 2023] https://www.mandragora.it/prodotto/il-nuovo-vocabolario-della-moda-italiana-ebook/

Blanks, T. (2020) *How Sunnei bucked the fashion system*. The Business of Fashion, 16 July. [Online] [Accessed 3rd April 2023] https://www.businessoffashion.com/articles/fashion-week/is-sunnei-the-future-of-milan-fashion/

Brain, E. (2020) *SUNNEI Is in a CGI world of its own* Hypebeast, 15 July. [Online] [Accessed 3rd April 2023] https://hypebeast.com/2020/7/sunnei-spring-summer-2021-collection-canvas-milan-fashion-week-exclusive-interview

Carù, A. and Cova, B. (2003) *Esperienze di consumo e marketing esperienziale: Radici diverse e convergenze possibili*. Micro & Macro Marketing [Preprint], (2/2003). https://doi.org/10.1431/9503

Cova, B. and Cova, V. (2002) 'Tribal marketing: The tribalisation of society and its impact on the conduct of marketing.' *European Journal of Marketing*, 36(5/6), pp. 595–620. https://doi.org/10.1108/03090560210423023

Csikszentmihalyi, M. (1997) *Finding flow: The psychology of engagement with everyday life*. New York: Basic Books (Finding flow: The psychology of engagement with everyday life), pp. ix, 181.

Davalli, C. (2021) 'S/S 22 Canvas Reality di SUNNEI porta il concetto di moda custom a un altro livello', 21 June. [Online] [Accessed 3rd April 2023] https://i-d.vice.com/it/article/88n5kg/sunnei-canvas-reality-ss-22

Edvardsson, B., Tronvoll, B. and Gruber, T. (2011) *Expanding understanding of service exchange and value co-creation: A social construction approach*. [Online] [Accessed 3rd April 2023]. https://doi.org/10.1007/s11747-010-0200-y']

Eytan, D. (2017) *Sunnei: The story of a young, Thriving Italian menswear brand discovered on Instagram*. Forbes, 26 March. [Online] [Accessed 28th September 2023] https://www.forbes.com/sites/declaneytan/2017/03/26/sunnei-the-story-of-a-young-thriving-italian-menswear-brand-discovered-on-instagram/

Fuat Firat, A., Dholakia, N. and Venkatesh, A. (1995) 'Marketing in a postmodern world.' *European Journal of Marketing*, 29(1), pp. 40–56. https://doi.org/10.1108/03090569510075334

Gentile, C., Spiller, N. and Noci, G. (2007) 'How to sustain the customer experience: An overview of experience components that co-create value with the customer.' *European Management Journal*, 25(5), pp. 395–410. https://doi.org/10.1016/j.emj.2007.08.005

Grönroos, C. and Ravald, A. (2011) 'Service as business logic: Implications for value creation and marketing.' *Journal of Service Management*, 22(1), pp. 5–22. https://doi.org/10.1108/09564231111106893

Haenlein, M. et al. (2020) 'Navigating the new era of influencer marketing: How to be successful on Instagram, TikTok, & Co.' *California Management Review*, 63(1), pp. 5–25. https://doi.org/10.1177/0008125620958166

Hjarvard, S. (2008) 'The mediatization of society. A theory of the media as agents of social and cultural change.' *Nordicom Review*, 29(2), pp. 102–131. https://doi.org/10.1515/nor-2017-0181

Holbrook, M.B. and Hirschman, E.C. (1982) 'The experiential aspects of consumption: Consumer fantasies, feelings, and fun.' *Journal of Consumer Research*, 9(2), pp. 132–140. https://www.jstor.org/stable/2489122

Hwang, J. and Choi, L. (2020) 'Having fun while receiving rewards? Exploration of gamification in loyalty programs for consumer loyalty.' *Journal of Business Research*, 106, pp. 365–376. https://doi.org/10.1016/j.jbusres.2019.01.031

Iannilli, V.M. and Linfante, V. (2022) 'Exploring disrupting scenarios in the fashion retail and communication paradigms.' *Luxury Studies: The In Pursuit of Luxury Journal*, 1(1), pp. 45–65. https://doi.org/10.1386/ipol_00005_1

Kamble, S.S. et al. (2022) 'Digital twin for sustainable manufacturing supply chains: Current trends, future perspectives, and an implementation framework.' *Technological Forecasting and Social Change*, 176, p. 121448. https://doi.org/10.1016/j.techfore.2021.121448

Kumar, A. et al. (2016) 'From social to sale: The effects of firm-generated content in social media on customer behavior.' *Journal of Marketing*, 80(1), pp. 7–25. https://doi.org/10.1509/jm.14.0249

LaSalle, D. and Britton, T. (2003) *Priceless: Turning ordinary products into extraordinary experiences*. Boston, MA: Harvard Business School Press..

LeDoux, J.E. (1996) *The emotional brain. The mysterious underpinning of emotional life*. New York: Simon & Schuster.

Leitch, L. (2023) *Fewer collections, steady growth: How Milan's Sunnei sees its future*. Vogue Business, 22 February. [Online] [Accessed 4th April 2023] https://www.voguebusiness.com/fashion/fewer-collections-steady-growth-how-milans-sunnei-sees-its-future

Lemon, K.N. and Verhoef, P.C. (2016) 'Understanding customer experience throughout the customer journey.' *Journal of Marketing*, 80(6), pp. 69–96. https://doi.org/10.1509/jm.15.0420

Lim, K.Y.H., Zheng, P. and Chen, C.-H. (2020) 'A state-of-the-art survey of digital twin: Techniques, engineering product lifecycle management and business innovation perspectives.' *Journal of Intelligent Manufacturing*, 31(6), pp. 1313–1337. https://doi.org/10.1007/s10845-019-01512-w

LUISAVIAROMA (2020) *SUNNEI Intervista | Luisaviaroma*. www.luisaviaroma.com. [Online] [Accessed 3rd May 2023] https://www.luisaviaroma.com/it-it/lvr-magazine/interviews/lvr-in-conversation-sunnei

Mouratidou, E. (2022) 'Fashion as leisure: Experience and entertainment through brands' digital narratives,' in Cantista, I. and Delille, D. (eds.) *Fashion heritage: Narrative and knowledge creation*. Cham: Springer International Publishing, pp. 263–287. https://doi.org/10.1007/978-3-031-06886-7_11

Nobre, H. and Ferreira, A. (2017) 'Gamification as a platform for brand co-creation experiences.' *Journal of Brand Management*, 24(4), pp. 349–361. https://doi.org/10.1057/s41262-017-0055-3

Pareigis, J., Echeverri, P. and Edvardsson, B. (2012) 'Exploring internal mechanisms forming customer servicescape experiences.' *Journal of Service Management*, 23(5), pp. 677–695. https://doi.org/10.1108/09564231211269838

Pine, B.J. and Gilmore, J.H. (1999) *The experience economy: Work is theatre & every business a stage*. Boston, MA: Harvard Business Press.

Ramaswamy, V. (2009) 'Co-creation of value — Towards an expanded paradigm of value creation.' *Marketing Review St. Gallen*, 26(6), pp. 11–17. https://doi.org/10.1007/s11621-009-0085-7

Resciniti, R. (2005) 'Il marketing orientato all'esperienza,' in *4th International Congress "Marketing Trends", ESCP-EAP*. Paris.

Rocamora, A. (2017) 'Mediatization and digital media in the field of fashion.' *Fashion Theory*, 21(5), pp. 505–522. https://doi.org/10.1080/1362704X.2016.1173349

Rogers, D.L., Vrotsos, K.L. and Schmitt, B.H. (2003) *There's no business that's not show business: Marketing in an experience culture*. FT Press.

Salamone, L. (2020) *Sunnei's digital platform to create custom collections*. nss magazine, July. [Online] [Accessed 3rd April 2023] https://www.nssmag.com/en/article/22959

Salibian, S. (2019) *Sunnei to show collection in requalified urban area.*, WWD, 14 June. [Online] [Accessed 29th September 2023] https://wwd.com/fashion-news/fashion-features/sunnei-show-requalified-urban-area-1203167896/

Salibian, S. (2021a) *Sunnei canvas experience gets physical at Milan fashion week.*, WWD, 19 June. [Online] [Accessed 3rd April 2023] https://wwd.com/feature/sunnei-canvas-collection-irl-experience-milan-fashion-week-1234850731/

Salibian, S. (2021b) *Sunnei to present canvas collection through video game concept.* WWD, 15 January. [Accessed 3rd April 2023] https://wwd.com/feature/sunnei-canvas-collection-videogame-concept-1234696493/

Salibian, S. (2022) *Who is joe boffer? Sunnei Teases fashion jobs in new capsule collection.* WWD, 4 October. [Online] [Accessed 28th September 2023] https://wwd.com/fashion-news/fashion-scoops/sunnei-launches-tshirts-capsule-collection-mocking-fashion-jobs-1235376904/.

Salibian, S. (2023) *Why Sunnei Is tweaking its business model.* WWD, 19 January. [Online] [Accessed 4th April 2023] https://wwd.com/fashion-news/fashion-features/sunnei-vanguards-group-ceo-discusses-brand-potential-business-model-tweaks-1235480882/.

Sashi, C.M. (2012) 'Customer engagement, buyer-seller relationships, and social media.' *Management Decision*, 50(2), pp. 253–272. https://doi.org/10.1108/00251741211203551

Schivinski, B. and Dabrowski, D. (2016) 'The effect of social media communication on consumer perceptions of brands.' *Journal of Marketing Communications*, 22(2), pp. 189–214. https://doi.org/10.1080/13527266.2013.871323

Schmitt, B.H. (1999) *Experiential marketing. How to get customers to sense, feel, think, act and relate to your company and brands.* New York: The Free Press.

Shen, B. et al. (2021) 'How to promote user purchase in metaverse? A systematic literature review on consumer behavior research and virtual commerce application design.' *Applied Sciences*, 11(23), p. 11087. https://doi.org/10.3390/app112311087

Sunnei (2023) *SUNNEI Company Profile* [Online] [Accessed 5th April 2023] https://www.linkedin.com/company/sunnei/

Tagwalk (2020) 'SUNNEI is ready to write its next chapter through an investment with Vanguards.' *Tagwalk*, 24 September. [Online] [Accessed 5th April 2023] https://www.tag-walk.com/it/news/897

Tancorre, M. (2021) *Sunnei, la nuova collezione Canvas Reality è una tela bianca tutta da personalizzare.* Vogue Italia, 30 June. [Online] [Accessed 3rd April 2023] https://www.vogue.it/moda/article/moda-primavera-estate-2022-sunnei-progetto-canvas-reality-collezione

Tom Greyhound (2018) *Sunnei interview, Tom Greyhound Paris.* [Online] [Accessed 28th September 2023] https://tomgreyhound.com/blogs/journal/sunnei-interview

Turra, A. (2020) *Dancing "Macarena" With Sunnei Avatars.* WWD, 15 July. [Online] [Accessed 3rd April 2023] https://wwd.com/feature/dancing-macarena-with-sunnei-avatars-1203678751/

Venezia, A. (2022) *Sunnei: «Non abbiamo mai voluto creare un marchio per diventare famosi ma un movimento».* [Online] [Accessed 3rd May 2023] https://www.editorialedomani.it/idee/sunnei-moda-milano-chi-sono-intervista-tm9z3fau

Verhoef, P.C. et al. (2009) 'Customer experience creation: Determinants, dynamics and management strategies.' *Journal of Retailing*, 85(1), pp. 31–41. https://doi.org/10.1016/j.jretai.2008.11.001

Wang, C.L. (2021) 'New frontiers and future directions in interactive marketing: Inaugural Editorial.' *Journal of Research in Interactive Marketing*, 15(1), pp. 1–9. https://doi.org/10.1108/JRIM-03-2021-270

Williams, R. (2020) *Nanushka's owner launches New Fashion Group, buying Milan's Sunnei.* The Business of Fashion. [Online] [Accessed 5th April 2023] https://www.businessoffashion.com/articles/luxury/nanushkas-owner-launches-new-fashion-group-buying-milans-sunnei/

Wongkitrungrueng, A., Dehouche, N. and Assarut, N. (2020) 'Live streaming commerce from the sellers' perspective: Implications for online relationship marketing.' *Journal of Marketing Management*, 36(5–6), pp. 488–518. https://doi.org/10.1080/0267257X.2020.1748895

Zhou, L. et al. (2022) 'Understanding the role of influencers on live streaming platforms: When tipping makes the difference.' *European Journal of Marketing*, 56(10), pp. 2677–2697. https://doi.org/10.1108/EJM-10-2021-0815

Further reading and resources

Sunnei website: https://sunnei.it/
Sunnei official Instagram page: https://www.instagram.com/sunnei/
Sunnei YouTube channel: https://www.youtube.com/@sunnei4734
Sunnei Canvas 'Macarena' video: https://www.youtube.com/watch?v=tYhGPb0GL5k&ab_channel=
    SUNNEI
Sunnei Endless Game: https://www.youtube.com/watch?v=vMZwtLl6Q-E&ab_channel=SUNNEI
Radio Sunnei: https://sunnei.radio/

Definitions

Mediatisation: The process whereby society and fields of cultural production are increasingly influenced or dependent on the media and the way they present and transmit information.

6.4   Glossier: instigating phygital customer experience in the beauty and skin care market

Anna Mangas and Laura Costin

Learning objectives

On completion of this case study, learners should be able to:

1   Explore strategies implemented by Glossier in delivering compelling customer experiences.
2   Understand the role of customer centricity in creating phygital experiences that build engagement and emotional connection.
3   Examine how co-creation and user generated content (UGC) can facilitate community building to add value to the customer experience.
4   Evaluate future customer experience opportunities in the beauty and skin care sector.

Introduction

Glossier's history

Emily Weiss, a former fashion assistant at Vogue and avid beauty enthusiast, launched her blog 'Into the Gloss' in 2010 (Mintel, 2018). Into the Gloss was transformed into Glossier, a sleek yet affordable beauty and skin care brand for the millennial market. It launched with four products after receiving USD 2 million in funding (Turk, 2020). The brand now sells a wider range of products across beauty and skin care, alongside fragrance, body and GlossiWear – clothing and accessories. Weiss attributes the success of Glossier to understanding the changing beauty consumer. Whilst the fashion industry was witnessing a seismic shift in power dynamics between consumers and brands, the beauty industry was arguably still directing their audiences. Beauty bloggers were paving the way as industry disruptors, developing authority that signalled change was under way (Turk, 2020).

Weiss took the opportunity to re-shape the narrative in beauty and skin care with Glossier by using the social media platform Instagram as a direct communication channel with the consumer (Morosini, 2022). Glossier created a customer feedback loop (Mintel, 2018) whereby education and influence work side by side, Glossier educating its community about skin care and beauty whilst followers in turn influenced product design. This resulted in a range of must-have items with distinctive appeal (Danziger, 2018).

Website

Glossier.com, part of the first wave of direct-to-consumer (DTC) brands that prioritised a digital-first approach, benefited from low barriers to market entry (Greifeld, 2023). At the time of Glossier's launch, millennials were the most digitally native demographic, embracing technology to discover brands and make ecommerce purchases (McClure, 2022). Weiss understood the target customer valued beauty conversation, building this into Glossier's website to create a unique, content-rich customer experience (Moraes, 2020). This included communicating in an informal copywriting style and pioneering the inclusion of UGC and how-to videos (Gibson, 2018). Glossier.com marked a shift in how beauty and skin care could be experienced online, paving the way for subsequent brands.

Physical stores

Glossier experimented with pop-up stores from its first year of trading (Into the Gloss, n.d.) with its first permanent flagship store opening in 2018 in New York. When Glossier's London pop-up store opened in 2019, it served over 100,000 visitors in ten weeks, the highest average daily sales of any of Glossier's previous pop-ups, and planned to stay open on a longer-term basis (Bertolino, 2021). However, Glossier closed its stores during the global pandemic in 2020, announcing all stores would permanently close later that year. By 2023, Glossier operated ten US stores and one UK store (Glossier, n.d.-a).

Sephora partnership

In 2023, Glossier's products became available in Sephora's stores in the US and Canada, as well as online via its website and app (Chitrakorn, 2022). After nine years of operating a DTC model, Glossier's retail partnership reflects market trends that show multi-brand retailers are advancing post-pandemic (Edited, 2023) as consumers now want products to be available wherever they are shopping (Strugatz, 2022). In 2023, the Sephora partnership expanded to the UK, Glossier's second biggest market (Hill, 2023), making the brand available in-store, online and via the app, marking another chapter in Glossier's retail strategy (Sandler, 2022) (see Figure 6.4.1 for a timeline of Glossier's history).

Glossier and the beauty sector

The global beauty and personal care industry is thriving; in 2022 it was valued at USD 534 billion and is expected to grow by almost 6% annually until 2026 (THG Ingenuity, 2022). With a a sales value of USD 1.8 billion in 2021, Glossier commands around 0.3% market share (Mondalek and Strugatz, 2021). Glossier's product offer encompasses

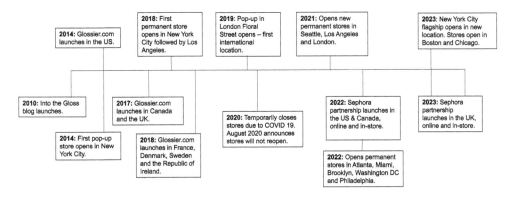

Figure 6.4.1 A history of Glossier timeline.

Source: Author's own.

both skin care and cosmetics; the global market is driven by these sectors, with skin care accounting for 27% of market share, and cosmetics achieving 16% share (Statista, 2022a). Despite a stream of new niche market entrants, the industry remains largely homogenous, dominated by key firms including L'Oreal, P&G, Unilever and Shishedo (Statista, 2022a).

Glossier's primary market is the US. This market generates the most skin care and cosmetics revenue globally, with skin care accounting for USD 20 billion (Statista, 2023a) and cosmetics generating USD 19.43 billion (Statista, 2023b). In 2022, Glossier achieved approximately 0.1% brand share of the beauty and personal care market in the US (Euromonitor, 2023). Outside of the US, Glossier operates in Canada, the UK, the Republic of Ireland, France, Denmark and Sweden (Glossier, n.d-b). According to Similar Web (2023a), 67% of website traffic to Glossier.com comes from the US, illustrating the importance of its domestic customer base.

The beauty consumer

The beauty industry has been more resilient in the face of global economic factors such as the aftereffects of COVID-19 and rising inflation (Mintel, 2023). Generation Z and millennials are purchasing skin care more than other beauty categories (Statista, 2022b), demonstrating a reshaping of the sector as beauty ideals alter. The largest demographic of visitors to Glossier.com are 25–34-year-olds, accounting for 36% of visitors, followed by 18–24-year-olds making up 20% of visitors (Similar Web, 2023b), evidencing the continued youth appeal of the brand.

Expanding the brand universe: a phygital store strategy

Glossier's physical stores allow the brand to experiment with immersive retail design to create unique environments geared towards social media content and community building (Flora, 2021). The generation of online conversation in the physical space creates a phygital customer experience, with IRL (in real life) and digital interactions working in union. Phygital is defined as physical and digital channels coexisting that lead to blended customer experiences (Goldsgeyme, 2021). As bricks-and-mortar retail returned post the pandemic, consumers expected brands to bridge the gap between the online and offline worlds with immersive phygital experiences (Rees and Sagresse, 2023). Physical retail is important to Glossier's target audience, with 55% of Generation Z and 65% of millennials in the US identifying physical stores as their leading shopping channel (Statista, 2023c).

Designing Glossier's in-store customer experience

Glossier stores take an experimental approach to how a beauty brand can be presented and experienced by the customer. Each store is unique, playing on the individualism of the location to create a bespoke experience that relates to the place and the community (Huber, 2019). For its 2019 London pop-up location on Floral Street in Covent Garden, Glossier looked at the history of London design for inspiration. The space featured hand-drawn floral wallpaper inspired by William Morris (Tse, 2020) and patterned prints to reflect the ornate style of 19th-century parlours and members clubs (Levy, 2019). Similarly, the Miami pop-up interior was influenced by the city's Art Deco architecture; the design included architectural columns and tropical palms (Lam, 2019).

London flagship

Whilst Glossier's pop-ups are playful, its flagship stores have a more refined aesthetic. Glossier's London flagship is its only international location. Situated in a townhouse in Covent Garden, the foyer is branded with an ornate Glossier 'G' reflecting the building's 17th-century heritage (Englefield, 2021). A large pink bench invites customers to dwell in the space where selfies can be taken at a large mirror inscribed with Glossier's affirmation statement, 'YOU LOOK GOOD'. The chamber-like spaces achieve an airy and inviting environment where customers can spend time browsing, testing products and interacting. As in all Glossier stores, orders are placed via Glossier 'Editors' on iPads using a point-of-sale system. The system syncs online and offline purchases and gives customers the flexibility to start orders in-store and finish them on desktop or mobile devices (Lacombe, 2018), thus providing a phygital purchase experience (Goldesgeyme, 2021).

Store localism

A further aspect of uniqueness is Glossier merchandise, a range of items specific to each store location. Glossier partners with non-profits that are local to Glossier stores on the merchandise items, contributing a sales donation of USD 5 (or currency equivalent) for each item sold (Glossier, n.d.-c). According to Edelman (2022), 73% of Generation Z shoppers would purchase from a brand that aligns with their own beliefs and values. Therefore, these partnerships affiliate Glossier with its target audience values.

Glossier's stores are sophisticated spaces that entice customers to spend a generous amount of time discovering products, experimenting and connecting. Further store openings remain a key part of its strategy (Sandler, 2023).

Utilising the better model to appraise Glossier's customer experience

Glossier's approach to phygital customer experience can be analysed using the BETTER Creative Model (Smilansky, 2018: 75). This model is designed to aid the creation of authentic, interactive brand experiences. Glossier has translated its online offer into the physical store environment to achieve an immersive branded experience. Each letter within the BETTER acronym represents a different stage of experience to be examined (Smilansky, 2018).

B – Brand Personality
E – Emotional Connection
T – Target Audience
T – Two-Way Interaction
E – Exponential Elements
R – Reach

Brand personality

"Brand personality pillars" (Smilansky, 2018: 82) are human-like qualities that bring the brand to life in an experiential way and should be the starting point when developing an IRL experience. Glossier defines its approach to beauty using three personality-like statements: celebrating individuality, freedom of expression and having fun (Glossier, n.d.-d). Glossier's brand voice has been inspired by its youthful audience; the brand communicates in an authentic, conversational tone across website, store and social media, achieving authentic appeal by speaking directly to the customer like a friend. Glossier's personality is communicated on its website through product videos and demonstrates the ease of applying products in a simple visual style that reflects TikTok content and UGC. The relatable and fun personality is consistently communicated in retail stores via Editors (sales associates). Their role is to enhance the customer experience by educating and connecting with customers in a down to earth manner.

Emotional connection

Glossier has cultivated a loyal relationship online with its audience through social media community building, making the transition from content to commerce (Ravi, 2018). Instagram remains Glossier's top social media platform with 2.7 million followers globally (Instagram, 2023a). The brand continues to use Instagram to build a personal connection with its community through a daily blend of product posts, creator videos and UGC, achieving an attainable and engaging content style. Glossier's engagement is stronger on Instagram than that of its core competitors (Similar Web, 2023c), evidencing its customer connection (see Table 6.4.1).

Given the strength of its online community, customers visit Glossier stores with some prior loyalty, providing opportunities in the IRL customer experience to facilitate a deepening of the relationship. Emotional connection is achieved by multisensory experiences (Smilansky, 2018). In Glossier's stores this is through individual design features, tactile finishes and product testing (Morris, 2022) where customers can relax, interact and take photos. The spaces integrate the brand personality through Glossier's branding to develop memorable experiences.

Target audience

Glossier defines itself as a "people powered beauty ecosystem" (Instagram, 2023b) placing the customer at the centre of its brand story through personal interaction and co-creation. From Glossier's origins as the Into the Gloss blog, Weiss discussed products and tips,

Table 6.4.1 Glossier Instagram engagement vs competitors

Company	Instagram profile	Average number of comments per post	Engagement rate	Source
Glossier	@glossier	754	0.68%	(Social Blade, 2023a)
e.l.f. Cosmetics	@elfcosmetics	188	0.17%	(Social Blade, 2023b)
Milk Makeup	@milkmakeup	37	0.06%	(Social Blade, 2023c)

interacting directly with an audience that was beauty obsessed. In the Into the Gloss blog feature 'Top Shelf', individuals were interviewed about their beauty routine in detail, providing a democratic take on beauty content (Meltzer, 2019). By building a legion of online followers, Glossier is positioned as a brand authority, understanding the values and preferences of the target audience through frequent interaction.

The dominant use of pink in Glossier's branding is significant in its successful creation of products and experiences that aesthetically appeal to the target audience. A pop-cultural phenomenon, 'millennial pink' was coined as a term in 2016 (Hyland, 2016). Glossier's early use of this specific shade communicated their cultural kudos to the consumer through actual product characteristics (Kotler, 2020). Fun packaging including a free bubble wrap make-up bag and stickers with each order developed brand affinity (Sandler, 2022). 'Insta-worthy' packaging inspires UGC, with the hashtag #glossierpink being used over 26,000 times to date (Instagram, 2023c). Glossier continues to prioritise social media, establishing 579.5k followers and 9.5 million likes on TikTok (TikTok, 2023a), continually evolving with customers across relevant platforms and content.

Two-way interaction

Bringing together the prior themes outlined, the core of Glossier's success is how it uses interaction, listening to and taking input from its audience to generate advocacy. Co-creation and community combine across the brand's touchpoints to facilitate a phygital customer experience. The broad definition of co-creation can be understood as creating together (Sarasvuo et al., 2022), comprising the interactions between firms and customers for the purpose of creating value (Prahalad and Ramaswamy, 2004). Glossier created a community on Instagram as part of its original DTC strategy, recognising that a shift towards customer centricity meant consumers had a role to play in the development of products (Turk, 2020). Glossier's latest co-created product is deodorant, having developed the product over five years based on customer feedback (Glossier, 2023). On launch, Glossier ran an interactive feature on Instagram Stories, with customers invited to ask questions about the new product and Glossier re-posting these with answers. This customer-centric approach to launching a new product demonstrates the brand's continued focus on community as its core strength, promoting a sense of customer value and ownership.

Glossier's physical stores are also customer-centric, placing importance on human interaction. When launching its post-pandemic stores, Weiss discussed the value of the customer experience being centred on discovery and feeling a sense of belonging, with a "people first, products second" approach (Salpini, 2021).

Exponential elements

Smilansky (2018) theorises that brand experiences should include moments that encourage social media sharing to spread content and positive sentiment beyond the initial experience. Glossier's stores can be defined as "content generating journeys" (Smilanksy, 2018: 111) that encourage social sharing. Through its social media platforms, Glossier consistently shares UGC to encourage more followers to chronicle their experience, thus creating a continuous stream of content.

Reach

The exponential elements link intrinsically with reach. In the context of social media, reach refers to the number of users that view content; it can be applied to a single piece of content or overall reach of all content (Michaels, 2023). Glossier's customer experience revolves around brand-generated content and UGC working together, the blend of which drives its community engagement. Glossier's experience reach is maximised by a customer-led narrative; the customer is involved in shaping the storytelling and amplifies the message. An example of this is the 'You Look Good Tour', a 2023 travelling pop-up experience to three US university cities – Columbus, Austin and Nashville. The tour brought the Glossier IRL experience to customers in locations where the brand has a large following on social media, thus responding to online customer engagement by providing a one-to-one physical experience (Spruch-Feiner, 2023).

Glossier was ranked as the fourth most popular skin care brand on TikTok in the US in 2021 in terms of reach (Statista, 2022b). In 2023, the TikTok hashtag #glossier had 1.9 billion views (TikTok, 2023b), with customer content on the platform including tutorials, product unboxing and product rankings. TikTok is known for product virality; the 'TikTok made me buy it' phenomenon signifies the culture of compelling products recommended on the platform (Jennings, 2021). This viral product drives wider brand appeal beyond beauty and skin care products and broadens Glossier's reach. The volume of interaction and reach across social platforms affirms the strength of Glossier's human-like brand personality (Smilansky, 2018) and genuine emotional connection with customers, further supporting the notion that Glossier customers are active participants in the brand universe.

Conclusion

The impact of Glossier

This case demonstrates Glossier's strengths in delivering a compelling customer experience, including its distinctive brand personality, co-created products and ability to build emotional connection. Now approaching its tenth anniversary, Glossier is powered by its ability to use these strengths to create value for its customers and differentiate its position as an innovative market leader. Glossier's reach is further amplified by its loyal customers sharing their experiences, thus extending the brand universe organically. According to McKinsey & Company (2023), the beauty industry is expected to increase by 5% over the next five years, as well as become more competitive due to independent brands looking to scale up; further innovation is therefore crucial to keep consumers engaged (Mintel, 2023). As technology, including generative AI, becomes more sophisticated and both beauty and fashion continue to explore its use to enhance phygital customer experiences, Glossier must consider innovation in its future strategies. Generation Z will represent a quarter of the world's population by 2030 (Business of Fashion, 2023); therefore remaining relevant to this audience is fundamental.

Case questions

1   Drawing on the case study, assess any weaknesses or threats that could impact Glossier's future success in delivering compelling customer experiences.
2   How should Glossier continue to appeal to Generation Z? Propose ideas for Glossier stores, website, social media channels and touchpoints, using evidence to support your decisions.

3   Identify and discuss digital technologies Glossier could use to enhance its phygital customer experience.
4   Use the BETTER Creative Model (Smilansky, 2018: 75) to appraise a beauty or fashion brand of your choice. Apply each area of the framework to assess the brand's current approach and identify new customer experience opportunities and ideas.

References

Bertolino, H. (2021) *Glossier is officially reopening its stores and a new permanent London spot.* [Online] [Accessed 26th June 2023] https://www.dazeddigital.com/beauty/article/53232/1/glossier-is-officially-reopening-stores-london-permanent-shop

Business of Fashion. (2023) *The state of fashion beauty.* [Online] [Accessed 6th June 2023] https://cdn.businessoffashion.com/reports/The_State_of_Fashion_Beauty_2023.pdf

Chitrakorn, K. (2022) *Glossier to sell in Sephora as DTC darling shifts to wholesale.* [Online] [Accessed 29th June 2023] https://www.voguebusiness.com/beauty/glossier-to-sell-in-sephora-as-dtc-darling-shifts-to-wholesale

Danziger, P. (2018) *5 reasons that Glossier is so successful.* [Online] [Accessed 26th June 2023] https://www.forbes.com/sites/pamdanziger/2018/11/07/5-keys-to-beauty-brand-glossiers-success/?sh=7ec77757417d

Edelman. (2022) *2022 Edelman trust barometer special report: The new cascade of influence.* [Online] [Accessed 26th June 2023] https://www.edelman.com/trust/2022-trust-barometer/special-report-new-cascade-of-influence

Edited. (2023) *The state of multi-brand strategies.* [Online] [Accessed 26th June 2023] https://app.edited.com/#retail/article/retail-mixed-strategy-multi-brand-030523

Englefield, J. (2021) *Glossier opens London flagship in Covent Garden's oldest building.* [Online] [Accessed 26th June 2023] https://www.dezeen.com/2021/12/14/glossier-make-up-store-covent-gardens-oldest-building/

Euromonitor. (2023) *Brand shares – Beauty and personal care (USA).* Passport Euromonitor [Online] [Accessed 26th June 2023] https://www.euromonitor.com/beauty-and-personal-care-in-the-us/report

Flora, L. (2021) *Glossier is betting big on experiential retail again.* [Online] [Accessed 26th June 2023] https://www.glossy.co/beauty/glossier-is-betting-big-on-experiential-retail-again/

Gibson, E. (2018) *UX review: Glossier and it's winning UX features.* [Online] [Accessed 26th June 2023] https://medium.com/@emmaegibsonux/why-i-wish-i-d-seen-the-glossier-website-before-designing-my-e-commerce-site-6a5f936f9655

Glossier. (2023) 'ICYMI we're launching an aluminium-free deodorant on January 17!' [Instagram]. 11 January. [Online] [Accessed 26th June 2023] https://www.instagram.com/stories/highlights/17938030595541897/

Glossier. (n.d.-a) *Our locations.* [Online] [Accessed 26th June 2023] https://uk.glossier.com/pages/locations

Glossier. (n.d.-b) *Help & FAQ.* [Online] [Accessed 8th September 2023] https://uk.glossier.com/pages/help

Glossier. (n.d.-c) *Glossier for good.* [Online] [Accessed 8th September 2023] https://uk.glossier.com/pages/glossier-for-good

Glossier. (n.d.-d) *Welcome to glossier. You look good.* [Online] [Accessed 8th September 2023] https://www.glossier.com/pages/about

Goldsgeyme. (2021) *Phygital: The future of retail.* [Online] [Accessed 6th September 2023] https://www.thedrum.com/opinion/2021/08/10/phygital-the-future-retail

Greifeld. (2023) *Insiders #147: Glossier's controversial site redesign: Bold move or epic fail?* [Online] [Accessed 12th September 2023] https://www.futurecommerce.com/posts/glossiers-controversial-site-redesign-bold-move-or-epic-fail

Hill, E. (2023) *Glossier joins forces with Sephora under first UK retail partnership*. [Online] [Accessed 15th August 2023] https://www.retailgazette.co.uk/blog/2023/09/glossier-sephora-partnership/

Huber, H. (2019) *We're living for Glossier's art deco–inspired Miami pop-up*. [Online] [Accessed 26th June 2023] https://www.architecturaldigest.com/story/glossier-miami-pop-up

Hyland, V. (2016) *Why is millennial pink suddenly so popular?* [Online] [Accessed 26th June 2023] https://www.thecut.com/2016/07/non-pink-pink-color-trend-fashion-design.html

Instagram. (2023a) *'Glossier'* [Instagram]. [Online] [Accessed 26th June 2023] https://www.instagram.com/glossier/?hl=en

Instagram. (2023b) *'Glossier Instagram Bio'* [Instagram]. [Online] [Accessed 26th June 2023] https://www.instagram.com/glossier/?hl=en

Instagram. (2023c) *'#glossierpink'* [Instagram]. [Online] [Accessed 28th June 2023] https://www.instagram.com/explore/tags/glossierpink/

Into the Gloss. (n.d.) *A look inside Glossier's 2014 pop-up*. [Online] [Accessed 26th June 2023] https://intothegloss.com/2014/10/glossier-pop-up-shop/

Jennings, R. (2021) *TikTok made me buy It*. [Online] [Accessed 26th June 2023] https://www.vox.com/the-goods/22555723/tiktok-viral-products-cerave-sky-high-mascara-amazon-leggings

Kotler, P., Armstrong, G., Harris, L. and He, H. (2020) *Principles of marketing*. Harlow: Pearson Education Limited.

Lacombe, G. (2018) *Glossier opens first NYC flagship*. [Online] [Accessed 28th June 2023] https://uk.fashionnetwork.com/news/Glossier-opens-first-nyc-flagship,1031895.html

Lam, T. (2019) *Glossier's Miami pop-up opens this week – Look inside the Instagram friendly space*. [Online] [Accessed 26th June 2023] https://hypebae.com/2019/3/glossier-miami-pop-up-store-interior-makeup-skincare-beauty-emily-weiss

Levy, N. (2019) *Glossier's floral pop-up store in London blooms with colour*. [Online] [Accessed 26th June 2023] https://www.dezeen.com/2019/11/28/glossier-pop-up-london-floral-print-interiors/

McClure, E. (2022) *Digital natives: How to win the trust of Gen Z and Millennials*. [Online] [Accessed 7th September 2023] https://www.the-future-of-commerce.com/2022/05/05/digital-natives-definition-stats-marketing-strategies/

McKinsey & Company. (2023) *The Beauty Market in 2023: A special state of fashion report*. [Online] [Accessed 16th June 2023] https://www.mckinsey.com/industries/retail/our-insights/the-beauty-market-in-2023-a-special-state-of-fashion-report

Meltzer, M. (2019) *How Emily Weiss's Glossier grew from millennial catnip to billion-dollar juggernaut*. [Online] [Accessed 26th June 2023] https://www.vanityfair.com/style/2019/10/how-emily-weiss-grew-glossier-from-millennial-catnip-to-billion-dollar-juggernaut

Michaels, G. (2023) *Reach vs. impressions: What's more important to track in 2023?* [Online] [Accessed 15th September 2023] https://blog.hootsuite.com/reach-vs-impressions/

Mintel. (2018) *Beauty influencers and educators – UK-2018*. [Online] [Accessed 13th June 2023] https://store.mintel.com/report/uk-beauty-influencers-and-educators-market-report

Mintel. (2023) *Beauty and personal care retailing – UK – 2023*. [Online] [Accessed 16th June 2023] https://store.mintel.com/report/uk-beauty-and-personal-care-retailing-market-report

Mondalek, A. and Strugatz, R. (2021) *Glossier raises $80 million Series E, valuing company at $1.8 Billion*. [Online] [Accessed 26th June 2023] https://www.businessoffashion.com/articles/beauty/glossier-raises-80-million-series-e-valuing-company-at-18-billion/

Moraes, M. (2020) *Why Glossier owns customer relationship building*. [Online] [Accessed 15th June 2023] https://content-is-me.medium.com/why-glossier-owns-customer-relationship-building-5f3a5cd180ae

Morosini, D. (2022) *Does Instagram still matter for beauty Brands?* [Online] [Accessed 12th June 2023] https://www.voguebusiness.com/beauty/does-instagram-still-matter-for-beauty-brands

Morris, L.G. (2022) *Immersive Tactility: Glossier's secret to engaging, sensory beauty spaces*. [Online] [Accessed 26th June 2023] https://www.frameweb.com/article/retail/immersive-tactility-glossiers-secret-to-engaging-sensory-beauty-spaces

Prahalad, C.K. and Ramaswamy, V. (2004) 'Co-creation experiences: The next practice in value creation.' *Journal of Interactive Marketing*, 18(3), pp. 5–14.

Ravi, K. (2018) *How glossier built a cult following on social media*. Unmetric, 19 September. [Online] [Accessed 26th June 2023] https://blog.unmetric.com/glossier-social-media-strategy https://blog.unmetric.com/glossier-social-media-strategy

Rees, A. and Sagresse, B. (2023) *Shopper forecast 2023*. [Online] [Accessed 6th September 2023] https://www.wgsn.com/insight/article/63bda896db6ac2ee7a12a064

Salpini, C. (2021) *Glossier gets back into physical retail with plans for 3 stores*. [Online] [Accessed 26th June 2023] https://www.retaildive.com/news/glossier-gets-back-into-physical-retail-with-plans-for-3-stores/602064/

Sandler, E. (2022) *Glossier goes full omnichannel with Sephora partnership*. [Online] [Accessed 26th June 2023] https://www.glossy.co/beauty/glossier-goes-full-omnichannel-with-sephora-partnership

Sandler, E. (2023) *Glossier's CEO talks new hires and promotions, and why 'beauty is a feeling'*. [Online] [Accessed 29th June 2023] https://www.glossy.co/beauty/glossiers-ceo-talks-new-hires-and-promotions-and-why-beauty-is-a-feeling/

Sarasvuo, S., Rindell, A. and Kovalchuk, M. (2022) 'Toward a conceptual understanding of co-creation in branding.' *Journal of Business Research*, 139, pp. 543–563.

Similar Web. (2023a) *Geography & country targeting*. [Online] [Accessed 8th September 2023] https://www.similarweb.com/website/glossier.com/#geography

Similar Web. (2023b) *Glossier.com audience demographics*. [Online] [Accessed 8th September 2023] https://www.similarweb.com/website/glossier.com/#demographics

Similar Web. (2023c) *Similar sites & Glossier.com competitors*. [Online] [Accessed 26th June 2023] https://www.similarweb.com/website/glossier.com/#competitors

Smilansky, S. (2018) *Experiential marketing: A practical guide to interactive brand experiences*. 2nd ed. London: Kogan Page.

Snelling, B. (2022) *Why Glossier's stores are uniquely successful in this economy*. [Online] [Accessed 26th June 2023] https://www.forbes.com/sites/brinsnelling/2022/11/30/why-glossiers-stores-are-uniquely-successful-in-this-economy/?sh=209820127f57

Social Blade. (2023a) *Glossier*. [Online] [Accessed 28th June 2023] https://socialblade.com/instagram/user/glossier

Social Blade. (2023b) *e.l.f. Cosmetics and Skincare*. [Online] [Accessed 28th June 2023] https://socialblade.com/instagram/user/elfcosmetics

Social Blade. (2023c) *Milk Makeup*. [Online] [Accessed 28th June 2023] https://socialblade.com/instagram/user/milkmakeup

Spruch-Feiner, S. (2023) *Glossier hits the road for its first college campus tour*. [Online] [Accessed 24th September 2023] https://www.glossy.co/beauty/glossier-hits-the-road-for-its-first-college-campus-tour/

Statista. (2022a) *Beauty & personal care report 2022*. [Online] [Accessed 8th June 2023] https://www.statista.com/study/55499/cosmetics-and-personal-care/

Statista. (2022b) *Gen Z and the beauty industry in the United States*. [Online] [Accessed 4th September 2023] https://www-statista-com.mmu.idm.oclc.org/study/110937/gen-z-and-the-beauty-industry-in-the-united-states/

Statista. (2023a) *L'Oreal – statistics & facts*. [Online] [Accessed 7th September 2023] https://www.statista.com/topics/1544/loreal/#topicOverview

Statista. (2023b) *Cosmetics worldwide*. [Online] [Accessed 7th September 2023] https://www-statista-com.mmu.idm.oclc.org/outlook/cmo/beauty-personal-care/cosmetics/worldwide#global-comparison

Statista. (2023c) *Millennial and Gen Z in the US: Consumer goods and shopping behaviour*. [Online] [Accessed 4th September 2023] https://www.statista.com/study/19374/us-millennials-shopping-behavior-statista-dossier/

Strugatz, R. (2022) *Glossier will sell products at Sephora next year*. [Online] [Accessed 15th August 2023] https://www.businessoffashion.com/articles/beauty/glossier-will-sell-products-at-sephora-starting-next-year/

THG Ingenuity. (2022) *The evolution of the beauty industry*. [Online] [Accessed 8th June 2023] https://www.thgingenuity.com/resources/reports/the-evolution-of-the-beauty-industry

TikTok. (2023a) *'Glossier'* [TikTok] [Online] [Accessed 26th June 2023] https://www.tiktok.com/@glossier?lang=en

TikTok. (2023b) *'#glossier'* [TikTok]. [Online] [Accessed 26th June 2023] https://www.tiktok.com/search?q=%23glossier&t=1687951111659

Tse, S. (2020) *Glossier's London pop-up will stay for the rest of the year*. [Online] [Accessed 26th June 2023] https://www.forbes.com/sites/samanthatse/2020/01/31/glossiers-london-pop-up-will-stay-for-the-rest-of-the-year/?sh=2d86e36c3766

Turk, V. (2020) *How Glossier turned itself into a billion-dollar beauty brand*. [Online] [Accessed 8th June 2023] https://www.wired.co.uk/article/how-to-build-a-brand-glossier

Further resources

Business of Fashion. (2018) *The potential of conversational commerce Emily Weiss with Alexandra Shulman*. 12 March. [Online] [Accessed 15th September 2023] https://www.youtube.com/watch?v=Njfpm6_5fXQ

Business of Fashion. (2023) *Where to focus retail technology investment in 2023*. 23 March. [Online] [Accessed 15th September 2023] https://www.youtube.com/watch?v=nZwRJXEHq6U

Fabulous Magazine. (2021) *There is now a permanent Glossier shop in London and its doors are now open!* 9 December. [Online] [Accessed 27th September 2023] https://www.youtube.com/watch?v=CKI-7J_SEJY

Glossier. (2018) *Glossier presents: A tour of the New York flagship store feat*. Paloma. 4 December. [Online] [Accessed 27th September 2023] https://www.youtube.com/watch?v=23XLFh4unH0&t=2s

Matilda on Video. (2019) *Beauty tour: Glossier showroom Los Angeles, USA*. 3 October. [Online] [Accessed 27th September 2023] https://www.youtube.com/watch?v=4RWlqsPMiio

The Next Web. (2017) *Emily Weiss (Glossier) on a non-traditional approach to community TNW conference 2017*. 1 June. [Online] [Accessed 27th September 2023] https://www.youtube.com/watch?v=MyRQsK6sf3w

Definitions

- **Customer-centric/customer centricity:** Placing the customer at the heart of the organisation, shaping offerings including products and experiences based on the customers' wants and needs.
- **DTC:** Direct to consumer.
- **IRL:** In real life.
- **Phygital:** The concept of using technology to bridge the digital world with the physical world with the purpose of providing a unique interactive experience for the user.
- **UGC:** User generated content.

Sustainable customer experiences

7.1 Ræburn Lab: more than a store – responsible retail for contemporary consumers

Natascha Radclyffe-Thomas

Learning objectives

On completion of this case study, learners should be able to:

1 Analyse sustainable visual merchandising and store design.
2 Explore innovation in customer experience through Lab Tours and Making Workshops.
3 Evaluate the potential for communicating sustainability and circularity through branded retail spaces.
4 Explore how lessons learned from RÆBURN's sustainable customer experience could be extrapolated and adopted by other players in the sector.

Introduction

Christopher Raeburn is the creative force behind the eponymous UK-based luxury label RÆBURN, founded in 2008 as Christopher Raeburn. Originally trained in womenswear, Raeburn made his name with functional menswear inspired by military and technical garments. Christopher's unusual and innovative make-do-and-mend approach to design, that of re-appropriating military fabrics as raw material for high-fashion pieces, attracted media and industry attention from the outset. However, he maintains his upcycling approach – unpicking and remaking military surplus – was initially less about sustainability and more about getting access to quality materials at a low price. After showing off-schedule in Paris in 2009, Christopher received an International Ethical Fashion Forum award, and support from Esthetica (a British Fashion Council initiative supporting design excellence and sustainable fashion), enabling him to show his menswear collection at London Fashion Week, featuring a range of outerwear constructed from a single military parachute. Christopher Raeburn's leadership in sustainable design gained him fans globally and he was soon retailing at style meccas including Liberty London and Barneys in New York.

RÆBURN's business expansion coincided with a greater consumer awareness of sustainable and ethical fashion. Christopher was mentored by Fashion Revolution

DOI: 10.4324/9781003378099-10

co-Founder Orsola de Castro – a sustainable fashion role model who had run an upcycling label, and believed in fashion as a power for positive change and was steering the British Fashion Council's sustainability work. The last decade has seen rising awareness of the unethical practices and negative environmental impacts emanating from the fashion industry, creating opportunities for businesses whose core values align with sustainability and transparency (Radclyffe-Thomas, 2024). Christopher Raeburn has accrued multiple awards for his sustainability work reflecting the strength of the brand across design and business. Orsola de Castro describes Christopher Raeburn as 'the original pioneer of the present generation of upcyclists and someone who has beautifully integrated the endemic use of waste in all his practice' (de Castro, 2021:174).

Christopher's early work used military surplus materials and he continues to source surplus materials including parachute canopies, air brake parachutes and 1950s Royal Air Force silk maps. Including the provenance of these rescued materials on website product pages enhances the brand's sustainable messaging. Christopher Raeburn's creative approach to sustainability and circularity has seen him engaged in a series of collaborations with brands. These have included fashion labels, and also extended into sportswear, upcycling deconstructed football shirts for Umbro x RÆBURN, footwear, Vans x RÆBURN incorporated responsibly sourced natural rubber and organic canvas, skin care, producing a roll-up carrier for Aesop x RÆBURN including limited-edition RÆMADE Adventurer Roll Ups made from reclaimed 1960s aeronautical navigation maps, and working with watchmakers Instrmnt and car manufacturers Cupra. Named the first Global Creative Director at Timberland in 2018, Christopher Raeburn worked on a series of sustainable product offers and although he subsequently stepped down from this role in 2022, he continues his affiliation with parent company VF Corporation, recently being appointed Global Creative Director for Napapijri (Kennedy, 2023).

Having won the British Fashion Award for Emerging Designer back in 2011, after more than a decade in business, and in an increasingly competitive space, Christopher Raeburn is still winning awards. The year 2020 saw him selected as a British Fashion Council Honouree in its Environmental category, an award decided by 800 key members of the global fashion industry. The same year RÆBURN won Brand of the Year at the inaugural Drapers Sustainable Fashion Awards, a feat repeated in 2021 and 2022. In 2022 Christopher Raeburn was also recognised as one of the Winners of the Common Objective Leadership Award celebrating ambition for, and commitment to, business practices that transform lives as well as solve environmental challenges. The year 2022 also saw him make the finalist list for the 2022 Zalando Sustainability Award celebrating brands driving positive change and contributing to a more responsible fashion industry.

But it is not just with product and leadership that Christopher Raeburn has excelled. This case explores the ways in which Raeburn has translated his own passions and interests in sustainable making, functionality and responsible business and woven these into RÆBURN-branded experiences, including a series of experimental pop-ups, a flagship store in London's East End and a store in the Carnaby area of London's West End which opened in 2021, winning Most Sustainable Store Design in the 2022 Drapers Sustainable Fashion Awards before closing in 2023.

The case traces the brand's development against the context of contemporary customer sentiment and expectations and asks readers to evaluate pro-environmental customer experience in physical retail spaces applying Lehner's (2015) concept of retailers as sustainability translators. Furthermore, it provides opportunities to consider the alignment between customer experience in RÆBURN stores delivered through events and entertainment – including store tours and making workshops – with Elg and Welinder's (2022) retail marketing strategy.

Sustainability translation in retail

In today's fashion retail landscape, stores play a crucial role extending beyond that of mere distribution outlet. A store's ability to contribute to brand development, communication and customer engagement is now considered critical for business success (Varley and Trigoni, 2019). However, whilst there has been much talk of consumers' increased interest in sustainability, in a study of food retailers, Lehner highlighted the 'considerable risk and uncertainty' (2015:387) retailers face implementing more sustainable operations, especially where they attempt to adopt the role of '"translators" of the sustainability discourse' (2015:386). Before expanding on how RÆBURN has employed their competitive advantage in sustainability to create engaging retail experiences, it is important to define some terms.

Common Objective (CO) defines sustainable fashion as an approach 'that maximises benefits to people, and minimises impact on the environment as well as being commercially successful' (CO, n.d.). As such, sustainability covers environmental issues, social issues and business governance. Under the UN Global Compact's Ten Principles, corporate sustainability in relation to human rights and environmental responsibility includes requirements for businesses to ensure that they are 'not complicit in human rights abuses' as well as undertaking 'initiatives to promote greater environmental responsibility' (UNGC, n.d.). Organisations including the Ellen MacArthur Foundation (EMF) highlight how unsustainable levels of fashion production in a linear system negatively impact the environment and propose circular fashion as an alternative. Circular fashion, with its zero waste approach, supports efforts to achieve UN Sustainable Development Goal 12 responsible consumption and production (UN, n.d.) A circular economy comprises three core principles:

- Design out waste and pollution
- Keep products and materials in use
- Regenerate natural systems

In using pre-existing materials as the base for collections, with the addition of responsibly sourced recycled and/or organic fabrics, Christopher Raeburn embraced zero waste and circular fashion as the founding principles of his brand. His design references and make-do-and-mend approach stretch back into his childhood. On panels and in interviews, Christopher frequently refers to his formative years and rural upbringing in Kent, England, and how this influenced how he sees the world. Christopher speaks fondly of the types of creative experiments and activities he and his family engaged in, including designing and building tree- houses and robots and adapting and improving the kit he was issued as an Air Cadet (Athleisure, 2019; Finney, 2023). It isn't hard to see how these sorts of family activities, paired with the habits and skills he would have developed as an enthusiastic Air Cadet, later translated into a fascination with materials and military designs that blend efficiency, functionality and symbolism. And whilst this is most evident in his design work, the vividness of Raeburn's childhood memories is also translated into the playful approach he takes to creating fashion retail experiences.

Elg and Welinder (2022:1) expand Lehner's argument of sustainability translation, positioning the retail store as 'an arena where sustainability is made visible and tangible to consumers' (2022:1). RÆBURN uses their stores to educate and inspire, and in so doing has created award-winning fashion retail spaces that encapsulate and communicate a brand philosophy illustrated by a Venn diagram that appears on store windows illustrating how each area of work intersects and supports each other (See Figure 7.1.1).

Figure 7.1.1 Intersecting 4Rs of RÆBURN: RÆMADE, RÆDUCED, RÆCYCLED and RÆ-BURN painted on an exterior window at the RÆBURN Lab, Hackney.

Source: Reprinted with permission of Christopher Raeburn.

- RÆMADE represents the founding principles of the brand, the reuse and reimagining of surplus materials, products and artefacts.
- RÆDUCED reflects the consideration of environmental impact in design decisions, minimising carbon footprint through local manufacturing, and reducing textile waste by utilising surplus materials for making new products and small batch production.
- RÆCYCLED focuses on how the brand selects what they consider to be the most sustainable materials and seeks out responsible manufacturing partners.

The Ræburn Lab, Studio 1, the textile building, Hackney, London

A flagship store is the canvas upon which a brand creates and communicates its ideal image. A flagship store has become a key facet of brand strategy for fashion retailers, allowing full rein to communicate an ideal brand image and positioning. Moving into a custom-designed space gave Raeburn the opportunity to embody his founding principles into a physical space as well as extend the brand's customer-engagement opportunities. Opening in 2016, the RÆBURN Lab is an experiential flagship retail store located in Hackney, East London, an area imbued with fashion manufacturing history (Sutherland, 2016). The physical site of a brand's flagship store is a key decision and brands often situate their flagship in a significant or historic building as a way to acquire or reinforce their heritage and status (Varley and Trigoni, 2019). In the case of RÆBURN's flagship, in a serendipitous alignment, given the founder's fascination with adventure and exploration, the RÆBURN Lab is not only located in the former Burberry Textile factory, but situated where Burberry's own archive was stored, which would have included such items of significance as those belonging to the great polar explorer Sir Ernest Shackleton. The provenance of the building is not lost on Raeburn; it is highlighted on the brand's own website and is frequently referred to in media pieces and at customer-engagement events hosted in the store.

Flagships are the place where brands can display a full range of their products in their most preferential way and as such are often used as the site of PR and customer-engagement events (Varley and Trigoni, 2019). The naming of the brand's flagship store as the RÆBURN Lab conjures associations with innovation and experimentation. RÆBURN's innovative design approach is reflected in the multi-functionality of the flagship retail space, which includes a making space and storage for the RÆBURN archive as well as provides a venue for a diverse range of sales, promotional and customer-experience-focused activities that help translate the RÆBURN ethos for customers and visitors. The Lab takes full advantage of its ground-floor double-aspect position, using the windows not only to feature garments but also to promote its sustainable mission (see Figure 7.1.2). Inside, the Lab's retail space is divided into two main functions: making and selling. A studio area The RÆMADE atelier, where cutting tables and sewing machines are situated providing working space for the design team, and an area that includes a fabric shop selling previous season fabrics and trims as well as the more expected space showcasing the brand's latest men's and women's collections. In addition, the Lab holds RÆBURN's extensive archive of original designs and pieces made for brand collaborations, which are close at hand so the team can draw on for inspiration and also for the studio tours which have become part of the brand's customer experience offer.

For several years, RÆBURN has offered behind-the-scenes tours of the Lab offering individuals and small groups a chance to explore the retail space, making atelier

Figure 7.1.2 An exterior window at the RÆBURN Lab, Hackney, decorated with the founder's call for systems change.

Source: Reprinted with permission of Christopher Raeburn.

and archive. A key driver for these tours is to showcase what a contemporary, creative responsible business looks like in action. For forty minutes visitors are guided through each area of the store by a member of the team who highlights key features of the brand story and opens the archive showing the development of the brand from its earliest days. Following this, there are opportunities for questions and shopping the latest RÆBURN collections. RÆBURN is very much embedded into its community and the small fee charged for non-Hackney residents goes to a local charity supporting local young people. Taking advantage of collaborating with other social engagement bodies, the studio tours have also featured as part of the Open House festival, London, an annual event encouraging members of the public to explore architectural spaces that are usually out-of-bounds.

RÆBURN's zero waste philosophy has led to a range of creative outputs; any off-cuts from making garments are collected and reused in other projects. For example, RÆBURN's seasonal #OffCutAnimals has included sharks, pandas and dogs (see Figure 7.1.3). RÆBURN prides itself on craft, creativity and community. The RÆBURN

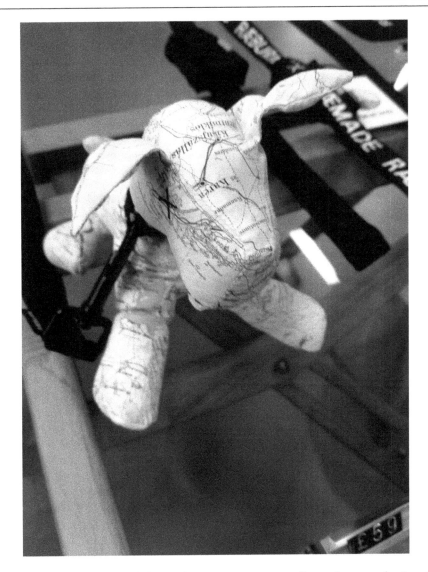

Figure 7.1.3 RÆBURN Lab workshop, where customers use off-cuts from production to create their own #OffCutAnimal.

Source: Reprinted with permission of Christopher Raeburn.

Atelier is very much a maker-space and it has been used to create experiential activities by hosting workshops where members of the public can craft their own RÆBURN products and accessories. For example in 2019, to coincide with the launch of a range of RÆ-BURN dog accessories, an Off-Cut Dog workshop took place using a range of RÆBURN fabric off-cuts and guided by members of the RÆBURN team. Although an attendance fee was charged, proceeds were donated to RÆBURN's chosen global charity WWF.

This respect and celebration of craft was highlighted in a collaboration with London Craft Week in 2020 where visitors could watch first-hand whilst the RÆBURN team transformed a one-person emergency raft into a limited-edition capsule, taking each opportunity to convey their brand story and mission for innovation and sustainability. In addition to these types of open engagements, RÆBURN offers the Lab for private tours and events and they have produced a 360-degree online tour for those curious brand fans who cannot access the store in real life. The Fabric Shop at the Lab is another way in which RÆBURN promotes circularity in-store. In 2021 a new initiative, the LAB Takeover, was launched, whereby young designers sold limited-edition capsules made from RÆBURN deadstock fabrics. The first takeover 'guest' was Melina Trapezanlidou, a Greek fashion designer who made macramé totes using cord from RÆBURN signature air brake parachutes.

From East End to West End

Creating sustainability-related events and entertainment is a key strategy to broaden customer experience (Elg and Welinder, 2022), one which was reproduced and extended when RÆBURN took a permanent store space in London's West End. Following a series of pop-ups, RÆBURN opened in a 900 sq ft, two-storey unit at 2 Marshall Street, Carnaby, in London's West End. Taking the brand into such a highly competitive retail area, RÆBURN sought to attract customers to its new store through an imaginative environment designed as a physical representation of the RÆBURN ethos. One way in which this was created was by using shop fixtures made from materials that were reused, recycled and/or designed to be easily repurposed.

One of Raeburn's aims with the store was to disrupt the status quo of our throwaway culture by changing customers' perception of waste. Raeburn's work has elevated waste materials, viewing them as a valuable resource, and the store showcased original raw materials such as military parachutes, Cold War silk maps and RAF anti-gravity trousers. In April 2022, on winning the Drapers Sustainable Store Design of the year RÆBURN reflected on their success in creating a store where design is elevated and customers are inspired by the use of eco-conscious and recycled materials (Raeburn, 2022). At the time, the Drapers' judges commented on how well thought through the no-waste store concept was. Using an easily adaptable modular design, storage and display plinths on wheels, packable and flexible shelving, with ski poles used as rails, hung with rock-climbing carabiners and suspended on a pulley system, designing for reconfiguration makes sense for store flexibility and it is not a stretch to see how this approach links back to Christopher's experience and fascination with military functionality.

In November 2018, Christopher Raeburn had announced via Instagram that he was closing their East London store and the e-commerce section of the website for the day in protest at the fast-fashion model of low prices and high sales volume exemplified in extremis by the US phenomenon of Black Friday sales. In so doing, Christopher Raeburn joined a growing group of retailers disrupting a sales promotion whereby retailers offer heavily discounted deals in the hopes of creating in-store and online shopping frenzies and shifting high volumes of stock in the process. Given the immense pressure for sales in retail spaces, especially for businesses based in high-rental areas such as London's West End, it was a bold move when instead of joining the host of UK businesses who have added Black Friday to their sales promotions calendar, RÆBURN closed their Marshall Street store for the day in 2021. The store was transformed into a re-commerce station with RÆBURN's circularity partner Responsible authenticating and valuing RÆBURN and other premium streetwear brands, becoming a venue for customer education and just the sort of unique and playful retail experiences that add value for brands (Varley and Trigoni, 2019).

Conclusion

The RÆBURN brand has grown up during a period of immense change in the fashion industry. Sustainability, which was once a minor concern, is now front of mind for many consumers and has become central to business strategies (Radclyffe-Thomas, 2024). Elg and Welinder (2022) argue that consumers are less influenced by general corporate sustainability communications, but are engaged and motivated by messages, practical examples and examples of sustainability displayed in-store. The rise of digital retail and pandemic lockdowns threatened the future of the physical store and post-pandemic digitally savvy customers have elevated retail expectations (Briedis et al., 2020).

Christopher Raeburn's Earth Day 2020 RÆSTART manifesto committed the brand to disrupt, innovate and inspire. This case has outlined some of the tangible and intangible ways RÆBURN has used its retail spaces to further these commitments through its visual merchandising, store design and range of engagement opportunities. As such RÆBURN has built brand loyalty through innovative customer experiences, receiving industry plaudits and fuelling retail expansion. Arguably, the level of recognition and reward Christopher Raeburn has received shows how he and the brand have been trailblazers not only in sustainability and circularity, but in how they translate this into retail spaces. Christopher recently announced on social media that the brand will undergo a restructuring, starting with the closing of the RÆBURN Lab, seeing it as a time to reset, recharge and renew (Kennedy, 2023). This is an opportune time to consider how RÆBURN can continue to differentiate themselves and evolve as sustainable retailers in an increasingly complex and competitive market, how is it possible to disrupt and innovate avoiding RÆPETITION? And what are the lessons for other brands wishing to emulate RÆBURN's award-winning sustainable retail strategy aside from mere RÆPLICATION?

Case questions

1   Elg and Welinder (2022) highlight the challenge for retailers of balancing a large number of interests and messages that compete for consumer attention in-store. Using examples from the case, analyse the extent to which RÆBURN has successfully incorporated sustainability messaging into their visual merchandising and store design.
2   Research and describe the range of innovative customer experience opportunities created by RÆBURN through Lab Tours and Making Workshops. As a member of the RÆBURN Customer Experience team can you suggest how further playful retail experiences could be created across the selling season and for a range of existing and potential customers.
3   RÆBURN has demonstrated several ways in which sustainability and circularity can be communicated through branded retail spaces. Given that these are complex topics, draw up guidance including credible definitions of these terms, for a brand team wanting to roll out a sustainability and/or circularity initiative in-store.

4   Imagine you are designing a range of in-store customer-engagement opportunities for a small sustainable brand you are familiar with. Taking the lessons learned from RÆBURN's sustainable customer experience as a starting point to design immersive, imaginative experiences that allow for discovery and education without causing information overload or detracting from the purpose of the store as a retail space.

References

Athleisure. (2019). *Sustainable by design: Christopher Raeburn*. Athleisure Mag. [Online] [Accessed 12th October 2023] http://www.athleisuremag.com/the-latest/2019/3/13/sustainable-by-design-christopher-raeburn

Briedis, H., Kronschnabl, A., Rodriguez, A. and Ungerman, K. (2020) *Adapting to the next normal in retail: The customer experience imperative*. McKinsey & Company, 14 May. [Online] [Accessed 12th October 2023] https://www.mckinsey.com/industries/retail/our-insights/adapting-to-the-next-normal-in-retail-the-customer-experience-imperative

de Castro, O. (2021) *Loved clothes last: How the joy of rewearing and repairing your clothes can be a revolutionary act*. London: Penguin Life.

Elg, U. and Welinder, A. (2022) 'Sustainability and retail marketing: Corporate, product and store perspectives.' *Journal of Retailing and Consumer Services*, 64, p. 102810. https://doi.org/10.1016/j.jretconser.2021.102810

Finney, A. (2023) *"I've seen the entire narrative change" around sustainable fashion says Christopher Raeburn*. Dezeen, 28 March. [Online] [Accessed 12th October 2023] https://www.dezeen.com/2023/03/28/christopher-raeburn-sustainable-fashion-interview/

Kennedy, J. (2023) *Napapijri taps Christopher Raeburn as Global Creative Director*. Business of Fashion, 15 November. [Online] [Accessed 19th November 2023] https://www.businessoffashion.com/news/retail/napapijri-taps-christopher-raeburn-as-global-creative-director/

Lehner, M. (2015) 'Translating sustainability: The role of the retail store.' *International Journal of Retail & Distribution Management*, 43(4/5), pp. 386–402. https://doi.org/10.1108/IJRDM-02-2014-0013

Radclyffe-Thomas, N. (2024) 'Managing fashion responsibly,' in Varley, R., Roncha, A., Radclyffe-Thomas, N. and Gee, L. (eds.) *Fashion management: A strategic approach*, 2nd edn. London: Bloomsbury.

Raeburn. (2022) *RÆSTART 6.0*. April 21. [Online] [Accessed 12th October 2023] https://www.raeburndesign.co.uk/blogs/round-up/raestart-6-0

Sutherland, E. (2016) *Hackney walk is shaking up outlet fashion*. Drapers, 2 September. [Online] [Accessed 12th October 2023] https://www.drapersonline.com/companies/hackney-walk-is-shaking-up-outlet-fashion

Varley, R. and Trigoni, M. (2019) 'Fashion retail management,' in Varley, R., Roncha, A., Radclyffe-Thomas, N. and Gee, L. (eds.) *Fashion management: A strategic approach*, 1st edn. London: Bloomsbury, pp. 193–210.

Further resources

https://www.raeburndesign.co.uk/.
https://www.youtube.com/channel/UCT2H1O8O_C3yLUxoslnal_w/videos.

7.2   ECOALF: retail experience – visceral, behavioural and reflective design for engaging a sustainability community

Silvia Pérez-Bou, Javier Antón Sancho and Nicola Arcenas

Learning objectives

On completion of this case study, learners should be able to:

1   Understand the retail store customer experience (CX) of the Spanish brand, ECOALF, whose DNA is based on sustainability.
2   Reflect on the visceral, behavioural and reflective design applied to ECOALF stores and how they are aligned with the mission and vision of the brand.
3   Apply the three-level emotional design model to other retailers' physical stores.
4   Reflect on the role that fashion companies could play in involving consumers in more sustainable patterns of consumption (Sustainable Development Goal – SDG 12).

Introduction

ECOALF's history and values

ECOALF started in 2009 as a sustainable fashion company based in Spain, founded by Javier Goyeneche. He was an entrepreneur who, after graduating, launched Fun&Basics in 1993, a bag business that introduced him to the fashion industry. With ECOALF, he was a pioneer in envisioning a fashion brand that did not indiscriminately use natural resources to protect the natural environment. As cited,

> I wanted to create a truly sustainable fashion brand and I believed the most sustainable thing to do was to stop using natural resources in a careless way to ensure those of the next generation. Recycling could be a solution if we were able to make a new generation of recycled products with the same quality and design as the best non-recycled.
>
> (Goyeneche, 2021)

Goyeneche started to explore recycling processes. However, he faced two challenges. First, he wanted to ensure the use of recycled and recyclable materials, but consumer perceptions were that recycled fabrics were of lesser quality. Second, there was a lack of sustainability-focused suppliers (Ind and Iglesias, 2022:19). He saw this as an opportunity to research textile production techniques that made use of recycled plastic bottles, recycled nylon using discarded fishing nets and other new materials.

ECOALF started selling T-shirts, coats and jackets, widening its portfolio to include trousers, vests, knitwear, dresses, skirts, etc. Besides clothing, it also produces shoes and accessories, for women, men and children. In 2023, ECOALF extended its offer by adding a line of cosmetics, ECOALF Wellness, and ECOALF Sports specialised in clothing for running, cycling, yoga and surfing.

ECOALF is a slow fashion brand (Núñez-Barriopedro and Llombart, 2021; Velasco-Molpeceres et al., 2022). It is considered one of the promising Spanish fashion retailers, offering burgeoning competition to the dominant incumbents (Inditex, Mango, Cortefiel, etc.) that have driven Spanish fashion to leading positions in the international market (Viaña and Osorio, 2018). ECOALF is recognised worldwide and stands out for its innovative projects linked to caring for the environment, such as Upcycling the Oceans (Velasco-Molpeceres et al., 2022). It started this initiative in 2015, through the ECOALF Foundation with the support of the fishing industry, to recover marine litter from the ocean and turn it into fabric (Ecoalf, 2022:13). As Goyeneche says,

> we started with 3 fishermen from the East coast of Spain. All the waste that they collected in the ocean, when they pulled up the nets with the fish, instead of throwing it back into the ocean, they would put it in a container and take it to the port.
>
> (World Economic Forum, 2020)

By 2022 the project had grown, reaching more than 54 ports in Spain, Thailand, Greece, Italy and France, with more than 3,300 fishermen involved, and more than 1,000 tonnes of waste collected since its inception (Ecoalf, 2022:86). Figure 7.2.1 shows how fishermen are acknowledged at the Milan store.

Figure 7.2.1 Milan store fishermen acknowledgement.

Source: Reprinted by permission of ECOALF.

Figure 7.2.2 Tokyo Shibuya store.
Source: Reprinted by permission of ECOALF.

ECOALF's values are focused on commitment, coherence, transparency and integrity, sustained in three pillars: sustainability, innovation and design. They do not follow trends but rather opt for quality and timeless design as product hallmarks (Ecoalf, 2022).

ECOALF is a sustainable lifestyle brand leading change with every product (Ecoalf, 2022:8). They are demonstrating their intent to do good by driving positive change and embracing brand transcendence (Fabian, 2023). ECOALF's motto 'because there is no planet B®'[1] has contributed to consumers' sustainability perception of the brand. This motto was trademark registered in 2018 together with the brand name ECOALF, for many categories of products (see Figure 7.2.2). #becausethereisnoplanetb has begun an international media movement followed by more than 1 million people (Ecoalf, 2023a).

Sustainability and circularity in the fashion industry

European regulatory framework in the textiles and fashion sector

The Circular Economy Action Plan (European Commission, 2020) identified the textile sector as one of the seven key value chains to achieve circularity in Europe. Sustainability is no longer seen as an option, but an obligatory regulated aspect. In 2022, the European Commission adopted a package of measures including a Strategy for Sustainable and Circular textiles (European Commission, 2022a) with specific requirements for products, including eco-design, recyclability, repairability, recycled content, minimising waste, introducing clearer information on textiles and a digital passport, among many others.

The building and construction sector is another of the key value chains for circularity in Europe. The proposal for Construction Products Regulation (European Commission, 2022b) also includes addressing the sustainability performance of product construction, the introduction of recycled content requirements and energy efficiency targets in buildings.

In 2023, a proposal for a directive on substantiation and communication of explicit environmental claims (Green Claims Directive) was launched for all sectors. It aims at empowering consumers to make better-informed decisions and to play an active role in the ecological transition (European Commission, 2023). As claiming to be green and sustainable has become a competitive factor, a framework is needed for these environmental claims to be compared and verified. When this proposal comes into force, the environmental claims of products or services in European markets should be science-based, using life-cycle assessments by third parties. It means that any reference to 'eco', 'zero emissions', 'responsible', etc., in a product must be substantiated in scientific data, and made public with the claim.

With the current shift in mindsets and regulations, fashion players increasingly feel the pressure to show their efforts to become more sustainable throughout their operations, including across their retail channels – physical and digital (Euromonitor, 2023). Some brands have included their stores in their strategy to reduce greenhouse gas (GHG) emissions, to improve their energy efficiency and to evidence commitment to circular design practices (Pérez-Bou et al., 2021). ECOALF is one of these leading companies.

ECOALF's development

ECOALF can be considered a successful brand in terms of its business model. Their turnover has multiplied by 156% in the last ten years, reaching €37.48 million in 2021 (Orbis, 2023), growing from 18 employees in 2016 to 153 in 2021.

They sell in 33 countries, both business-to-business (B2B) (through 1,261 multi-brand stores and partners) and direct-to-consumer (B2C) (e-commerce, 7 retail stores and 18 corners) (Ecoalf, 2022:15). Their retail prices range from €50 to €930. ECOALF 1.0, their premium collection, started in 2021, merging a timeless design, minimalist forms and neutral colours with technical filaments with lower environmental impact (Ecoalf, 2023b). In 2021, 56% of ECOALF's revenue came from Spain (Ecoalf, 2022), and the company was acquired by Treïs, a French family-led investment group specialised in long-term returns and responsible investments.

ECOALF obtained the BCorp® certification in 2018. It is a designation that a business is meeting high standards of verified performance, accountability and transparency on social and environmental aspects (BCorp, 2023). ECOALF was the first Spanish clothing company to obtain this certification and was ranked Best in the World, 2022, in the category of Environment. Today (2023) there are around 350 clothing brands globally certified by BCorp, including Patagonia, Mud Jeans, North Sails and Vestiaire Collective.

In 2023, ECOALF had seven stores in four countries (Spain, France, Italy and Germany) and two under a joint-venture agreement with Sanyo Shokai group in Japan. Since 2019, ECOALF adopted the NET ZERO 2030 pledge to eliminate GHG emissions, prompting an evolution in the ECOALF stores' design, to make more visible their commitment to decarbonisation and circularity. The store, also as a point of interaction between retailers and consumers, fulfils an important role in the process of achieving sustainable consumption, not only as a place of physical exchange, but also as a place for the exchange of information, ideas and understanding of what it means to consume sustainably (Lehner, 2015).

This case study explores the elements ECOALF is using to engage consumers in sustainable awareness and experiences through their physical stores, with reference to their architectural design. The brand is a pioneer in addressing sustainability and circularity in their products and it is leading the way in extending these values to their stores. This case study applies Stephens' model of CX (2017) and Norman's Levels of Emotional Design (visceral, behavioural and reflective) (2005) to highlight the sustainability experience at ECOALF stores.

CX in retail spaces: fashion retail 4.0

The term 'experience' has become the foremost biggest buzzword in retail (Scapin et al., 2012). This concept presents a gateway for innovation in the interaction between fashion brands and customers: a relationship that goes beyond mere transactions and visual encounters within a store. Within physical stores, the need to design experiences that help enhance a user's encounter with the product and the brand is fundamental. There is growing demand for spaces that can deliver meaningful experiences.

The evolution of retailing can be explained in three phases, each informing retail design (Quartier, 2011). Retail 1.0 was dominated by manufacturers, minimising the need for retail designers. In Retail 2.0, retailers took charge and engaged designers to align store design with their brand identity. Retail 3.0 is where customers exert significant influence. This phase requires designers to go beyond translating identity and consider creating emotionally engaging shopping experiences. As customer centricity has accelerated in the development of retail design, so has credence to creating compelling, engaging experiences to satiate their needs and desires, manifest in the evolution to Retail 4.0. Here boundaries among consumers, creatives, architects and retailers are dissolving, enabling the convergence and co-creation of remarkable experiences. Doug Stephens, founder of Retail Prophet, argues that many retailers are guilty of limiting CX to mere store refurbishment (online or offline), the refreshing of brand aesthetics (e.g. identity, layouts, etc.) generating 'enhanced experiences' to drive sales (2017). However, he argues such tweaks do not provide meaningful CX, and rather than perpetuating the sales per square foot model that produces average and forgettable experiences, the focus should be on creating customer-centric experiences that seek to generate superior and memorable CX. He suggests retailers can create genuine CX design by deconstructing the entire customer journey – physical, digital and social channels – and then reconstructing each element to manifest a distinct look, feel and functionality that is consumer-centred and woven into every consumer touchpoint – to truly evidence Retail 4.0.

Emotional design to enhance CX

In 'Emotional Design', Don Norman (2005), design psychologist and usability expert, explores the idea that design is not just about functionality but also about the emotional connection between people and the objects they use. He explains three different levels of connection:

- *Visceral design* – focuses on the initial, instinctual and immediate reaction to a design. This visceral reaction is based on sensory input and aesthetics. Norman asserts that people often make quick judgements about products and their desirability based on their appearance, colour, texture and form. He argues that good design should elicit positive visceral responses, creating a sense of attraction.

- *Behavioural design* – is concerned with how products and systems influence our behaviour and how they function in our daily lives. Norman emphasises the importance of usability and functionality. He discusses how well-designed products should support the user's actions, making tasks easier and more efficient. Behavioural design focuses on the experience during interaction and how a product fits into the user's life.
- *Reflective design* – explores the deeper, reflective aspects of design. This is where the user's emotions, values and meaning come into play. He suggests that truly great design not only provides utility but also offers a sense of satisfaction, accomplishment and identity to the user. Products that have reflective appeal often carry a story or narrative that resonates with the user on a personal level.

Norman argues that all three design levels – visceral, behavioural and reflective – are crucial for creating successful and emotionally engaging products. Moreover, successful design should aim to create a positive emotional experience for users. We can create a parallelism and understand the CX in fashion retail stores through these three levels. By drawing parallels between products and stores, we emphasise the importance of considering the emotional and connectional aspects of CX within a store. Just as in product design, all three levels are crucial for creating a holistic and emotionally engaging CX that fosters brand loyalty and customer satisfaction. Next, we look at how these three levels are applicable within ECOALF's physical stores.

ECOALF's visceral level: establishing intuitive attraction and sustainability values discovery

- *Customer attraction*: based on creating an immediate and instinctual attraction to the brand and products. The initial reaction is based on sensory input and aesthetics.
- *Store ambience*: The store's physical appearance, window displays, messages and product presentation should evoke positive emotions and desires in customers. The aesthetics of the store can play a significant role in drawing customers in.

ECOALF uses both physical and digital elements to initiate an immediate and intuitive connection with its customers. Their motto 'because there is no planet B®' is present in windows, on walls and screens, as well as other encouraging messages: 'It is not what we do but how we do it', 'I do care', 'Help us Clean the Oceans', etc. Some designed elements (such as counters made from marine debris in the Tokyo stores, a plastic waste mannequin in Milan or the 3D printed shelves at Las Rozas, Madrid, see Figures 7.2.3–7.2.5) act as triggers, evoking visceral responses of immediate attraction to the brand.

ECOALF's behavioural level: immersive engagement and deep connection

- *Visiting the store*: The behavioural level in CX relates to the ease and functionality of shopping but also to experiencing the store itself. It's about making the shopping process and/or the visit to the store enjoyable and meaningful for customers.

Figure 7.2.3 Ocean's waste counters, Tokyo Futakotamagawa.

Source: Reprinted by permission of ECOALF.

Figure 7.2.4 Plastic waste mannequin, Milan store.

Source: Reprinted by permission of ECOALF.

Figure 7.2.5 3D printed shelves, Las Rozas store, Madrid.
Source: Reprinted by permission of ECOALF.

- *Store navigation and interaction*: The store's layout, signage and organisation should facilitate a meaningful shopping experience. This includes factors like product placement, fitting rooms and checkout processes, but also interaction with the store personnel and getting to know the products, the store environment, the retailer and its values.

ECOALF's stores clearly display a curated selection of limited products on shelves and tables, evoking the need to buy less (see Figure 7.2.6). The store personnel receive training every season about the collection, on innovation, composition and impact, to interact with the customers (ECOALF interview, 2023). Curated content is shown on large screens to educate and engage people (see Figure 7.2.7). Some stores have dedicated event spaces, like the 'Act Now' activities, which include talks, roundtable discussions and workshops. Beyond the products, the experience at the store deepens the connection, providing a holistic understanding of the brand's sustainability principles that impels consumers to act.

ECOALF's reflective level: emotional connection and brand loyalty

- *Emotional connection*: At the reflective level, CX involves creating a deeper emotional connection between customers and the brand, where meaning and satisfaction are key.

Figure 7.2.6 Curated products display, Madrid Caleido.
Source: Reprinted by permission of ECOALF.

Figure 7.2.7 Large screen, Paris store.
Source: Reprinted by permission of ECOALF.

- *Brand storytelling*: Fashion retailers may use storytelling and brand narratives to create a sense of identity and meaning for customers. This connection can lead to brand loyalty and advocacy.

ECOALF's website provides information about the sustainable design of the store, including material selection, energy consumption and use of recycled or discarded waste from construction, which may be difficult to appreciate on first sight at the store, but are recognised and appreciated after reading and learning about their pro-planet decision-making. In the Las Rozas, Madrid store, 3.3 tonnes of plastic waste have been used in 3D printing to produce a melting glacier installation (see Figure 7.2.8). ECOALF Madrid Caleido is the first net zero store, as it produces the energy needed for its operation through solar panels (see Figure 7.2.9), and in the Paris store, cotton waste has been mixed with cement for interior walls and floors.

Retail 4.0 also means the use of digital tools, and information is available to align ECOALF's customers with its core values of sustainability, circular economy and social responsibility. The brand seeks to transcend transactional interactions by encouraging customers to reflect on their own values and aspirations. ECOALF's distinctive brand narrative and mission invite customers to become stakeholders in this transformative journey. This deeper values alignment culminates in brand loyalty and customer satisfaction, as customers identify with the values underpinning ECOALF's mission, ultimately fostering a desire to be active participants in the brand's sustainability community.

Table 7.2.1 presents a summary of the three emotional design levels at ECOALF's stores. Although many resources have been used in all the stores, a specific feature in each one has been highlighted. These features cover most of the issues related to sustainability: climate change, oceans, waste and recycling.

Figure 7.2.8 Glacier interior, Las Rozas store, Madrid.

Source: Reprinted by permission of ECOALF.

Figure 7.2.9 Zero-energy building, Madrid Caleido.
Source: Reprinted by permission of ECOALF.

Conclusion

In synthesising these three design levels of CX – visceral, behavioural and reflective – ECOALF's approach reflects a deliberate commitment to fostering profound and enduring customer relationships that transcend mere transactions. This multifaceted strategy results in customer loyalty and satisfaction anchored in values and a collective vision of a more sustainable world. ECOALF's approach exemplifies a contemporary imperative for fashion retailers: bridging the gap between commerce and conscience, thereby not only enhancing the bottom line but also contributing to a broader societal and environmental narrative.

The demand for products and experiences that resonate on visceral, emotional and values-driven levels, especially among conscious consumers, is poised for continued growth. ECOALF's journey underscores the pivotal role that fashion retailers play in addressing this demand and reshaping the fashion industry. It highlights the significance of integrating aesthetics, functionality and sustainability values into the CX, recognising that in an era defined by conscious consumerism, these elements are paramount.

As we navigate the evolving retail milieu, critical questions emerge: How can ECOALF further evolve its CX strategy to remain at the forefront of sustainability-driven retail? How will it continue to differentiate itself through its hyper-physical experiences and engage consumers on deeper emotional and values-driven levels? Additionally, what valuable lessons can other fashion retailers glean from ECOALF's innovative approach?

Table 7.2.1 ECOALF's store elements of emotional design (visceral, behavioural and reflective)

Store	Year	Feature	Visceral	Behavioural	Reflective
1 Madrid Caleido	2023	Net zero: climate change	Big screen with messages and informative videos because there is no planet B® motto on walls	The products themselves. Product display: curated, limited quantity to reduce consumption. Educational activities to promote sustainable behaviour: Act Now events. Employee training	Net zero emissions: solar photovoltaic (PV) panels, locally sourced wood beams, benches and tables, table ceramics, natural raffia in benches, recycled polyester in cushions, natural terracotta in walls to regulate heat and humidity, natural light and LEDs, aluminium hangers, few different materials
2 Las Rozas	2023	Melting glaciers	Large screen with informative content, glacier's melting in installations, hangers, counters, tables and shelves	The products themselves. Curated, limited quantity to reduce consumption. Employee training	3.3 tonnes of recycled plastic used in 3D printing to produce the melting glacier installation. Recyclable product at end-of-life. The created environment invites customers to reflect on climate change, rising temperatures, and the risk of melting glaciers
3 Milan	2023	Fishermen heroes	Large windows, fishermen photography, mannequins with plastic bottles, motto because there is no planet B® on walls	The products themselves. Messages about Upcycling the Oceans and ECOALF Foundation, through photographic storytelling. Employee training	Natural light, Cimento floors, walls and furniture: using 90% recycled production waste and CO$_2$ neutral basis. Lateral panels from recycled textiles. Ecological painting (Airlite). 3D plastic waste curtains. Furniture made of recyclable HONEXT® panels. WELL™ and LEED™ certifications
4 Barcelona	2022	Waste in materials	Brand values wall displays, large screen with motto and inspiring content, motto and brand's mission in storefront: because there is no planet B®	Corner with large screen and sofas to sit and watch videos with informative content. Employee training	Locally sourced wood on wall, floor, ceiling and division panels. Material reduction (e.g. no false ceiling, minimum colour palette, concrete), recycled cardboard mannequins, bio-resin and jute. Greenery (planters). Cross ventilation and natural light to reduce energy consumption, using LEDs

(Continued)

Table 7.2.1 (Continued)

Store	Year	Feature	Visceral	Behavioural	Reflective
5 Paris	2021	Oceans	Brand values wall displays, large screen with motto and inspiring content, motto and brand's mission in storefront: because there is no planet B®. 'It's what we do and how we do it'	Products themselves. Multidisciplinary room dedicated to oceans and education: ECOALF Foundation activities to drive engagement. Act Now events	Minimal use of new materials; mono- and timeless material; interior walls and floor made from recycled cotton mixed with cement. Minimum colour palette: black for windows frames and metals, and raw white for rest
6 Madrid	2021	Recover	Circular screen with oceans images at store entrance. Different zones for displaying collections: yoga, kids, furniture, etc.	Products themselves. Renovation of XIX building. Space for Act Now events. Employee training	Natural light, use of natural and recycled materials: recovered wood (old doors, tables), recycled stainless steel, and old ceramics from existing site. Recycled mannequins made from bio-resin, jute and recycled cardboard
7 Tokyo Futakotamagawa	2020	Plastic counters	Large screens with informative content, motto. Informative wall displays about fashion industry pollution: '650,000 tonnes of plastic on the bottom of the sea' Counters made from plastic waste	Screen with curated content showing information about water and CO_2 emissions reduction, circularity, mono-materiality, etc. Act Now events. Employee training	Counters made from marine debris to raise awareness (plastic bottles, fishing nets), natural wood (absorbs CO_2), local materials: bamboo hangers, greenery (planters); natural light
8 Tokyo Shibuya	2019	Remix: recycle, reuse, reduce	Brand values wall displays, counters and windows: 'Help us Clean the oceans', 'Act Now', 'I do care'	Large screens with curated content about recycled products and recycling processes. Employee training	Steel and concrete; natural light; use of recycled materials. Floor decoration with glass boxes containing marine waste; discarded fishing nets and plastic bottles
9 Berlin	2017	Biophilia	Large screens with motto: because there is no planet B®	Products themselves. Zones for Act Now events with sofas, books to read about the sea and large circular screens. Employee training	Limited, selected materials: mainly concrete for floor and walls, no false ceiling, recycled wood for furniture (from demolitions), recycled metal, LED lighting, greenery: linear planters, vertical gardens

Case questions

1   Research and discuss the range of customer experience opportunities ECOALF generates in-store. As part of the customer experience team, brainstorm how ECOALF can evolve its CX strategy through a series of immersive and provocative content creation and activations that generate visceral, behavioural and reflective customer responses.

2   Drawing on the case study, what valuable lessons can other responsible retailers learn from ECOALF's innovative approach to CX?

3   Select a sustainable fashion brand of your own choice. As the Director responsible for creating the experiential strategy, apply the Emotional Design – visceral, behavioural and reflective – Model to devise a distinctive store experience.

4   How do you think fashion retailers can promote more sustainable consumption habits in society (SDG12)? What 'calls to action' do you propose that haven't been fully explored so far?

Note

1   https://euipo.europa.eu/eSearch/#advanced/trademarks/1/100/n1=MarkVerbalElement Text&v1=there%20is%20no%20planet%20b&o1=AND&c1=CONTAINS&sf=Application Number&so=asc.

References

BCorp. (2023) *Make business a force for good.* [Online] [Accessed 8th September 2023] https://www.bcorporation.net/en-us/

Ecoalf. (2022) *Sustainability report 2021. Don't think it's a Utopia.* [Online] [Accessed 8th September 2023] https://cdn.shopify.com/s/files/1/0553/2804/7279/files/ECOALF_SUSTAINABILITY_REPORT_2021_EN.pdf?v=1668091431

Ecoalf. (2023a) *Because there is no planet B.* [Online] [Accessed 8th September 2023] https://ecoalf.com/en-int/pages/because-there-is-no-planet-b

Ecoalf. (2023b) *About ECOALF.* [Online] [Accessed 8th September 2023] https://ecoalf.com/en-int

European Commission. (2020) *Circular economy action plan. For a cleaner and more competitive Europe.* [Online] [Accessed 8th September 2023] https://environment.ec.europa.eu/strategy/circular-economy-action-plan_en

European Commission. (2022a) *Proposal for a regulation of the European Parliament and of the council laying down harmonised conditions for the marketing of construction products.* [Online] [Accessed 8th September 2023] https://eur-lex.europa.eu/legal-content/EN/TXT/?uri=CELEX%3A52022PC0144

European Commission. (2022b) *Communication from the commission to the European Parliament, The European Economic and Social Committee and the Committee of the regions EU Strategy for Sustainable and Circular Textiles.* [Online] [Accessed 8th September 2023] https://eur-lex.europa.eu/legal-content/EN/TXT/?uri=CELEX%3A52022DC0141

European Commission. (2023) *Proposal for a directive of the European Parliament and of the Council on substantiation and communication of explicit environmental claims (Green Claims Directive).* [Online] [Accessed 8th September 2023] https://eur-lex.europa.eu/legal-content/EN/TXT/?uri=COM%3A2023%3A0166%3AFIN

Fabian, J. (2023) *10 Brands that really take responsibility.* [Online] [Accessed 20th August September 2023] https://www.ispo.com/en/sustainability/10-brands-really-take-responsibility

Goyeneche, J. (2021) *Letter to the customers.* [Online] [Accessed 8th September 2023] http://ecoalf.com/es-int/pages/historia

Ind, N. and Iglesias, O. (2022) *In good conscience. Do the right thing while building a profitable business.* Cham: Palgrave Macmillan-Springer Nature.

Lehner, M. (2015) 'Translating sustainability: The role of the retail store.' *International Journal of Retail & Distribution Management*, 43(4–5), pp. 386–402.

Euromonitor. (2023) *Why integrating sustainability in fashion retail is becoming a must.* [Online] [Accessed 19th September 2023] https://www.euromonitor.com/article/why-integrating-sustainability-in-fashion-retail-is-becoming-a-must

Norman, D.A. (2005). *Emotional design: Why we love (or hate) everyday things.* New York: BasicBooks.

Núñez-Barriopedro, E. and Llombart, M.D. (2021) 'New trends in marketing aimed at the fourth sector in the fashion industry,' in Sánchez-Hernández, M.I. et al. (eds.), *Entrepreneurships in the fourth sector*, Studies on Entrepreneurship, Structural Change and Industrial Dynamics. Cham: Springer Nature.

Orbis. (2023) *Database. ECOALF RECYCLED FABRICS SL.* [Online] [Accessed 11th May 2023] https://orbis-r1-bvdinfo-com.ezproxy.unav.es/version-20230324-3-3/Orbis/1/Companies/Report

Quartier, K. (2011) *Retail design: Lighting as a design tool for the retail environment.*, PhD Thesis Dissertation, Hasselt University, pp. 46–74. [Online] [Accessed 8th September 2023] 2023] https://documentserver.uhasselt.be/handle/1942/13488

Pérez-Bou, S., Valerio, M. and Eugui, P. (2021) Fashion stores as potential educators of conscious consumers. 2 case studies: H&M Group and Inditex. In *20th European Round Table on Sustainable Consumption and Production Graz*, September 8–10, 2021. [Online] [Accessed 8th September 2023] https://openlib.tugraz.at/download.php?id=613715d37cf0c&location=browse

Scapin, D., Senach, B., Trousse, B. and Pallot, M. (2012) 'User experience: Buzzword or new paradigm?' In *ACHI 2012, The Fifth International Conference on Advances in Computer-Human Interactions.* [Online] [Accessed 8th September 2023] https://www-sop.inria.fr/axis/pages/best-paper/dlsPaper20153ACHI2012.pdf

Velasco-Molpeceres, A., Zarauza-Cano, J., Pérez-Curiel, C. and Mateos-González, S. (2022) 'Slow fashion as a communication strategy of fashion brands on Instagram.' *Sustainability*, 15(1), p. 423. https://doi.org/10.3390/su15010423

Viaña, E. and Osorio, V (2018). *El Ganso, Ecoalf, Scalpers... la nueva moda española atrae al capital riesgo.* Expansión. [Online] [Accessed 8th September 2023] https://www.expansion.com/empresas/distribucion/2018/03/31/5abfb27846163f5f6b8b45fc.html

World Economic Forum. (2020) *Sustainability in the fashion industry: Turning seabed waste into clothing.* [Online] [Accessed 8th September 2023] https://www.youtube.com/watch?v=EyyWQwXQJcY

Stephens, D. (2017). *Reengineering retail: The future of selling in a post-digital world.* Publishers Group West.

Treïs (2023) *About us.* [Online] [Accessed 15th August 2023] https://treis-group.com/about-us/

Further resources

ECOALF Youtube. https://www.youtube.com/@ecoalf_.

ECOALF Las Rozas (2023) https://youtu.be/2uE-HPeqLuY.

Voices United for a Planet Beyond Next Season. Webinar around Black Friday https://www.youtube.com/watch?v=0OH-bkPg6eA.

7.3   Loanhood: on a mission to fix fashion through swap shop experiences

Bethan Alexander

Learning objectives

On completion of this case study, learners should be able to:

1   Understand collaborative (fashion) consumption models as experiences to engage young shoppers.
2   Explore community-based enterprises' approaches to creating customer experiences through swap shops.
3   Assess the potential for communicating circularity through IRL (in real life) collaborative retail spaces and events.
4   Reimagine future mission-led stores in fostering social capital and community engagement.

Introduction

Loanhood, a UK community-based social and circular enterprise founded in 2018 by two young changemakers, from the outset, was fixated on fixing fashion's negative sustainability reputation through pioneering swap shops and rental. 'Everything we do is about circulating clothes that are already in existence' (Founder interview, 2023). Intrinsic to collaborative consumption (CC) ways of doing business, swapping and renting extends the lifespan while reducing the dominant throw-away culture of clothing.

Loanhood was conceived by Jade McSorley, who returned to education as a mature student to study a Masters in Fashion Futures at London College of Fashion, and was learning about alternative business models. Prior to this, she had worked as a fashion model for ten years and had observed that most clothing exchanges were based on borrowing, rather than buying, i.e. a stylist would borrow clothes from a public relations (PR) agency for a shoot. Merging her prior experience with new learning, the idea of Loanhood was born, based on creating a digital and physical platform for people to access each other's wardrobes to borrow or swap rather than buy new clothing. Lucy Hall, the co-founder, shared Jade's vision and Loanhood became a reality.

Realising from the offset that young fashion-forward customers were not necessarily going to stop buying clothes when it is so integral to their self-expression, but they could satiate their desire for new fashion through offering swap shop experiences. Educating and empowering consumers to consider the way they consume and be more conscious with their choices has been critical from the get-go. Loanhood started with physical swap shops, as a way of building community and engaging with different audiences, before launching their rental app in July 2022, focusing on emerging designers and independent brands. The rental side of the business has been slow to start, requiring funding and investment from a combination of crowdfunding and Angel investors (Loanhood currently has over five Angel investors), launching into an already crowded space, comprising market leaders like HURR, Le Closet, GlamCorner, Rent the Runway and Hirestreet, as well as a plethora of micro enterprises, like Loanhood. It is the swap shops, however, that have been most popular so far, predominantly because they are free (no monetary transaction required) and are very community engaging (Founder interview, 2023).

'*Loanhood is its community*' is boldly communicated on its website, reinforcing that it is a community-based enterprise, entirely established on co-creation and collaboration with multiple stakeholders, including customers, stylists, emerging designers, students, fashion activists, retail partners, local councils, universities and third sector charities and other social enterprises. Building its community is central to their development, hosting talks, workshops and panel discussions with different audiences and locales about sustainable alternatives to consuming fashion, and often integrating these educational initiatives into the swap shop events, to make them more experiential. Loanhood pioneer both a business-to-business (B2B) and a peer-to-peer (P2P) business model, depending on which partner they are collaborating with and their objectives. For example, they have a long-term arrangement with Hackney Council, London, offering a swap shop service to the local residents. The regular swaps they run are about accessibility and affordability for the local Hackney community, whilst driving sustainability awareness. To date, around 10,000 clothing items have been swapped at Hackney Council x Loanhood events. Other swaps have been done in partnership with charities such as Hubbub and retailers like MatchesFashion, as a form of employee engagement. Most recently, Loanhood has extended its swapping reach into luxury by collaborating with Selfridges as part of its Worn Again campaign. Loanhood has been called 'clothing cupids', because it brings people together, stimulates happiness and excitement in the swapping experience, facilitates social connection and care for the environment (Founder interview, 2023).

Loanhood usually acts as a consultant, offering a fee-based service to other business partners for the swap shops, by providing the expertise on setting them up and hosting them, but also, importantly, reporting on their effectiveness, including attendance, consumer (e.g. age range) and swap (e.g. number of items and types of clothing swapped) statistics. Data analytics are important to these businesses in evidencing their sustainability endeavours. The Loanhood rental app is focused on P2P only, enabling individuals to rent their products directly to others.

This case study focuses on the swap shop community enhancing experience, specifically the cashless luxury Swap Shop by Loanhood in collaboration with Selfridges. It provides the opportunity to explore in-depth collaborative (fashion) consumption models, the role of community-based enterprises in keeping fashion circulating through swapping experiences, the ways in which collaborative swap shops can cultivate and enhance client and customer experiences, whilst critically changing the way we consume and do business to betterment the planet.

CC and clothes swapping

The fashion industry has gained a sustained negative reputation for fuelling excessive levels of clothing production and consumption, resulting in extreme waste (McNeill et al., 2020). On average 30 kg of clothing are disposed of in the UK per capita and the industry is recognised as the second most environmentally polluting after oil (Henninger, 2019, 2021). To address the clothing industry's negative environmental impact, new types of consumption practices have emerged, from renting, to secondhand retail, to swapping. These practices, collectively known as collaborative consumption (CC), attempt to reduce acquisition of new products, promote clothing reuse and lifespan or recirculation (Armstrong et al., 2016). CC is defined as 'people coordinating the acquisition and distribution of a resource for a fee or other compensation' (Belk, 2014, p. 1597). Recently *Time Magazine* named CC as one of the ten ideas that will change the world (Karpova et al., 2022). As a socio-economic model, it is part of the sharing economy, in which assets are owned and shared by a community. Some forms of CC require monetary transaction (e.g. renting); others rely on exchange, without payment. Swapping specifically increases clothing reuse and lifespan through exchange, and aligns with the UN Sustainable Development Goal 12: responsible production and consumption (United Nations, 2023).

The notion of swapping isn't new; it has been around for decades. In the UK the venerable children's Saturday morning TV programme *Swap Shop,* which ran from 1976 to 1982, was based on children sharing and swapping items and collections with each other. The travelling 'Swaporama' became one of the most popular aspects of the show, attracting thousands of children to show up at swaps across the country. However, swapping has seen a recent resurgence due to growing awareness of overconsumption and the need to reduce fashion waste (Henninger, 2019; Medeiros, 2023), attracting increasing attention from academics, practitioners and social enterprises alike.

Clothes swapping is described as the exchange of clothing or accessories during which ownership is redistributed from one person to another (Henninger et al., 2019) and can be categorised into four forms, determined by collaborative (CC) intensity (from P2P to mediated; i.e. organised by individual consumers or organisations) and channel (swaps hosted offline, online or both), as shown in the matrix (see Figure 7.3.1). While these forms are not mutually exclusive, meaning that they can cross over into other segments, for the sake of simplicity, the predominant approach is applied here. Swishing or swap parties (1) tend to be in-person P2P events often hosted for friends and family.

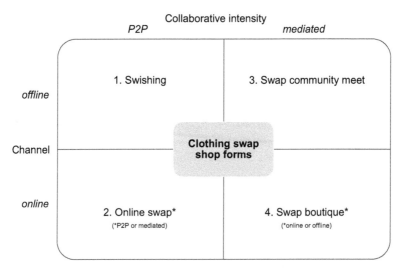

Figure 7.3.1 Matrix of swap shop forms.

Source: Author's own.

Online swap sites or apps (2) facilitate swaps digitally, through either a mediator or an individual. Swap community meets (3) tend to be open to the public, in-person and mediated by an organiser. Finally, swap boutiques (4) can be run online or offline, mediator operated, often by invite only, and tend to focus on premium or luxury items (Pocinková et al., 2023; Rathinamoorthy et al., 2019). Loanhood operates in segment 3 – they mediate community-based swaps that predominantly happen offline. The recent collaboration with Selfridges sees Loanhood entering segment 4, facilitated offline. Offering the possibility for customers to bring their pre-loved premium pieces to exchange for stamps to shop a curation of secondhand items to take home. In doing so, they provide another way to revive and refresh wardrobes while reducing fashion consumption (Selfridges press release, 2023). Before expanding on how this collaboration has driven social value whilst creating engaging retail experiences, it is important to first outline both Loanhood's swapping strategy and Selfridges' sustainability strategy, to demonstrate their complementary values, and how these are leveraged to synergistic effect.

Loanhood's cashless swap shop experience

The secondhand market has been intrinsic to British clothing consumption habits for decades, renowned for its jumble sales, car boot sales, flea markets, charity shops (or thrift stores) swap meets and vintage that burgeoned since the 1990s (Appelgren and Bohlin, 2015). Yet, even until recently there remained a stigma associated with acquiring secondhand clothing, it was therefore vital to Jade and Lucy to make the act of swapping more experiential (Founder interview, 2023). They have done this in a number of ways. Loanhood's team of advocators are knowledgeable about circularity and are excited to share the benefits of swapping with potential swappers. They have invested in elevating the visual swap shop environment, investing in modular recycled equipment that can be used at the various venues, from church halls to luxury retail department stores. This includes rails, branded hangers, signage and hang tags featuring circular fashion messages, mirrors and mobile changing rooms made by someone in their community, from Glastonbury festival forgotten tents that the founders personally collected on site. Budget allowing, they have an area dedicated to social sharing, set up as a studio, encouraging swappers to take pictures and share on their favoured platforms, encouraging user-generated content, word of mouth and furthering community relationships. The physical experience is a critical aspect of the swap shop, fuelling community involvement, interaction and engagement. According to Loanhood, this is what stands it apart from competitors like Nuw or Don't Swap Shop that tend to focus on digital swaps. 'In person events are so important to us, people have to feel even if they haven't left with an item, that they've still had an amazing IRL (in real life) experience' (Founder interview, 2023). Commensurate with Schmitt's (1999) strategic experiential modules (SEMs) that seek to categorise the type of experiential response a customer has to brand stimuli (e.g. an event, service, spatial environment, people, communications, etc.), Loanhood emphasises the feel, think, act and relate modules through their physical swap shops. Specifically, they trigger strong positive emotions of joy and excitement through the swapping experience, they appeal to people's intellect, using bold displays and educational workshops to communicate the benefits of circularity, they prompt people to act and change behaviours by offering a novel, interactive alternative fashion consumption experience and, lastly, but arguably most importantly, they appeal to people's desire for meaningful relationships through offering accessible, inclusive community-based interactions that actuate storytelling and social capital (Tan, 2023). Mission-led stores, founded on community-building and facilitating social connections, altruism and activism, is predicted to be a key success strategy for future retailing (Saunter and Medeiros, 2023), which intersects with Loanhood's pursuit of collaborative fashion consumption through community-based commitment.

Reselfridges and Project Earth

Reselfridges is part of Selfridges' Project Earth scheme, an initiative launched in August 2020 that aims to reinvent retail and change the way we shop and how we do business by 2025. It is built on three pillars: transitioning to environmentally friendly materials, exploring new business models and challenging mindsets. It is the latter pillar that the Swap Shop by Loanhood residency was aligned with (Selfridges press release 2023; Founder interview, 2023). As part of its Worn Again summer 2023 sustainable series, Loanhood took up residency in Selfridges, starting in Manchester on 1 June, followed by Birmingham and finishing in London for a three-week swap shop that closed at the end of July. Selfridges already offers a wide range of sustainable services focused on reducing waste, including renting, shopping and selling pre-loved, repair, refill, reuse sourcing archive fashion pieces and upcycling. Its bold ambition is for Reselfridges to make up 45% of customer transactions by 2030 (Faithfull, 2022). Worn Again featured a season of experimental secondhand and circular events and collaborations as part of its ten-year journey to realising their Project Earth strategy.

A swap shop by Loanhood x Selfridges

According to recent figures by Wrap (2022), the average UK adult owns 118 items of clothing but has not worn 26% of them in the last year, triggering calls for new ways to extend the life of unworn items that could reduce the environmental footprint. This is how the swap shop residency was conceived. Known for its London centric physical swap shops, Selfridges reached out to Loanhood in January 2023 to ask them to partner as part of their summer Reselfridges and recommerce initiatives. The global recommerce market is estimated to double, reaching USD 350 billion by 2027, growing 3× faster on average than the global clothing market overall and opening up new opportunities for brands, retailers and start-ups (Russell, 2023). In addition to market growth, consumer concerns over environmental impact is forcing fashion firms to invest in long-term initiatives, with Generation Z shoppers in particular, viewing recommerce services as a loyalty driver (Medeiros, 2023). This experimental collaboration therefore resonates with the growing 'shop-to-sell' consumer mindset. Following Selfridges' Stock Market, at The Corner Shop, an activation that 'traded' between May and June, comprising tailors, upcyclers, repairers, valuers and resellers, who were introduced to customers by Selfridges' 'stockbrokers' to help (re)discover the value of the clothes they already owned, came the Swap Shop by Loanhood residency.

At the luxury swap shop in-store experience, customers were invited to bring clothes they no longer wanted in exchange for stamps that could be used in the swap shop for something new. Selfridges saw this experience as 'dialling up the fun and desirability of shopping secondhand' (Selfridges press release, 2023). For Loanhood it meant taking the essence of their tried and tested accessible and inclusive swap shop model but elevating it to a luxury status, which determined the types of clothes that were accepted and the type of swappers that would attend.

As the first luxury department store to host a swap shop, Selfridges was naturally cautious about ensuring a luxury experience and needed assurances from Loanhood about how this would be delivered. Different criteria to a regular swap were established, centred on customer service, which included Loanhood devising a Swap Shop Handbook to help Selfridges' staff team understand how it would work. They also created Swap Shop Mindset posters to display in-store, to get customers into the mindset of making peace with the letting go of their pieces, whilst communicating the merits of circularity. As part of the internal communications, Loanhood engaged in 'Good Morning Selfridges' staff training to help them understand about the swap shop and also attended press breakfasts at each Selfridge location not only to share the swap shop story but for journalists to experience it firsthand (Founder interview, 2023). In advance of the swap shop opening, Loanhood had to source hundreds of premium products, pulling favours from its community of stylists, influencers and fashion friends for donations, in exchange for early access to the swap. This reassured Selfridges and its customers about the premium quality of products and brands included in the swap.

In terms of operating the swap, each customer could bring up to five items of men's and women's clothing with a resale value of between £50 and £300. A dedicated team was available to value items in exchange for stamps based on product type, brand and condition. Loanhood worked with Selfridge's in-house resident Vintage Threads, to help authenticate, assess and value the product, before accepting it. To manage footfall and generate a more personal experience, customers were asked to sign up via the Selfridges Eventbrite to attend. Tickets were complimentary and were bookable in two-hour swap slots, between noon and 9 pm daily. Customers were checked in at the welcome desk to the swap lounge and given stamps, according to the value of their swappable items. Swappers could then browse for pre-loved clothing and the stamps could be used to select new-to-them pieces from the swap shop, before checking out. If swappers did not use their stamps, they could book another session and use the same swap card (see Figures 7.3.2–7.3.4).

Swapping's only similarity to fast fashion is that the clothing constantly changes; therefore repeat visits were a common occurrence as customers, especially new, FOMO (fear of missing out) swappers, became 'addicted' to finding something new to them (Founder interview, 2023). Interestingly, many swappers talked about being 'hooked' by swapping and wanted 'permanent swaps' in-store. Loanhood refer to swappers' emotional experiences as a 'double dopamine hit', in that they experience joy and excitement from seeing someone else in their piece, as well as joy and excitement from getting a new piece for themselves (Founder interview, 2023).

Consumer involvement in swapping is integral to its effectiveness, assuming the dual role of provider and obtainer simultaneously. In other words, to obtain clothing from the swap, consumers need to first provide clothing. Some scholars have written about the significance of this, highlighting that swapping is referred to as letting go or voluntary disposition, which implies that the garment may have reached end of life for one consumer, but may have a second life for someone else, as opposed to disposal that implies a finite end (Pocinková et al., 2023). Letting go of a garment can be laden with emotion and memories (positive or negative) and can impact the decision-making process, in terms of deciding to part with it or not (Pocinková et al., 2023). This was evidenced at the Swap

Figure 7.3.2 Selfridges Swapshop by Loanhood.

Source: Reprinted by permission of Selfridges.

Figure 7.3.3 Selfridges Swapshop by Loanhood.

Source: Reprinted by permission of Selfridges.

Figure 7.3.4 Selfridges Swapshop by Loanhood.
Source: Reprinted by permission of Selfridges.

Figure 7.3.5 Selfridges Swapshop by Loanhood, Thursday Late.
Source: Reprinted by permission of Selfridges.

Shop by Loanhood, which elicited many shared stories between providers and obtainers. Loanhood collated over 30 customer stories during the residency, predominantly involving joyful interactions and acts of kindness between providers and obtainers. This social exchange and social value generation were inherent to the swap experience.

To augment the experience, *Thursday Lates* were hosted by Loanhood, offering a series of evening swap shop slots that included upcycler workshops, teaching guests how to transform items of clothing and complimentary cocktails from Whitebox Cocktails, ice cream from Little Moons and a live DJ. Tickets to these events were £10 with all proceeds going to charity Oxfam, which helps create lasting solutions to poverty injustice (Burke, 2023) (see Figure 7.3.5). Loanhood demonstrates that collaboration (beyond Selfridges) and community co-creation is intrinsic to the success of its swap shops. Creating a prosperity loop by cultivating community through swapping experiences and then co-creating new experiences with its community to further bolster its community. In other words, what it says – *Loanhood is its community* – is what it practises.

Conclusion

Loanhood's modus operandus (MO) is based on community that swaps, rents and changes fashion for the better (Founder interview, 2023). It forms part of a social and environmental movement that recognises the need to do business differently, for the good of people and the planet, while forging more meaningful relationships. By integrating and harnessing principles based on (re)circulation, collaboration, co-creation and community, it is carving out space in the growing secondhand fashion market and generating synergistic emotional, social, cognitive and behavioural experiences for its growing altruistic and activist swapper community.

WGSN's latest report on Stores in 2024 (Saunter and Medeiros, 2023) signals community and service-led formats like swap shops as an emerging format to watch for 2025 and beyond. With recommerce and community-led retailing burgeoning, this case study raises a number of questions for further consideration. For example, how should retailers experiment with hosting swapping experiences to engage consumers, especially Generation Z, in the future? And how can swap shops be experientially augmented whilst educating people about their responsible retailing habits? Moreover, as a niche newcomer, Loanhood faces challenges around financially resourcing its endeavours. As a social enterprise with scaling ambitions, how can they monetise swap shops and grow the business, while maintaining their ethos of community, accessibility and inclusivity?

Case questions

1   Research and discuss the variety of experiential opportunities Loanhood offers through their physical swap shops. Now consider what further swap shops experiences could be created to augment and elevate community engagement about circularity and responsible retailing.

2   To date, Loanhood focuses on in-person swaps as a way to foster and build its community. Charged with devising Loanhood's growth strategy, argue your case for or against it extending into digital swaps, ensuring that its values of recirculation, collaboration, co-creation, community, accessibility, inclusivity and experience are fully considered. Present your growth strategy as an elevated pitch.

3   Inspired by WGSN's store report that forecasts community and service-led retail formats to be important in the future (Saunter and Medeiros, 2023), you are asked to create a spatial design for a swap shop for a sustainable brand of your choice. In addition, to design a series of community-led, interactive, educational experiences that drive engagement for existing and potential customers. You are expected to draw on the learnings from the Loanhood case study as a starting point. Present these as a collection of annotated mood boards, using visuals and text to bring your concepts and creations to life.

References

Appelgren, S. and Bohlin, A. (2015) 'Growing in motion: The circulation of used things on second-hand markets.' *Culture Unbound: Journal of Current Cultural Research*, 7, pp. 143–168. https://doi.org/10.3384/cu.2000.1525.1571143.

Armstrong, C.M., Niinimäki, K., Lang, C. and Kujala, S. (2016) 'A use-oriented clothing economy? Preliminary affirmation for sustainable clothing consumption alternatives.' *Sustainable Development*, 24(1), pp. 18–31.

Belk, R. (2014) 'You are what you can access: Sharing and collaborative consumption online.' *Journal of Business Research*, 67(8), pp. 1595–1600.

Burke, J. (2023) *Selfridges readies swap shop*. Drapers. [Online] [Accessed 15 August 2023] https://www.drapersonline.com/news/selfridges-readies-swap-shop

Faithfull, M. (2022) *Selfridges wants resale, repair, rental or refills to near half of transactions by 2030*. Retail Gazette. [Online] [Accessed 15 August 2023] https://www.retailgazette.co.uk/blog/2022/09/selfridges-reselfridges-sustainability/

Founder Interview. (2023) *Case author interview with Loanhood's Founder Jade McSorley*, 14 August.

Henninger, C. (2021) 'Creative marketing and the clothes swapping phenomenon,' in Pantano, E. (ed.) *Creativity and marketing*. Bingley: Emerald Publishing.

Henninger, C.L., Bürklin, N. and Ninnimäki, K. (2019) 'Clothes swapping phenomenon – When consumers become suppliers.' *Journal of Fashion Marketing and Management*, 23(3), pp. 327–344. https://doi.org/10.1108/JFMM-04-2018-0057

Karpova, E., Jestratijevic, I., Lee, J. and Wu, J. (2022) 'An ethnographic study of collaborative consumption: The case of temporary clothing swapping.' *Sustainability*, 14. https://www.mdpi.com/2071-1050/14/5/2499

McNeill, L.S., Hamlin, R.P., McQueen, R.H., Degenstein, L., Wakes, S., Garrett, T.C. and Dunn, L. (2020) 'Waste not want not: Behavioural intentions toward garment life extension practices, the role of damage, brand and cost on textile disposal.' *Journal of Cleaner Production*, 260. https://doi.org/10.1016/j.jclepro.2020.121026

Medeiros, C. (2023) *Revitalising the department store 2023*. WGSN. [Online] [Accessed 15 August 2023] https://www.wgsn.com

Pocinková, L., Henninger, C.E., Le Normand, A. and Balzquez Cano, M. (2023) 'Exploring the role of community based enterprises in consumers' voluntary clothing disposition via UK swapping events using theory of social practice.' *Social Enterprise Journal* (ahead-of-print). https://doi.org/10.1108/SEJ-02-2023-0017

Rathinamoorthy, R., Surjit, R. and Karthik, T. (2019) 'Clothing swap: Gateway to sustainable ecofriendly,' in Martínez L., Kharissova O. and Kharisov B. (eds.) *Handbook of ecomaterials*. Springer, pp. 1599–1622.

Russell, M. (2023) *Secondhand apparel market soaring as awareness improves – Report*. Just Style. [Online] [Accessed 23 August 2023] https://www.just-style.com/news/secondhand-apparel-market-soaring-as-awareness-improves-report/?cf-view

Saunter, L. and Medeiros, C. (2023) *Stores in 2024: Community & service-led formats.* WGSN. [Online] [Accessed 15 August 2023] https://www.wgsn.com

Schmitt, B.H. (1999) 'Experiential marketing.' *Journal of Marketing Management,* 15(1/3), pp. 53–67.

Selfridges press release. (2023) *Selfridges opens UK's first in store swap shop.* [Online] [Accessed 24 August 2023] https://selfridgespress.com/2023/07/13/selfridges-opens-uks-first-in-store-swap-shop/

Tan, E. (2023) *Gen Z: The new hype cycle.* WGSN. [Online] [Accessed 24 August 2023] https://www.wgsn.com

United Nations (2023) *Sustainable development goals.* [Online] [Accessed 15 November 2023] https://sdgs.un.org/goals

Wrap (2022) *Nation's wardrobes hold 1.6 billion items of unworn clothes.* Wrap. [Online] [Accessed 23 August 2023] https://wrap.org.uk/media-centre/press-releases/nations-wardrobes-hold-16-billion-items-unworn-clothes-people-open-new

Further reading and resources

Fashion Swap Shop Enterprises

A stitch to wear: https://www.facebook.com/stitchtowearswapandthrift/
A Swap Shop by Loanhood video: https://www.youtube.com/watch?v=MCZH0vYFpaI
Don't Shop Swap: https://www.dontshopswap.co.uk/
Loanhood website: https://www.loanhood.com/
Nuw website: https://www.thenuwardrobe.com/
Swap Society: https://www.swapsociety.co/
Verte London: https://www.instagram.com/verte.london/

Selfridges Sustainability Schemes

Selfridges Project Earth site: https://www.selfridges.com/GB/en/features/project-earth/
Selfridges (Reselfridges site): https://www.selfridges.com/GB/en/cat/reselfridges/

Swap Shop by Loanhood Press Articles and Videos

Drapers: https://www.drapersonline.com/news/selfridges-readies-swap-shop
Glamour magazine: https://www.glamourmagazine.co.uk/article/preloved-fashion-swap-shop
Selfridges: A swap shop by Loanhood: https://www.selfridges.com/GB/en/features/info/stores/events/swap-shop-by-loanhood-selfridges-exchange/#bookingLink

Swapping and Collaborative Consumption Articles

Circular. (2021) *Pandemic drives 'clothes swapping' among UK youth.* [Online] [Accessed 15 August 2023] https://www.circularonline.co.uk/news/pandemic-drives-clothes-swapping-among-uk-youth/
Clarke, R. (2020) *Global Fashion Exchange launches new digital swapping system.* Forbes. [Online] [Accessed 15 August 2023] https://www.forbes.com/sites/roddyclarke/2020/05/27/global-fashion-exchange-launches-new-digital-swapping-platform/?sh=23fb609f6df1
Clube, R. (2020) *The rise of community fashion swaps.* Ecologist Informed by Nature. [Online] [Accessed 15 August 2023] https://theecologist.org/2020/jan/13/rise-community-fashion-swaps
GFX (no date) *Global fashion exchange youth project.* [Online] [Accessed 15 August 2023] https://www.globalfashionxchange.org/gfxyp

GFX (no date) *Global fashion ecosystem swappertunity model.* [Online] [Accessed 15 August 2023] https://www.globalfashionxchange.org/work?pgid=j6aneqjg-5091cdd4-53f7-4edb-a9be-3fcadfe5f2b8

Gray, S., Druckman, A., Sadhukhan, J. and James, K. (2022) 'Reducing the environmental impact of clothing: An exploration of the potential of alternative business models.' *Sustainability*, 14. https://www.mdpi.com/2071-1050/14/10/6292

Lang, C. and Armstrong, C.M.J. (2018) 'Collaborative consumption: The influence of fashion leadership, need for uniqueness, and materialism on female consumers' adoption of clothing renting and swapping.' *Sustainable Production and Consumption*, 13, pp. 37–47. https://doi.org/10.1016/j.spc.2017.11.005

Ramtiyal, B., Johari, S., Vijayvargy, L. and Prakash, S. (2023) 'The impact of marketing mix on the adoption of clothes rental and swapping in collaborative consumption.' *Journal of Global Operations and Strategic Sourcing* (ahead-of-print). https://doi.org/10.1108/JGOSS-04-2023-0027

Visceral customer experiences

8.1   Aesop Sensorium: providing sensorial excellence within the physical fashion store

Ben Butling

Learning objectives

On completion of this case study, learners should be able to:

1   Identify the stimuli Aesop uses in their Sensorium and explain how they are used to deliver a sensorial experience.
2   Describe how a multi-sensory experience can contribute to a successful brand experience.
3   Assess the role of the Sensorium in Aesop stores and explain how it creates value for consumers.
4   Analyse and explain how the multi-sensory experiences used by Aesop help communicate the brand's identity.
5   Evaluate the successful sensory elements of Aesop's in-store experience and translate learnings into strategic recommendations for wider industry incumbents.

Introduction

Aesop's background

Aesop is an Australian premium skin, hair and body care, fragrance and accessories brand that was founded in 1987 by Dennis Paphitis. Since its inaugural store opening in 2003, the company has grown its operations to amass a global footprint of more than 300 stand-alone stores and over 120 counters in selected department stores, across more than 25 countries worldwide (Mohammed, 2022, Aesop to author, 2023). After purchasing a 65% stake in 2012 for USD 68 million (Sams, 2023), the brand underwent a complete sale to Natura and Co in 2016 (Natura&Co, 2023). In its most recent change of ownership, the skincare brand was formally acquired by the French beauty conglomerate L'Oreal in 2023 at a valuation of USD 2.5 billion – joining the likes of Maybelline, Garnier and YSL Beauty in the company's portfolio (Toh, 2023). Tapped as the global

DOI: 10.4324/9781003378099-11

beauty leader, L'Oréal's global market share amounted to 14% in 2022 (Statista, 2023a); however, in Europe this figure rises to 20%, with consolidated sales nearing €11.4 billion in the region (Statista, 2023b). Aesop's product offering spans gender-neutral formulations for skin, body and hair. The brand added fragrances in 2005 and homeware in 2018 (Mason, 2018). Aesop has positioned its product offering around a meticulous attention to detail, quality and sensory pleasure (Aesop, 2023a). These attributes have become synonymous with the brand and are translated into its physical spaces. To this effect, Aesop's approach to store design leads with sensibility; they consider the local community, design history and cultural nuances, resulting in unique, off-beat in-store customer experiences that underscore its upmarket positioning (Cosentino, 2023). Aesop stores further demonstrate a commitment to the brands' values as they adopt analogue and intimate customer experiences, favouring human interaction over store technology with a focus on small-format locations (Chitrakorn, 2022).

The importance of in-store experiences in the beauty and personal care market

The global beauty and personal care market generated USD 430 billion in revenue in 2022 and is projected to grow to USD 622 billion by 2028 (Mckinsey, 2023; Mordor Intelligence, 2023). Consequently, the market has become attractive for new companies and investors to enter, forcing existing brands to revaluate their differentiation strategies amidst increased industry competitiveness. In conjunction, specialised physical stores are threatened as e-commerce continues as the fastest growing sales channel for beauty products at a projection of 12% year-on-year (Mckinsey, 2023). Among other factors, this is catalysed by the expanding offerings from online retail giants and proliferation of direct-to-consumer brands. With the convenience and speed of digital channels often surpassing that of in-store retailing, brands are having to amplify their physical stores using exceptional experiences (Alexander and Nobbs, 2016), offering memorable and compelling interactions that add value beyond products and services (Kandampully et al., 2021). Echoed by industry voices, the bifurcation of retail means brands failing to deliver exceptional experiences may become obsolete by way of experience mediocrity (Dennis, 2020). Shifting consumer demand also intensifies the requirements of exceptional store experience; nearly four in five consumers point to experience as an important factor in their purchasing decision (PWC, 2018), while 61% expect more floor space devoted to experiential offerings in the future (Shopify, 2021).

Aesop is well regarded as an industry leader for in-store experiences, embodying what is described by the brand's CEO Michael O'Keeffe as an "engagement-centric model" (Powell, 2016). Their success with this approach is underlined as 77% of total sales are generated from physical retail spaces (Mohammed, 2022). With the experience economy growing, however, competing brands are fast adopting similar strategies; retailers like Lush, Diptyque, Le Labo and L'Occitane are among their competition, and all are placing strong emphasis on the physical store experience. Staying true to its innovative status, in late 2021, Aesop expanded its store offering and unveiled its first 'fragrance experience' inside its Sydney flagship named the Sensorium (Hui-Miller, 2021) – an added room devoted to its perfume category. The Sensorium was expanded into select Aesop stores globally, signalling the brand's intent on developing store experiences that prioritise sensory retailing techniques.

The role of sensory retailing

A brand experience is an intangible, non-material retail offering that stimulates consumer emotions through interactions between objects, environments and people (Holbrook and Hirschman, 1982; Oh et al., 2007). Researchers attest a positive brand experience can strengthen consumer-brand relationships (Trudeau and Shobeiri, 2016), increase consumer satisfaction (Tsaur et al., 2007; Becker and Jaakkola, 2020; Happ, 2021; Cachero-Martínez and Vazquez Casielles, 2021) and store patronisation (Cassel, 2021) and reinforce brand loyalty (Schmitt et al., 2009; Sahin et al., 2011).

Sensory experiences are one dimension of brand experience, often accompanied by cognitive, affective, physical and relational dimensions (Schmitt, 1999). Schmitt's seminal framework, the Strategic Experience Module (SEM), conceptualises sensory experiences – the activation of visual, olfactory, aural, tactile and gustatory senses through brand-related stimuli – as one dimension of a consumer's brand experience. These sensory experiences work in unison and further catalyse the remaining dimensions of brand experience – affective, cognitive, behavioural and relational experiences (Schmitt, 1999). Hulten (2011: 265) argues retailers can apply sensory expressions "to be closer and more deeply imprinted in the customer's mind". Wider extant research further outlines the importance of sensorial experiences for creating a successful consumption environment (Kandampully et al., 2021), developing pleasure (Dubé and Le Bel, 2010), emotional connection (Helkkula, 2011), gathering information (Holbrook and Hirschman, 1982; Schmitt, 2010) and the creation of a holistic brand experience (McCarthy and Wright, 2004; Schmitt et al., 2009; Lemon and Verhoef, 2016).

This case explores how Aesop's physical retail store design leverages sensorial experiences to create a successful consumer experience, drawing particular attention to the brand's use of visual, olfactory, aural, tactile and gustatory sensations. Within this, it enables readers to critically analyse Aesop's multi-sensory strategy through the lens of Schmitt's (1999) SEM framework, encouraging the application of extant theory to the brand's retail environment, and exploring how sensory experiences are connected to brand experience. In conjunction, the case refers to immersive and congruent experiences, asking the reader to consider the method in which Aesop delivers its store experiences, and how this may benefit the consumers' brand experience further.

Aesop's approach to sensorial design

Aesop primarily targets sophisticated consumers who are independent, intelligent, well-travelled and appreciative of both art and culture (Kearney, 2019). Aesop takes a holistic approach to store design, aiming to best reflect this audience by curating pleasurable experiences throughout the store that are congruent with their consumers' desires. Consequently, the brand ensures their servicescapes and products not only have a functional purpose, but also emotionally align with consumers' personal and social-life context (Hulten, 2011).

In addition, Aesop also curates immersive experiences, promoting consumers to actively engage with the brand, products and the wider service environment. Such experiences have the propensity to ignite stronger – or more 'complex' (Schmitt, 2010: 70) – brand experiences, as sensorial stimulation triggers a combination of cognitive, affective, physical and relational outcomes. Aesop chooses to conjoin sensorial stimuli throughout its store experiences, resulting in experiences that host an interplay between different senses – stimulating visual, olfactory, tactile, gustatory and auditory senses in one (Schmitt, 1999). As a result, Aesop creates multi-sensory and complex brand experiences, catalysing affective experiences where emotions like joy or excitement are developed, cognitive experiences where information processing occurs and behavioural experiences where further actions are taken by consumers (Schmitt, 1999; Schmitt et al., 2009). The following section of the case outlines the brand's application of sensorial design across each sensory dimension.

Aesop's application of sensorial design

Visual experiences

The brand first develops its store experience through its interior and facade design. Aesop partners with architects that consider the cultural nuances of store locations, forming a design language using contextual materials and subtle cues towards local history. Summarised in Aesop's print publication, Paphitis, the brand's founder, expresses how each space responds to its setting and their desire is always to integrate with the streetscape (Paphitis and Down, 2019) (see Figures 8.1.1 and 8.1.2). Although each store differs visually, Aesop finds unity in concept, seeking cohesion through design principles as opposed to replicable aesthetics (Simon, 2015). This approach is largely unique to the brand as competitors like Lush and L'Occitane's store footprints predominantly follow

Figure 8.1.1 Aesop store exterior, Regent Street, London.

Source: Reprinted by permission of Aesop.

Figure 8.1.2 Aesop store exterior, Sounds Hannam, Seoul.
Source: Reprinted by permission of Aesop.

a systematic approach, irrespective of location. Exemplifying these differences, Aesop's Cape Town, South African store, draws on local art deco influences and integrates the architectural vernacular of Sea Point suburb (Moss, 2022); conversely, in Germany, its Leipzig store draws heavily on metal fixtures, low-level lighting and dark green hues that are informed by the city's industrial heritage (Kwok, 2016).

In London, Aesop's Regent Street store takes inspiration from neoclassical colonnades seen in the streets original design from 1819. Architects further repackaged historically British aesthetics such as oversized, stately basins, building grandeur through visual references while maintaining connection to place (Aesop, 2023b) (see Figure 8.1.3).

While Aesop experiments with unique store designs, they maintain strict consistency with product design, using apothecary-style brown glass or plastic bottles for nearly all their products. As such, product displays within each store are congruent and promote a sense of cohesion within the store.

Olfactory experiences

A positive olfactory experience has been found to have a decisive impact on consumers' emotional state and moods (Rinaldi, 2007; Hulten, 2011), as well as being a powerful catalyst for strengthening brand recognition and developing memorable consumer experiences. Some argue olfactory stimuli are powerful because the experience and corresponding emotion are stored in the same memory for consumers (Walsh, 2020). Conversely, unsuccessful or overpowering applications of sensory stimulus can be highly disruptive

Figure 8.1.3 Aesop's interior design, Regent Street, London.

Source: Reprinted by permission of Aesop.

of cognitive processing, fuelling a negative consumer experience (Schmitt, 1999; Schmitt et al., 2009; Hulten, 2011). As a skin, hair and fragrance brand, Aesop products develop olfactory experiences as they revolve around scents and aromas. To further elevate the communication of their fragrance collection, Aesop chooses to enhance the consumption experience within a specifically designed section of the store – the Sensorium. The Sensorium is a unique conceptual space found in select Aesop stores that possesses theatrical design qualities – a place the brand describes as an "intriguing portal into the art of fragrance" (Aesop, 2023c). While its aesthetic differs by store, each Sensorium is underpinned by some identifiable design consistencies. Fragrances are lined along the walls, allowing consumers to select and test each one. In addition, Aesop provides individual ceramic discs where visitors can spray perfume – replacing the paper strips found in competing retailers. The Sensorium also houses the brand's fragrance armoire translating to fragrance cabinet in English (Aesop, 2023c). Here consumers can leave an item of clothing inside the infusion chamber with a select perfume, imbuing it with a scent that stays with the wearer once they leave the store (Callahan, 2021). Referring to the value of this experience, some have suggested the Sensorium offers consumers a place for experimentation and self-discovery (Thwaites, 2022) (see Figures 8.1.4 and 8.1.5).

Arguably, Aesop's Sensorium is both novel and sophisticated, distancing the brand's consumption experience from its competitors. What's more, some suggest a brand experience is made more valuable if it is both memorable and enduring (Pine and Gilmore, 2014; Gao and Lan, 2020) – something which Aesop looks to achieve through imbuing scents to the visitors' clothes. The Sensorium adds further differentiation from

Figure 8.1.4 Aesop's Sensorium and Fragrance Amoire, Regents Street, London.
Source: Reprinted by permission of Aesop.

competing brands such as Le Labo, Glossier and Byredo, as they choose not to separate their fragrance offering and wider product lines in-store, whilst Aesop provides a secluded space for consumers to experience their scents (Markidis, 2022). In this regard, it could be argued consumers are able to better process product information

Figure 8.1.5 Aesop's Sensorium, Regents Street, London.
Source: Reprinted by permission of Aesop.

because there are less additional stimuli to distract them (Hulten, 2011), likely facilitating a clearer cognitive response to product stimuli (Schmitt, 1999).

Tactile experiences

Touch is one of the most important senses in physical retailing environments as tactile stimulation boosts consumers' ability to evaluate brand and product information (Karangi and Lowe, 2021). These experiences are largely provided through a retailer's deployment of materials, surface and product, while also influenced by temperature, form and weight (Hulten, 2011). Aesop is well-known to concentrate their store experience around their wash basins; in an interview with *Esquire* (2019), the brand's CCO (Chief Customer Officer), Suzanne Santos, posits: "There is a special reverence for the sink in every Aesop space". The brand takes inspiration from handwashing and good hygiene within Japanese culture, conducted as a ritual of purification before visiting religious venues (Kyo-Suzume, 2020). In doing so, the brand aims to embody more intellectual reference points and romanticise the ritual of handwashing to their consumers (Fetto, 2018). Aesop's London and Seoul stores are some examples where the basins are the centrepiece of the physical space (see Figures 8.1.6 and 8.1.7) (Kolnaar, 2019). Alongside its connection to the brand's values, they also place focus on the wash basins to enhance the stores' consumer experience. In the context of omnichannel retailing, tactile experiences are arguably more important to consumers in physical retail stores, as the absence of tactile stimuli within e-commerce sites are their biggest disadvantage. In Aesop's physical

Figure 8.1.6 Aesop's wash basins, Regents Street, London.

Source: Reprinted by permission of Aesop.

Figure 8.1.7 Aesop's wash basins, Sounds Hannam, Seoul.

Source: Reprinted by permission of Aesop.

stores, visitors can touch and apply a range of trial products, as the brand hosts multiple basins in unison with numerous items beside each station (Radcliffe-Moore, 2021). As handwashing is the focal point of their store design, the brand's design choices successfully signpost – and thus encourage – consumers to use the products. Aesop's concentration on tactile experiences arguably allows consumers to derive greater value. A tactile experience is also likely to enhance their brand experience, as Hulten (2011) suggests the use of goods enhances affective value – feelings of enjoyment and fun – while also providing cognitive value – arising through increased product understanding.

Gustatory experiences

Gustatory experiences are applied less frequently in retail environments yet have been found to have a positive effect on consumer experience when conducted successfully. Some suggest this is because gustatory stimuli further contribute to a multi-sensory experience and serve as another sensorial facet for consumers to draw affective and cognitive experiences (Hulten, 2011; Alexander and Nobbs, 2016). In keeping with Japanese cultural references, Aesop emulates historical custom as consultants have been offering liquorice root, rosehip and peppermint leaf tea to browsing customers since 2008.

The brand's inspiration is exemplified in an interview with *L'Officiel Magazine* (2023), as Santos notes, "our relationship with our customers is never simply a transactional one – it is also educational, prescriptive, and sensorial, where we treat our customers as guests". Aesop intends to use gustatory experiences to create an intimate connection with visitors and curate a welcoming store experience (Argosino, 2021). These strategic elements further serve to communicate the brand's identity, summarised in an article by Batchelor (2022), "It is these well-thought-out and intimate gestures that make Aesop's customers appreciate the brand".

Auditory experiences

Music in the retail environment has been found to influence enjoyment, store dwell time and mood (Morrison et al., 2011), mediated by variables such as pitch, tempo and volume (Li et al., 2022). Extant research expresses positive auditory experiences further contribute to a consumer's brand experience through the development of feelings and emotion (Hulten, 2011). Aesop carefully selects music that contains both intellectual and cultural nuances – aligning with their brand identity. Aesop acknowledges the transportive qualities of auditory experiences (Cosmetic Business, 2022), and aims to create these in their retail spaces, offering a sense of escapism to consumers (Gim Ean, 2020). Their considered playlists are also used to set the pace of the store experience, encouraging visitors to be unhurried and thoughtful. In doing so, the brand's auditory selection aligns with another one of their core values – slow beauty (Nair, 2022).

Conclusion

Sensory experiences are a core component of a wider brand experience and are effective in developing memorable brand interactions and emotional connection, while improving product understanding and patronage intentions. Aesop's physical retail strategy successfully employs a plethora of multi-sensory experiences, combining visual, olfactory, tactile, gustatory and auditory stimuli to promote a stronger brand experience. Bolstering the effectiveness of their multi-sensory experiences, the brand ensures stimuli are mutually congruent, developing positive interplay between each design feature without being overpowering or disjointed. Visually, their application of unique interior design in response to cultural cues and local contexts successfully generates aesthetic appeal, positioning the brand as both luxury and unique. The Sensorium offers an olfactory experience that brings discovery and novelty to the consumption experience. Aesop's focus on wash basins further delivers a successful tactile experience, signposting consumers towards opportunities to trial their products. Their provision of tea attaches connotations of care to a gustatory experience in-store, assimilating Aesop with wider luxury brand services. Finally, their use of calming music within an auditory experience develops an atmosphere in alignment with the brand's identity. In creating these sensorial experiences, Aesop catalyses wider brand experiences as the stimuli serve to enhance positive emotions – boosting affective experiences – while also communicating product and brand information – developing cognitive experiences. In creating a stronger brand experience, Aesop offers consumers increased intellectual and emotional value, while assisting in clearly translating the brand's identity.

Aesop's retail strategy exemplifies careful consideration and successful application of sensorial experiences within the physical store. Their cult following and recent acquisition only further highlights the positive progress of the brand, something which arguably stems from its in-store experience. As a segment leader in sensory retailing, industry stakeholders should look to the brand when assessing examples of effective sensory experience strategies.

Case questions

1   Identify the retail design features used by Aesop to deliver a sensory experience and explain how they successfully stimulate each human sense. Consider visual, olfactory, tactile, gustatory and auditory stimulus in turn.
2   How, and why, does Aesop's use of sensory experiences successfully contribute to a wider brand experience for consumers?
3   How, and why, do Aesop's sensory experiences successfully provide value for consumers?
4   How does Aesop use sensory experiences to communicate their brand identity?
5   Select a familiar fashion brand that you believe does not currently have an effective sensory retail strategy. Using the learnings from this case, recommend strategic sensorial design changes towards your chosen brand and, using Schmitt's (1999) SEM framework, evaluate how these changes could enhance their consumers' brand experience.

References

Aesop (2023a) *Our story*. Aesop UK. [Online] [Accessed 2nd October 2023] https://www.aesop.com/uk/r/about/
Aesop (2023b) *Aesop Regent Street | Signature store*. Aesop UK. [Online] [Accessed 2nd October 2023] https://www.aesop.com/uk/r/aesop-regent-street/

Aesop (2023c) *Aesop Sydney*. Aesop UK. [Accessed 6th November 2023] https://www.aesop.com/uk/r/aesop-sydney-city/

Albert Review (2021) *Aesop sensorium in Sydney takes olfactory pleasure to the next level*. Albert Review, 15 December. [Online] [Accessed 2nd October 2023] https://albertreview.com.au/design/aesop-sensorium/

Alexander, B. and Nobbs, K. (2016) 'Chapter 17: Multi-sensory fashion retail experiences: The impact of sound, smell, sight and touch on consumer-based brand equity,' in Vecchi, A. and Buckley, C. (eds.) *Handbook of research on global fashion management and merchandising*. IGI Global, pp. 420–443. ISBN 9781522501107.,

Argosino, I. (2021) *How Aesop builds compelling customer experiences through thoughtful design*. PURVEYR. [Online] [Accessed 2nd October 2023] https://purveyr.com/2021/01/07/how-aesop-builds-compelling-customer-experiences-through-thoughtful-design/

Batchelor, R. (2022) *Inside the world of Aēsop: Intimate, aesthetic, and beautiful*. ELLE SINGAPORE, 15 November. [Online] [Accessed 2nd October 2023] https://elle.com.sg/2022/11/15/inside-the-world-of-aesop-intimate-aesthetic-and-beautiful/

Becker, L. and Jaakkola, E. (2020) 'Customer experience: Fundamental premises and implications for research.' *Journal of the Academy of Marketing Science*, 48(4), pp. 630–648. https://doi.org/10.1007/s11747-019-00718-x.

Cachero-Martínez, S. and Vázquez-Casielles, R. (2021) 'Building consumer loyalty through e-shopping experiences: The mediating role of emotions.' *Journal of Retailing and Consumer Services*, 60, p. 102481. https://doi.org/10.1016/j.jretconser.2021.102481

Callahan, A. (2021) *Aēsop Sensorium | Snøhetta*. Architecture & Design. [Online] [Accessed 2nd October 2023] https://www.architectureanddesign.com.au/projects/office-retail/aesop-sensorium-sn%C3%B8hetta

Cassel, E., Jacobs, B. and Graham, M. (2021) 'Effects of the four realms of experience and pleasurable experiences on consumer intention to patronise pop-up stores.' *Journal of Consumer Sciences* [Preprint]. https://doi.org/10.4314/jfecs.v49i

Chitrakorn, K. (2022) *Forget the indie locations, Aesop is going mainstream. Can it keep its edge?* Vogue Business. [Online] [Accessed 2nd October 2023] https://www.voguebusiness.com/beauty/forget-the-indie-locations-aesop-is-going-mainstream-can-it-keep-its-edge

Cosentino (no date) *Aesop stores – Cosentino South Africa*. [Online] [Accessed 2nd October 2023] https://www.cosentino.com/en-za/blog/aesop-stores/

Cosmetic Business (2022) *Aesop teams up with Worldwide FM for new radio series*. [Online] [Accessed 2nd October 2023] https://cosmeticsbusiness.com/news/article_page/Aesop_teams_up_with_Worldwide_FM_for_new_radio_series/198927

Dennis, S. (2020) *Remarkable retail: How to win & keep customers in the age of digital disruption*. 1st edn. Vancouver, BC: LifeTree Media. [Accessed 2nd October 2023] https://stevenpdennis.com/remarkable-retail/.

Dubé, L. and Bel, J. (2010) 'The content and structure of laypeople's concept of pleasure.' *Cognition & Emotion*, 17(2), pp. 263–295. https://doi.org/10.1080/02699930302295

Esquire (2019) *How an Australian hairdresser built an empire out of status hand wash*. Esquire. [Online] [Accessed 2nd October 2023] https://www.esquire.com/uk/design/a27888878/aesop-founder-interview-store-design/

Fetto, F. (2018) *From Aesop to DS & Durga, The brands that mix beauty with culture*. British Vogue. [Online] [Accessed 2nd October 2023] https://www.vogue.co.uk/article/the-culture-of-beauty-arts

Gao, F. and Lan, X. (2020) 'Sensory brand experience: Development and validation in the Chinese context.' *Frontiers in Psychology*, 11, p. 1436. https://doi.org/10.3389/fpsyg.2020.01436

Gim Ean, T. (2020) *Aesop store design speaks sensitively to local surroundings, honouring neighbourhoods and heritage*. Options. [Online] [Accessed 2nd October 2023] https://www.

optionstheedge.com/topic/haven/aesop-store-design-speaks-sensitively-local-surroundings-honouring-neighbourhoods-and

Happ, E. et al. (2020) 'Insights into customer experience in sports retail stores.' *International Journal of Sports Marketing and Sponsorship*, 22(2), pp. 312–329. https://doi.org/10.1108/IJSMS-12-2019-0137

Helkkula, A. (2011) 'Characterising the concept of service experience.' *Journal of Service Management*, 22(3), pp. 367–389. https://doi.org/10.1108/09564231111136872.

Holbrook, M.B. and Hirschman, E.C. (1982) 'Hedonic consumption: Emerging concepts, methods and propositions.' *Journal of Marketing*, 46(3), pp. 92–101. https://doi.org/10.2307/1251707

Hui-Miller, J.-A. (2021) *Step inside Aesop's world-first fragrance experience, The Sensorium.* Inside Retail Asia. [Online] [Accessed 2nd October 2023] https://insideretail.asia/2021/11/25/55729/

Hulten, B. (2011) 'Sensory marketing: The multi-sensory brand-experience concept.' *European Business Review*, 23, pp. 256–273. https://doi.org/10.1108/09555341111130245

Kandampully, J., Bilgihan, A. and Amer, S.M. (2022) 'Linking servicescape and experiencescape: Creating a collective focus for the service industry.' *Journal of Service Management* (ahead-of-print). https://doi.org/10.1108/JOSM-08-2021-0301.

Karangi, S.W. and Lowe, B. (2021) 'Haptics and brands: The effect of touch on product evaluation of branded products.' *Journal of Consumer Behaviour*, 20(6), pp. 1480–1496. https://doi.org/10.1002/cb.1959

Kearney, T. (2019) *How this luxurious Australian beauty brand dominates by distribution.* LinkedIn. [Online] [Accessed 6th November 2023] https://www.linkedin.com/pulse/how-luxurious-australian-beauty-brand-dominates-toni-kearney/

Kolnaar, T. (2019) *7 stores showcasing Aesop's dedication to design.* Archello. [Online] [Accessed 2nd October 2023] https://archello.com/news/7-stores-showcasing-aesops-dedication-to-design

Kwok, N. (2016) *einszu33 develops Aesop store with historical references to Leipzig, designboom.* Architecture & Design Magazine. [Online] [Accessed 2nd October 2023] https://www.designboom.com/architecture/einszu33-aesop-leipzig-historical-references-12-27-2016/

Kyo-Suzume (2020) *Kyo-suzume culture and tourism.* [Online] [Accessed 2nd October 2023] https://kyosuzume.or.jp/en/

Lemon, K.N. and Verhoef, P.C. (2016) 'Understanding customer experience throughout the customer journey.' *Journal of Marketing*, 80(6), pp. 69–96.

Levy, L. (2018) *What's the next status hand wash (That Isn't Aesop)?* The Strategist. [Online] [Accessed 2nd October 2023] https://nymag.com/strategist/article/best-hand-soaps-restaurants-homes-status-luxury.html

Li, P., Guo, X., Wu, C. and Spence, C. (2022) 'How multisensory perception promotes purchase intent in the context of clothing e-customisation.' *Frontiers in Psychology*, 13. https://www.frontiersin.org/articles/10.3389/fpsyg.2022.1039875

L'Officiel (2023) *The luxury of living with Aesop.* L'Officiel Philippines. [Online] [Accessed 2nd October 2023] https://www.lofficielph.com/culture/the-luxury-of-living

Markidis, S. (2022) *Aesop adds "Sensorium" to Sydney store.* Australian Design Review, 24 January. [Online] [Accessed 2nd October 2023] https://www.australiandesignreview.com/interiors/projects-interiors/aesop-adds-sensorium-to-sydney-store/

Mason, M. (2018) *Aesop launch their first homewares product & yes, it's ridiculously luxe.* PEDESTRIAN.TV, 5 September. [Online] [Accessed 2nd October 2023] https://www.pedestrian.tv/style/aesop-oil-burner-homewares-australia/

McCarthy, J. and Wright, P. (2004) 'Technology as experience.' *Interactions*, 11(5), pp. 42–43. https://doi.org/10.1145/1015530.1015549.

Mckinsey (2023) *The beauty market in 2023: New industry trends.* McKinsey. [Online] [Accessed 2nd October 2023] https://www.mckinsey.com/industries/retail/our-insights/the-beauty-market-in-2023-a-special-state-of-fashion-report

Mohammed, H. (2022) *Aesop's new regent street store is all about Georgian and Regency architecture.* WWD, 12 August. [Online] [Accessed 2nd October 2023] https://wwd.com/beauty-industry-news/beauty-features/aesop-regent-street-store-georgian-regency-architecture-1235295043/

Mordor Intelligence (2023) *Personal care industry analysis – Market overview.* Mordor Intelligence. [Online] [Accessed 2nd October 2023] https://www.mordorintelligence.com/industry-reports/global-beauty-and-personal-care-products-market-industry

Morrison, M. et al. (2011) 'In-store music and aroma influences on shopper behavior and satisfaction.' *Journal of Business Research*, 64(6), pp. 558–564. https://doi.org/10.1016/j.jbusres.2010.06.006.

Moss, J. (2022) *Aesop stores: A visual history of interior architecture.* wallpaper.com. [Online] [Accessed 2nd October 2023] https://www.wallpaper.com/gallery/lifestyle/a-visual-history-of-aesops-best-designer-stores

Nair, S. (2022) *Aesop's Suzanne Santos on slow beauty, and why it's so important today.* Lifestyle Asia Singapore, 20 April. [Online] [Accessed 2nd October 2023] https://www.lifestyleasia.com/sg/beauty-grooming/skin/aesop-suzanne-santos-on-slow-beauty-and-why-its-so-important-today/

Natura&Co (2023) *Aesop, Natura &Co.* [Online] [Accessed 2nd October 2023] https://www.naturaeco.com/brands/aesop-2/

Oh, H., Fiore, A.M. and Jeoung, M. (2007) 'Measuring experience economy concepts: Tourism applications.' *Journal of Travel Research*, 46(2), pp. 119–132. https://doi.org/10.1177/0047287507304039

Paphitis, D. and Down, J. (2019) *Aesop: The book.* 1st edn. New York: Rizzoli International Publications (1, 1). [Online] [Accessed 2nd October 2023] https://books.google.co.uk/books/about/Aesop.html?id=bLmxDwAAQBAJ&redir_esc=y

Pine, J.B. and Gilmore, J.H. (2014) 'A leader's guide to innovation in the experience economy.' *Strategy & Leadership*. Edited by R. Randall and Brian Leavy, 42(1), pp. 24–29.

Powell, D. (2016) *How Aesop chief executive Michael O'Keeffe helped craft a $250 million business model.* SmartCompany. [Online] [Accessed 2nd October 2023] https://www.smartcompany.com.au/entrepreneurs/influencers-profiles/how-aesop-chief-executive-michael-okeeffe-helped-craft-a-250-million-business-model/

PWC (2018) *Experience is everything: Here's how to get it right.* PwC. [Online] [Accessed 2nd October 2023] https://www.pwc.com/us/en/services/consulting/library/consumer-intelligence-series/future-of-customer-experience.html

Radcliffe-Moore, L. (2021) *The Opulence that is Aesop.* Sinkfluencer, 23 March. [Online] [Accessed 2nd October 2023] https://sinkfluencer.wordpress.com/2021/03/23/the-opulence-that-is-aesop/

Rinaldi, A. (2007) 'The scent of life. The exquisite complexity of the sense of smell in animals and humans.' *EMBO Reports*, 8(7), pp. 629–633. https://doi.org/10.1038/sj.embor.7401029

Sahin, A., Zehir, C. and Kitapçı, H. (2011) 'The effects of brand experiences, trust and satisfaction on building brand loyalty: An empirical research on global brands.' *Procedia – Social and Behavioral Sciences*, 24, pp. 1288–1301. https://doi.org/10.1016/j.sbspro.2011.09.143

Sams, L. (2023) *How Aesop turned into a billion-dollar brand.* Australian Financial Review. [Online] [Accessed 2nd October 2023] https://www.afr.com/life-and-luxury/fashion-and-style/how-aesop-quietly-turned-cult-handsoap-into-a-billion-dollar-brand-20221215-p5c6m8

Schmitt, B. (1999) 'Experiential marketing.' *Journal of Marketing Management*, 15, pp. 53–67.

Schmitt, B., Brakus, J. and Zarantonello, L. (2009) 'Brand experience: What is it? How is it measured? Does it affect loyalty?' *Journal of Marketing*, 73(3), pp. 52–68. https://doi.org/10.1509/jmkg.73.3.052

Schmitt, B. (2010) 'Experience marketing: Concepts, frameworks and consumer insights.' *Foundations and Trends® in Marketing*, 5(2), pp. 55–112. https://doi.org/10.1561/1700000027

Shopify. (2021) *Experiential Retail 101: How to host in-store events your shoppers love.* Shopify. [Online] [Accessed 2nd October 2023] https://www.shopify.co.uk/retail/experiential-retail

Simon, P. (2015) *The architecture of meaning: Aesop*. Medium, 13 December. [Online] [Accessed 2nd October 2023] https://medium.com/@parkersimon/the-architecture-of-meaning-aesop-6dab269000dc

Statista. (2023a) *Topic: L'Oréal*. Statista. [Online] [Accessed 2nd October 2023] https://www.statista.com/topics/1544/loreal/

Statista. (2023b) *Aesop's revenue 2022*. Statista. [Online] [Accessed 2nd October 2023] https://www.statista.com/statistics/1238231/aesop-revenue/

Thwaites, M. (2022) *The sensorium at Aesop Sydney by Snøhetta – Issue 08 Feature*. The Local Project, 20 March. [Online] [Accessed 2nd October 2023] https://thelocalproject.com.au/articles/the-sensorium-at-aesop-sydney-by-snohetta-issue-08-feature-the-local-project-the-commercial-project-feature/

Toh, M. (2023) *L'Oréal buys Aesop in $2.5 billion deal, its biggest acquisition* ever. CNN Business. [Online] [Accessed 2nd October 2023] https://www.cnn.com/2023/04/04/business/australia-aesop-loreal-natura-deal-intl-hnk/index.html

Trudeau H. and Shobeiri, S. (2016) 'The relative impacts of experiential and transformational benefits on consumer-brand relationship.' *Journal of Product & Brand Management*, 25(6), pp. 586–599.

Tsaur, S.-H., Chiu, Y.-T. and Wang, C.-H. (2007) 'The visitors behavioral consequences of experiential marketing.' *Journal of Travel & Tourism Marketing*, 21(1), pp. 47–64. https://doi.org/10.1300/J073v21n01_04

Walsh, C. (2020) *How scent, emotion, and memory are intertwined — And exploited*. Harvard Gazette, 27 February. [Online] [Accessed 2nd October 2023] https://news.harvard.edu/gazette/story/2020/02/how-scent-emotion-and-memory-are-intertwined-and-exploited/

8.2 To Summer: leveraging Chinese cultural identity to drive a sensorial customer experience

Ying Gao

Learning objectives

On completion of this case study, learners should be able to:

1 Understand To Summer's brand identity and positioning in the Chinese fragrance market.
2 Analyse how To Summer enhances the emotional and sensory experience for customers through its marketing mix.
3 Understand how cultural identity can influence the creation of an immersive customer experience (CX).
4 Evaluate how To Summer delivers CX across different channels and touchpoints.
5 Explore how lessons learnt from To Summer's emotional and sensory CX could be adopted by other fragrance and beauty players in the Chinese retail sector.

Introduction

To Summer is a Chinese fragrance brand that was founded by Huipu Liu, Li Shen and Khoon in 2018, initially selling through online channels only (Runwise Consulting, 2022). The brand name was invented by the founders, who were impressed by the atmosphere of "watching summer in tranquility" (Lun, 2023) as they sat in the Lingering Garden, a famous classical garden in Suzhou, Jiangsu Province, China. From the brand's inception, Chinese culture was intrinsically associated with the brand aesthetic (LinkFlow, 2023).

By 2019, *To Summer* had reached a million subscribers to its WeChat official account and a product repurchase rate of 60%. The company then received investment from IDG Capital and the Zenith Fund which enabled the brand to open physical retail stores in three first-tier cities (Shanghai, Shenzhen and Beijing) based on a quiet confidence in the expansion of their channel network (Topher, 2022). In 2022, the brand entered large e-commerce platforms, such as the Chinese versions of Tmall and TikTok, which contributed to the generation of USD 143 million in sales revenue (Luxe.Co, 2021). In five years, the brand had built strong brand awareness and associations, to the extent that whenever 'oriental fragrances' are mentioned, many young consumers think of *To Summer* (Lin, 2022). Indeed, the 'oriental mood' is the essence of *To Summer's* brand identity, storytelling and CX, which has fostered over 100,000 loyal customers (Fang, 2023).

To Summer was developed because daily fragrance experiences are increasingly valued by Chinese consumers; indeed, data suggests that the Chinese olfactory economy will experience rapid growth in the near future (Kantar, 2021; Runwise Consulting, 2022; Euromonitor, 2023). Chinese fragrances brands, however, are much less experienced than their international competitors; they have limited reach and reputation, and sub-optimal formulae. International brands such as Dior, Chanel, Jo Malone, Tom Ford and Diptyque still lead China's perfume market, commanding a market share of around 70% (Euromonitor, 2023).

The development of 'China-Chic' and a growing cultural confidence means that an increasing number of Chinese consumers are now supporting domestic brands, preferring to choose Chinese fragrances to express their personality and cultural identity (Xin, 2021; Euromonitor, 2023). Previously, scholars have found that the effective development of cultural capital can improve the competitive advantage for local brands when facing international competitors (Strizhakova and Coulter, 2015; Steenkamp, 2019; Yeboah-Banin and Quaye, 2021). Indeed, 27% of Chinese consumers consider the cultural story behind the brand, and the related CX, to be essential to their fragrance choice (Hu, 2021; Social Book, 2021), which has led to the rapid development of local brands such as Scent Library, Boitown, The Beast, Document and *To Summer* (Hall, 2021; Winning Business Network, 2021). They incorporate traditional Chinese cultural elements to different degrees in their development and promotion. Some of them have invested more focus on exploring traditional Chinese cultural heritage, using elements such as osmanthus, tea, native animals, architecture and philosophy to launch corresponding fragrances, opening up a new Chinese fragrance scene (Euromonitor, 2023). For example, high-end brand Document bases its brand on a blend of Confucianism, Buddhism and Taoism, and the physical store is inspired by Chinese temples (Mu, 2023), while The Beast has leveraged its cultural codes through collaboration with Manner Coffee, launching a 'Panda Latte', which comes with a limited-edition sample of The Beast's Panda Poof fragrance (SocialBeta, 2021). While many local brands focus on an expression of traditional culture in the presentation of the product, retailers are interested in ways to better infuse cultural identity into the CX, both online and offline (Hu, 2021).

To Summer has outstanding performance in terms of the online and offline CX. The company started with a WeChat account where traditional cultural and fragrance storytelling was integrated into online retail scenarios (An, 2022). The brand creates an exclusive story, with corresponding images, for each product when publishing online so that consumers experience traditional stories, scenes and poems related to the fragrance through the product copy they receive (Runwise Consulting, 2022). These visual experiences stimulate and evoke memories of the aromas associated with the product's story, which drives consumers into the stores to smell the products that resonate with them (Liu, 2022). Meanwhile, the brand incorporates both its core Chinese cultural storytelling and aesthetic concepts into its physical stores by designing CX that stimulate cultural memories (LinkFlow, 2023). For example, when *To Summer* opens a flagship store in a new city, the company often chooses a site with a local heritage (GrowthHK.cn, 2022). A prominent local identity supports a consumer's positive connection to local cultural values and traditions, which enhances brand recognition and experience (Yeboah-Banin and Quaye, 2021), which becomes the key to a great brand performance within a short time (Runwise Consulting, 2022; Topher, 2022). By 2023 *To Summer* had a network of nine physical retail outlets in China (including in Beijing, Shanghai, Shenzhen, Hangzhou, Nanjing and Chengdu) as well as a counter in the luxury department store Lane Crawford, Beijing.

This case details the various ways that *To Summer* uses traditional Chinese cultural identity to deliver unrivalled CX. It illustrates the ways in which traditional cultural stories can be used to deliver emotional experiences in an online retail environment, as well as the motivation these experiences create for consumers to travel to the offline store. The case also focuses on exploring the multi-sensory experience *To Summer* creates for their flagship store based on local culture, and provides the reader with a basis for reflection on the interconnections between the brand's emotional experience, sensory experience and cultural identity.

Imbuing Chinese cultural identity into the brand experience

Cultural identity is defined by Jensen (2003) as a broad set of beliefs and lifestyles that people share with their local communities. Specifically, some Chinese brands portray a sensitive perception of local traditional culture related to consumer needs, which is often reflected through a strong brand image (Swoboda *et al.*, 2012; Fang, 2023). *To Summer* differentiates its product positioning based on Chinese cultural identity (Grewal and Roggeveen, 2020). Its product matrix is based on core competencies regarding the creation of oriental scents, blended with Chinese aesthetic design and continuous product innovation, to provide consumers with a continuous flow of fresh experiences (Xu, 2019). The founders of *To Summer* state, "the product itself is the way to deliver the Chinese aesthetic experience of the brand" (Wang, 2020).

The key ingredients used in the fragrances are plum blossom, orchid, bamboo and chrysanthemum, all culturally symbolic scents from plants that are used to raise the goodness and perseverance of character (Liu, 2022). These culturally symbolic ingredients evoke a sense of identification with Chinese aromas (CBNData, 2023). In addition, *To Summer* extends a lot of care into the packaging design of its products. For example, the jade-like octagon cap of the perfume bottle was inspired by the shape of traditional garden windows in southern China (GrowthHK.cn, 2022). Besides this, the packaging design is minimalist with a lot of white space, in line with the national Chinese aesthetic (Ju, 2023). Moreover, *To Summer* launches gift boxes for different Chinese festivals and seasons, such as the recent Year of the Rabbit limited-edition design (Figure 8.2.1), which emphasises the gift-giving traditions of the season and enhances the visual experience.

The brand extends and enriches the product experience by creating multiple lines with common scents, including perfume, solid perfume, essential oils, candles, diffusers, wax tablets, wax warmers and body care products that reflect a wide range of usage scenarios (Zhou and Ding, 2022). The price structure reflects its high-end positioning; a 30 ml perfume is priced at 598RMB (approx. £68). In the flagship stores, there are no *To Summer* prices on display as they are incorporated into individual product story tags. Although many young consumers have expressed their willingness to pay a premium for a national brand that expresses Chinese cultural identity, some have expressed concern over the perceived high pricing, which is comparable to that of established international brands (Luxe.Co, 2021).

Enhancing emotional cultural storytelling experiences through online communications

Emotional experiences are associated with values and feelings (Mishra *et al.*, 2016). Previous studies have found that the aim of creating emotional experiences in online retailing is to attract the attention of consumers by enhancing resonance with them (Das *et al.*, 2019; Cahero-Martínez and Vázquez-Casielles, 2021). *To Summer* is committed to

Figure 8.2.1 To Summer's gift packaging.

Source: Reprinted by permission of To Summer.

communicating the cultural identity of its products through online channels. The brand creates expressive content about their fragrances by exploring stories related to local humanities, arts, folkways and history that are deeply rooted in Chinese memory (Li, 2021; CBNData, 2023). For example, the 'Too Sweet to Miss Beijing' story collection is a response to the folk culture of Beijing, and has a high emotional resonance (Digitaling, 2022). This collection is based on the sweet and sour scent of hawthorn, which is the main ingredient in the most popular Beijing children's dessert – sugar-coated haws. The brand depicts a story scene through texts and pictures of playing in the snow while eating sugar-coated haws in the first snowfall of winter in Beijing (Hu, 2021). By exploring the fragrances and cultural stories that are relevant to the location of their flagship stores, the brand is better able to integrate into the local culture via online and offline brand space. Product stories and scenic images are released online to create emotional experiences, evoking childhood memories of tasting sugar-coated haws in the winter and fuelling their desire to visit a store to smell the scent and reminisce about their childhood.

To Summer was one of the first Chinese fragrance brands to offer an online emotional experience by connecting with customers through cultural storytelling (Wang, 2020); however, the competitive advantage gained is being eroded by copy-cat competitors (Li, 2021; An, 2022). This was what prompted the brand owners to expand their physical channels, to provide consumers with more immersive experiences of traditional Chinese culture through sensory interactions.

Enhancing the Chinese aesthetic sensory experience through physical stores

Physical shops play an important role as experiential space for brands to communicate their cultural values (Kent *et al.*, 2018; Shavitt and Barnes, 2020). Pine and Gilmore (1999) suggest that the aim of the experience is to create memories that enhance perceptions of the brand and build emotional connections, while Grewal and Roggeveen (2020) find that perceptions, emotions and behaviours towards a brand depend on a range of situational factors such as culture and technology. These factors are the result of conscious design decisions that leverage in-store elements such as atmosphere, products and displays, and various digital cues (Lemon and Verhoef, 2016; Grewal and Roggerveen, 2020).

Multi-sensory brand experiences occur when more than one of a consumer's senses of sight, smell, touch, sound and taste are stimulated (Hultén *et al.*, 2009); this creates a cognitive experience that is emotionally engaging (Hultén, 2011), which is particularly important for fragrance brands that emphasise sensory experiences (Shreya and Nilesh, 2022). Specifically, consumers can be guided through an immersive store experience to learn how to use fragrance products in a physical setting, by creating spaces that resonate with their lifestyle and cultural sentiments to create a deep connection with the product. It was necessary to evolve To Summer's Chinese aesthetic philosophy and lifestyle engagement from online to physical space to enhance multi-sensory stimulation, especially smell and touch (Wang, 2020; Lin, 2022). Indeed, industry analysts forecast that physical shops are expected to support more than 70% of To Summer's sales performance over the next three years (Zhou, 2022; Fang, 2023) and they are therefore strategically important to the brand's growth.

To Summer tends to open stores in historic neighbourhoods or heritage buildings, and the exterior of each store has a strong local cultural style (CBNData, 2023). For example, To Summer's Guozijian flagship store is located in a 700-year-old neighbourhood of Beijing and was originally a courtyard built during the time of the Qing Dynasty (Figure 8.2.2). The history and setting behind such architecture provide an additional sense of Chinese cultural charm to the brand (Xiao, 2023). The traditional shadow walls of the courtyard have been replaced with glass to bring in natural light, which changes constantly during the day and with the seasons.

Kotler (1973) suggests that the design of a store atmosphere can emotionally impact customers and encourage them to spend more time in the shop. To Summer's product storytelling atmosphere is inseparable from the olfactory experience. These offline stories

Figure 8.2.2 To Summer's Guozijian flagship store.
Source: Reprinted by permission of To Summer.

remain aligned to the online experience, with special ceramic scent testers and fragrance story cards corresponding to each product (Li, 2021); for example, the 'Osmanthus' perfume is inspired by the story of the osmanthus tree in the Summer Palace (Beijing) during autumn (Wang, 2020). The scene depicted on the story cards shows a person walking outside the red walls of the Palace, with the autumn wind carrying the faint scent of osmanthus blossoms. The smell and the story cards, combined with the cultural references to Beijing, enhanced by the store design, allow the customer to experience the fragrance in an immersive way, and develop relevant cultural identity associations. *To Summer* also focuses on tactile experiences, centred on the hands, with a hand washing station at the entrance of each shop offering a cleansing ritual (Figure 8.2.3); the purification of the hands is a metaphor for casting off distractions in traditional Chinese culture and is usually done before burning incense and lighting candles (iziRetail, 2020; An, 2022).

Customers are treated to an oriental herbal healing experience using the brand's essential oil hand soap and hand cream. The second courtyard of the Beijing Guozijian store is surrounded by walls made from handmade terracotta bricks, so customers walking past and touching the walls can be immersed in the charming culture of traditional Beijing handicrafts. Light music with a clearly traditional Chinese style is always playing in *To Summer's* stores (Fan, 2022). This is immediately recognisable as a form of cultural identity that accompanies the consumer on an immersive scented journey with a relaxing rhythm. In addition, *To Summer* regularly organises traditional cultural events and art exhibitions in the store, complemented by music, food and traditional specialties, where consumers can experience the brand's Eastern cultural atmosphere while socialising and interacting (Sina, 2022).

As a brand with Chinese culture as its core, *To Summer* takes advantage of the many traditional festivals to reinforce its brand cues by decorating stores and offering bespoke products and experiences related to the festival. For example, customers can participate in Chinese New Year festivities by writing 'Fu' characters, printing Chinese New Year

Figure 8.2.3 To Summer's hand washing station.

Source: Reprinted by permission of To Summer.

prints and receiving limited-edition red packets with any in-store purchase (Figure 8.2.4). This provides customers with a unique experience of traditional culture.

Brand communication via phygital touchpoints

The online *To Summer* experience often makes the connection between fragrance, local culture and lifestyle, visualising the product and reinforcing the sensory associations to inspire consumers to go offline (Xu, 2019). There are also digital touchpoints in the physical stores to integrate the online and offline experiences to encourage customer retention.

Figure 8.2.4 To Summer's in-store festival themed experiences.
Source: Reprinted by permission of To Summer.

For example, QR codes for the brand's WeChat account are provided on product posters placed in the waiting area at the store entrance, encouraging customers to look through interesting cultural stories while stimulating their interest in the brand. Moreover, consumers are also offered a coupon if they add the brand WeChat account when they check out. Furthermore, *To Summer* encourages consumers to revisit stores by regularly posting new product and cultural stories on their WeChat account (LinkFlow, 2022; Runwise Consulting, 2022).

Conclusion

To Summer's core brand concept is to tap into traditional cultural stories in the collective Chinese memory. Fragrance innovation, product packaging, online storytelling and physical store experiences are all deeply embedded with the essence of cultural identity. Consumers experience the brand's interpretation of Eastern aesthetics through emotional and multi-sensory experiences, as well as being guided and informed about traditional Chinese fragrance culture and lifestyle. This brand value, rooted in traditional Chinese culture and superior CX, makes *To Summer* more competitive with increased growth potential in the Chinese fragrance market.

Competition from local fragrance brands is intensifying, however, the adoption of oriental fragrances and the storytelling of traditions is increasingly being imitated by competitors in their online and offline experiences. Designing a more immersive and unique

CX based on cultural identity, to enhance the seamless emotional and sensory experiences, both online and offline, may be worth further exploration for the brand. In addition, some Chinese brands have reached a developmental ceiling in the domestic market in recent years and have started to expand into the wider international market (Kantar, 2021). More unpredictable challenges could be faced by *To Summer* in new markets, and shifts of strategy in response could be necessary. In particular, as a fragrance brand with such a distinct cultural identity, how should it adapt its culturally relevant experience to different consumer needs in new markets, with different consumer values? Looking ahead, this may be a direction for the brand to consider, but with caution.

Case questions

1   Analyse how *To Summer* has created a brand with an enhanced cultural identity and a differentiated position in the Chinese fragrance market. Use the marketing mix concept such as Booms and Bitner's (1981) 7P's to help frame your analysis.
2   Evaluate the benefits and drawbacks of delivering culturally aligned emotional and sensory customer experiences for fragrance and beauty brands.
3   Evaluate how *To Summer* has used online and offline touchpoints to build a sensory, emotional and immersive customer experience.
4   For a new international market of your choice, suggest how *To Summer* might need to adapt their customer experience for different consumer groups.

References

An, Q. (2022) *500 brand cases – To Summer: The premium sense of oriental incense.* [Online] [Accessed 20 May 2023] https://www.jiemian.com/article/7660346.html

Booms, B.H. and Bitner, M.J. (1981) 'Marketing strategies and organization structures for service firms,' in Donnelly, J.H. and George, W.R. (eds.) *Marketing of services.* Chicago, IL: American Marketing Association, pp. 47–51.

Cahero-Martínez, S. and Vázquez-Casielles, R. (2021) 'Building consumer loyalty through e-shopping experiences: The mediating role of emotions.' *Journal of Retailing and Consumer Services*, 60, pp. 1–10.

CBNData (2023) *Trends in the olfactory economy: Which 'smells' are consumers paying for?* [Online] [Accessed 6 March 2023] https://36kr.com/p/2233487956864642

Das, G., Agarwal, J., Malhotra, N.K. and Varshneya, G. (2019) 'Does brand experience translate into brand commitment? A mediated-moderation model of brand passion and perceived brand ethicality.' *Journal of Business Research*, 95, pp. 479–490.

Digitaling (2022) *From Chinese fragrance to Chinese sweetness, Guanxia's ability to storytell its brand has improved again.* [Online] [Accessed 20 March 2023] https://www.digitaling.com/articles/864016.html

Euromonitor (2023) *Fragrances in China.* [Online] [Accessed 2 March 2023] https://www.euromonitor.com/fragrances-in-china/report

Fan, X.X. (2022) *Explore To Summer's flagship store. Can a brand that sells $140 million a year retain its users?* [Online] [Accessed 3 October 2023] https://www.c2cc.cn/news/10008437.html

Fang, E. (2023) *How new fragrance brand To Summer achieved over $100 million in annual revenue in just 4 years with the DTC model.* [Online] [Accessed 2 March 2023] https://runwise.co/dtc/166276.html

Grewal, D. and Roggeveen, A. (2020) 'Understanding retail experiences and customer journey management.' *Journal of Retailing*, 96(1), pp. 3–8.

GrowthHK.cn (2022) *To Summer's path to oriental perfumery.* [Online] [Accessed 4 March 2023] https://www.growthhk.cn/quan/78393.html

Hall, C. (2021) *How China's new love affair with perfume is changing the market.* Business of Fashion. [Online] [Accessed 2nd March 2023] https://www.businessoffashion.com/briefings/china/how-chinas-new-love-affair-with-perfume-is-changing-the-market/

Hu, Y.F. (2021) *China investment trend of the five-sense industry: The rise and the study of olfactory economics.* [Online] [Accessed 2 March 2023] https://pdf.dfcfw.com/pdf/H3_AP202106021495483046_1.pdf?1622630616000.pdf

Hultén, B. (2011) 'Sensory marketing: The multi-sensory brand-experience concept.' *European Business Review*, 23(3), pp. 256–273.

Hultén, B., Broweus, N. and van Dijk, M. (2009) *Sensory marketing.* Basingstoke: Palgrave Macmillan.

iziRetail (2020) *In conversation with the manager, To Summer went from online to offline, what made it go popular?* [Online] [Accessed 20 May 2023] https://www.sohu.com/a/441327581_663226

Jensen, A.L. (2003) 'Coming of age in a multicultural world: Globalization and adolescent cultural identity formation.' *Applied Developmental Science*, 7(3), pp. 189–196.

Ju, M.L. (2023) *How imaginative can the breakout oriental fragrance be?* [Online] [Accessed 10 March 2023] https://36kr.com/p/2090562937115912

Kantar (2021) *2021 China beauty industry white paper.* [Online] [Accessed 2 March 2023] https://www.kantarworldpanel.com/cn-en/news/2021-Beauty-Industry-White-Paper

Kantar (2022) *2022 China perfume industry white paper.* [Online] [Accessed 2 March 2023] https://min.news/en/news/6408ed8df9456bdd71b3772c867f6b1b.html

Kent, A., Dennis, C., Cano, M.B., Helberger, E. and Brakus, J. (2018). 'Branding, marketing, and design: Experiential in-store digital environments,' in Information Resources Management Association (ed.) *Fashion and Textiles: Breakthroughs in Research and Practice.* IGI Global, pp. 275–298.

Kotler, P. (1973) 'Atmospherics as a marketing tool.' *Journal of Retail*, 49(4), pp. 48–64.

Lemon, K.N. and Verhoef, P.C. (2016) 'Understanding customer experience throughout the customer journey.' *Journal of Marketing*, 80(6), pp. 69–96.

Li, X.R. (2021) *Local fragrances go viral, how does To Summer tell the story of contemporary oriental fragrances? BrandStar Interview.* [Online] [Accessed 2nd March 2023] https://www.brandstar.com.cn/in-depth/1820

Lin, V. (2022) *The premium of self-definition: why niche perfume brands such as To Summer and documents are becoming mainstream.* [Online] [Accessed 2nd March 2023] http://news.winshang.com/html/069/6546.html

LinkFlow (2023) *Why we're willing to pay for To Summer's story when it's only a private domain with annual sales of over 100 million.* [Online] [Accessed 2nd March 2023] https://www.linkflowtech.com/blogs/pay-for-the-story-of-watching-the-summer

Liu, C.Z. (2022) *The middle class is in desperate need of culture behind the explosion of To Summer.* [Online] [Accessed 5 March 2023] https://m.thepaper.cn/newsDetail_forward_19264079

Lun, L. (2023) *How To Summer is creating a new high-end fragrance brand.* [Online] [Accessed 2 March 2023] https://www.gtn9.com/perspectives_show.aspx?ID=F9374978D557601B

Luke.co (2021) *How to break the pricing ceiling for Chinese fragrance brands? See how To Summer and DOCUMENTS are doing it.* [Online] [Accessed 2 March 2023] https://cn.fashionnetwork.com/news/shen-du---ru-he-da-po-zhong-guo-xiang-fen-pin-pai-de-ding-jia-tian-hua-ban---kan-kan-guan-xia---wen-xian-shi-zen-me-zuo-de,1329184.html

Mishra, P., Bakshi, M. and Singh, R. (2016) 'Impact of consumption emotions on WOM in movie consumption: empirical evidence from emerging markets.' *Australasian Market Journal*, 24(1), pp. 59–67.

Mu, L.J. (2023) *How DOCUMENTS, the Chinese perfume brand's pricing ceiling, uses luxury logic to make perfume.* [Online] [Accessed 2 March 2023] https://www.adquan.com/post-2-323713.html

Pine, J. and Gilmore, J. (1999) *The experience economy*. Boston, MA: Harvard Business School Press.

Runwise Consulting (2022) *How did To Summer, a new fragrance brand, manage to achieve annual revenue of over $100 million in 4 years?* [Online] [Accessed 2 March 2023] https://zhuan-lan.zhihu.com/p/615602049

Sina (2022) *To Summer's flagship store is located in the Quadrangle of Guozijian.* [Online] [Accessed 3 October 2023] https://fashion.sina.com.cn/b/nw/2022-07-08/1529/doc-imizirav2499146.shtml

Shavitt, S. and Barnes, A.J. (2020) 'Culture and the consumer journey.' *Journal of Retailing*, 96(1), pp. 40–54.

Shreya, K. and Nilesh, G. (2022) 'Online sensory marketing: Developing five-dimensional multi-sensory brand experiences and its effectiveness.' *Cardiometry*, 24, pp. 567–576. [Online] [Accessed 20 June 2023] https://www.proquest.com/openview/706c0241d46571f63f5da3eb8bf16d79/1?pq-origsite=gscholar&cbl=2045095

SocialBeta (2021) *MANNER × The beast launches 'Panda Latte'.* [Online] [Accessed 2 March 2023] https://socialbeta.com/c/7692

Social Book (2021) *A new trend in the "smell economy", To Summer has created an oriental fragrance.* [Online] [Accessed 2nd March 2023] https://www.amz123.com/thread-794402.htm

Steenkamp, J.B.E. (2019) 'Global versus local consumer culture: Theory, measurement, and future research directions.' *Journal of International Marketing*, 27(1), pp. 1–19.

Strizhakova, Y. and Coulter, R.A. (2015) 'Drivers of local relative to global brand purchases: A contingency approach.' *Journal of International Marketing*, 23(1), pp. 1–22.

Swoboda, B., Pennemann, K. and Taube, M. (2012) 'The effects of perceived brand globalness and perceived brand localness in China: Empirical evidence on Western, Asian, and domestic retailers.' *Journal of International Marketing*, 20(4), pp. 72–95.

Topher (2022) *500 brand case study – To summer: A premium oriental fragrance.* [Online] [Accessed 2 March 2023] http://topherglobal.com/?p=12657

To Summer (n.d.) [Online] [Accessed 3 March 2023] https://weibo.com/u/6850300065?refer_flag=1005050010_

Wang, J. (2020) *Conversation with to summer: 90% of the brand companies of the future will be content companies.* [Online] [Accessed 6 March 2023] https://socialone.com.cn/guanxia-brand-of-the-future/

Winning Business Network (2021) *How many more "To Summer" fragrances are missing in the domestic fragrance circuit to be the light of the country?* [Online] [Accessed 2 March 2023] https://36kr.com/p/1400396631709315

Xiao, M. (2023) *To Summer: Why popular brands love to tell the story of the old city.* [Online] [Accessed 20 June 2023] https://36kr.com/p/2154135799976193

Xin, Y.H. (2021) *2021 China diffusion industry: New fashion for Z Generation, new type of olfactory economy.* [Online] [Accessed 2 March 2023] https://www.leadleo.com/report/details?id=617674f2701ce534c3497a08

Xu, Z. (2019) *To SummerLab: Enhancing the olfactory economy with 'facial attractiveness'.* [Online] [Accessed 6 March 2023] https://36kr.com/p/1723523186689

Yeboah-Banin, A.A. and Quaye, E.S. (2021) 'Pathways to global versus local brand preferences: The roles of cultural identity and brand perceptions in emerging African markets.' *Journal of Global Marketing*, 34(5), pp. 372–391.

Zhou, R. (2022) *With 70% of future performance likely to rely on offline channels, what other new content will To Summer create?* [Online] [Accessed 20 May 2023] https://www.cbo.cn/article/id/50767.html

Zhou, Y.K. and Ding, Y.R. (2022) *With over $100 million in annual revenue from private domains alone and a reorder rate of over 60%, how does this niche brand do it?* [Online] [Accessed 20 May 2023] https://www.cmovip.com/detail/18423.html

8.3   Anya Hindmarch: pioneering hyper-physical customer experiences

Bethan Alexander

Learning objectives

On completion of this case study, learners should be able to:

1   Explore the meaning of customer experience and how it has been brought to life by niche luxury accessories brand Anya Hindmarch.
2   Assess the different types of customer experiences that retailers can leverage in creating experiences and the types of consumer responses to them.
3   Understand how customer experience theories can be applied to real-life fashion retailers.
4   Propose a prognosis for the future of customer experience in a highly competitive global luxury market.

Introduction

Brand background

Anya Hindmarch, aged just 18, founded her eponymous luxury accessories brand in 1987, predominantly focusing on the handbag category (Imms, 2019). From the outset, she attracted a dedicated following amongst celebrities and royalty for her renowned whimsical, witty, creative designs and fastidious craftsmanship (BoF, 2014; Kent, 2019). The business grew quickly expanding via wholesale partners, like high-end department stores Bergdorf Goodman, Harrods and Barneys. By 2014, the brand was producing four collections per year, selling its bags internationally with 56 stores in nine countries and was the only accessories brand to present catwalk shows at London Fashion Week (BoF, 2014).

Playfulness, humour, irreverence and personalisation signify the brand personality that have been reflected in the collections since inception, offering surprise and intrigue and serving to differentiate it from the oft seriousness and perfectionism associated with typical luxury (Chitrakorn, 2015). The success of Anya's leather stickers typifies this tongue-in-cheek approach, which by 2015 were generating £12 million in sales alone. Inspired by childhood memories of wearing a school uniform, where children stickered books to define themselves, the act of taking recognisable cultural motifs and luxurifying them in leather was the motivation, and, in doing so, injecting playfulness to the traditional world of leather goods (Mellery-Pratt, 2015). This obsession with labelling and personalising products stuck and has been incorporated into other collections. These brand codes are embedded across all lines, including the mainline, sticker (shop), bespoke (personalisation) and special projects. As Anya says, "We have a story and inspiration which changes seasonally, but wit has always been at the heart of what we do. It's part of our DNA" (Chitrakorn, 2015).

Global brand attention was garnered with a number of special philanthropic projects. 'Be a Bag', launched in 2001, enabling customers to print personalised images directly onto bags with a donation of £10 for every bag sold to charity. The initiative was key in establishing the brands' connectivity to personalisation, a "key part of our brand values" (AH interview, 2023). This was followed in 2007 by "I'm Not a Plastic Bag", heralded as one of the first environmentally friendly fashion bags that used wit to reframe the notion of shopping with reusable bags, whilst drawing attention to the issue of single-use plastic waste (Chitrakorn, 2015). Antithetical to standard luxury practices, Anya Hindmarch partnered with supermarkets as well as high-end boutiques to sell the £5 bag, which became a huge success worldwide. As the brand asserts, "I think we as a brand, very naturally can play with that high-low position, without it damaging our brand" (AH interview, 2023). The success and demand that ensued has led to additional product development projects allied to positive environmental and regenerative practices; "I am a plastic bag" was launched in 2020, concerned with reusing plastic waste to develop new products. This was followed by the "Return to nature" project, focused on producing a biodegradable, compostable leather that decomposes at end of life. Anya's latest initiative is the "Universal bag", an iteration of the "I'm not a plastic bag", that aims to be a genuine bag for life, which comes with a ten-year guarantee, and is recyclable yet stylish. The brand has again partnered with multiple supermarkets globally with the ambition for this £10 bag to become the co-branded bag of choice for all consumer grocery shopping (AH interview, 2023). According to the brand, "it's these special projects that help the brand stand out from competitors", enabling brand elasticity and stretch, from luxury into mainstream (AH interview, 2023).

Personal luxury goods market

The global market for luxury personal goods grew 34% to reach €225 billion in 2021, and is forecast to increase to €462 billion by 2027 (Mintel, 2022). Fashion and leather goods make up the largest segment, accounting for 48% of total sales in 2021, and is also the fastest growing sector. However, the sector is highly concentrated, with ten luxury groups commanding 68% of total sales. Anya Hindmarch sits within the remaining fragmented and highly competitive 32%, all vying for a slice of market share (Mintel, 2022). According to the company, articulating its competitors is challenging, reflecting the breadth of the brand's activities, ranging from Loewe on leather handbags to Smythson on personalised goods (AH interview, 2023).

Despite the acceleration of online shopping during the pandemic, global luxury shoppers still prefer to shop in-store in their own home country for luxury goods. Today, online accounts for an estimated 16% of global luxury sales and its predicted continuous growth has precipitated increasing omnichannel practices by luxury brands (Mintel, 2022).

Of these global luxury shoppers, millennials and Generation Z consumers make up at least 30% and are forecast to increase to 45% by 2025, and are driving demand for luxury goods and experiences (Euromonitor, 2023a/b). As a result, increasingly, luxury brands are shifting their strategies to satiate the desires and demands of this important consumer segment, whose appetite for visceral, physical (and digitally amplified), memorable experiences are at an all-time high (Mintel, 2022).

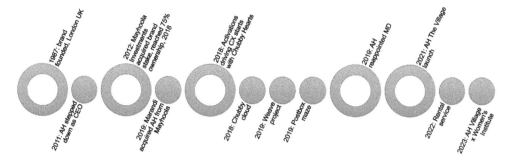

Figure 8.3.1 Anya Hindmarch brand timeline.

Source: Author's own.

Brand turnaround

Since 2017, Anya Hindmarch entered a difficult period of restructuring, with the business struggling to retain sales and profit. It reported pre-tax losses of £28.2 million in 2017 on sales of £37.2 million (Kent, 2019; O'Connor, 2019) falling to £13.5 million in 2020. This resulted in the closure of most of its international stores and focusing on its UK home market, and strategic markets Hong Kong and Japan. On reassuming the role of managing director in 2019, Anya stated, "It's time for businesses to be brave and decisive, we have been transforming our business model … I'm incredibly excited for the next phase" (Berezhna, 2019). Recently the company has turned a corner, with latest reported sales of £15.7 million in 2022 (Fame, 2023). This turnaround is a result of investment in e-commerce, physical store rationalisation, experimenting with consumer-facing mesmeric experiences and digital marketing campaigns to drive customer experience and engagement (O'Connor, 2019; Wright, 2020; Jain, 2022). Radically rethinking its direct-to-customer approach sits at the heart of the turnaround, centred on creating immersive and interactive customer experiences. Figure 8.3.1 presents a summary of the brand's timeline.

This case study allows readers to explore the experiential practices of niche luxury player Anya Hindmarch and critically appraise their pioneering hyper-physical approach to effectuating customer experience implemented to differentiate the brand in a highly competitive and fragmented luxury accessories market.

Customer experience

As discussed in Part 1, customer experience has received extensive academic and practitioner attention over the past 40 years, and is recognised as a strategic priority for retailers and brands today (Khan et al., 2020; Euromonitor, 2023a/b). Seminal authors Holbrook and Hirschman (1982) identified an experiential view of consumption "involving a steady flow of fantasies, feeling and fun" (Holbrook and Hirschman, 1982: 132). Pine and Gilmore (1998) were instrumental in their depiction of customer experiences as "when a company intentionally uses services as the stage, and goods as the props to engage individual customers in a way that creates a memorable event" (Pine and Gilmore, 1998: 98). The metaphor of a stage or performance has since become common in customer experience literature (Gobe, 2010). The concept of customer experience gives credence to entertainment, fun and fantasy, and what can be considered a hedonic experience. Subsequent studies recognise the importance of not only retailer-controlled aspects of customer experience but the role of consumers in the co-creation of an experience (Bäckström and Johansson, 2006). Whilst scholarly divergence remains on defining and characterising the customer experience construct, a commonly shared view is that it is both a retailer process (i.e. experience creation) and a customer response (cognitive, affective, emotional, social and physical) to a retailer (specifically the retail experience offered). Pine and Gilmore's (1998) Experiential Realms Model (that takes the retailer's perspective) and Schmitt's (1999, in Rhea, 2014) Strategic Experiential Modules (SEMs) (that takes a customer's perspective) are useful to consider customer experience holistically – from both the retailer and the customer viewpoint. Pine and Gilmore classify experiences into four realms: entertainment, educational, escapist and esthetic. Schmitt categorises the consumer's response into five experiences: sensory (SENSE), affective (FEEL), cognitive (THINK), behaviours and lifestyle (ACT) and social (RELATE).

Pine and Gilmore's experience realms model

According to the author an experience occurs when a company intentionally uses services as the stage, and goods as props, to engage customers in a personal and memorable way (1998: 98). The experience realms model helps depict the characteristics of experiences. It conceives experiences across two dimensions, according to customer participation, ranging from passive to active, and according to the connection that unites customers with the experience, ranging from absorption (in the experience) to immersion. Four categories of experiences ensue (see Figure 8.3.2):

- Entertainment – customers tend to passively participate and their connection is likely to be one of absorption.
- Educational – involves more active participation but their connection is likely to be outside of the event than immersed in the action.
- Escapist – can teach or entertain (like the above two modes) but they tend to involve more customer immersion.
- Esthetic – customers tend to be immersed in an activity or environment but they have little effect on it.

Pine and Gilmore posit that the richest experiences encompass all of the four realms, forming a "sweet spot" (1998: 102). Asking the question "what specific experience will my company offer" helps retailers to define their experience strategy. In alignment with Schmitt (1999, 2015), the authors assert that the more senses an experience engages, the more effective and memorable it is likely to be for customers.

Schmitt's SEMs model

Schmitt (Rhea, 2014) posits that retailers can use the SEMs model to create different types of experiences for their customers to generate specific experiential outcomes (see Figure 8.3.3).

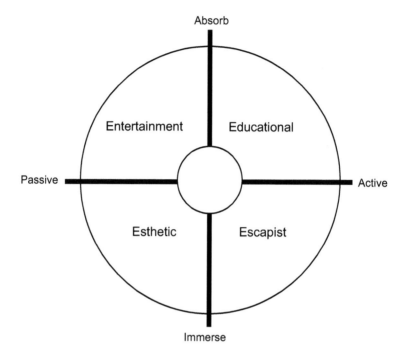

Figure 8.3.2 Experience Realms Model (Pine and Gilmore, 1998).

Source: Reprinted by permission of Harvard Business Review Press. From book The Experience Economy, Pine and Gilmore. Boston, MA, 2020, p. 39.

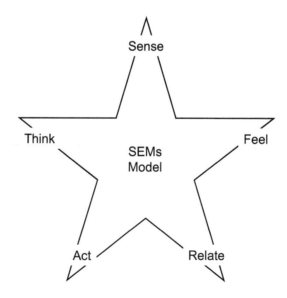

Figure 8.3.3 SEM Model (Schmitt, 1999).

Source: Reprinted by permission of author Bernd Schmitt.

- The SENSE module appeals to the senses, with the objective of creating sensory experiences through sight, sound, touch, taste and smell to generate sensory appeal.
- The FEEL module appeals to customers' inner feelings, with the objective of creating affective experiences that range from mild mood enhancing to strong emotions of joy and excitement.
- The THINK module appeals to the intellect, with the objective of creating cognitive, problem-solving experiences that engage customers creatively, through offering surprise, intrigue and provocation.
- The ACT module serves to enrich customer's lives by targeting their physical experiences, by showing them different lifestyles, ways of behaving and doing things.
- The RELATE module contains aspects of the above four modules, but extends beyond the individual state to relate with others and to a broader social system.

These SEMs are implemented through experience providers (or ExPros) which include visual identity, communications, spatial environments and people, etc. ExPros must be coherent, consistent and detailed to potentialise experience creation (Rhea, 2014).

In the subsequent sections, these two constructs are applied to Anya Hindmarch to show how the brand co-creates customer experience.

Customer experience: the Anya Hindmarch way

Anya Hindmarch's unconventional approach to doing luxury was cemented in 2018, eschewing the traditional, exclusive catwalk show, synonymous with fashion week, in pursuit of playful, immersive and inclusive customer experiences that placed consumers at the centre (O'Connor, 2019). As Anya said at the time, "It just makes sense. It just feels more modern" (O'Connor, 2019). What makes these projects unique is that they're conceived entirely in-house by a small team with Anya at the helm. This creative control and attention to detail ensures that each element is fully considered and connected, from choice of location, collaborators, interactive workshops, limited edition merchandise to the café's cakes. However, it also allows for a test, try and iterate approach (AH interview, 2023).

Chubby Hearts experience

Anya Hindmarch's first venture into the realm of experience creation was the Chubby Hearts project, which saw giant inflatable hearts flown over different London landmarks in February 2018. It was conceived as a love letter to London, a city-wide civic celebration for people (AH interview, 2023). The experiment not only coincided with Valentine's Day, but resonated with customers desire for more co-created brand experiences. It proved impactful, only generating over 12 million Instagram impressions (O'Connor, 2019) but also in terms of raising brand awareness and emotional attachment with a global audience (AH interview, 2023).

The Chubby Cloud experience

With consumers increasingly redirecting spend from products towards experiences, Anya Hindmarch's Chubby Cloud immersive experience, inspired by the Chubby collection, resonated with people who participated during London Fashion Week,

September 2018. Hosted at London's Banqueting House, the experience included a giant Chubby Cloud beanbag that people could lie on while admiring the ceiling painted by 17th-century artist Ruben, as well as live readings of bedtime stories, lullabies, guided meditations and talks from the likes of Poppy Delevingne and Richard E Grant. An onsite shop sold the Chubby collection and Chubby Cloud one-off merchandise and people could sit and soak up the atmosphere at the Chubby-themed café (O'Connor, 2018) (see Figure 8.3.4). The three-day experience attracted 3,000 participators, and the brand used it as an opportunity to amplify and engage directly with consumers (O'Connor, 2019). For Anya, it was about offering consumers an

Figure 8.3.4 Chubby Cloud.

Source: Reprinted by permission of Anya Hindmarch.

experience that they couldn't replicate online. The curation of all elements was a key part of delivering that strategy. At the time Anya said this: "can speak to a customer as much as an advertising campaign with the latest handbag" (O'Connor, 2018). Breaking with conventions, the experience was ticketed, with prices ranging from £7.50 to £15, with all sales going to charities. The notion of paying for experiences, much like we do to experience theatre or art, resonates with Pine and Gilmore's (1998) experience economy theorisation that suggests people are willing to pay for experiences that they value.

Weave Project experience

Building on the success of Chubby Cloud, Anya Hindmarch changed location to Brewer Street multi-storey car park in Soho, London, for its next fashion week activation to support the launch of its Spring/Summer 2020 collection (O'Connor, 2019a). The Neeson bag launched at the Weave Project has since become one of its best performing styles (O'Connor, 2019). The immersive weave installation created in collaboration with art collective Numen/For Use took over the entire carpark floor, encouraging people to climb into it and explore its labyrinth like hand-netted tube construction (see Figure 8.3.5). Alongside the mammoth installation, the brand offered an interactive weaving workshop, enabling people to learn the art of weaving – "At any one time

Figure 8.3.5 Weave Project.

Source: Reprinted by permission of Anya Hindmarch.

we have between 80 and 100 people sitting on the floor learning to weave" (Anya Hindmarch interview, O'Connor, 2019), as well as a café, selling weave decorated sweet treats, and the pop-up store featuring the weave collection and event-specific merchandise for sale. The three-day event attracted over 4,000 participators in the experience (O'Connor, 2019).

Postbox maze experience

Again taking over the top floor of Brewer Street multi-storey car park in Soho, London, the brand hosted its giant maze, in pillar box red, evoking traditional British letter boxes to promote its Spring/Summer 2020 Postbox handbag. The activation was inspired by MC Escher's Metamorphosis III mural that was designed for the Hague Post Office. Again, shunning with tradition, the brand charged for the experience. Participants paid £12.50 to work their way around the maze, discovering postal artefacts and listening to recordings by Letters Live and celebrities like Benedict Cumberbatch reciting words from literary heroes like Charlotte Bronte. Visitors were encouraged to participate in the calligraphy workshop, to learn the skill of decorative handwriting and to scribe a letter to loved ones that the brand would then post for them. In addition, they could shop the Postbox collection and limited edition Postbox maze merchandise and consume Postbox-themed edible treats at Anya's café (O'Connor, 2019). In an age of digital acceleration, such human-centric, analogue, interactive, craft-based experiences served to resonate with consumers. Anya Hindmarch cleverly melded the offline experience, online, generating social media fans and strengthening brand engagement and reach. As expounded by one commentator, "today, luxury is more democratised than ever and it's about things like co-creation, personalisation, initiatives that bring the consumer into the experience, rather than it being closed off" (O'Connor, 2019).

The Village experience

The Village on Pont Street, Belgravia, London, poignant as the place of Anya's first store and its proximity to Anya's own home, epitomises the brand's obsession with crafting customer experience and also resonates with a resurgence in neighbourhood retail. Post the pandemic, hyper-local has been a significant driver for consumers shopping physically in a quest for socialisation whilst supporting local business. The Village concept that opened in May 2021 offers a nostalgic nod to the traditional shopkeeper of yesteryear, where clienteling was critical and customer service paramount (O'Connor, 2021).

Anya's unique Village retail concept brings the brand's playful wit to life through a cluster of five permanent spaces dedicated to different product collections and a café. Each store has its own identity. The "Plastic Store" sells the "I am a Plastic Bag" collection, focusing on the recycled product offering. The "Labelled Store" houses the best-selling organisation-focused collections. The "Village Hall" store hosts a rotating roster of pop-up concepts that change every six weeks, which, to date, has included a hair salon, a greengrocers, Santa's grotto (at Christmas), the Dry-drinker (i.e. non-alcoholic store in January), Houndmarch (to launch the dog collection), the Garden centre (to celebrate Chelsea Flower Show), Ice-cream parlour, AH Stationery (for back-to-school), Anyzzzzz (sleep store) and "It Takes a Village" concept (in collaboration with the Women's Institute) (see Figures 8.3.6–8.3.10).

The "Bespoke Store", which is the original location of Anya's first store, offers the Bespoke collection and personalisation service, with a craftsperson working onsite to show the art of bag making. The newest addition is the "World's Smallest Department Store" shop, a tongue-in-cheek nod to traditional service orientated retailing from the 1950s (featuring an edited collection of product, made especially for the store, celebrating British makers) (AH interview, 2023). Finally, the Anya Café sells Anya-branded

Figure 8.3.6 Village Hall Grotto.

Source: Reprinted by permission of Anya Hindmarch.

Figure 8.3.7 Village Hall Grocers.

Source: Reprinted by permission of Anya Hindmarch.

Figure 8.3.8 Village Hall Butchers.

Source: Reprinted by permission of Anya Hindmarch.

Figure 8.3.9 Village Hall Ice-cream Parlour.

Source: Reprinted by permission of Anya Hindmarch.

Figure 8.3.10 Village Hall Women's Institute (WI).

Source: Reprinted by permission of Anya Hindmarch.

confectionary and cakes (see Figures 8.3.11–8.3.13). The Village concept brings to life Anya's vision to create a hub,

> where we could pour all of the creative energy that we have traditionally been pouring into fashion weeks and into pop-ups … it becomes my blank canvas for projects that we care about … and it can be ever changing. If [physical] retail is to exist, its needs to be special.
>
> (O'Connor, 2021)

The five preceding experiential concepts are applied according to Pine and Gilmore and Schmitt's customer experience models in Table 8.3.1.

Figure 8.3.11 Village café.

Source: Reprinted by permission of Anya Hindmarch.

Figure 8.3.12 The Village Bespoke Store.

Source: Reprinted by permission of Anya Hindmarch.

Figure 8.3.13 The Village Department Store.

Source: Reprinted by permission of Anya Hindmarch.

Table 8.3.1 CX theory applied to Anya Hindmarch

AH experience	Pine and Gilmore's experience realms (2020)	Schmitt's (1999) SEMs
Chubby Hearts	Entertainment, esthetic	Sense, feel, relate
Chubby Cloud	Entertainment, esthetic, escapism	Sense, feel, think, act, relate
Weave Project	Entertainment, esthetic, escapism,	Sense, feel, think, act, relate
Postbox Maze	educational	
The Village		

Conclusion

The Anya Hindmarch brand has consciously eschewed typical luxury practices by making the brand accessible across market levels through its product offering and by pioneering a direct-to-consumer approach with its experiential strategy. The brand leverages all categories of experience (four realms), arguably creating a sweet spot that appeals to consumers' senses, feelings, thinking, acting and related response attributes (SEMs). The demand for luxury goods and experiences that generate visceral and memorable affects, especially from young consumers, is forecast to increase. How Anya Hindmarch, a relatively small player within a highly competitive global luxury market, is able to continue to carve out experiential sweet spots remains to be seen. How can they continue to differentiate themselves through their hyper-physical experiences? And what can other fashion retailers learn from Anya Hindmarch's experiential approach?

Case questions

1   This case study explores how Anya Hindmarch has created customer experiences. What does customer experience mean to you?
2   Which recent fashion retail experiences do you recall and why? Now apply the Experience Realms and the Strategic Experiential Modules (SEMs) frameworks to these experiences to identify the types of experiences created and your personal response.
3   Anya Hindmarch exemplifies a hyper-physical approach to customer experience. Can such immersive customer experiences be replicated online? With advancements in Web 4.0, research, identify, discuss and evaluate at least three ways that fashion retailers are delivering immersive customer experiences online.
4   Customer experience is recognised as a strategic priority for fashion retailers to survive and thrive today. Given the rapidly evolving marketplace, what is your prognosis for the future of customer experience? Support your assertions with robust evidence-based insight.

References

Bäckström, K. and Johansson, U. (2006) 'Creating and consuming experiences in retail store environments: Comparing retailer and consumer perspectives.' *Journal of Retailing and Consumer Services*, 13(6), pp. 417–430.

Berezhna, V. (2019) *Anya Hindmarch to take back reins of her business*. Business of Fashion. [Online] [Accessed 22 April 2023] https://www.businessoffashion.com/articles/luxury/anya-hindmarch-to-take-back-reins-of-her-business/

BoF (2014) *Anya Hindmarch: A world of creativity and humour.* Business of Fashion. [Online] [Accessed 22 April 2023] https://www.businessoffashion.com/articles/workplace-talent/anya-hindmarch-world-creativity-humour/

Chitrakorn, K. (2015) *'Oh so serious' fashion industry, brands make wit work.* Business of Fashion. [Online] [Accessed 21 April 2023] https://www.businessoffashion.com/articles/luxury/in-oh-so-serious-fashion-industry-brands-make-wit-work/

Euromonitor. (2023a) *Competitor strategies in luxury goods.* Passport Euromonitor. [Online] [Accessed 21 April 2023]

Euromonitor. (2023b) *Where consumers shop for luxury goods.* Passport Euromonitor. [Online] [Accessed 21 April 2023] https://www.euromonitor.com/where-consumers-shop-for-luxury-goods/report

Fame. (2023) *A.S.H.S Ltd financial statement.* Fame. [Online] [Accessed 21 April 2023]

Gobe, M. (2010) *BrandJam: Humanizing brands through emotional design.* New York: Allworth Press. [Online] [Accessed 4 July 2021] https://ebookcentral.proquest.com/lib/ual/detail.action?docID=1321663#

Holbrook, M.B. and Hirschman, E.C. (1982) 'The experiential aspects of consumption: Consumer fantasies, feelings and fun.' *Journal of Consumer Research,* 9(2), pp. 132–140.

Imms, K. (2019) *Anya Hindmarch returns to brand as MD.* Drapers. [Online] [Accessed 21 April 2023] https://www.drapersonline.com/news/anya-hindmarch-returns-to-brand-as-md

Jain, R. (2022) *Anya Hindmarch: What's it really like to run a fashion business in the 2020's?* [Online] [Accessed 22 April 2023] https://fashionunfiltered.com/news/2022/anya-hindmarch-whats-it-really-like-to-run-a-fashion-business-in-the-2020s/

Khan, I., Hollebeek, L.D., Fatma, M., Ul-Islam, J. and Riivits-Arkonsuo, I. (2020) 'Customer experience and commitment in retailing: does age matter?' *Journal of Retailing and Consumer Services,* 57, pp. 1–9.

Kent, S. (2019) *Anya Hindmarch sold to Marandi family.* Business of Fashion. [Online] [Accessed 21 April 2023] https://www.businessoffashion.com/articles/news-analysis/anya-hindmarch-sold-to-marandi-family

Mellery-Pratt, R. (2015) *Anya Hindmarch's luxury sticker success.* Business of Fashion. [Online] [Accessed 21 April 2023] https://www.businessoffashion.com/articles/news-analysis/anya-hindmarchs-luxury-sticker-success/

Mintel. (2022) *Luxury goods retailing international 2022.* Mintel Group Ltd. [Online] [Accessed 21 April 2023] https://store.mintel.com/report/international-luxury-goods-retailing-market-report

O'Connor, T. (2018) *Anya Hindmarch to host consumer-facing event at London Fashion Week.* Business of Fashion. [Online] [Accessed 21 April 2023] https://www.businessoffashion.com/articles/news-analysis/anya-hindmarch-to-host-immersive-consumer-facing-event-during-lfw/

O'Connor, T. (2019) *At fashion week, Anya Hindmarch continues to put consumers front and centre.* Business of Fashion. [Online] [Accessed 21 April 2023] https://www.businessoffashion.com/articles/fashion-week/anya-hindmarch-london-fashion-week-event-postbox-maze/

O'Connor, T. (2021) *Anya Hindmarch to open five-store 'Village' in London as part of new retail strategy.* Business of Fashion. [Online] [Accessed 21 April 2023] https://www.businessoffashion.com/articles/retail/anya-hindmarch-to-open-five-store-village-in-london-as-part-of-new-retail-strategy/

Pine, B.J. and Gilmore, J.H. (1998) 'Welcome to the experience economy.' *Harvard Business Review,* 76(4), pp. 97–105.

Pine, B.J. and Gilmore, J.H. (2020) *The experience economy: Competing for customer time, attention and money.* Boston, MA: Harvard Business Publishing.

Rhea, D. (2014) 'Experiential marketing: A new framework for design and communications By Bernd Schmitt.' *Design Management Review,* 25, pp. 19–26. [Online] [Accessed 14 July 2023] https://onlinelibrary.wiley.com/doi/epdf/10.1111/drev.10298

Schmitt, B.H. (1999) 'Experiential marketing.' *Journal of Marketing Management,* 15(1/3), pp. 53–67.

Schmitt, B.H. (2015) 'Experiential marketing: A new framework for design and communications.' *Design Management Review*, 40th Anniversary Issue.

Wright, G. (2020) *Anya Hindmarch takes back half her company*. Retail Gazette. [Online] [Accessed 22 April 2023] https://www.retailgazette.co.uk/blog/2020/01/anya-hindmarch-takes-back-half-her-company/

Further reading and resources

Anya Hindmarch website: https://www.anyahindmarch.com/

Anya Hindmarch Chubby Hearts: https://www.youtube.com/watch?v=_hqwMj-Wgxk

Anya Hindmarch The Chubby Cloud: https://www.youtube.com/watch?v=6eScZXTXaOw

Anya Hindmarch Weave Project: https://www.youtube.com/watch?v=0_ZoORMAKjk

Anya Hindmarch Postbox Maze: https://www.youtube.com/watch?v=4zIBX-f3mLI

Anya Hindmarch The Village: https://www.youtube.com/watch?v=3PSTJungMCw

Anya Hindmarch 'I am a plastic bag': https://www.youtube.com/watch?v=zG30a_GQIos

Afterword

Gary Warnaby

A territoriological perspective on consumer experience in fashion retailing?

Until the latter part of the last century, consumer experience in retailing would almost invariably have taken place within the arena of the physical store. However, as this book has well demonstrated, retailers now operate beyond the bounds of the traditional physical outlet into digital and virtual worlds, manifest by their increasingly multi- (and even omni-)channel activities. This evolving retail practice – explored through the various contributions to the second and third parts of this volume – forces us perhaps to re-evaluate our conceptual and theoretical understandings of retail customer experience to incorporate the multifarious places and spaces within which this experience now occurs.

These places and spaces range from the physical and the digital, to some blend of the two (i.e. the 'phygital', discussed in the first part of this volume). Such places and spaces are, moreover, increasingly personalised and thus responsive to individual customer requirements; in other words, placing people at the centre of customer experiences (explored in the first and third parts of this volume), and also harmonising the customer experience through the integration of these different places and spaces (discussed in the second part). The increasing plurality of the nature of retail place and space does, I suggest, require us to broaden our thinking about retail customer experience, incorporating new framings to structure our explorations of this constantly evolving subject area. One possible new framing, mentioned in the first part of this volume, is the notion of *experiential retail territories*, and in this afterword, I seek to explore some implications of this novel notion.

Delimiting 'territory'

In layman's terms, the concept of a 'territory' can refer to a distinct, boundaried space wherein a regular set of behaviours might occur, and which is to some degree under the control of an entity (linked to notions of territoriality – which can be thought of in terms of the exercise of power over blocs of space). In his discussion of 'territorology' (which he describes in terms of a general science of territory and territorial phenomena), Brighenti states that territory is "not an absolute concept. Rather, it is always relative to a sphere of application or a structural domain of practice" (2010: 61). In this volume, the 'sphere of application' is the retail industry.

The development of 'territoriology' (Brighenti and Kärrholm, 2020) as a subject of study has a range of multidisciplinary theoretical antecedents and the concept of territory has been applied in numerous academic disciplines (see Brighenti and Kärrholm, 2020), including architecture, where Kärrholm (2008, 2012) has discussed territory in the context of pedestrian shopping precincts within urban space. Narrowing the spatial scale further, an individual physical retail store could be considered in territoriological terms in that it is a distinct boundaried space whose nature and characteristics are under the control of the retailer that owns/occupies it.

However, the notion of territory can be delimited in terms other than the physical/material. Referring to the behaviour that occurs within its boundaries, Brighenti argues that a territory can be "better conceived as an act or practice rather than an object or physical space" (2010: 53), and that it has both expressive and functional components. In other words, a territory is a product of human and institutional relations, which resonates with discussions of customer experience in the retail places and spaces mentioned earlier in this volume. I posit here that this leads to a range of both spatial and relational implications which are worthy of further consideration, and which could potentially form the basis of a future research agenda for retail customer experience.

Spatial implications

Inherent in stereotypical ideas of a territory is the extent of its spatial coverage, delineated by territorial boundaries. Brighenti emphasises the importance of *boundaries*, which he argues "are a constitutive prerequisite of territory" (2010: 60). The making of a territory is, he thus argues, "inherently related to the drawing of certain boundaries" (2014: 2), which can be accomplished in a range of ways. In the traditional physical retail context, these boundaries would constitute the four walls of the retail store, but now with increasingly multi- (and even omni-)channel retail operations (with multiple customer 'touchpoints'), such territorial boundaries will arguably be more porous, as a shift occurs from traditional separate, singular channels (i.e. 'places', such as individual retail stores) to a convergence of on- and off-line (and possibly interstitial) *spaces* of retail consumption. Thus, instead of sites of retail experience and consumption being restricted to material, fixed spatial entities, they can be considered as having much broader socio-material and relational attributes, becoming non-exclusive, overlapping and intersecting constructs whose shapes, characteristics and experiences are constantly being renegotiated.

Here, the concept of the *milieu*, described by Deleuze and Guattari in terms of "a block of space-time" (1987: 312), could be considered as one way in which these convergent and conjunct territorial spatialities may be further explicated. Chapter 2 of this volume applies the different types of milieus – *interior, intermediary, exterior and annexed* – to the context of customer experience in fashion retailing, exploring their potential to conceptualise the increasingly multi- and omni-channel nature of the contemporary retail industry. Thus, customer experience potentially becomes more 'holistic', not only restricted to the physical territory of the retail store itself, but also incorporating a related digital experience in other retail channels which could be conceptualised as virtual 'territories'.

Relational implications

Linked to the conceptualisation of territory as an act or practice (Brighenti, 2010), in a retail experience context, retailer-customer interactions (and also customer-customer interactions) within these retail milieus could be a part of the overall customer experience, and, as such, contribute to territorial creation. In other words, particular combinations of actions/behaviours – which could be choreographed by the retailer to some degree by placing parameters (spatial and/or procedural) around these actions – could be constitutive of territorial creation (in physical and/or digital worlds). Thus, retail customer experience can be cocreated (see Overdiek and Warnaby, 2020, in the specific context of pop-up retailing), through "patterns of relations" (Brighenti, 2010: 57). Indeed, Brighenti notes that

> only once relations among actors, rather than space, are put at the conceptual core of territory, does it become possible to capture the ways in which spatial and non-spatial territories are superimposed one onto the other and endowed with multiple linkages.
>
> (ibid: 51)

This relational dimension also resonates with the fluid and amorphous nature of the retail 'territories' that are described throughout this volume.

Inevitably the 'experiential retail territories' created through the interplay of such spatial-social relations will be dynamic, which will in turn influence the processual nature of territorial creation through what Brighenti (2010) terms 'territorial movements'. Drawing on Deleuze and Guattari (1987) who identify three interrelated movements in the territorial process, namely, *deterritorialisation*, *reterritorialisation* and *territorialisation*, Brighenti argues that territories are only actualised when one leaves them because as one leaves a territory another territory is created (which is the reason for Deleuze and Guattari beginning with deterritorialisation in their explication of 'territorial movements'). Processes of de- and re-territorialisation are arguably evident in consumers' interplay between different retail channels as new behaviours are encouraged (or perhaps even proscribed) in order to experience – and 'consume' – to optimum effect within these different channels, thereby contributing to the creation of different experiential retail territories across different physical and digital retail channels.

Concluding comments

Mindful of Kurt Lewin's maxim that "there's nothing so practical as a good theory" (1951: 169), I would argue that the concept of retail spaces and places as 'territories' could serve as a useful conceptual framework for future investigation into retail customer experience. The inherent flexibility in how territories are defined and delineated could provide both academics and practitioners with new perspectives through which to view the constantly evolving nature of the topic as both technological and social developments over the coming years. Volumes such as this one will play an important role in framing the parameters of – and setting the agenda for – further research into this important topic.

References

Brighenti, A.M. (2010) 'On territorology: Towards a general science of territory.' *Theory, Culture & Society*, 27(1), pp. 52–72.

Brighenti, A.M. (2014) 'Mobilizing territories, territorializing mobilities.' *Sociologica*, 1, pp. 1–25.

Brighenti, A.M. and Kärrholm, M. (2020) *Animated lands: Studies in territoriology.* Lincoln: University of Nebraska Press.

Deleuze, G. and Guattari, F. (1987) *A thousand plateaus: Capitalism and Schizophrenia* (trans. Massumi, B). London: The Athlone Press.

Kärrholm, M. (2008) 'The territorialisation of a pedestrian precinct in Malmo: Materialities in the commercialisation of public space.' *Urban Studies*, 45(9), pp. 1903–1924.

Kärrholm, M. (2012) *Retailising space: Architecture, retail and the territorialising of public space.* Farnham: Ashgate Publishing.

Lewin, K. (1951) 'Problems of research in social psychology,' in D. Cartwright (ed.) *Field theory in social science: Selected theoretical papers.* New York: Harper & Row, pp. 155–169.

Overdiek, A. and Warnaby, G. (2020) 'Co-creation and codesign in pop-up stores: The intersection of marketing and design research?' *Creativity and Innovation Management*, 29(S1), pp. 63–74.

Index

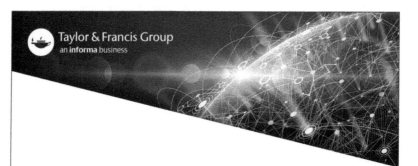

For Product Safety Concerns and Information please contact our EU
representative GPSR@taylorandfrancis.com
Taylor & Francis Verlag GmbH, Kaufingerstraße 24, 80331 München, Germany

www.ingramcontent.com/pod-product-compliance
Ingram Content Group UK Ltd.
Pitfield, Milton Keynes, MK11 3LW, UK
UKHW050930180425
457613UK00015B/356